Land and Society in Medieval South India

Notes

The responsibility for the facts stated or opinions expressed is entirely of the author and not of the editors.

Land and Society in Medieval South India

Perspectives on Socio-economic and Cultural Traditions

Edited by

K. Mavali Rajan
V. Palanichamy

KALPAZ

First Published, 2021

Published by

Kalpaz Publications
C-30, Satyawati Nagar,
Delhi – 110052
Ph.: 011-47034999, 9811692060
www.kalpazpublications.com
E-mail: kalpaz@hotmail.com

Printed at: Gyan Press, Delhi.

Cataloging in Publication Data--DK

Courtesy: D.K. Agencies (P) Ltd. <docinfo@dkagencies.com>

Land and society in medieval South India : perspectives on socio-economic and cultural traditions / edited by K. Mavali Rajan, V. Palanichamy.
pages cm
Contributed articles.
ISBN 9789353243166

1. Land use--India, South--History. 2. India, South--Social conditions. 3. India, South--Politics and government. 4. India, South--History. 5. India, South--Religious life and customs. I. Mavali Rajan, K., editor. II. Palanichamy, V., editor.

LCC DS484.5.L36 2021 | DDC 954.8 23

Contents

Dedicated to

Parents

&

Teachers

Acknowledgement

This book is a collection of essays by distinguished historians and scholars from Tamil Nadu, West Bengal, Sikkim and Karnataka focusing the social, economic and cultural facets of early and medieval south India covering the period from the early historic to the pre-modern times. They highlighted the agrarian patterns and practices, irrigation system, social aspects, and cultural milieu of medieval south India. The volume would not have been possible without the support and co-operation from contributors. The contributors of the volume responded promptly to all our queries and furnished us with all complementary notes and information whenever required. At first, we wish to acknowledge our sincere indebtedness to the contributors of this edited volume. We remain grateful for their co-operation and for having shared with us their research work by way of their sincere efforts and commitments.

We would be failing our duty if we do not thank our parents who dedicated their life to us. We are also thankful to our teachers, who introduced us to the knowledge of the world and guided us at every stage of academic careers and advised us in every aspect of a studious life. They rendered their full moral support when we were in school and college days. We express our deepest gratitude to all our friends and well-wishers for their encouragement in completing this work. We owe a special thanks to research scholars of the department of Ancient Indian History, Culture and Archaeology, Visva-Bharati University, Santiniketan for their assistance in bringing this volume in a successful manner.

Finally, We are am very thankful to Shri Amit Garg, Kalpaz Publications, New Delhi for publishing this volume within a short time.

Visva-Bharati
Santiniketan

K. Mavali Rajan
V. Palanichamy

Abbreviations

A.R.E.	Annual Report on Epigraphy
A.R.I.E	Annual Report on Indian Epigraphy
A.R.S.I.E.	Annual Report on South Indian Epigraphy
A.S.I	Archaeological Survey of India
A.S.I.A.R.	Archaeological Survey of India Annual Report
Dt.	District
E.C.	Epigraphia Carnatica
E.I.	Epigraphia Indica
Ibid.	'Ibidem', in the same place of work
Idem	the same author and work
I.P.S.	Inscriptions of Pudukkottai State
M.E.R.	Madras Epigraphical Reports
op.cit.	'opera citato', in the work cited
P.S.I.	Pudukkottai State Inscriptions
S.I.I.	South Indian Inscriptions
S.I.T.I	South Indian Temple Inscriptions
T.A.S.	Travancore Archaeological Series
Tk.	Taluk

Scheme of Transliteration and guide to Pronunciation

Vowels:

a	as u in	cut
ā	as ea in	heart
i	as i in	it
ī	as ee in	need
u	as u in	put
ū	as oo in	cool
ṛ	as ri in	brick
e	as e in	end
ē	as a in	cake
ai	as y in	why
o	as o in	bow
ō	as o in	over
au	as ow in	cow
aṃ	as m in	hum
aḥ	as h in	verandah

Consonants:

ka	as c in	cat
kha	as ch in	chaos
ga	as g in	gift
gha	as gh in	ghana

ṅ	as ng in	swing
ca	as ch in	chart
cha	as tch in	fetch
ja	as j in	jar
jha	as ja in	jhahir
ña	as ñ in	spañol
ṭa	as t in	top
ṭha	as dh in	matha
ḍa	as d in	disk
ḍha	as dh in	adhesive
ṇ	as n in	want
ta	as th in	breathe
tha	as th in	thunder
da	as th in	that
dha	as th h in	withheld
na	as n in	north
pa	as p in	paper
pha	as ph in	prophet
ba	as b in	bat
bha	as bh in	abhor
ma	as m in	mother
ya	as y in	yes
ra	as rr in	carry
la	as l in	low
va	as v in	van
śa	as ch in	German pronunciation of ch
ṣa	as sh in	shine
sa	as s in	sea
ha	as h in	home
ḷa	as l in	clumsy

l̤a	as ge in	genre
r̲a	as r in	rope
r̤	as tt in	little

Notes on the Contributors

B.S. Chandrababu is Emeritus Professor of UGC in Madurai Kamaraj University and retired Professor and Chairperson from the Department of Medieval History, School of Historical Studies, Madurai Kamaraj University, Tamil Nadu. His area of specialization is socio-economic history, issues relating to women, Dalit and marginalised sections. He served as a faculty in the department for more than 32 years. He is authored 13 well-researched books and edited three volumes. Guided 31 Ph.D. scholars and done 10 project studies. His major publications include 'Essays on Societal History: Some Interpretations (2012)', 'Trade in Kongu (up to 16th century A.D.) (2003)', 'Women: Her History and Her Struggle for Emancipation (2009)' along with Dr. Mrs. L. Thilagavathi, 'Social Protest in Tamil Nadu (1993)' and 'Battered Women of Madras (1998)'. He served as Indian Editor to six volume of Encyclopedia on Daily Life through history, published by Greenwood publishing Groups, USA. He is associated with South Indian History Congress as editor, General Secretary and president. He has published more than hundred research articles in reputed journals of national and international.

Binay Barman is Assistant Professor of History in Saldiha College, Saldiha, Bankura, West Bengal. His area of research interest includes historical geography, religion and regional studies. He was awarded the Dadhi Mahanta Memorial Social Science Research Award in 2014. Barman has conducted Minor research project funded by University Grant Commission, New Delhi. He is the editor of the books 'Ambedkar's Thoughts on Dalits, Politics and Women Empowerment' (New Delhi, 2017), 'Understanding of Historie Geographic Approaches' (Jorhat, 2016), 'Life and Time of Panchanan Barma', (Jorhat, 2014), and jointly edited three volumes, 'History and Culture of North-Bengal', (Kolkata, 2015),

'Uttar Banger Itihas O Sanskriti Vol. I & II' in Bengali (Kolkata, 2012). He has jointly published a research work "Buddhist Monasteries in Assam-Field Survey Basis" (Kolkata, 2014). His several articles have been published in national and international journals and in edited volumes.

C. Premnaseer is Assistant Professor of History at Jairam Arts and Science College, Salem, Tamil Nadu. His area of research includes Ethno-history and Tribal studies of south India. He completed his M. Phil. degree from the School of Historical Studies, Madurai Kamaraj University and his M.Phil. dissertation is entitled "The Position of Brahmanas and Vellalas in Kongu Region (9th century A.D. to 14th century AD.)" and also awarded Indian Council of Historical Research (ICHR) Fellowship in 2012. He was also awarded Indian Council of Social Science Research (ICSSR) Fellowship in 2014 for his Ph.D. research work entitled "The Malaiyali Tribes of Pachaimalai: An Ethno-historical Study 1947-2007" which he completed from Arignar Anna Government Arts College, Musiri, (Affiliated to the Bharathidasan University, Thiruchirappalli). He participated in many state level, national level workshops and seminars in various colleges and universities. He is a member of Tamil Nadu History Congress and South Indian History Congress. He has published few articles in journals, edited volumes and conference proceedings.

K. Ashok is Assistant Professor of History at Madras Christian College, Chennai. His area of research is transportation studies and economic history. His area of interest includes History of Science and Technology and Socio-Political and Cultural History of Tamil Nadu. He obtained his Ph.D. degree for his research "Chennai on Wheels"- A Historical Study of the Automobile Industries in and around Chennai" from the University of Madras in 2019. He was awarded Teacher Fellowship under Faculty Development Programme (FDP) during the 12th Plan Period (2012-2017) by UGC. His articles have been published in national and international journals and in edited volumes. He is associated with the Tamil Nadu Text Book Committee in writing text book for schools. He has written two chapters for Class XII History text book for the Government of Tamil Nadu.

K. Mavali Rajan is Assistant Professor in the Department of Ancient Indian History, Culture and Archaeology, Visva-Bharati University, Santiniketan, West Bengal. He specialises in various aspects of socio-economic history of early India and History of ancient and medieval South India. He completed his Ph.D. research on "Socio-Economic Conditions of Agrestic Slaves of Medieval Tamil Country" from Madurai Kamaraj University in 2007. He is the author of three books "Medieval Tamil Society and Agrarian Slavery" (Maha Bodhi Book Agency, Kolkata, 2014), "Temple and Society in South India" (Kaveri Books, New Delhi, 2016) and "Facets of Temple Culture: Perspectives on Religious and Social Traditions in Early Medieval India" (Edited Book with co-editors) (Kaveri Books, New Delhi, 2018). His various research works has been published in several reputed national and international journals.

K.R. Sankaran is Associate Professor in the Department of History, A.V.C. College (Autonomous), Mannampandal, Tamil Nadu. He specialises in various aspects of socio-economic history of medieval south India, irrigation history and agrarian history of south India. He completed his Ph.D. research on "Irrigation in the History of Tamil Nadu with special reference to Pudukkottai Region from c. 800 to 1800 A.D" from Tamil University, Thanjavur in 1999. He is very active researcher and completed an UGC research project on the "The Nomenclature of the Water Resources as Gleaned from the Inscriptions of Pudukkottai Region from c. 800 to 1800 A.D". He is the author of more than ten books. Of them "Studies in the History of Tamil Nadu: Irrigation, Society and Temple" (2001), "Aspects of the History of Pudukkottai Region" (2003), "Water Rights in the History of Tamil Nadu: from Sangam Age to c. 1600 A.D." (2011), "South India: State and Society" (2013) and "South Indian History" (2012) are very notable publications. He is also the editor and publisher of the journal 'Arivottam' (bi-lingual). His various research works has been published in several reputed national and international journals.

K. Thangapandian is Assistant Professor in the Department of History, School of Social Science, Central University of Tamil Nadu, Thiruvarur. His area of specialisation is social, economic and cultural history of medieval south India, and Tribal study. He completed his Ph.D. research on "State and Society under the Rule of the Pandyas of Tamil Nadu (c.1251-1308 A.D.)" from Madurai Kamaraj University, Madurai, Tamil Nadu in 2016. He was awarded Dr. S. Radhakrishnan National Post Doctoral Fellowship 2017-2018 by University Grant Commission (UGC), New Delhi. He was also awarded Doctoral Fellowship by Indian Council of Social Science Research, New Delhi. He has published twenty research articles in both national and international journals and in edited volumes.

L. Thilagavathi is a retired professor from the Department of History, Arulmigu Palaniandavar Arts College for women, Palani, Tamil Nadu. She served as faculty in the department of history for 25 years. Her subject specialisation is gender studies and socio-economic history of south India. A studious researcher of social concern having worked for her Ph.D. programme on "History of Secularism in Tamil Nadu" from Madurai Kamaraj University, Madurai. For her credit she has published four books and more than thirty articles in reputed journals. Her major publications are 'Women: Her History and Her Struggle for Emancipation' (2009), and 'Trade in Kongu (up to 16th century A.D.)' (2003). She is associated with various academic bodies and contributed a few articles on five temples in Udumalaipettai region of Coimbatore district. She has been actively involved in social service work to help the poor students belonging to all castes and communities.

Palas Kumar Saha, is formerly research scholar in the department of Ancient Indian History, Culture & Archaeology, Visva-Bharati University, Santiniketan, West Bengal. His area of research includes ancient Indian socio-cultural and art history, history of Buddhism especially in the east coastal region and study about Buddhist sites across the India. He was awarded his M. Phil. degree in 2013 from the same department. He received his Ph.D. on the topic "Social and Cultural History of Buddhism in the East-Coast of India (c 5th C.E. to 12th century C.E.)" from the same university in May 2019. He was awarded the Rajiv Gandhi National Fellowship Award in 2011 for his doctoral research. He is also qualified UGC NET in 2019. Several of his research articles have been published in national and international journals, edited volumes and conference proceedings.

Priya Thakur is presently Assistant Professor at the Department of Studies and Research in History and Archaeology at Tumkur University in Karnataka. Previously, she has worked as a Research Trainee under a DST project related to Archaeo-astronomy at the Indian Institute of Astrophysics, Bangalore. She has done her M.A. in Ancient Indian History Culture and Archaeology from DDU Gorakhpur University. She was an UGC-JRF and obtained her Ph.D. from the University of Mysore in Ancient History and Archaeology. She has published a book, "Secular Architectural Landscape of the Vijayanagara Period", in 2019. Her research interests lie mainly in cultural studies, archaeology, art history and epigraphy. She has carried research projects funded by ICHR and UGC. She has published more than forty research papers and has presented papers in national and international conferences and seminars. Priya is associated with national and international associations like the Indian Society for Prehistoric and Quaternary Studies, Epigraphical Society of India, Indian Art History Congress and Society for South Asian Archaeology.

R. **Govindaraj** is Assistant Professor of History at Kamaraj College, Thoothukudi, Tamil Nadu. In 2008, he completed his master degree in history from the Pondicherry University, Puducherry. From the same university he completed his M.Phil. dissertation on 'Historical and Archaeological Study of Virudhunagar District with Special Reference to Rajapalayam Taluk'. He received Indian Council of Historical Research Junior Research Fellowship in 2013 for his Ph.D. research on 'Historical and Cultural Geography of Vadipatti Taluk up to 13th century A.D.', awarded from the Madurai Kamaraj University, Madurai, Tamil Nadu in 2018. His area of research includes cultural geography, territorial administrative division, epigraphical studies, ancient and medieval South Indian history. Several of his articles have been published in national and international journals and in edited volumes. He is very active member in various professional societies such as Avanam (Tamil Nadu Archaeological Society), Indian History Congress, South Indian History Congress and Tamil Nadu History Congress.

S. **Jeevanandam** is Assistant Professor at the Department of History, Sikkim University, Sikkim. Earlier he served in the department of history in Assam University, Silchar. He completed his research work on topic "The Evolution and Reformulation of Devadasis System in Tamilakam- Historical Study" from Hyderabad University. His area of interest is on gender history, religious history and history of medieval South India. He is the author of the book "Devadasis in South India: A Journey from Sacred to a Profane Spaces" (Kalpaz Publishers, New Delhi, 2017). He has published several articles on south Indian history and society. He is associated with the Indian History Congress, South Indian History Congress and Tamil Nadu History Congress.

Sabarni Pramanik Nayak is Assistant Professor at the Department of History, Maharaja Nandakumar Mahavidyalaya, West Bengal. She has obtained doctoral degree from University of Calcutta for her work on the society and economy of Andhra from the 6th to the 10th centuries CE. Her specialisations on the aspects of south Indian history and social and economic history of Andhra Pradesh,

Odisha and West Bengal based on the epigraphic evidences. She has published several articles in various reputed journals and proceedings. Her publications includes "Movements and Migration of Brahmins in Andhra from Epigraphy 7th -10th CE", (Proceeding of Indian History Congress, 2013), "Traders and Centres of Trade in the Inscriptions of Srikakulam (11th -15th century CE", (Kolkata, 2014), "Women in Epigraphy: A case Study of the Srikakulam Region (11th -13th century CE)", (Kolkata, 2012).

Saumalya Mali is Assistant Professor in the Department of English at Saldiha College, under Bankura University, West Bengal. In teaching his area of interest spans English literature, literatures in English, language, Indian classical literature, Diaspora literature, Dalit literature, travel literature, history of English literature, critical theories and literary criticism. At present he is doing his doctoral research on Sufism and Sufi literature. This area specially falls under translation studies. He has presented research papers in many national and international seminars. He is eager to continue his research both in English and History discipline.

Sourav Sen is a Research Scholar at the department of Ancient Indian History, Culture and Archaeology, Visva-Bharati, Santiniketan. His area of interest includes social history, cultural history and epigraphical studies on early medieval India and medieval south India. He completed his under graduation in History from Maulana Azad College under the University of Calcutta. He obtained his post graduation and M. Phil. degrees from the department of Ancient Indian History, Culture and Archaeology, Visva-Bharati, Santiniketan. He has done his M. Phil. on "Mode of Communication in Early India – A Study (From c. 3rd Century BCE. to c. 3rd Century C.E.)". Currently he is working on the topic "Temple Functionaries in Kaveri Delta Region – A Study (from 9th to 13th Century C.E.)" for his Ph.D. research.

Sreebarna Ghosh is an UGC Senior research fellow working on the research topic 'Rock-cut Architecture in Western Deccan: a study from Social Perspective- 2nd century BCE to 9th century CE in the department of Ancient Indian History Culture and Archaeology', Visva-Bharati University, Santiniketan. Her area of research includes ancient Indian history, art and architecture and archaeology. She has an article entitled 'Temple: The Abode of God and the Pride of the King' published in the edited book 'Facets of Temple Culture: Perspective on Religious and Social Traditions in Early Medieval India' edited by K. Mavali Rajan, Remya V.P.

and S. Khettry (Kaveri Books, New Delhi, 2018). She is an active member of few historical associations.

Sudip Narayan Maitra is Associate Professor of History at Chandidas Mahavidyalaya, Birbhum, under the University of Burdwan, West Bengal. His area of the study includes Ancient Indian History, Culture and Archaeology broadly with polity, kingship, state formation, agriculture, water resource management, irrigation and the like. He obtained his Ph.D. from Visva-Bharati University, Santiniketan for his research work on 'Kingship in Early Medieval India: A Comparative Study of the Cholas and the Eastern Gangas'. He completed two research projects funded by UGC (MRP) and also by ICHR. Published a book on 'Kingship and Polity in Early Medieval India: Kāveri Delta Region and the Chōḷas', (J.N. Chakraborty, Kolkata, 2018) and jointly edited volumes on "Development & Politics in India" (2015), and "State, Nation & Multiculturalism: Problem in Perspectives" (2013). His various articles have been published from the journals of national and international.

Suman Saha is a Research Scholar at the department of Ancient Indian History, Culture and Archaeology, Visva-Bharati, Santiniketan. His area of interest includes social history, agrarian history of south India, cultural history, epigraphical studies on early medieval India and medieval south India. He completed his post graduation in Ancient Indian History. Culture and Archaeology from Visva-Bharati University, Santiniketan. Currently he is working on the topic "Land Use and Water Management in the Krishna and Kaveri Delta Regions (600- 1200 A.D)" for his Ph.D. research. He has published many research articles in refereed journals, edited volumes and conference proceedings. He is very active member in various professional bodies like Indian History Congress, West Bengal History Congress, etc.

V. Palanichamy is presently Assistant Professor of History in Arignar Anna Government Arts College, Musiri, Tamil Nadu (India) since 2013. His specialisations on the history of medieval south India and social and economic history of early modern south India. He obtained his post graduation (2002) in History with first class from H.K.R.H. College, Uthamapalayam, Tamil Nadu and M.Phil. Degree (2003) with first class from Pondicherry University, Puducherry. He completed his Ph.D. (2010) under the guidance of Dr. Venkata Raghotham from Pondicherry University. His various research works has been published in different journals of national and international level. He is very active member in various professional bodies as life member of Epigraphical Society of India, Place Name of Society, Archaeological Society of Ancient Science and Archaeology, Andhra Pradesh History Congress, South Indian History Congress, Tamil Nadu History Congress and as annual member of the Indian History Congress.

Introduction: Historiographical Overview on the South Indian Studies

K. Mavali Rajan and V. Palanichamy

Many south Indian historians, social scientists, and foreign scholars have done very sincere efforts in studying the social, economic, and cultural history of early and early medieval South India. In their efforts of writings, they used a variety of source materials both archaeological and literary data in interpreting the historical traditions of the early period. The South Indian historical writings in the early sixties or seventies or even in the beginnings of the twentieth century were essentially concerned with the cultural and political history. The pioneering work in the reconstruction of the early Tamil history was done by V. Kanakasabhai, who was a lawyer and became historian, concentrated in writing of the Tamil history and culture. In 1904, V. Kanakasabhai published his memorable work '*The Tamils Eighteen Hundred Years Ago*'[1] which examined the life and culture of the early Tamils; geographical features, trade and commerce, religion and philosophy of the early Tamil people based on the description in two early Tamil epics *Silappadhikāram* and *Manimēkalai*. It is considered to be a classic and as one of the first noteworthy efforts in the writings of the history of early *Tamilakam*. He was the first person to date early Tamil literature to the early centuries of the Christian era.

The credit of writing the beginning of south Indian history goes to S. Krishnaswami Aiyangar, who is considered as the true first historian of south India. Pioneers in the south Indian studies are S. Krishnaswami Aiyangar and K.A. Nilakanta Sastri, both of them vigorously produced a great many of foundational works. Noboru Karashima characterises their period as 'the first golden age of south Indian historical studies'.

S. Krishnaswami Aiyangar[2] produced certain historical works- '*The Beginning of South Indian History*' (1918), '*Some Contributions of South India to Indian Culture*' (1923), '*Evolution of Hindu Administrative Institutions in South India*' (1931), etc. Of them '*The Beginning of South Indian history*' is a monumental work based on the Tamil classical literature of the *Sangam* Age as well as south India, which highlights the social, economic, and cultural history of early south India. The various source materials have been analyzed from the Greek, Chinese, Arabian traveler's points of view. In the introduction part of the book, the contribution from the literary sources in Tamil, Sanskrit, Kanarese, and Telugu has been adequately illustrated.

Along with Robert Sewell, Krishnaswami Aiyangar edited the volume '*Historical Inscriptions of South India (Collected till 1923) and Outlines of Political History*' (1932).[3] He started a praiseworthy project on the '*Sources of Vijayanagar History*' (1920) and his method of historical writing is neither argumentative nor interpretative.[4] For the historical reconstruction he discovered the wide range of source materials on areas of art, society, culture and social and political institutions. The technological framework to south Indian history provided by Krishnaswami Aiyangar. His another important work is '*Manimēkalai In Its Historical Settings*' (1928), which critically analyzed the different philosophical systems that existed at the time of *Sangam* Age, the historical personalities existing at their time, the cream of Buddhist philosophy and the activity and lifestyle of the people of the post-*Sangam* age.[5] The main purpose of the work is to consider the philosophical systems and the religious conditions in the Tamil country as described in *Manimēkalai* throw upon the important question of the work and *Sangam* literature generally.

K.A. Nilakanta Sastri, K.K. Pillai, N. Subramanian, and some other historians focused on the society of early *Tamilakam* based on *Sangam* text but failed to see the interrelationships between the political, social, and economic aspects. They adopted the conventional pattern of describing the economy, society, religion, etc. Among them K.A. Nilakanta Sastri was the most popular and eminent historian who contributed much for the writing of south Indian history, using both archaeological and literary sources. In his work on '*A History of South India from Prehistoric Times to the Fall of Vijayanagar*' (1958) discussed some of the aspects of the political, socio-economic and cultural history of medieval south India in brief manner.[6]

Professor K.A. Nilakanta Sastri is considered as the earliest historian to write a comprehensive history of south India. He contributed immensely to South Indian history and worked on multiple aspects, such as culture, society, and polity. He also worked extensively on the *Sangam* literature and history of the Tamil region. He used a large number of epigraphical evidence and literary sources in the reconstruction of south Indian history. His works[7] include '*The Pandyan Kingdom*' (1929), '*Historical Method in Relation to Problems of South Indian History*' (1941), '*The Colas*' (1955), '*Development of Religion in South India*' (1963), '*The Culture and History of Tamils*' (1964), '*Sangam Literatures: Its Cults and Cultures*' (1972), etc. Though Nilakanta Sastri was primarily concerned with political history, he did not neglect its social, economic, and cultural facets. He was able to restructure the history of south India from the earliest times to the modern period, with a fairly reliable chronology of political developments. His significant contribution is the reconstruction of the history of the Cholas, which is largely based on inscriptions, highlights the aspects of the Chola history such as agriculture, land tenure, taxation, industry, trade and commerce, coinage, etc.

K.A. Nilakanta Sastri's work on '*Studies in Cola History and Administration*' (1932),[8] deals with the *Sabha* and *Mahāsabha* and their administrative system. He has mentioned that the later Chola inscriptions contain specific examples of royal orders communicating certain rules to regulate the qualifications of the members and the conduct of the meeting of the *Sabha*. The economic status (landholding rights) was an important criterion for becoming a member of these corporate bodies. The *Sabha* strictly was the assembly of Brahmin villages (*Brahmadēyas*) which usually had names ending with *Chaturvēdimangalam*. The Brahmin *Sabha* was associated with several administrative committees called *Vāriyam*, which is frequently appeared in the Uttiramerur inscription of the tenth century C.E. This study is based on the evidence of contemporary inscriptions which gives interesting details of the economic and social life of the village and the part played by the assembly in it.

The Cōlas (1955)[9] by K.A. Nilakanta Sastri is a milestone work in the realm of the social, political, and cultural history of south India, celebrated all over the world as a pioneering work in the Chola history. It emphasises the social groups of the *valangai* and *idangai* division and also discussed the taxation system, land measurement, agriculture, fertility of the land, various cropping patterns, the agricultural labourers, and land tenures of medieval Tamil Country. He also emphasised the standard of rates of land per *vēli*, which are figures in the Thanjavur inscriptions of the reign of Rajaraja I like the share of the temple on *dēvadāna* lands, the fertility of the land and the total produce. The Thanjavur inscription represents the state's share on the lands made over the temple. The villages situated on the bank of the river Kaveri and its branches had sometimes to take special measures for keeping the river bund in good repair to avoid overflow during the floods; such villages had to levy a special tax for this intention. The book also discussed the *ēkabhōga-brahmadēya* lands (land rights to the single Brahmin) and the privileges of the Brahmins in the village and their actual distribution too.

Footsteps of Nilakanta Sastri were followed by many historians. The scholars like A. Appadorai and T.V. Mahalingam followed the path of Nilakanta Sastri and produced some works on the social and economic history of south India in the early period. '*Economic Conditions in Southern India (A.D. 1000-1500)*' (1936) by A. Appadorai[10] is an important work on the economic history of medieval south India based on epigraphic sources. It studies the land tenures, agriculture, and the nature of south Indian village communities, commerce, guilds, towns, industries, and foreign trade from 1000 to 1500 A.D. The book also deals with the economic role of the state and concludes based on the foreign accounts and epigraphic references. His approach of writing is descriptive and portrays the main features of the economic conditions of the region and he shows a general awareness of some of the basic issues on Indian historiography. T.V. Mahalingam's works '*Administration and Social Life under Vijayanagar*' (1940), '*Early South Indian Paleography*' (1967), '*Inscriptions of Pallavas*' (1974), etc. are considerable importance for the reconstructions of the social and cultural history of the Pallava and the Vijayanagar Empires.[11]

Land Grants and Agrarian Reactions in Cola and Pandya Times (1987) written by R. Thirumalai analyzed the modes of Chola land assessment and explains the rates of assessments followed in Chola and Pandya regions.[12] N. Subramanian's '*Sangam Polity: The Administration and Social Life of the Sangam Tamils*' (1980) is a comprehensive study on the various aspects of a highly advanced Tamil society and polity of the *Sangam* period. It deals with the administration, military organisation, law and justice, revenue system, agriculture and trade and commerce, etc.[13]

The historical writings of south India were revolving around the solid foundations laid by S. Krishnaswami Aiyangar and K.A. Nilakanta Sastri up to the 1960s. Then a group of American scholars worked on medieval south Indian History. They provided new interpretations, using modern methodology. Burton Stein, George W. Spencer, Kenneth R. Hall, Richard Kennedy, and Aidan Southall are important historians' contributed much to the historical writings of south India. They have been working on south Indian history highlighting the tradition of relationships between the different social groups and their economic connectivity. They have borrowed much from modern sociologists to projects an explanatory model for the development of south Indian polity and society.

The medieval South Indian history has attracted a good deal of attention since 1980 when Burton Stein published his monumental work, '*Peasant State and Society in Medieval South India*'.[14] In his work, he introduced a new theory of 'segmentary' state system. He questioned the concept of 'centralized monarchy' of K.A. Nilakanta Sastri. The arguments of Burton Stein revolved around the nature of state formation in medieval south India and the processes, both economic and political that resulted in the emergence of the Chola state in the Kaveri delta region in the middle of the ninth century C.E. Burton Stein painted the broad historical canvass and subsequently, we have the work of Noboru Karashima and Y. Subbarayalu. When Burton Stein's work first appeared, more than three decades back he was firmly criticized for suggesting that the Chola state was not a centralised bureaucracy. After nearly three decades historians have finally begun to realize that given the material conditions existing in the medieval period and the complex distribution of Land rights, it would have been impossible for the Chola state (segmentary/feudal state) to acquire the trappings of a bureaucratic state.

Burton Stein's another work[15] '*All the Kings' Mana: Papers on Medieval South Indian History*' (1984), brought to light the kingship and polity of medieval south India, the Brahmanical ritual power and their legitimisation in the Chola polity and involvement as priests, kings, gods, and the multiplicity of ranked groupings (castes) capable of being replicated in territorial segments of larger political systems as an ideology of homologies. Burton Stein discussed in his book about the local chiefs, e.g., the heads of dominant agricultural groups and the economic functions of medieval south Indian temples particularly, Tirupati *dēvasdhānam* temple. He also discussed elaborately the integration of the agrarian system of south India, the Coromandal trade with China and the Southeast Asian countries by the merchant communities from the Pallavas to the Vijayanagara period, focused on the historical geography of Tamil country, the social mobility, the medieval south Indian Hindu sects and the cultural activities of South India.

'*Trade and Statecraft in the age of Cholas*' (1980) of Kenneth R. Hall criticized the concept of centralised state during the Chola period.[16] His work mainly deals with the assembly of regional commercial centers known as *nagaram*, and its administrative and marketing functions. This book also discusses the local commercial centers of each nādu unit and their formal relationships with several supra-regional commercial organisations, whose activities extended beyond the local *nādu's* marketing community. He argues that the activities of the eleventh-century monarch allowed the development of regional centres of political power which during the late twelfth and thirteenth centuries were to changes the authority of the Chola kings themselves. South India's commercial system has confined its attention to the itinerant trade organisations which seem to have developed during the Chola period.

Noboru Karashima, a Japanese historian worked on the south Indian studies, who is familiar to the Indian readers by his earlier scholarly writings and lectures. Karashima published his popular work '*South Indian History and Society: Studies from Inscriptions A.D. 850-1800*' in 1984,[17] which followed the publication of the '*Concordance of the Names in the Chola Inscriptions*' (1978), which he wrote with T. Matsui and Y. Subbarayalu and '*A Concordance of Nayaks: The Vijayanagar Inscriptions in South India*' (2002).[18] In his '*Ancient to Medieval: South Indian Society in Transition*' (2009),[19] Karashima moved into a new study on social discord and its causes. In his work, he argues that there were some changes took place in medieval south Indian society, Chola's state policy of land grants, development of maritime trade in the Indian Ocean, the decline in the traditional landowning class, and the emergence of the new *jātis* in the agrarian order. This social disorder also saw the birth of new religious faith and thoughts. '*A Concise History of South India: Issues and Interpretations*' (2014) is an edited volume of Noboru Karashima, a unique collection of articles on the different aspects of south India's history from the pre-historic times to the present, contributed by both Indian and Japanese scholars.[20] The most distinctive features of Karashima's academic approach were that he went through thousands of unpublished and published south Indian inscriptions, analyzed them intensively and widely using statistical analysis, and attempted to reconstruct the history of south India.

Noboru Karashima's contribution to the historiography of the later period is impressive and valuable. Karashima inaugurated a new trend in reconstructing the South Indian past by looking intensely at localities of *nādu* units based on the epigraphic sources. Unlike Burton Stein who relied mostly on published inscriptions, Karashima and his group worked with both published and unpublished inscriptions. The terms which appear in the records are assembled in time series and the statistical and ecological distribution of the terms, particularly revenue terms, is studied. Thus, Karashima was among the first historians to suggest that the political and social structure of the dry regions was different than that which existed in the river belt regions.

Noboru Karashima's associates Y. Subbarayalu is a well-known epigraphist who studied extensively the social and economic history of the Cholas based on epigraphic sources. His research work '*Political Geography of the Chola Country*' (1973) is the only in-depth study of the settlement pattern and social geography of the Chola during the eleventh century C.E.[21] Those who are familiar with '*Kaveri*' and '*Studies in Cholas History*' will find some of these papers in this book. However, the books bring together important contributions made by Y. Subbarayalu[22] over the years. The trade guilds and their activities have been studied very closely and Y. Subbarayalu does break new ground in the study of the Tamil inscription found in Southeast Asia. Though only six Tamil inscriptions have been found, ranging in dates from the seventh century till the fourteenth century C.E., historians have expanded expressively on Tamil participation in the trade with Sumatra and the rest of Srivijaya.

Y. Subbarayalu's study of the Barus inscription from Sumatra is interesting and well-argued. His study of the *vatteluttu* inscriptions discovered at Pulānkurrichi (Sivagangai District), datable to the fifth century C.E, is undoubtedly a valuable contribution as he explicitly rejects the use of the unpredictable and incorrectly labeled '*Sangam* literature' as the basis for dating the earliest record giving details of the land structure in the dry regions of the Pandyan territory. 'The significance of the inscriptions is that they are the first detailed inscriptions relating to land grants to the temple and Brahmin an inkling of the developments in the agrarian system during the post-*Sangam* centuries' says Y. Subbarayalu in his work '*Studies in Cola History*'. Another interesting finding which needs to be considered is the fact that after a detailed study of the personal names found in Chola records, Y. Subbarayalu finds that only seven percent of the 'officers' of the Chola state came from this social group. It has become the grist to the mill of Tamil historiography to date 'Brahmin domination' to the patronage extended to the Brahmins by the medieval rulers. Such important contributions from a historian of the integrity of Subbarayalu will certainly influence public debate on the politically convenient myth of Brahmin domination. Noboru Karashima was the first to point out that non-Brahmin village called *ūr* practiced social exclusion as there is mention of *tīndāchchēri* (living quarters of outcastes) in inscriptions.

The resource base of the medieval state is always an interesting issue. Earlier historians had maintained that the level of taxation was rather high and with the grant of *sarvamānya* tax-free (*iraiyili)* status to more and more villages as they came under the control of temples of the villages and *nādus*. Very noteworthy work of Y. Subbarayalu is '*South India under the Cholas*' published by Oxford University in 2012, analysis different aspects of state-society interactions in medieval south India under the Cholas. The book highlights the socio-economic setting, merchant guilds, and other sociological characteristics. It also traces the evolution of the Chola states, economy, and society and emphasises the land surveys, revenue system of the Cholas, sale deeds, and property rights. The author examines, in detail, the emergence of new agrarian units like *ūr*, *sabha*, *nādu*, *periyanādu*, trade guilds, and agrarian population like landowners, cultivators, landless peasants, slave labourers and the peculiar social divisions *valangai* and *idangai*. Y. Subbarayalu's work on the Chola territory has helped the readers to understand a few extremely difficult questions on the productivity of the land or the extent of the land under cultivation. P. Shanmugam's '*The Revenue System of the Cholas (A.D. 850-1279)*' (1987) dealt with the subject in the context of important contributions made by the Cholas to the development of the state economy. He consulted a large number of the Chola inscriptions to identify the different revenue terms and land surveys undertaken in the Chola period.[23]

David Ludden's monumental work '*Peasant History of South India*' (1985),[24] provides an exhaustive account of the structures of the peasant history throughout a full millennium of India's history. He points out that the change in the agrarian system began during the last century of the Pandya rule. He emphasised the local activity and transformation of social relations and rural society in the Tirunelveli region and the historical change. He has mentioned in his book the villages assemblies of landowners appear to have played a dominant role in temple management and finance under the Pandyas rule and also emphasised that the local institution control in the southern Pandya country seems rather have been dominant-caste assemblies in single settlements or circuits of villages. During the transformation of the early modern period, local initiatives helped in proper changes in South Indian economy, politics, and culture and peasants participated forcefully in making a modern world system of exchange of power relations.

Trade, Ideology and Urbanization South India 300 BC to AD 1300 (1996) of R. Champakalakshmi,[25] covering a vast period of sixteen hundred years, deals with the economic history of early and early medieval South India. This is an analytical study, emphasised the factors which responsible for the emergence and growth of the urban centres, city centres and temple towns, which includes royal as well as cultural centres like Kanchipuram and Madurai, *Nagaram* centres, port towns, *Brahmadēya* and *Dēvadāna*, Trade and merchant centres during the Pallava and Pandya periods. According to the view of R. Champakalakshmi and other scholars, the land grants to the religious institutions like temples, mutts, Buddhist and Jain monasteries, creation of new settlements for Brahmins, *Dēvadāsis*, artisans, construction of temples, etc. were the responsible for the emergence of urban centres during the early medieval period.

James Heitzman's work '*Gifts of Power: Lordship in an Early Indian State*' (2001),[26] discusses the medieval state, the interpretation of the various 'intermediaries' between the agrarian labourers and the king. James Heitzman views that the proliferation and increased specification of property terms through the Chola period was a process furthered by the extension of the Chola state and its functions. He also scrutinises the urban culture, transaction networks, and social relations that grew up around the temple, which increasingly became recipients of property and defrayed tax revenue from royal agents and local nobles seeking association with the Chola court through donatives ritual culture. Early medieval urbanism depended on agrarian expansion through land reclamation by temples which mobilised land cultivators to supervise labour in return for various cultivation rights. The dominant landowning class concentrates in its own hands the exercise of political functions, a situation markedly different from the capitalist state in which the state apparatus remains 'autonomous' from the ruling class.

Kesavan Veluthat's '*The Early Medieval in South India*' (2010) explores the polity, society, and economy of the early medieval period in south India.[27] It examines the historiography of early medieval south India and debates the structural formation of economy, society, polity and culture, the role of temples, corporate bodies, land-rights, surplus production, nature of the state, landlordism, and regional identity written over two decades. The author re-examines the problems and patterns in the early history of *Tamilakam* in general and early medieval Kerala and Karnataka in particular. '*Social Formations of Early South India*' (2012) of Rajan Gurukkal[28] presents a critical analysis of social formation in Tamil Nadu and Kerala from pre-historic times to early medieval period. It observes the transformation from agro-pastoral to the agrarian social formation by searching areas like economy, technology, and historical processes of state configuration. The book specifically focuses on the transition from clan to lineage to the traditional occupation of a social group, and the social implications of the spread of writing. In the works of Rajan Gurukkal attempts are made to analyze the nature of the social and economic structure of *Tamilakam* in general and the forces of change or development within it.

K. Sivathamby's[29] works refer to a considerable change in south Indian historiography. In his interpretation, he used various types of source materials, adopted anthropological methods, and applied the concept of historical materialism in understanding the '*tinai*' or physiographical divisions and the socio-economic milieu of ancient Tamil society. S. Manickam's[30] work '*Slavery in the Tamil Country: A Historical Over-View*' (1982) highlights the social and economic conditions of slavery in the early and medieval Tamil country. The book intends to make a historical probe into the origin and development of slavery in its varied forms- hereditary, penal, temple slaves, agrestic slavery i.e. slavery connected with land and bonded labourers of both voluntary and non-voluntary nature- by citing some literary and inscriptional evidence to indicates the existence of formal slavery as a considerable phenomenon in the Tamil country.

Many scholars have worked on the agrarian history of medieval south India, but very limited works have been done on the artisans and craftsmen of early and early medieval South India. Vijaya Ramaswamy who has been working on the search of artisans and craftsmen for more than three decades published several articles and research monographs on the skilled labourers of medieval south India. Her major works[31] include; '*Vishwakarma Craftsmen in Early Medieval*

Peninsular India' (2004), *'Vishwakarma in South Indian History'* (2018), *'Craftwork & Wages in Medieval Tamilnadu (based on Inscriptions from the 8th to 13th century)* (1993)', *'Traditional Crafts, Technology and Society in pre-Colonial Peninsular India'* (2008), etc. They are extremely commendable works in the field of art and craft activities and give a vivid picture of the social, economic, and cultural aspects of the artisans and craftsman communities.

Vijaya Ramaswamy in her recent edited volume[32] *'In Search of Vishwakarma: Mapping Indian Craft Histories'* published in 2019 emphasised the various aspects relating to the craftsmen and their divine skill. Based on her view the Vishvakarma community who is a specialist in the making of crafting icons and building monumental structures. This volume on the search of 'Vishvakarma' seeks to explore the hermeneutics of Vishvakarma and to document a rich tapestry of images as well as historical information regarding crafts and craftsmen through the ages. Further, Vijaya Ramaswamy's presidential address[33] delivered at the 38th annual session of South Indian History Congress on *'Vishwakarma in south Indian History'* focuses the Vishvakarma craftsmen and their social and economic life, based on epigraphic evidence. In her address she is attempted to answer the following questions; (1) who were the Vishwakarma craftsmen? (2) What constitutes the essential difference between artisan and craftsman? (3) Where did they live? and (4) what did they do in terms of their role function in medieval society and economy?. She logically tried to answer those questions and highlights the role and function of the Vishvakarma community in the growth of art and craft activities. Another work 'C*raftwork & wages in Medieval Tamilnadu'* focuses on the employment and wages paid to the Vishvakarma craftsmen based on inscriptional evidence.

Besides the historical works, quite a few scholars worked on Tamil literature and their traditions. In the collection and compile of Tamil literary texts many Tamil and foreign scholars were involved and spent their precious epoch in collecting and publishing of the early Tamil literary works. Among them U.Ve. Swaminatha Iyer is popularly known as *'Tamil Thāttā'* (Grant father of Tamil) was instrumental in bringing many long-forgotten works of Classical Tamil literature to light. He was a Tamil scholar and eminent researcher. His painstaking works over five decades brought to light major literary works in Tamil. He contributed to a great extent for the enrichment of Tamil literary heritage and published over a hundred books in his lifetime, on a variety of information connected to classical Tamil literature.

He collected 3,067 paper manuscripts, palm-leaf manuscripts, and notes on various kinds. At first, he published *Civakacintāmani*, a Jain classical in 1887. Being the first time, Swaminatha Iyer and his associates had to face a lot of difficulties in understanding the original texts, with missing leaves, textual inaccuracies, and unknown terms. He started to collect the *Sangam* classics with the aim of editing and publishing them. Swaminatha Iyer's long search for the original Tamil texts of early periods during which he regularly worked with C.W. Damodaram Pillai. They were accountable for collecting and cataloging several old Tamil manuscripts and preparing them in compilations and modern form. Both Swaminatha Iyer and Damodaram Pillai visited every hamlet and knocked at every door to collect manuscripts. They employed all the resources at their command to get at the works. Both of them printed and published the *Tolkāppiyam*, *Pattupāttu*, *Puranānūru*, *Silappadhikāram*, *Manimēkalai*, etc. which received great attention among the Tamil lovers with a lot of keenness.[34]

Constantine Joseph Beschi, popularly known as 'Viramāmunivar', was an Italian Jesuit priest, who is commonly identified as a Tamil scholar, contributed much for the Tamil literary traditions. He compiled the first Tamil Lexicon, a Tamil-Latin dictionary. He translated and explained in Latin the *Thirukkural*, an epic poem of Thiruvallur. He is credited with the translation of several important Tamil literary texts such as *Tēvāram*, *Thiruppāvai*, *Nannōl*, and *Āthichchūdi* into European languages. He wrote a grammar for the common use of Tamil which at times led him to be referred to as the 'Father of Tamil Prose' (Tamil *Urainadai Ilakkiyathin thanthai*). His greatest poetical work is the '*Thēmbāvani*', an ornament of poems as sweet as honey. The *Thēmbāvani* was presented for ratification as a classic in the academy of poets and received their approval and Constantine Joseph Beschi was given the title '*Viramāmunivar*' (the courageous ascetic).[35] He is one of the earliest and most distinguished pioneers in the field of Tamil Studies. It is important to note Albertine Gaur's comments on him. He says that "his fame rests partly on brilliant linguistic achievements, partly on a rare poetic sensitiveness that enabled him to penetrate the complex thoughts and ornate techniques of Tamil poetry and produce some highly original works in so alien a medium".[36]

In the translation work of Tamil literature, scholars undertook their sincere efforts. Among them, A.K. Ramanujan was an Indian poet and scholar of Indian literature who wrote in both English and Kannada. He was also an author, folklorist, translator, and play writer. He has been recognized as the world's most profound scholar of South Asian language and culture. His academic research ranged across five languages; Tamil, Kannada, Telugu, Sanskrit, and English. A.K. Ramanujan's '*Poems of Love and War: From the Eight Anthologies and the Ten Long Poems of Classical Tamil*', is an excellent work on *Aham* and *Puram* poems.[37] Another distinguished scholar in the field of Tamil literature is Kamil V. Zvelbil, who is an eminent foreign scholar in Indian literature and linguists. He is generally concerned with the poetic genre, chronology, and the contents of the early Tamil texts. In the course of discussing the literary works, he provides some information on the socio-cultural aspects. He published several volumes on different Indian Dravidian languages such as '*Dravidian Linguistics: An Introduction*' (1995), '*Smile of Murugan: On Tamil Literature of South India*' (1973), '*Companion Studies to the History of Tamil Literature*' (1991), '*Lexicon of Tamil Literature*' (1994), '*Classical Tamil Prosody: An Introduction*' (2014), etc.[38] His '*Smile of Murugan: On Tamil Literature of South India*' is a fundamental text for scholar those who want to study the Tamil literature.

The historiographical survey has attempted here to highlights the earlier studies on the social, economic, and cultural history of medieval south India from the early times to the pre-modern period. The works cited and reviewed above are of valuable contribution to the history of early and early medieval south India with the proper endeavour. These works explore the process of social and economic changes that unfolded in rural agrarian and urban industrial society, especially the formation of stratified land relations with the agrarian community and other occupational groups.

The present edited volume '*Land and Society in Medieval South India: Perspectives on Social, Economic and Cultural Traditions*' consists of seventeen research papers, afford a welcome enlargement of the scope of the social, economic and cultural discourse, which dealt with the some of the facets like geopolitical settings, Nayakas of Srikakulam-Vishakhapatnam regions, colonial diarchy in the Pudukkottai princely state, Tamil-Tulu linkages, agrarian patterns and practices of early and medieval south India, water resource management systems, the medieval Tamil society and class transformation, the ritual functionaries of the Hindu temples, hero stone traditions of early medieval Karnataka, *Bhakti* movements, Buddhist monastic orders, the rock-cut architecture of the Pallavas and other aspects of the early and early medieval South India.

The importance of the publication of this book lies in the fact that it would not only help the academic world but also all those who are interested in understanding of early medieval agrarian history and socio-cultural facets of medieval south India. Towards a fuller perceptive of the society, economy, and culture in early medieval India, the present volume contributes in an enormous way and we hope that this will stimulate further research in the field of the socio-economic and cultural history of early medieval South India. The strength of this edited volume spotlight the wide range of aspects on the subject as well as projections of the learned scholars on the theme of this book. It is hoped that the readers would be immensely benefitted from the learned exposition of the social, economic, and cultural milieu of the early medieval period of south Indian history.

References

1. V. Kanakasabhai, *The Tamils Eighteen Hundred Years Ago*, Higginbotham & Co., Madras, 1904.
2. S. Krishnaswami Aiyangar, *The Beginnings of South Indian History*, Modern Printing Works, Madras, 1918; *Some Contributions of South India to Indian Culture*, University of Calcutta, Calcutta, 1923; *Evolution of Hindu Administrative Institutions in South India*, First Published by University of Madras, Madras, 1931.
3. Robert Sewell and S. Krishnaswami Aiyangar (eds.), *The Historical Inscriptions of Southern India (Collected till 1923) and Outlines of Political History*, The Diocesan Press, Madras, 1932.
4. S. Krishnaswami Aiyangar, *Sources of Vijayanagar History*, University of Madras, Madras, 1920.
5. S. Krishnaswami Aiyangar, *Manimekalai in Its Historical Setting*, The Diocesan Press, Madras, 1928.
6. K.A. Nilakanta Sastri, *A History of South India: from Pre Historic times to the Fall of Vijayanagar*, Oxford University Press, New Delhi, 1958.
7. K.A. Nilakanta Sastri, *The Pandyan Kingdom from the Earliest Times to the Sixteenth century*, Luzac & Co., London, 1929; *The Colas*, Second Edition, University of Madras, Madras, 1955; *Historical Method in Relation to Problems of South Indian History*, University of Madras, Madras, 1941; *Development of Religion in South India*, Orient Longmans, Madras, 1963; *The Culture and History of Tamils*, K.L. Mukhopadhyay, Calcutta, 1964; *Sangam Literatures: Its Cults and Culture*, Swathi Publishers, Madras, 1972.
8. K.A. Nilakanta Sastri, *Studies in Cola History and Administration*, University of Madras, Madras, 1932.

9. K.A. Nilakanta Sastri, *The Colas*, Second Edition, University of Madras, Madras, 1955.
10. A. Appadorai, *Economic Conditions in Southern India (A.D. 1000-1500)*, University of Madras Historical Series, No.12, in two volumes, University of Madras, Madras, 1936.
11. T.V. Mahalingam, *Administration and Social Life under Vijayanagar*, University of Madras, Madras, 1940; *Early South Indian Paleography*, University of Madras, Madras, 1967; *Inscriptions of the Pallavas*, Indian Council of Historical Research, New Delhi, 1974.
12. R. Thirumalai, *Land Grants and Agrarian Reactions in Cola and Pandya Times*, University of Madras, Madras, 1987.
13. N. Subramanian, *Sangam Polity: The Administration and Social Life of the Sangam Tamils*, Ennes Publication, Madurai, 1980.
14. Burton Stein, *Peasant State and Society in Medieval South India*, Oxford University Press, New Delhi, 1980.
15. Burton Stein, *All the Kings' Mana: Papers on Medieval South Indian History*, New Era Publications, Madras, 1984.
16. Kenneth R. Hall, *Trade and Statecraft in the age of Cōlas*, Abhinav Publications, New Delhi, 1980.
17. Noboru Karashima, *South Indian History and Society: Studies from Inscriptions A.D. 850-1800*, Oxford University Press, New Delhi, 1984.
18. Noboru Karashima, Y. Subbarayalu and Toru Matsui, *A Concordance of the Names in the Chola Inscriptions*, Sarvodaya Ilakkia Pannai, Madurai, 1978; Noboru Karashima, *A Concordance of Nayaks: The Vijayanagar Inscriptions in South India*, Oxford University Press, New Delhi, 2002.
19. Noboru Karashima, *Ancient to Medieval: South Indian Society in Transition*, Oxford University Press, New Delhi, 2009.
20. Noboru Karashima (ed.), *A Concise History of South India: Issues and Interpretations*, Oxford University Press, New Delhi, 2014.
21. Y. Subbarayalu, *Political Geography of the Chola Country*, Tamil Nadu State Archaeology Department, Madras, 1973.
22. Y. Subbarayalu, *Studies in Cola History*, Surabhi Pathippakam, Chennai, 2001; "Changes in Agrarian Relations in Kaveri Delta, c.900-1300", *Social Scientist*, Vol. 38, No.7/8 (July-August 2010), pp.44-52; *South India under the Cholas*, Oxford University Press, New Delhi, 2012; S.Rajagopal, (ed.), *Kaveri: Studies in Epigraphy, Archaeology and History –Professor Y.Subbarayalu Felicitation Volume*, Panpattu Veliyittakam, Chennai, 2001.
23. P. Shanmugam, *The Revenue System of the Cholas, 850-1279*, New Era Publications, Madras, 1987.
24. David Ludden, *Peasant History of South India*, Princeton University Press, Princeton, 1985.

25. R. Champakalakshmi, *Trade Ideology and Urbanization South India 300 BC to AD 1300*, Oxford University Press, New Delhi, 1996.
26. James Heitzman, *Gifts of Power: Lordship in an Early Indian State, Oxford University Press, New Delhi*, 2001 (first published in 1997).
27. Kesavan Veluthat, *The Early Medieval in South India*, Oxford University Press, New Delhi, 2010.
28. Rajan Gurukkal, *Social Formations of South India*, Oxford University Press, New Delhi, 2012.
29. K. Sivathamby, *Studies in Ancient Tamil Society: Economy, Society and State Formations*, New Century Book House, Chennai, 1998; "Early South Indian Society and Economy: The *Tinai* Concept", *Social Scientist*, Vol.29, 1974.
30. S. Manickam, *Slavery in the Tamil Country: A Historical Over-View*, The Christian Literature Society, Madras, 1982.
31. Vijaya Ramaswamy, "Vishwakarma Craftsmen in Early Medieval Peninsular India", *Journal of the Economic and Social History of Orient*, Vol. 47, No. 4, 2004, pp. 548-582; "Vishwakarma in South Indian History" *South Indian History Congress Thirty Eight Annual Session Proceedings*, Calicut, 28-30 January 2018; Craftwork & Wages in Medieval Tamilnadu (based on Inscriptions from the 8th to 13th century)', in Narayani Gupta, *Craftsmen and Merchants: Essays in South Indian Urbanism*, Chandigarh, 1993; 'Traditional Crafts, Technology and Society in pre-Colonial Peninsular India', in Rajat Datta (ed.), *Rethinking A Millennium: Perspectives on Indian History from the Eighth to the Eighteenth Century*, AAKAR Books, Delhi, 2008.
32. Vijaya Ramaswamy (ed.), *In Search of Vishwakarma: Mapping Indian Craft Histories*, Primus Books, New Delhi, 2019.
33. Vijaya Ramaswamy, "Vishwakarma in South Indian History" *South Indian History Congress Thirty Eight Annual Session Proceedings*, Calicut, 28-30 January 2018, pp.954, 955.
34. U.Ve. Swaminatha Iyer, *En Sarithiram: Autobiography of Swaminatha Iyer*, published by S.Kalyanasundar Ayyar, U.Ve. Swaminathayyar Library, Chennai, second edition, 1982.
35. Leon Besse, *Father Beschi of the Society of Jesus: His Times and Writings*, St. Joseph's Industrial School Press, Trichinopoly, 1918.
36. Albertine Gaur, "Father Beschi and His Grammar of High-Tamil", *The British Museum Quarterly*, Vol.32, No.3/4 (Spring 1968), pp.103-108.
37. A.K. Ramanujam, *Poems of Love and War: From the Eight Anthologies and the Ten Long Poems of Classical Tamil*, Columbia University Press, Columbia, 2011.
38. Kamil V. Zvelbil, *Dravidian Linguistics: An Introduction*, Pondicherry Institute of Linguistics and Culture, Pondicherry, 1995; *Smile of Murugan: On Tamil Literature of South India*,

E.L. Brill, Leiden, 1973; *Companion Studies to the History of Tamil Literature*, Brill Academic Publishers, Leiden, 1991; *Lexicon of Tamil Literature*, Brill Academic Publishers, Leiden, 1994; *Classical Tamil Prosody: An Introduction*, New Era Publications, Chennai, 2014.

PART - I

STATE, POLITY AND SOCIETY- LINKAGES

1

Geo-Political Settings of the Early and Medieval Tamil Country

Binay Barman and Saumalya Mali

Contribution of Geography is fathomless to measure when it comes to the culture of history in any region. History and Geography are two inseparable entities indeed. It is said that Geography 'is the foundation of all historical knowledge.'[1] Historical Geography is the part of that Human Geography where people interact with nature; in other words, it is the relation between habit and habitat. Historical geography focuses mainly on emphasis on location, society-land relation, and regional analysis. While defining Historical Geography, Golden Berg said, "the apparent conflict of views and definitions of the concept of 'historical geography' can be resolved only on the condition of recognizing unified historical geography both geographical and historical as an independent scientific discipline located in the transition zone between geography and history".[2] B.S. Cohn said about Historical Geography, "Regions are far from fixed, enduring things, especially if any historical perspective is taken. They are not absolutes and they are difficult, if not impossible to define by objective criteria".[3]

The historical geography is mainly the study of the very geographic pattern of a particular region and how people interact with that environment and landscape through times. According to the World Commission on Environment and Development (WCED), the environment is that very entity where we live and development is what we do to improve our well being. Both environment and development are inseparable. Historical Geography exists in natural phenomena and biodiversity and these two forms a unit of the region. Smith talked of four different approaches to the study of Historical Geography. Those are the operation of geographical factors in history, the evolution of the cultural landscape, reconstruction of the past geography, and the study of geographical change through time.[4] A remarkable development came in the study of Historical Geography in the post-independence era in India. In that time, archeological field works resulted, mainly, in the accumulation of vast quantity of geographical data on ancient sites and settlements. Many archeologists determined the pre and proto-historic periods based on cartographic presentation.

In Indian history, works and research on Historical Geography are very limited in number. In this field, an important work is Alexander Cunningham's '*Ancient Geography of India*' which gives an account of the routes, followed by Hiuen Tsang. Despite the plain description and narration, we need to consider this book as the first document in the field of Historical Geography, in India. Brajdulal Chattopadhyay[5] who is an eminent scholar of India criticized the works of Historical Geography encapsulating early and early-medieval India. According to him, most of the earlier works were the accounts of locating the different countries, regions, mentioning the names of the places, rivers, hills, mountains which were mentioned in ancient literature and inscriptions. He also said that the authors who penned these earlier works did not attempt to relate geographical information to any chronological framework or general problems of history.[6] Many scholars enriched Historical Geography through reconciliation between history and geography after Alexander Cunningham left his first imprint on this field. Some of these scholars who are worth mentioning are H.D. Sankalia, B.C. Law, D.C. Sircar, and Y. Subbarayalu. H.D. Sankalia was the founder of Scientific Archaeology in India. He studied the inscriptions and found the personal names and the names of places in Gujarat. He also depicted the impact of Sanskrit language, Sanskrit literature, and culture on the people of that region.

In ancient Indian texts, the Indian subcontinent is divided into five geographical zones and one of these five is '*Daksinapatha*'.[7] The '*Daksinapatha*' is defined in many ways with different new meanings but to take it in a broad sense we need to understand that the term '*Daksinapatha*' which refers to the region from the Narmada valley to the middle of the foothills of Vindhya mountain.[8] Hence, the '*Daksinapatha*' refers to the entire Indian peninsula. Generally, we can say that it stretches out to the valleys of river Narmada, Tungabhadra and Krishna. On the other hand, south India is also termed as 'Deccan' and the word 'Deccan' is derived from '*Daksinapatha*'.[9] Greeks and the early Indian authors termed the regions in the far south of India as '*Damirica*' or '*Drāvida*' respectively.[10] In a few *silpa* texts of south India, the region from Krishna river to Kanyakumarika is mentioned as '*Drāvidadēsa*'. The *Drāvida* style of art flourished in that region.[11] The term '*drāvida*' is not popular in the study of history in south India.[12] While talking of history of south India, Ganapathy Subbiah comments that 'south India' refers to the Tamil speaking region or what is known as *Tamilakam*; since early times it is found in the writings of other historians too.[13] According to Kesavan Veluthat, "south India is equated with the region known to early sources as *Tamilakam*, generally corresponding to the present linguistic states of Kerala and Tamilnadu".[14]

The geographical location of Tamil Nadu helped to construct the society and culture of the state. The present state of Tamil Nadu was known as '*Tamilakam*' and 'Tamil country' in the ancient period and early medieval period respectively.[15] In the Tamil literature, the geographical portrait of Tamil Nadu is depicted. In those literatures, it is said that Tamil Nadu is located in the region from Venkatam Tip (presently known as Tirupati Hill) in the north to Cape Comorin in the south and from the Bay of Bengal in the east to the Arabian Sea in the west.[16] Andhra Pradesh came within the borderline of Tamil country in the north which showed Venkatam Tip as an important landmark. It is worth to mentioning that ancient *Tamilakam* and early medieval Tamil Country are different in geographical areas and boundaries. Due to its peninsular location, Tamil Nadu differed from north Indian style and culture. Kaveri, Vaigai, Palar, and Thenpennai, the four important rivers of south India formed the Tamil region. Some other rivers are Noyyal, Cheyyar, Vellar, Moyar, Pampar, Vaippar, etc. These rivers flow on Tamil country and help to enrich Tamil culture and civilisation. Apart from these rivers, several other hills, hillocks, and mountains are there in Tamil country. Some of these are Palani, Velliangiri, Doddabeta peak, Meghamalai, Perumal peak, and Cairn hill. These rivers and hills played a key role in the formation of sub-regional dialects and culture of Tamil country.

Impact of Geographical Factors on Tamil Culture

Geographical characteristics, especially rivers, hills, mountains, climate, and landscape of a particular region cast a firm impact on the social life, livelihood, and economy of that region. In terms of geographical location, the plain of Tamil country which stretches from

Vindhya Mountain in the north of the Deccan plateau to Mysore in the south is situated in the coastal part. The average depth of the south-west Tamil country plateau is 1500 ft. Two very important mountain ranges of this region are the Eastern Ghats and the Western Ghats. Doddabeta peak (8000 ft.) is the highest peak of the Nilgiris and in Palghat region, the gap between Mysore and Palghat is 20 miles.[17] Of all the hills and mountains of Tamil country, Palani, Anaimalai, Kodaikanal, Podiyil Hill are the hills of south Tamil country. At Dinbam, north of Satyamangalam, Tekkadi west of Madurai and Anaimudi, south-west of Pollachi natural concentration is charming.[18] It is said about the plains of Tamil country that it is the south of Tirupati and east of the Western Ghats and Tamil country is a monotonous plain.[19] Of the rivers of Tamil country, Kaveri, Palar, Vaigai, etc. are mentioned in *Sangam* literature. We come across special mention of *Silappadhikāram* where it is said that water of all the rivers mentioned above was used in irrigation in the Tamil region.[20] A main characteristic of the rivers of Tamil country is that all the rivers in the extreme south in the Indian peninsula run from west to east, since the landscape slopes eastwards.[21] We need to mention that most parts of the plains of Tamil country are situated in the east and west coastal region.

Geographical Division of Tamil Country

From the early Tamil texts, we find a mention of five ecological and cultural regions in this area. These five regions are *Kurunji*, *Mullai*, *Marutam*, *Neytal*, and *Pālai* which have their occupational patterns, festivals, deities, etc. Ganapati Subbiah's 'Order of Hierarchy in the Realm of Religion and Society' notes that classical Tamil poetry was governed by the concept of *tinai* where five eco-zones were correlated to each other. And all these five zones are named after the flora typical to the region.[22] From the five *tinais* geographical and social history of early Tamil country is revealed. In Tamil literature '*Kurunji*' refers to the mountainous regions. One of the main characteristics of these regions was slash and burn cultivation. According to the Tamil Lexicon, the Kuravars and the Kanvars were the aboriginal people in *Kurunji* regions. These people would live on primitive hunting habits, shifting culture, and honey collection from forests. In *Mullai* regions, traces of shifting cultivation and animal husbandry are found. We also come to know that minor millet was cultivated in this region. The *Marutam* was a fertile region in Tamil country where paddy cultivation was remarkable due to the fertility of the soil that suited for paddy plants. Therefore, the Chera, Chola, Pandya and some other dynasties established their political powers in the fertile regions. In *Sangam* literature, we come across references to the *Marutam* region. The aboriginal people of *Marutam* regions were the Ulavars and the Toluvars. In early Tamil literature, these people were called as the Kalamars and the Arinars whose main occupation was cultivation.[23] The coastal region is known as *Neytal*. It is to note that the occupation of the people of this region was fishing. Of the early inhabitants of *Neytal* land, the Paratavars or Valainars were worthy of mention. In Tamil literature we come across a depiction of the Paratavars.[24] *Palai* of Tamil country mainly refers to sandy and dry regions. The Maravars, the Malavars, and the Eyinars who mainly belonged to the martial groups were the inhabitants of the *Pālai* region. There was a stark difference in character and behaviour between these people and the people of the other regions of the early Tamil country. These people would mainly depend on fighting, robbing, and killing wayfarers to earn their livelihood.

The five regions (*tinais*) of Tamil country are mentioned in *Tolkāppiyam* and various other Tamil literary works. We know geography, ecology, social life, and economic condition of the people of Tamil country from these works. These unique geographical factors of Tamil country helped the state to get established as a separate cultural unit. Besides, the early Tamil tradition was neither Vedic nor influenced by Sanskrit culture.

While talking about the impact of climate on geographical units of Tamil country, Burton Stein states that, "Farther south, ranges of mountains and plateau run down the Peninsula to the southern tip and tend to compartmentalise the terrain of the whole of peninsular India. These features make for the greater historical isolation and smaller political units of the south compared to the north. Thus, as will be seen, physiographic shaped the political as well as the economic and social history of the people".[25]

Information about the climate, geographical regions and lands of Tamil country are available in *Tolkāppiyam*. In *Tolkāppiyam*, we find references to '*Kādurai ulagam*', which were the forest regions; '*Maivarai ulagam*' refers to the hilly regions; '*Tiruppunal ulagam*' refers to the plain lands and '*Perumanal ulagam*' refers to littoral and sandy regions.[26] The term '*ulagam*' refers to the idea that all these regions are separate units. On the other hand, the five ecological regions were identified based on the trees, shrubs, vines, and their blooms which grew abundantly in the respective regions. In Tamil country, reservoirs of water were there so that it could be used in irrigation and people could use it in '*Marutam*' region for agriculture.

Generally, through irrigation dry crops were cultivated. In Tamil language, '*aruvi*' referred to the falls in '*Kurunji*' region, '*vellaruvi*' referred to the springs and streams from the mountains. All these were mentioned in the *Sangam* literature.[27]

Cultivation was the primary occupation of the people in Tamil country. In south India, in the 10th and 11th century C.E. the peasants enjoyed land ownership rights together in villages. From the contemporary inscriptions, we come to know that the landowners would donate their land for the well-being of local people.[28] In Tamil country, the lands where irrigation was available and cultivation was possible, were divided as '*Vellānvagai*', '*Jīvitham*' and '*Varam*'.[29] Apart from these lands, there were '*Brahmadēya*' (donated lands to the Brahmins) and '*Dēvadāna*' (donated lands to the temples) lands.[30] Not only that, the lands, donated to the Buddhists and the Jains were classified as '*Pallichandam*', the lands, donated to the heroes were classified as '*Salabhōgam*' and '*Vīrabhōgam*'.[31]

The cultivation fields, in Tamil country, were known as 'wet', 'dry' and 'garden land'. During the Chola dynasty, wetland, dry land, and garden land were known as '*nanjai*', '*punjai*' and '*thōttakal*' respectively, from their inscriptions.[32] The term '*nanjai*' came from Tamil word '*nal*' which means good and '*shai*' refers to agriculture. Hence, we can understand that irrigation was there in these fields. The term '*punjai*', related to irrigation, came from the Tamil word '*pun*' which refers to rice cultivation. Greens vegetables, and fruits were cultivated in *thōttakal* land which was watered from wells.[33] It is to be noted that, in Tamil country, '*nanjai*' and '*punjai*' were also known as '*nīrnilam*' and '*kollainilam*' respectively. Besides, we come to know from a medieval Tamil inscription that these lands were also called '*nērraramban*' and '*kattāramban*'.[34] In wet cultivation regions, farmers would harvest in two ways- '*kār*' and '*pāsānam*'.[35] According to K. Mavali Rajan, Tamil inscription speaks of two kinds of cropland in Tamil country and they are 'one-crop-land' and 'two-crop-land'. The one-crop-land was termed as '*oruppu vilayumnilam*' and 'two-crop-land' was termed as '*iruppu vilayaumnilam*'.[36] Besides, there was a 'three-crop-land' which was termed as '*kadaippu*'.[37]

In the dry lands agriculture would depend on local rainfall, but in wetlands irrigation was based on tanks, canals, and rivers. In garden lands artificial irrigation systems were adopted. Normal agricultural techniques were followed in both dry lands and wetlands. The wetlands were ploughed several to make the land fit for cultivation. Seeds were sowed manually by hand but sometimes bamboo drills were used to sow seeds. During the medieval period, the Chola kings played a key role in the development of agriculture. The Chola kings managed to build up a few dams on the river Kaveri, in the district of Tanjore for irrigation. Economy of the country was based on agriculture; hence the Chola kings took necessary steps to promote irrigation facilities. Of all the dams built by the Cholas, the *Kallanai* dam was important in the irrigation history of the south India. This dam was 1080 ft. long and 60 ft. wide and 18 ft. high.[38] The Chola kings in 11th century C.E. built up a dam on a canal which was connected to river Kaveri, to bring water for irrigation purpose and the dam was 300 mtr long, 18 mtr deep and 5.5 mtr high.[39]

In Tamil country, pearl cultivation and pearl trade developed during the Pandya kings. In the ancient period, Kaveri valley was famous for the cultivation of pearls. By the end of the 13th century C.E. Marco Polo who came to the Pandya Kingdom from Venice, Italy, wrote that this region made its glorious room in the world trade of pearl export.[40] Ginger and cinnamon were grown abundantly in Pandya kingdom. Camphor was produced in the foothills of the mountains between Quilan and Madurai.[41] In the old Tamil literature of 1st century C.E. there is a mention of the export of gemstones, corals, ivory, pearls, etc. from India. The main diamond mine of this period was in the Kadappa basin region. South India got enriched and forged ahead on the path of success depending on these resources. According to Dilip Chakrabarti, gold, found in Mohenjo-Daro probably came from the gold mines of south India.[42] In Tamil literature, trade, and commerce and travel of the foreigners to south India were mentioned frequently. A Tamil poet described how a *javan* ship, loaded with gold came to Musirish port to unload and returned to their land fully loaded with black pepper. In Tamil poetry, it is described that the rich *javan* traders would live on the bank of river Kaveri by its convergence.[43]

From Tamil literature we come to know that many rich towns got established in south India. During the reign of the Chola king Kulotunga I (1070 -1120 C.E.) Nagapattinam and some other ports became busy and popular as the ports for trade and commerce. It was easy to go from this port to the Pagan region which was to the east of the Bay of Bengal. The Cholas flourished in naval trade and commerce during the period between the 10th and 12th century C.E. Eastern coast of south India was the centre of trade and commerce with the Roman Empire and the Southeast Asian countries. At this time two important ports were Kaveripattinam and Arikamedu. Farmers, artisans, labourers, merchants, and other persons from many other jobs helped to build up a very strong economy in this region with the kind and whole-hearted help of the kings of Tamil country. The climate of the region, geographical location, natural resources, human resource, and sympathetic guidance of the local kings with vision, left a firm and promising imprint on the field of economic success in south India. Naval trade and commerce flourished due to the unique position of the land as it was surrounded by sea on three sides.

Political Background of Early Tamil Country

In south India and to the far south probably in 300 -200 B.C.E. the first historical era came into being. During this period the superiority of the Satavahana got established in south India. In the ancient *Tamilakam* region, political history started in the *Sangam* period. During this time three ancient Tamil kingdoms namely, the Cheras, the Cholas, and the Pandyas ruled *Tamilakam* roughly from 3rd century B.C.E. to 3rd century C.E. These three Tamil kingdoms got involved in ceaseless battles and skirmishes to keep their interest and superiority intact among these three and therefore they kept fighting with each other. In the 4th century C.E. in the peninsular region of India, several changes started to take place. The tradition of these changes resulted at the beginning of the second historical era. It is to be noted that during the reign of the Guptas, geographical and political influence made the kingdoms in south India battle against each other and this ultimately resulted in rising and fall or advent and extinction of many kingdoms. On the other hand, many kingdoms wanted to show and establish their pomp and power through battles in order to occupy many feudal states. In 6th century C.E. in south India, the geographical difference was the centre of imbroglio where the entire royal powers unleashed conflicts and clashes and started disturbing the political situation. As the valleys of Krishna, Kaveri and Godavari were fertile and suitable for agriculture, the kingdoms fought against each other to occupy this particular region. This enmity was more geographical than it was stately. While visiting south India, Chinese traveller Hiuen Tsang noticed that agricultural lands became sparse and scanty towards the south. No dynasty was based on agriculture because of the scarcity of the plains. Therefore, small kingdoms were there and those were based on the local and particularly regional enterprises and organisations. In comparison to north India, many states were formed on the basis of sheer loyalty and obedience.[44]

To the far south, in the early *Tamilakam*, there were three kingdoms; the Chera or Keralas of Malabar Coast (present Kochin and Travancore region), the Pandya kingdom at Tinnevelly in Madurai and the Cholas at the Kaveri delta region. The centre of Dravidian culture was the Pandya kingdom that developed a maritime trade connection with the Roman Empire in the 1st century B.C.E.[45] The Chola kingdom was between the Pandya kingdom and Pennar River and it was extended up to the east coast of Pennar river. The region under the Chola rule came to be known as '*Cholamandalam*'. In the *Sangam* period, to fight against each other was a common custom with these three kingdoms. In this rivalry the Chola king Karikala got the victory in 190 C.E. after he defeated his enemies in the battle of Venni and occupied all the Tamil speaking regions. He was even successful in establishing his rule on ancient Sri Lanka. While talking about the meaning of the word '*Karikala*', K.A. Nilakanta Sastri said that the term '*Karikala*' means 'the man with the charred leg', a reference to an accident by fire which befell the prince in early life.[46] Kaveripattinam port was built during his time and it is to be noted that Karikala was the patron of the then Tamil literature. In the *Sangam* period, the Pandya king was Nedunjeliyan and his capital was Madurai. K.A. Nilakanta Sastri commented on Nedunjeliyan that "Nedunjeliyan distinguished by the title 'he who won the battle at '*Talaiyālangānam*' may be taken to have ruled about 210 C.E".[47] He defeated the Cholas and the Cheras. During the *Sangam* period, another powerful king was Nedunjeraladan. He conquered Kadamba kingdom and defeated the enemies in the naval battle of Malabar. By the end of the *Sangam* period, Andhra and Kalabhra tribes intruded, into south India and due to this intrusion the political balance of the entire region got marred severely. As a result of this event, the Pallava dynasty rose in the far south.

The origin of the Pallavas is quite unclear. Many scholars and researchers came up with several different opinions about the origin of the Pallavas. According to R. Gopalan, the origin of the Pallavas was the most vexing problem in the history of ancient India.[48] In this regard, R.S. Tripathi commented that, "They find no place among the traditional sea powers of southern India, which, as mentioned above are the Cheras, the Pandyas and the Cholas".[49] Some historians think that the Pallavas were the outsiders who had a nexus with the north Indian culture. However, there is no such concrete evidence that can prove that the Pallavas came from outside of south India. Through another source, we come to know that the Pallavas were autochthonous of the land and they were associated with the Maravars, Kallars, Kurumbas, and other predatory tribes.[50] M.C. Rasanayagam views that the Pallavas were 'Cola-Naga extraction' and they belonged to the southern peninsular region.[51] According to

K.P. Jayasval, the Pallavas were neither foreigners nor Dravidians, but good Brahmin aristocrats from the north who would take fighting battles as their profession and they were the offshoots of the Vakatakas.[52] Jayasval also said that the ancient scripts of the Pallavas were written in Prakrit language. But it is thought that the Pallavas belonged to Tondaimandalam or southern India. The word 'Pallava' derived from 'Pulind' or 'Palad'. Evidence of the Pulinds is found in the inscription of Asoka. In 2nd century C.E. Kanchi, the capital of the Pallava dynasty, was under the Nagas. Therefore, we can understand that the power of the Nagas declined to make room for the Pallavas.

The period of the Pallava dynasty we come to know from the scripts of that time and those were written in Prakrit and Sanskrit. The Prakrit scripts reveal that the Pallavas ruled from 250 to 350 C.E. Later the Pallavas ruled from 352 to 575 C.E. Sanskrit was the court language of the Pallavas. During the early days when the Pallavas were strengthening their rule in the land, a set of Pallava rulers were there and a few of them were Bappadeva, Sivashkandavarman, and Viravarman. It remains unclear whether Bappadeva was the original founder of the Pallava dynasty but it is believed that Telugu Andhrapatha and Tamil *Tondaimandalam* were under his rule and that he, a very powerful ruler, operated from Dhanyakata (near Amaravati) and Kanchi (modern Kanchipuram) respectively at the same time.[53] Sivaskandavarman, son of Bappadeva, was one of the famous Pallava kings. He ruled in the first quarter of the 4th century C.E. His kingdom stretched from Krishna River to Bellari and his capital was Kanchipur. Another Pallava king was Visnugopa who ruled from 350 to 375 C.E. and he is mentioned in the Allahabad Pillar inscription as the ruler of Kanchi. Probably he was contemporary to king Samudragupta. Within the time frame of 350-375 C.E. we come to know about fifteen Pallava kings but there is nothing significant about them. After 575 C.E. we get regular and continuous information about the Pallava kings. In the last quarter of the 6th century C.E. we see the magnificent rise and glory that came to the crown of the Pallava king Simhavishnu who ruled from 575 to 600 C.E. and set this dynasty on a renewed path of glory, success, and vitality. He became successful to extend his empire from Kaveri valley to the coastal regions of the Cholas and he defeated the Pandyas and the Kalabhras and then he occupied *Cholamandalam*. King of ancient Sri Lanka bowed down to accept his sovereign power. It is significant to note that Mahabalipuram became one of the centres of culture during the reign of Simhavishnu who was the patron of the Sanskrit poet Bharvi.

Simhavishnu was succeeded by Mahendravarman I, his son who ruled from 600 to 630 C.E. Geographical boundaries of his kingdom are known from the script found in Kopeteswar temple in Guntur. The kingdom of Mahendravarman I extended from Krishna valley in the north to the Kaveri River in the south. Nellore and Guntur were in his kingdom. Harsavardhana in the north and Pulakeshin II of the Chalukya dynasty in the south were his contemporaries. During his reign, the rivalry between the Pallavas and the Chalukya dynasty started and it lasted for almost 100 long years. The main reason behind this rivalry was more geographical than it was political. And at the same time we need to mention that both the dynasties wanted to establish their rule on the Tungabhadra region. Pulakeshin II crossed the Tungabhadra region and attacked Kanchi, the capital of the Pallavas. Thus, the battle of Pallalur took place. Though Mahendravarman succeeded to save Kanchi, Aihole's inscription tells us a different story that denotes Mahendravarman's fall. But according to Kasakudi plate the Pallavas became victorious.[54] Among the Pallava kings, Mahendravarman had many qualities. He acquired a place of merit in the cultural history of south India. He adopted the old tradition of stone carving on hillocks for architecture instead of brick works or wood carvings. He established many temples by carving the stones of hillocks at Trichinapally, Chingalpet, and Arcot. He is considered one of the best kings of the Pallava dynasty. He also came to be known as Pallavamalla and his reign is called the age of creativity.

In 630 C.E., after the death of Mahendravarman I his son Narasimbavarman I sat on the throne. He adopted the title 'Mahamalla' and ruled from 630 to 668 C.E. During his reign the Pallavas touched the pinnacle of success and power. The rivalry between the Pallava kingdom and the Chalukya kingdom continued as before. From the Kurram plate, we come to know that Narasimhavarman I attacked the Chalukya king Pulakeshin II.[55] The commander-general of Narasimhavarman I, attacked Vatapi (Badami) in 642 C.E. and occupied it with his army. Narasimhavarman I adopted the title '*Vātāpikondān*' to celebrate his victory over the Vatapi. He defeated the Cholas, the Pandyas, the Kalabhras and Kerala kingdoms. He set his expedition to ancient Sri Lanka with his great naval power to throne Manabvarman as the king of ancient Sri Lanka. But this incident incurs much controversy and some scholars think that it is not true. One of the most memorable incidents of his time was the visit of Hiuen Tsang to Kanchi. According to the annals recorded by Hiuen Tsang, we come to know about the political, social, cultural, economic, and geographical history and the lifestyle of the people of Kanchi.

According to him, "the country, of which 'kin-chi-pu-lo'(Kancipura) is the capital, is known as 'Ta-lo-ti-cha'(Dravida). It is 6000 li in circuit. The soil is fertile and regularly cultivated, and produces abundant grains. There are also many flowers and fruits. It produces precious gems and other articles. The climate is hot and by character the people are courageous. They are deeply attached to the principles of honesty, truth, and highly esteemed learning: in respect of their language and written characters, they differ but little from those of Mid-India. There are some eighty Deva temples, and many heretics called these Nirgranthas."[56] During the reign of Narasimhavarman I, the chariot temple of Mahabalipuram was made and the architectural techniques of carving and shaping the stones on the entire hillocks met the epitome of success. This time marked the sheer excellence of Kanchi in the teaching and learning of Sanskrit and Kanchi flourished as a prestigious study centre of Sanskrit.

After Narasimhavarman passed away, his son Mahendravarman II ruled only for two years from 668 to 670 C.E. At that time the Chalukya king Vikramaditya I reached Pallava kingdom and defeated northern portion. In this critical situation, after the death of Mahendravarman II in 670 C.E, the Pallava king Paramesavarvarman I came to the throne. He saw that the northern part of the Pallava kingdom was under the Chalukya rule as they occupied that part by force. He had to battle against all the three big powers- the Chalukya, Ganga, and Pandya almost all the time. Finally, he became successful to keep his kingdom intact. Narasimhavarman II (695 -722 C.E.) who succeeded his father Paramesvaravarman I, adopted the 'Rajsimha' title. During his reign there is no evidence of Pallava-Chalukya conflict. Peace, law, and order prevailed during his time. As he was a devotee of Lord Siva, he built many Siva temples and contributed for the cultural developments. Scholars compared him to the Chola king Rajaraja I. It is to be noted that he was aware of the harmful and deleterious activities of the Arab merchants in south India and Southeast Asia. We notice a significant development in the study of Sanskrit in south India during his reign. After his death, Paramesvaravarman II came to power, but he failed to resist the Chalukya king Vikramaditya II, who occupied Kanchi. It is quite interesting to note that he was finally able to restore Kanchi from the Chalukya rule. Nandivarman II succeeded Paramesvaravarman II in 730 C.E. and he ruled for a long period (nearly 65 years). During his time the Pallava-Chalukya conflict started once again. The Chalukya king Vikramaditya II occupied Kanchi and enthroned Chitramaya, the rival of Nandivarman II. Chitramaya ruled for almost 20 years. During this period Nandivarman II was in exile but in 745-746 C.E. he became successful to restore the throne and his kingdom.

We see a change in the political scenario of south India in 745-746 C.E. because this very time marked the fall of the Chalukya kingdom and the rise of the Rashtrakuta power. Nandivarman II was aware of the Pandyas and Rashtrakuta kingdom which was potential threats to the Pallavas in south India. He made a master plan to build a strong relationship with the Rashtrakuta kingdom through marrying Reva, the princess of Rashtrakuta and thus he was successful to tame the kingdom which was once a threat to him. After the death of Nandivarman II, Dantivarman sat on the throne. The Rashtrakuta king Govinda III attacked Kanchi, the capital city of the Pallava kingdom in 804 C.E. and defeated the Pallava king. On the other hand, the Pandya king Varaguna I attacked the Pallavas and occupied the Kaveri region. Nandivarman III (828-851 C.E.), son of Dantivarman, sat on the throne and defeated the Pandyas at Vellaru. Nandivarman III was successful to establish his rule on Kaveri and Mailaipur regions. Nripatungavarman (851-876 C.E.), son of Nandivarman III, became ruler of the Pallava dynasty and faced a conspiracy, made by Aparajitavarman, his step-brother who joined hands with the Chola kingdom and Ganga kingdoms. In 876 C.E., Aparajitavarman defeated Nripatungavarman in the battle of Sripurambiyam with the help of the Chola and the Ganga kingdoms. However, Aparajitavarman ruled from 876 to 895 C.E. During his reign the Chola king Aditya gained power. It is thought that Aditya defeated and killed Aparajitavarman and thus the Pallava dynasty came to its end. The last free and sovereign king of the Pallava dynasty in Tamil country was Aparajitavarman.

Within the geographical boundaries of the Pallava kingdom, the provinces were called '*mandalam*'. Those provinces were also called '*kōttam*' or '*kōttamnādu*'. According to the ancient Tamil inscriptions of the 8th and 9th century C.E. the villages of Tamil country were called '*ūr*', '*sabha*' and '*nagaram*'. While elucidating these three- '*ūr*', '*sabha*' and '*nagaram*', K.A. Nilakanta Sastri commented that "The '*ūr*' was the common type of village which included all classes of the people who held the land in the village. The '*sabha*' was an exclusively Brahmin assembly of the village, given as a gift to Brahmins, where all the land belonged to them. The '*nagaram*' was quite another type of localities, where the traders and merchants were used to live".[57] In Tamil country, there were '*ēripatti*' which was a particular type of land which the village people could donate. During the time of the Pallavas, art, culture, learning, and literature flourished. We notice that the Dravidian style of art was introduced to the temples for the first time in south India by the Pallavas. Another aspect of the Pallava dynasty, worth to remembering is that Hinduism, along with the power of the Brahmin sect, flourished with full bloom and channelised its roots deeply into the ground of south India. The Pallava culture was not only village-centric; it also developed around the *nagarams* like Kanchi, Mahabalipuram etc.

After the Pallavas the Cholas came to power in the middle of the 9th century C.E. There are many opinions on the meaning of the word 'Chola'. The 'Chola' is sometimes referred to as '*cul*' (to hover). Some others think that the origin of 'Chola' is 'kola'. K.A. Nilakanta Sastri commented that the Cholas "in the early days designated the dark-coloured pre-Aryan population of southern India in general considered as Cholas".[58] Whatever is said about the origin of the Cholas, it is to be noted that in south India the Pandyas, the Cheras and the Cholas were indigenous people. Later, in literature and inscriptions, it is stated that the Cholas that they were a mythical descent from the sun.[59] The kingdom of the Cholas was known as '*chōlamandalam*'. The territory of the Cholas stretched from the Pennar River in the north to the middle of the Vellaru River in the south. It consisted of Tanjore, Trichirapally and a portion of Pudukottai state. Few names that denote the capital of the Chola kingdom, are Uragapura (Uraiyur which is near Trichirapally), Panjuvur (Tanjore), Gangaikonda, and Cholapuram. We come to know that the early history of the Cholas from the information, given by grammarian Katyana (4th century B.C.E.) and the *Mahabharata*.[60] According to the Rock Edicts II and XIII of King Asoka, we come to know that there was a nexus between Maurya and early Chola kingdom. On the other hand from *Mahāvamsa* (Buddhist text, found in Sri Lanka) we get the information that the Cholas had a relation with Ceylon (ancient Sri Lanka) in 2nd century B.C.E. From the same source, we also get references to Elara, a Chola king, ruled ancient Sri Lanka for a long time. Ptolemy's *The Geography* (c. middle of the 2nd century C.E.) tells us about the inland towns and ports of the Chola kingdom.

The founder of the Chola dynasty was Vijayalaya Chola (850 -871 C.E.). He started his victorious journey from Uraiyur and captured Tanjavur from the Muttaraiyar chiefs who were partisans of the Pandya monarch Varagunavarman. The region stretched from Vellore to the Kaveri River was under the rule of Vijayalaya. His capital was Tanjavur. Aditya I (871-907 C.E.) succeeded his father Vijayalaya. Aditya I defeated the Pallava king Aparajitavarman and occupied

Tondaimandalam.[61] He ruled the entire land from present Chennai city in the north to Kaveri River in the south. After the death of Aditya I, Parantaka I (907-953 C.E.) came to the Chola throne. Parantaka I attacked the Pandya kingdom and defeated the Pandya king Rajsimha who fled to ancient Sri Lanka. Then Parantaka I occupied the Pandya kingdom and adopted the title '*Maduraikondan*'. He even tried his naval power and reached ancient Sri Lanka but he could not manage to establish his rule there. After this, he 'uprooted two Bana kings and conquered the Vaidumbas'.[62]

By the end of his reign, Chola king Parantaka I got involved in the battle of Takkolam with Rashtrakuta king Krishna III in 949 C.E. In this battle, Krishna III defeated Parantaka I. Due to this defeat, the Cholas had to retreat and they had to wait for three decades. The golden and glorious age of the Cholas started during the reign of Rajaraja I (985-1014 C.E.). His kingdom stretched from the north to south in Tamil country. In the 11th century, the Cholas rose as the greatest political power in the south. Rajaraja I was the real founder of the Chola kingdom because, for the first time, set this dynasty on a firm base that could never be shaken easily and he unified the Tamil country as a single organised political unit and also introduced a bureaucratic administration which was unique in his time. He knocked down the military powers of ancient Ceylon (Sri Lanka) and Pandya kingdom. He led a powerful naval expedition to Ceylon and destroyed Anuradhapuram which was situated in the north of Ceylon. Thus, he established his rule in the northern part of the island country and made it a Chola province. He defeated the Chalukya forces in the west and Rashtrakuta kingdom as well. It was his time when the Maldives came under his direct rule.[63]

After the death of Rajaraja I, Rajendra I (Gangaikondan) (1014-1044 C.E.) sat on the Chola throne. Though it is recorded that Rajendra I ruled from 1014 C.E., actually he started ruling the Chola kingdom from 1012 C.E. as Rajaraja I proclaimed him to be the prince of the state.[64] In the very beginning of his rule he showed his valour by defeating the Ceylon king Mahinda V. Then he defeated the Pandyas who ruled Kerala and defeated the Western Chalukyas as well. Within a very short time, he included places like Idaiturainadu, Banavasi (north Kanara), Kollippakkai (Kulpak), Mannaikkadakkam (Malkhed), etc. in his empire. His military expeditions were not only restricted to the southern part of India, but he also targeted to bring the northern states under his rule and expand his empire. During his time the greatest power was Gauda which was rich in culture as the rulers were always the patrons of art and culture. Gauda was situated to the north of the Ganga and the rulers of Gauda were liberal. Probably between 1021-1025 C.E. Rajendra I attacked Gauda after crossing the Ganga River. He completely defeated Gauda and adopted '*Gangaikondan*' title to commemorate his victory.[65] He constructed a city called Gangaikondacholapuram and made it as the capital city of the Cholas.

As the Cholas attacked Gauda, direct or indirect influence of the Dravidian culture was seen in the regions and provinces around Gauda, western Kamarupa or Kamata, Radha, or present Birbhum, Barddhaman, Bankura, Tamralipta or Medinipur or a portion of present Bangladesh. The remarkable influence of Dravidian linguistics was seen in Kamata or Kamarupa which was a neighbouring state of Gauda. Tamil word '*punal*' means 'water' or 'river' and in the Kamata kingdom, it changed into '*pani*' which bears the same meaning. Tamil '*annai*' refers to 'mother' and in the Kamata kingdom; it became '*aai*' with the same meaning. Tamil '*arai*' means 'two and half'; in Kamata and Bengal, it remained unchanged both in spelling and meaning. Tamil '*atanam*' means 'excess', in Kamata, it became '*atla*'. Tamil '*attam*' refers to 'mirror'. In Kamata and Bengal, it changed into '*aayna*'. Tamil '*ottai*' means 'one' and in Kamata, it becomes '*otai*'.[66] Not only in language, but there was a Dravidian influence on festivals as well. Tamil festival '*Pongal*' and '*Charak*' festival of Gauda, Kamata, and Bengal have very close similarity.[67] Rajendra I brought many feudal rulers to Bengal from south India and those rulers settled permanently in the land. Those rulers later cemented the base on which the Sen Dynasty rose brightly.

From Tirumalai (situated in North Arcot district) inscription,[68] we come to know that Rajendra I succeeded to include many regions and provinces of north India like Odda-Visaya (Orissa), Kosalainadu (southern Kosala, Madhya Pradesh), Dharmapala Tandabutti (Danda-bhukti which was probably the district of Balasore and a part of Midnapore), Ranasuras Takkana-ladam (south Radha), Gobinda Candra's Vangaladesa (eastern Bengal), Uttira-ladam (north Radha), and Gauda (ruled by Mahipala who was on the throne from 992 to 1040 C.E.) on his 13th year as a king. But according to Merpadi inscription, this event took place on his 9th year as a king.[69]

Prior to Rajaraja I and Rajendra I the Chola kingdom was a small regional state in Tamil country. This state, under the leadership of king Rajendra I, not only expanded itself and crossed the Indian boundary and reached the neighbouring countries like Maldives and Ceylon (Sri Lanka) to establish its rule over there, but also with maritime expeditions and great naval power it reached several countries of south and Southeast Asia to bring Indian culture, ethics, values, learning, literature, and philosophy in those foreign lands. The Chola kingdom also managed to control and expands its maritime trades with the Southeast Asian countries. In 1025 C.E., Rajendra I made an expedition to present Malaysia and Indonesia and as a result of it, Sumatra, Java, Borneo, Penang, and some other places came under his control. He never wanted to control these places with a sword but he wanted to conquer the hearts of the local people of these foreign lands and keep a warm relationship with them on the basis of art, culture, trade, and commerce. Therefore, he never occupied these regions. The Cholas built up a strong naval power to thwart or stop the increasing presence of the Arab merchants on the sea nearby and the geographical location of their kingdom helped them a lot in this regard. Chola king Rajaraja I took the initiative to build up a navy and his son Rajendra I carried it on farther to make it invincible.

After the death of Rajendra I, Rajadhiraja I (1044-1054 C.E.) came to the throne and he dominated the rebellion of the Pandyas and the Cheras. He attacked Ceylon and made the Ceylon king flee away. After Rajadhiraja I died, the history of the Cholas becomes unclear as we find no concrete evidence that can tell what happened at the time. The next Chola king was Vira Rajendra (1064-1070 C.E.) who was able to thwart the attack of the Chalukyas from the west. In 1070 C.E., Kulottunga I (1070-1129 C.E.) came to the Chola power, ruled up to the 1129 C.E. After Rajendra I, Kulottunga I was a competent Chola ruler. Being a ruler with vision and talent, he was successful in merging the Cholas and the Chalukyas to form the Chola-Chalukya kingdom. He conquered many kingdoms and advanced up to Kalinga. He had a good relationship with the Gaharwals of Kanauj. The Chola Empire began to collapse after the death of Kulottunga I who was the last powerful, sovereign ruler of the Cholas. Some Chola kings of worth mentioning after Kulottunga I are Vikrama Chola (1118-1133 C.E.),[70] Kulottunga II (1133-1147 C.E.), Rajaraja II (1147-1162 C.E.), Rajadhiraja II (1162-1178 C.E.), Kulottunga III (1178-1216 C.E.),[71] and Rajaraja III (1216-1252 C.E.). During the reign of Rajaraja III, Tanjore was occupied by Maravarman Sundara Pandya I, a Pandya king. After this, we get no more important Chola king.

The glorious history of the Cholas was not restricted within India only; golden glory travelled to the foreign countries as well. One great achievement of the Cholas was the formation of a very strong naval power, undertaking naval expeditions and expansion of maritime trade and commerce. As the Mediterranean Sea was the supply line and lifeline to the Romans, the Bay of Bengal was the same as the Cholas. The naval power of the Cholas was so strong. About the naval power of the Cholas, many scholars think that it was the only Indian state which had a proper appreciation of sea power.

The Chola Empire was divided into provinces (*mandalams*) which were under the charge of the viceroys. Those provinces or the *mandalams* were divided into sub-divisions which were called '*kōttams*' or '*valanādus*' ('*nādu*' refers to district). Like the Pallavas, the Cholas also focused on irrigation systems and started many projects and built up many stone dams on the Kaveri River from which they would channelise water through canals.[72] Rajendra I built up an artificial lake near his capital Gangaikondacholapuram. The Chola kings built up many magnificent temples, cities, palaces, and mansions. Art, painting, sculpture, stone carving, religion, literature and quality learning touched the epitome of success during the Chola rule. Brihadeeswar temple at Tanjore (built up by Rajaraja I), Gangaikondacholapuram temple (built up by Rajendra I) are the two important temples that carry the past glory of the Cholas. The Chola kings applied the typical Dravidian form of carving temples from stone chunks, blocks, or hillocks with the special decoration of putting up multiple layers on the upper side. Religion mattered a lot to the Chola kings who were devotees of Lord Siva.[73] But it is important to note that they were not intolerant to the other sects of Hinduism like Vaishnavas and other religion like Buddhism. Being a Shaiva (devotee of Lord Siva), Rajaraja I was liberal enough to build up a Buddhist *Vihāra* at Nagapattinam.[74]

Next important political power in south India was the Pandyas. Trace the origin of the Pandyas is very mysterious. Many scholars think that the Pandyas were the descendants of the mythical three brothers of Korkai. Those three mythical brothers established three different kingdoms- the Pandya, Chola and Chera. Some other scholars think that the Pandyas belonged to the Dravidian origin and it is a claim to kinship with epic heroes which was advanced when the Aryans had established themselves and their religion and institutions in southern India.[75] The Pandyas were the rulers of the far south part of India and the Indian peninsula along with the east coast was under their rule. The political power of the Pandyas went through ups and downs. According to the general concept, the Pandya kingdom consisted of three main districts namely, Madurai, Ramnad, and Tinnevelly. The Madurai (Madura) was the capital of the Pandya kingdom. This city was called 'Mathura of the south'. Korkai was the earliest and the most famous port city of the Pandyas. The Pandya kingdom has high antiquity. In Panini's *Ashtaddhoyee* and *Rāmayana* the Pandya kingdom was referred to as a rich land. In *Mahāvamsa*, a Buddhist text of Sri Lanka, it is stated that the Sri Lankan prince Vijaya got married to a Pandya princess. In Koutilya's *Arthasastra*, it is referred to that pearls of a special kind were available at Kavataka which was known as Pandya country.[76] Even according to the reference, given by Megasthenese, we come to know that female ruler governed the Pandyan nation which was actually Pandya kingdom.[77] Strabo, in his writing, also mentioned Pandya kingdom with the term 'Modoura' which was the capital of Pandya kingdom.[78]

Two important Pandya kings of the early medieval period were Kadungon (590-620 C.E.) and his son, Maravarman Avanishulamani (620-645 C.E.). To the south of the Pandya kingdom was the land ruled by the Kalabhra dynasty. These Kalabhra rulers were also known as Kalvars, Kalappirars, or Kalabhras who were probably the followers of Buddhism or Jainism.[79] Some scholars think that they migrated from the present Karnataka. The reign of the Kalabhras is sometimes called, in the history of Tamil country, as the "dark period". Their capital was at present Madurai and during their rule; people were belonging to three religious faiths - Hinduism, Jainism and Buddhism.[80]

According to the Velvikudi inscription which was written in Tamil and Sanskrit on copper plates in 8th century C.E., Kadungon was the Pandyan king with whom the Pandyas revived after their obscure presence during the reign of the Kalabhras and therefore he was often treated as the bright sun who came with his burning radiance that dispersed the dark clouds of the Kalabhra rule. We need to mention here that Kadungon and his son Maravarman took the help of Pallava king Simhavishnu to put the Kalabhra rule to an end.[81] Maravarman succeeded his father Kadungon and sat on the Pandya throne. We don't get much information about him. Cheliyan Chendan (620- 650 C.E.) was the next king and after his reign came Arikesari Maravarman (670-700 C.E.) who succeeded to expand his kingdom by defeating Kerala and some other states. He joined hands with the Chalukya king Vikramaditya I and defeated Pallava king Parameswar. Arikesari Maravarman is said to have won battles at Pali, Nelveli, Uraiyur, and Sennilam.[82] According to some scholars he adopted the title 'Parakusan'.

The next Pandya king was Koccadayan (700-730 C.E.), son of Arikesari. He was also called Ranadhira. It is said that he proved his mettle on the battlefields and he was aggressive. He adopted titles like 'Kongarkoman' and 'Madurakarunatakan'.[83] After the death of Ranadhira, Maravarman Rajasimha I (730-765 C.E.) came to the throne and he won a few battles including the battle of Periyalur. He defeated the Malava king by crossing the Kaveri River. He renewed a few old cities. Nedunjadaiyan/ Varaguavarman I (or, Jatila Parantaka) was the next Pandya king who ruled from 765 to 815 C.E. During his reign the Pandya kingdom expanded with the inclusion of the Chola and the Chera kingdoms. He fought against the Pallava king Nandivarman who was also known as 'Pallavamalla' several times and occupied many places like Kongudesa (present Coimbatore and Salem district), Venadu (present south Travancore) and Tanjore, etc. Srimara Srivallabha (815-862 C.E.) succeeded Jatila Parantaka. He was one of the brave and great kings of the Pandya dynasty. He came to be known as 'Parachakra Kolahala' and this title refers to his valour. According to the Larger Sinnamanur Plates (the portion which was written in Sanskrit), Srimara Srivallabha defeated the king of Sri Lanka, the Chera (Kerala), the 'Mayapandya', the Vallabha and the Pallava. When Sena I was the king of Sri Lanka, he attacked his land and occupied the city of Anuradhapura. Being defeated to him, Sena I fled to Malaya. After making a pact with the Sri Lankan king, Srimara came back to his land. In the meantime, an alliance was made between the Gangas, the Pallavas, the Cholas, and the Rashtrakutas. They joined hands to defeat Srimara Srivallabha who was defeated by this alliance, led by the Pallava king Nandivarman III at the battle of Tellaru. Though the Pandya forces were compelled to retreat, Srimara, later, became successful to take revenge and in a battle, he completely defeated the alliance.[84] It was the battle of Arichil where Srimara was defeated by the Pallava king Nripatunga.[85] In the battle he was severely wounded and he succumbed to these injuries later. Varaguna II (862-880 C.E.) was a rebel Pandya prince who joined hands with Sena II of Sri Lanka secretly to dethrone Srimara. However, Sena II occupied Madurai and made Varaguna II the ruler of the Pandya dynasty. After the Pallavas, the Cholas occupied the Pandya kingdom and continued their rule till the 12th century C.E.

In the first half of 13th century, three Pandya kings came one after another; they were Maravarman Sundara Pandya I (1216-1238 C.E.), Sundaravarman Kulasekara Pandya II (1238-1240 C.E.) and Maravarman Sundara Pandyan II (1241-1251 C.E.).[86] But under the leadership of the next king Jatavarman Sundar Pandya I (1251-1272 C.E.) the Pandya kingdom revived and restored its lost strength. He was a patron of art, culture, and Dravidian architecture. During his reign, the Pandya kingdom saw the highest growth in economic power and territorial expansion. He made the kings of the Chola, the Chera, Ceylon (ancient Sri Lanka) and Kanchi to accept his sovereign rule and all those kings bowed down before him. Some scholars think that when Jatavarman Sundara Pandya attacked the Chera country, the Chera army was defeated and their king was killed in the battle. He defeated the Kavada king and he also occupied Kongu and Madagai countries. Jatavarman's kingdom stretched from Nellore in the north to Ceylon (Sri Lanka) in the south. He conquered Ceylon but he did not occupy the country. He made a pact with the ruler that the ruler of Ceylon would send him jewels, other valuables, and elephants every year as tribute. He also played a key role to beautify the Siva temple of Chidambaram and the Vishnu temple of Srirangam. He covered the roofs of these two temples with gold plates and he also contributed a lot to other temples. He accumulated a large store of gold and other valuables from several battles.[87]

After the death of Jatavarman Sundara Pandya, the Pandya kingdom became weak. Taking the advantage of the poor and cripple central administration and revolt of the provincial chieftains, the commander of the then Sultan of Delhi (Alauddin Khilji), Malik Kafur attacked Pandya kingdom and destroyed Madurai city. In the 16th century, the Pandya kingdom became a part of Vijayanagara and thus it lost its existence. Italian traveler Marco Polo visited the Pandya kingdom in 1293 C.E. and mentioned the capital city and the Kayel port of the kingdom in his writing. He also praised the glory and wealth of the Pandya kingdom. Though south India got involved in the political imbroglio and bloody battles like north India, the Aryan culture and civilisation found an entry in south India and therefore we see a development of that in the Tamil country. Though the Muslim invaders ravaged, ransacked north India, and then looted and destroyed the Hindu temples, the Muslim invaders failed to do the same to the temples in south India. Therefore, these Hindu temples of south India bear the ancient glory and visible history that baffle us with their very presence even today.

Conclusion

History has often been influenced by many scholars and therefore it lost its original flavour in many ways. People from north India tried to showcase everything from their perspectives so that north Indian history could be glorified and on the other hand, south India often denied the north Indian influence in their land. But based on the concrete evidence we can sum up and reach a neutral perspective so that history never loses its ground and comes to us as it was in the time which we are about to reveal or we want to. While discussing the history of south India we must admit a few facts. Innumerable battles were fought and through these, three main powers emerged in the early Tamil country; the Pandya, the Pallava and the Chola. They shaped south India and its art, culture, architecture, sculpture, literature, and learning. Besides, they also left a firm imprint on the religious history, agriculture, trade and commerce, and economy of the land. Those three great dynasties remained busy to showcase their power on homeland and foreign lands. They reached several countries of South and Southeast Asia with several intentions. Sometimes they wanted to conquer the foreign lands, occasionally they focused on maritime trade and commerce, and on occasion they developed indigenous political strategies to control the lands even by not conquering those. It is important to note that many kings of south India made pacts with foreign kings (especially of Ceylon) after conquering their lands only to get annual tributes of elephants or other valuables. And on the other hand, we see that some kings were only interested in showcasing their art, culture, learning, and literature in foreign lands. They never sought to occupy foreign countries; rather they helped them in many ways. Invaders from north India failed to bring south India under their control. It proves the unity of the land and understanding among the people in difficult times. The age-old cultural tradition is alive even today. In a way, therefore, we can say that south India always showed the true spirit of modern India.

Notes and References

1. H.G. Rawlinson, *A Concise History of the Indian People*, Delhi, 2011, p.1.
2. L.A. Goldenberg, 'About the Place of Historical Geography in the System of Sciences', in W.P. Adams and Helliner (eds.), *International Geography*, Vol.1, University of Toronto Press, Toronto, 1972, pp. 420-422.
3. Soumentara Mitra, *The State and Society in Early-Medieval Bengal*, unpublished Ph.D. thesis, submitted to the Department of Ancient History, Culture and Archaeology, Visva-Bharati University, Santiniketan, 2014, p. 22.
4. R.D. Dikshit, *Geographical Thought-A Contextual History of Ideas*, New Delhi, 2008, p. 212.
5. Brajdulal Chattopadhyay, *A Survey of Historical Geography of India*, Calcutta, 1994.
6. Y. Subbarayalu, "*Historical Geography of Ancient and Medieval India: A Comparative Study of Nadu and Vishaya*", General Presidential Address, Indian History Congress of 73rd session, University of Mumbai, December 2012, p. 1.

7. B.C. Law, *Historical Geography of Ancient India*, Paris, 1968, p. 3.
8. *Ibid.*, p. 15; see also G. Yazdani (ed.), *The Early History of Deccan*, London, 1960, p. 3.
9. *Ibid.*, p. 3.
10. *Ibid.*, p. 4.
11. R. C. Majumdar (ed.), *The History and Culture of the Indian People*, Vol. V, The Struggle for Empire, Bombay, 1957, p. 533.
12. Michael W. Meister (ed.), *Encyclopedia of Indian Temple Architecture*, American Institute of Indian Studies, 1983. And also see Ganapathy Subbiah, "*Daksinapatha: Where Does the Path Lead Us?*" Presidential Address, Ancient Indian History Section, 67th Indian History Congress Session, Farook College, University of Calicut, March 10-12, 2007, p. 8.
13. Ganapathy Subbiah, *op.cit.*, p. 9.
14. Kesavan Veluthat, *The Political Structure of Early Medieval South India*, New Delhi, 1993, p. IX.
15. *Ibid.*
16. K. Mavali Rajan, *Medieval Tamil Society and Agrarian Slavery*, Kolkata, 2014, p. 2.
17. K. Mavali Rajan, 'Geographical Features of Early Tamilakam as Portrayed by Tamil Literature Texts', *Modern Tamil Research*, Vol. 6, No. 3, 2018, p. 600.
18. *Ibid.*
19. N. Subrahmanian, *Social and Cultural History of Tamil land*, Udumalpet, 2005, pp. 5-6.
20. K. Mavali Rajan, *Medieval Tamil Society and Agrarian Slavery*, p. 4.
21. K. K. Pillay, *A Social History of Tamils*, Vol. I, University of Madras, 1975, pp. 24-28.
22. Ganapathy Subbaiah, 'Order of Hierarchy in the Realm of Religion and Society: An Introspective View from Back and Forth in Indian History', in K. Mavali Rajan, et. al. (eds.), *Facts of Temple Culture: Perspectives of Religious and Social Traditions in Early Medieval India*, New Delhi, 2018, p. 7.
23. Tamil Lexicon: 1046, 1134.
24. K. Mavali Rajan, *Medieval Tamil Society and Agrarian Slavery*, p. 5.
25. *Ibid.*
26. Burton Stein, *A History of India*, Oxford University Press, New Delhi, 2010, p. 7.
27. T.M. Srinivasan, "Agricultural Practice as Gleaned from the Tamil Literature of Sangam Age", *Indian Journal of Social Science*, 51(2-1), 2016, p. 170.
28. *Ibid.*

29. *Annual Report on Epigraphy* (*A.R.E.*), No.760 of 1929; see also K. Mavali Rajan, *Medieval Tamil Society and Agrarian Slavery*, p. 127.
30. *A.R.E.*, No. 111 of 1905.
31. K. Mavali Rajan, *Medieval Tamil Society and Agrarian Slavery*, p.127.
32. *A.R.E.*, No. 91 of 1918.
33. H.H. Wilson, *A Glossary of Judicial and Revenue Terms and the Usual Words Occurring in Official Documents Relating to the Administration of the Government of British India*, London, 1855, p. the relevant words.
34. Burton Stein, *The Peasant State and Society in Medieval South India*, Delhi, 1985, p. 26.
35. K. Mavali Rajan, *Medieval Tamil Society and Agrarian Slavery*, p. 128.
36. *Ibid.*
37. T.V. Mahalingam, *Administration and Social Life under Vijayanagara*, Part-II, University of Madras, Madras, 1975, p. 93.
38. Gourisankar Dey and Subhradip Dey, *Bharatbarsher Itihas* (in Bengali), Kolkata, 2017, p. 1084.
39. *Ibid.*, p. 1081.
40. *Ibid.*, p. 1084.
41. *Ibid.*, p. 1081.
42. Dilip Chakrabarti, *Bharatbarsher Pragitihas* (in Bengali), Kolkata, 1963, reprint 1999, p. 105.
43. Gourisankar Dey and Subhradip Dey, *op.cit.*, p. 1084.
44. Romila Thapar, *Bharatbarsher Itihas* (in Bengali), Calcutta, 1960, p. 125.
45. P. Maiti et.al., *Bharat Itihas Parikrama* (in Bengali), Kolkata, 2006, p. 599.
46. K.A. Nilakanta Sastri, *A History of South India*, Oxford University Press, Delhi, 1975, p. 112.
47. *Ibid.*, p. 114.
48. R. Gopalan, *History of the Pallavas of Kanchi*, University of Madras, Madras, 1928, pp. 15-27.
49. R.S. Tripathi, *History of Ancient India*, Delhi, 2014, p. 442.
50. *Ibid.*
51. M.C. Rasanayagam, *Indian Antiquity*, Vol. III, 1923, pp. 77-82.
52. *Journal of Bihar and Orissa Research Society*, 1933 (March-June issue), pp. 180-183.
53. R. Gopalan, *op.cit.*, p. 32
54. P. Maiti, et.al. *op.cit.*, p. 603.

55. *South Indian Inscriptions* (*S.I.I.*), Vol. I, Government Press, Madras, 1890, p. 52.
56. Samuel Beal, *Buddhist Records of the Western World*, London, 1884, pp. 228-229.
57. K.A. Nilakanta Sastri, *op.cit.*, p. 149.
58. K.A. Nilakanta Sastri, *The Colas*, The University of Madras, 1935, p. 24.
59. *Ibid.*, p. 38.
60. R.S. Tripathi, *op.cit.*, p. 457.
61. K. A. Nilakanta Sastri, *The Colas*, p.159.
62. *Ibid.*, p. 150.
63. *Ibid.*, pp. 211-215.
64. *Epigraphia Indica* (*E.I.*), Vol. IX, p. 217.
65. H.C. Roychowdhury, *The Dynastic History of Northern India*, Vol. I, New Delhi, 1973, p.318.
66. The Dravidian words are derived from T. Burrow and M. Bemenew, *A Dravidian Etymological Dictionary*, Oxford University Press, 1968, pp.6, 8, 12, 17, 70, 73, 113, 287. The Kamata region words are collected by Binay Barman and Saumalya Mali.
67. Dipak Kumar Roy delivered a lecture at Aai Bhandani, Mathabhanga, Coochbehar, October 10-12, 2016. In this programme Dipak Kumar Roy said that Malayalam word '*oti*' and Kamata region word '*odi*' bear the same meaning which is 'piece of land' and '*gundi*' is a Dravidian word and its Kamata region counterpart is '*gandja*' which means 'to bloom/ to blossom'.
68. *E.I.*, Vol. IX, pp. 229-33.
69. *S.I.I.*, Vol. III, Part I, 1899, pp. 27-29.
70. K.A. Nilakanta Sastri, *The Colas*, pp. 49, 61.
71. *E.I.*, Vol. VII, pp. 4-5.
72. *Tiruvaduturai Inscription* (*A.R.E.*, No.110 of 1925) refers to the rising banks of the Kaveri by Parakesari Karikala Chola.
73. R.S. Tripathi, *op.cit.*, p. 479.
74. *Ibid.*, p. 480.
75. *Ibid.*, p. 481.
76. Koutilya's *Arthasastra*, BK.I, Ch. XI: Eng. Trans., 1929, p. 76.
77. J.W. Mc Crindle, *Ancient India as Discussed by Megasthenes and Arrian*, London, 1926, p. 161.
78. R.S. Tripathi, *op.cit.*, p. 482.
79. Kesavan Veluthat, *The Early Medieval in South India*, Oxford University Press, New Delhi, 2010, pp. 45-46.
80. *Ibid.*
81. *Ibid.*
82. Sailendranath Sen, *A Textbook of Medieval Indian History*, New Delhi, 2013, pp. 45-46.

83. K.A. Nilakanta Sastri, *The Pandyan Kingdom from the Earliest Times to 16th Century*, London, 1929, p. 17.
84. *Ibid.*, pp.74-76.
85. Noboru Karashima, *A Concise History of South India: Issues and Interpretations*, Oxford University Press, 2014, pp. 88-89.
86. 'The Pandya Dynasty', www.tamilnation.org, dt.05 May 2020.web.
87. *Ibid.*

Bibliography

Adams, W.P. and Helliner (eds.), *International Geography*, Vol. 1, University of Toronto Press, Toronto, 1972.

Annual Report on Epigraphy (in various years), 1905, 1918, 1925, 1929.

Brajdulal Chattopadhyay, *A Survey of Historical Geography of India*, Calcutta, 1994.

Burrow, T and M.Bemenew, *A Dravidian Etymological Dictionary*, Oxford University Press, Delhi, 1968.

Burton Stein, *A History of India*, Oxford University Press, New Delhi, 2010.

Dikshit, R.D, *Geographical Thought-A Contextual History of Ideas*, New Delhi, 2008.

Dilip Chakrabarti, *Bharatbarsher Pragitihas* (in Bengali), Kolkata, 1963.

Epigraphia Indica, Vols. VII, IX.

Ganapathy Subbiah, *"Daksinapatha: Where Does the Path Lead Us?"* Presidential Address, Ancient Indian History Section, 67th Indian History Congress Session, Farook College, University of Calicut, March 10-12, 2007.

Gopalan, R, *History of the Pallavas of the Country*, University of Madras, Madras, 1928.

Gourisankar Dey and Subhradip Dey, *Bharatbarsher Itihas* (in Bengali), Kolkata, 2017.

Kesavan Veluthat, *The Political Structure of Early Medieval South India*, Orient Longman, New Delhi, 1993.

----------------, *The Early Medieval in South India*, Oxford University Press, New Delhi, 2010.

Law, B.C, *Historical Geography of Ancient India*, Paris, 1968.

Mahalingam, T.V, *Administration and Social Life under Vijayanagara*, Part-II, University of Madras, 1975.

Maiti, P., et.al., *Bharat Itihas Parikrama* (in Bengali), Kolkata, 2006.

Majumdar, R.C. (ed.), *The History and Culture of the Indian People*, Vol.V, The Struggle for Empire, Bharatiya Vidya Bhavan, Bombay, 1957.

Mavali Rajan, K, *Medieval Tamil Society and Agrarian Slavery*, Maha Bodhi Book Agency, Kolkata, 2014.

Mavali Rajan, K, et. al. (eds.), *Facts of Temple Culture: Perspectives of Religious and Social Traditions in Early Medieval India*, New Delhi, 2018.

---------------, 'Geographical Features of Early Tamilakam as Portrayed by Tamil Literature Texts', *Modern Tamil Research*, Vol. 6, No. 3, 2018.

Mc Crindle, J.W, *Ancient India As Discussed by Megasthenes and Arrian*, Trubner & Co, London, 1926.

Michael, W. Meister (ed.), *Encyclopedia of Indian Temple Architecture*, American Institute of Indian Studies, 1983.

Nilakanta Sastri, K.A, *The Pandyan Kingdom from the Earliest Times to 16th Century*, London, 1929.

--------- , *The Cōlas*, University of Madras, Madras, 1935.

--------- , *A History of South India*, Oxford University Press, Delhi, 1975.

Noboru Karashima, *A Concise History of South India: Issues and Interpretations*, Oxford University Press, 2014.

Pillay, K.K., *A Social History of Tamils*, Vol. I, University of Madras, 1975.

Rasanayagam, M.G, *Indian Antiquity*, Vol. III, 1923.

Rawlinson, H.G, *A Concise History of the Indian People*, Delhi, 2011.

Romila Thapar, *Bharatbarsher Itihas* (in Bengali), Jai Gyan Publisher, Calcutta, 1960.

Roychowdhury, H.C, *The Dynastic History of Northern India*, Vol. I, Munchiram Manoharlal Publisher Pvt. Ltd., New Delhi, 1973.

Samuel Beal, *Buddhist Records of the Western World*, Trubner & Co. Ltd., London, 1884.

Sailendranath Sen, *A Textbook of Medieval Indian History*, New Delhi, 2013.

Soumentara Mitra, *The State and Society in Early-Medieval Bengal*, unpublished Ph.D. thesis submitted to the Department of Ancient History, Culture and Archaeology, Visva-Bharati University, West Bengal, 2014.

South Indian Inscriptions, Vols. I, III, Part I.

Subbarayalu, Y, *'Historical Geography of Ancient and Medieval India: A Comparative Study of Nadu and Vishaya'*, General Presidential Address, Indian History Congress of 73rd session, University of Mumbai, December, 2012.

Subrahmanian, N, *Social and Cultural History of Tamil land*, Udumalpet, 2005.

Tripathi, R.S, *History of Ancient India*, Motilal Banarsidass Publishers Pvt. Ltd, Delhi, 2014.

Wilson, W.W., *A Glossary of Judicial and Revenue Terms and the Usual Words Occurring in Official Documents Relating to the Administration of the Government of British India, London*, 1855.

Yazdani, G (ed.), *The Early History of Deccan*, Oxford University Press, London, 1960.

2

Revisiting the Nāyakas from the Epigraphs of Srikakulam-Vishakhapatnam Region (10th-15th century CE.)

Sabarni Pramanik Nayak

Introduction

The political, social, economic, and cultural scenario of early medieval India greatly varied from region to region, and these variations went on multiplying during the medieval era. Apart from the emergence of numerous new *jātis* during the period, huge social change was visible regarding the status, rank, and status-titles which were reflected in the name-suffixes. In Kaliṅga, the area encompassing Odisha and parts of northern Andhra, which were ruled by the Gaṅga and Gajapati kings, a group emerged into prominence. It was the *nāyakas* figuring in the copper plate charters and donatives records at temples. They were mostly concentrated in the Srikakulam-Vishakhapatnam territory.

In the epigraphs of early India, the term *nāyaka* is used to mean royal officer, ruling chief, head of a district or general. Sometimes, it implies the title of a subordinate ruler.[1] In the context of early-medieval and medieval Orissa, the emergence of *nāyakas* is seen by Shishir Kumar Panda as a political move on the part of the Later Gaṅgas who are said to have introduced the *nāyaka* system.

According to him, after the Imperial Gaṅgas making grants to the *nāyakas*, the first ruler of the Later Gaṅga Vajrahasta III introduced the *nāyaka* system which was intensified in administration later by Anantavarman Choḍagaṅga. There has been found the operating of two systems of administration in the Kaliṅga province: first, ministerial rank of governor (*kaliṅga parikṣā*) and a group of Kaliṅga cadre officials appointed from the centre and posted at the provincial capital Kaliṅganagara and second, the peripheral locations, where the semi-autonomous *nāyakas* ruled. And, in this context, a comparative study has been done by him between the *amara nāyakas* of the Vijayanagara empire and the *nāyakas* of medieval Orissa. The military and administrative aspects are emphasised in this respect. They enjoyed service grants, were landlords, administrators, and revenue-collectors, and important persons in temple administration, supplied troops to central government, and fulfilled military, administrative, and financial obligations to the central government, and were not subject to transfer.[2] Panda says "...the *nāyakas* were local military leaders and they had to fulfill military, administrative and perhaps financial obligations to the central government for which they had been assigned with territories. But obviously, they were enjoying autonomous territories. It seems that the central government did not interfere into the internal administration of the *nāyaka* territories".

The *nāyakas* were not subject to transfer as in the cases of the governors and their officers. They besides their military obligations were responsible for other works in their territories."[3] On one occasion, as many as twelve villages including Velpura in Erada *viṣaya* were clubbed together and after renaming the *viṣaya* as Velpura, these all were gifted to Pāṅgusāmaya, son of Śrīkaṇṭhanāyaka and his wife Vedavī and the grandson of Aitana, resident of Chili (around Ragolu in Srikakulam).[4] Without at all challenging the factor of the political and administrative significance attached to the *nāyakas*, this paper attempts to show another aspect. It is how the *nāyakas* gradually projected themselves as a group in society and showed social mobility too. In that process, they gradually shed off their former name-suffixes or status-titles and encompassed themselves in the broader category called *nāyakas*. Gradually, this name-suffix became very common in the area of the study. In this article, I have tried to show their emergence in the local level and have attempted to make a comparison with their counterparts in the Kākatīya Andhra. Because, the Kākatīyas ruled in the Andhra region up to the 1323 CE whereas the Vijaynagara rule in Andhra lasted between 1336 and 1660 CE. As the Kākatīya rule precedes the Vijaynagara rule, the comparison with the Kākatīya territory would be fruitful. And more so, as Shishir Kumar Panda and others have already noted that the *nāyaka* system originated in the Dravidian south and most probably in the Telugu speaking areas.[5] However, from 1327-1434 CE, some features of the nāyaka system of the Vijaynagara Empire could indeed enter into our study-area. During 1327-1434 CE, we find seventy five epigraphs mentioning this title (Table 1). And it is also not improbable that some features of the nāyaka system in our territory entered into the Vijaynagara area during this later phase.

It is undeniable that some of the *nāyakas* came from the south. In the 11th century CE, the village Sattivāḍa located in the *viṣaya* of Erada was given in favour of Gaṇapati Nāyaka, son of Kutāḍi Nāyaka and his wife Śrīdevī and the grandson of Gaṇapati Nāyaka, who was the resident of Valutavuru of Kāñchi-deśa.[6] It certainly implies the territory around Kāñchīpuram in Tamil Nadu.

Table 1: Mention of *nāyakas* (prepared from 'Nāyaka System in Medieval Orissa', by Shishir Kumar Panda, p. 94)

Period	*Modern districts*	*Numbers of epigraphs mentioning about nāyakas*	*Total number of epigraphs*
1038-1078 CE	Srikakulam	8	9
	Vishakhapatnam	1	
1078-1211 CE	Srikakulam	81	98
	Vishakhapatnam	17	
1211-1263 CE	Srikakulam	6	13
	Vishakhapatnam	7	
1263-1327 CE	Srikakulam	3	24
	Vishakhapatnam	21	
1327-1434 CE	Srikakulam	8	75
	Vishakhapatnam	67	

Nāyaka as a status-title in Srikakulam-Vishakhapatnam area

The individuals bearing the name-ending 'nāyaka' figure in the epigraphs of the Srikakulam-Vishakhapatnam region right from the beginning of the 10th century to the end of the 15th century CE. During the period of the Later Gaṅgas (from 1038 to 1434 CE) we find a total number of 220 inscriptions (Table 1) in the districts of Srikakulam and Vishakhapatnam.[7] Interestingly, in Central Orissa, the number of epigraphs speaking about the *nāyakas* are invariably small. While all of the names of the *nāyakas* are mentioned as donees in the charters, the stone-inscriptions, more accurately saying the temple-inscriptions, present them as donors and as being engaged in other activities as well, be it related to temple or independent of it. In most cases, their paternal identity is recorded which give us scope of investigating in their emergence as a category which was not affiliated to any particular *varṇa* and/or even not a *jāti* and also show the continuity and change in terms of their status-titles. While a large number of persons opted to continue with the status-title *nāyaka*, the cases are not rare where it could change to anything else from the father to the son. Some tried to retain the title *nāyaka* while taking up other titles or preferring to get themselves acquainted according to their professions or offices. There are also the cases where the son of an *nāyaka* father did not use this title, and the grandson again resumed it. There are only seven cases where the son acquired the title *nāyaka* and the father was not a *nāyaka*. Therefore, was it difficult to enter into the fold of the *nāyaka* category? But, after entering this group, a person was not debarred from continuing with it or changing it and his son too could take up other titles as well.

Nāyaka encompassing all varṇas

Nāyaka as a status-title was not exclusive to any particular *varṇa*. In other words, it was extended to the *brāhmaṇa*, *brahma-kṣatriya*, *vaiśya* and śūdra *varṇa*, evidence in support of the last one comes from the 13th century Vishakhapatnam region (and absent in the Srikakulam area). In the 11th century Srikakulam area, there is the reference to three-hundred *brāhmaṇas* headed by Māpayanāyaka, son of Karaṇṭamanāyaka and Rekapā and grandson of Pilliśarman.[8] It would be a logical conclusion to suggest that the first change of title from śarman to *nāyaka* was entertained by Māpayanāyaka's father at the end of the 10th century or a little later. Originally being the inhabitants of Jalambura (Jalamuru), he settled at Kuddam (Kudda); both in Srikakulam. In the 11th century, Ayitananāyaka, born of a brāhmaṇa (*vipra-samudbhava*), his wife *veśya* (*vaiśya*) Vuddhama and their son Nārāyaṇa received the village Māṭura in Samva *viṣaya* (between Bobbili in Vishakhapatnam and Chipurupalli in Srikakulam) from the king.[9] Interestingly, Ayitananāyaka's father was brāhmaṇa, but his mother's identity is not given and rather than calling himself a brāhmaṇa, he calls himself *vipra-samudbhava*. Moreover, even being the son of a brāhmaṇa, he married a *vaiśya* woman. And further interesting is the fact that their son Nārāyaṇa was not mentioned as Nārāyaṇanāyaka either. Was the name-suffix *nāyaka* likely to spare him the inferiority of being marked as the son of a *vaiśya* woman and a man whose father was a brāhmaṇa and mother was probably not? An 11th century epigraph from the Madhukeśvara temple of Mukhaliṅgam refers to Daddapanāyaka, the son of Ketanāchārya, the minister of Choḍagaṅgadeva, the king.[10] He was a brāhmaṇa. Another 12th century inscription mentions from the Kūrmeśvara temple of Śrīkūrmam refers to Meḍapota pradhānī, son of the brāhmaṇa Erapota nāyaka as the donor.[11] A 13th century inscription from Śrīkūrmam recorded the donation of perpetual lamp by brāhmaṇa Kūrmmi Nāyaka, son of Māṃkki Nāyaka and his wife Māṃkyama Nāyakāni.[12]

Not like any other title, the term *nāyaka* had developed a feminine rendering, though there is doubt whether *nāyakāni* was considered Māṃkyama's status-title apart from being an indicator of her identity as the wife of a *nāyaka*. In this context, we can cite the 12th century Mukhaliṅgam inscription where Erakama Nāyakāni gave a perpetual lamp, 5 *māḍas* to the temple, and also 2 *puṭṭis* of land as āchārya-bhoga and another 5 *māḍas* to the *sthānapati*. Erakama was the wife of Vanapati-peggaḍa of Siṃhapura and her parents were Daṇḍama nāyaka and Sudāma nāyakāni of Piṣṭapura (in the Godavari territory).[13] As Erakama's husband was identified as a *peggaḍa* or general and not a *nāyaka*, at first sight we are prone to think that Erakama must have got the suffix *nāyakāni* as the daughter of a *nāyaka* and *nāyakāni*. The items of donation also point to her well-to-do condition. But, another donative record from the same temple dated three years earlier informs us that Vaṇapati-peggaḍa's[14] father was Rāyapa Nāyaka and mother Rekama Nāyakāni.[15] So, it is difficult to conclude that why Erakama was a *nāyakāni*: as a daughter of a *nāyaka* or a daughter-in-law of a *nāyaka*. Another 13th century Lakṣmī-Nārāyaṇa temple epigraph mentions about Purāi Nāyakāni, the donor, as the mother of Lakṣmaṇa Nāyaka who was the son of Bhavapati-ṭhakkura of Kauśika *gotra*.[16] It seems unlikely that Purāi Nāyakāni was called a *nāyakāni* because her son was a *nāyaka*. Rather, it seems right that her father was a *nāyaka*. However, we do not know anything about the name-suffixes used by Bhavapati-ṭhakkura's father. But, a 12th century Mukhaliṅgam inscription refers to Somamu-Nāyakāni, wife of the *māṇḍalika* Kāpari, son of the *māṇḍalika* Sāhasagaṅga.[17] It is evident that this lady had *nāyaka* father. It cannot be concluded based upon one or two epigraphs that the intermarriage among the *nāyaka* families was a regular phenomenon and regarded as a custom.

In any case, the title *nāyaka* had attained a place of distinction. A piece of interesting inscriptional evidence comes from the Lakṣmī-

Narasiṃhasvāmī temple of Siṃhāchlam in Vishakhapatnam. This 13th century donative record speaks about the *brahma-kṣatriya* Gajādhara (Gadādhara) nāyaka, the son of Pṛthivīdeva, belonging to Ḍāhala as the donor to temple.[18] The interesting point is that this is the only evidence of a person of *brahma-kṣatriya* origin being introduced as *nāyaka* and this person did not belong to the Srikakulam-Vishakhapatnam region but came from Ḍāhala or Chhattisgarh. *Brahma-kṣatriya* identity is taken by scholars as the signature of a subordinate and landlord brāhmaṇa's aspiration of being an independent ruler. However, the concerned epigraph does not speak anything about the donor's political status. In Srikakulam-Vishakhapatnam area, we do not find any person with the name-ending *nāyaka* who has defined himself as a *kṣatriya*. Does that indicate that in the study area, the term '*kṣatriya*' and *nāyaka* gradually came to be synonymous much in the same way as the term '*rajput*' and '*kṣatriya*'? In this context, we also may refer to two 15th century Lakṣmī-Narasiṃha temple epigraphs of the same year which record two persons of Vatsa *gotra*, both from Rāyapura of Ḍāhala as the donors of perpetual lamps; one named Ghughghulu Nāyaka, son of Lakavu Nāyaka,[19] and another known as Harirāja Nāyaka, son of Maheśvara Nāyaka.[20]

In the 15th century Siṃhāchlam inscription, there is the reference to Rikudāsa, son of Prayāga Nāyaka and son-in-law of the Kaliṅga merchant Viṣṇudāsa Upādhyāya.[21] A 15th century Kūrmeśvara temple inscription refers to the same Viṣṇudāsa Upādhyāya, but this time his son was mentioned as Prayāga Upādhyāya.[22] Another 15th century epigraph from the same temple mentions the father of Viṣṇudāsa Upādhyāya as Vyāsa Upādhyāya.[23] It is evident that Prayāga used both the titles 'nāyaka' and 'upādhyāya', and he was the first to take the title 'nāyaka'. His was a brāhmaṇa-vaiśya family. Thus, a brāhmaṇa married to a *vaiśya* lady (which we have seen earlier), or a brāhmaṇa taking to the profession of *vaiśya*- both could be introduced by the term *nāyaka*.

In the Srikakulam region, the *vaiśya* or merchant *nāyakas* were present side by side with the brāhmaṇa *nāyakas* as early as the 11th century CE. Apart from the well-known upādhyāya family mentioned in the temple inscriptions, there were other merchants who liked to be addressed as *nāyaka*. The 11th century Chicacole copper plate charter informs that Erapanāyaka, the son of Mañchināyaka of the family of merchants (*vaiśya-kula-vaṁśa*) hailing from Paḍuṇi-*grāma* and residing at Dantapura, was granted Paḍuṇi-*grāma*, Hoṇḍaravanto and Morakhiṇo collectively as a *vaiśyāgrahāra* though Erapanāyaka had to give 150 *rupya* for it.[24] It is very interesting to note that they were not introduced as being included in the *nāyaka kula* and their *vaiśya* origin was emphasized in the naming of the grant as well as in addressing the family which was entitled both as a *kula* and a *vaṁśa*. Also, the 11th century Māḍagrāma copper plate charter speaks about the donation of the village Māḍagrāma of Bhiliṅgṅā-bhoga to Viṭhana, son of Prollama and Pāṇḍava, son of Reuchianāyaka, the merchant or *vyāpārī* of Māḍagrāma.[25] These epigraphs do not give us any evidence that the merchant *nāyakas* were militarily active, or were administrators. A 12th century Mukhaliṅgam inscription refers to Pommapa-nāyaka, the best of the merchants, who gave a perpetual lamp to the god Madhukeśvara.[26] Did the superiority of his position among the merchants accord him the title of *nāyaka*? Another 12th century epigraph from the Sūryanārāyaṇa temple of Arasavalli refers to the donation of 5 *puṭṭis* of land located in the village of Ārṣavalli by śrīkaraṇa, *rāja-paḍihasta* and *puravari* Surapotu, who was a *vaiśya* and the son of Māliya *nāyaka*.[27] So, here also we find the reference to a *nāyaka* who was *vaiśya*. Another 13th century Madhukeśvara temple inscription speaks about the *mahājanas* (used in the sense of merchants) named Surupa *nāyaka* and Eruma *nāyaka* of Valaṅga with whom 5 *māḍas* and 2 *puṭṭis* of land gifted to the temple were entrusted by a *daṇḍanāyaka*.[28] Also the 13th century Śrīkūrmam inscription records the donation of 25 cows for a perpetual lamp by Arjama-seṭṭi, the *nāyaka* of Aṃgaḍi, who was the son of Bhīma-seṭṭi and grandson of Chiṃgama-seṭṭi, a resident of Oḍḍavāḍi.[29] This epigraph shows that in this particular case, the donee did not shed off the title 'seṭṭi', which was the indicator of his identity of trader, but was regarded as the *nāyaka* of Aṃgaḍi; and here the term *nāyaka* was not a status-title, but denotes head or chief. Probably, he enjoyed the headship of Aṃgaḍi while his residence was Oḍḍavāḍi or Vaddadi in the Chodavaram taluk of Vishakhapatnam.We do not know whether the word *aṃgaḍi* was applied here in the sense of a place, or a market. If the latter sense is taken, then this might be located either in Śrīkūrmam, or in Oḍḍavāḍi. Probably, the next generation of Arjama-seṭṭi would have the advantage of being addressed as *nāyaka*. In a 14th century inscription found from the temple of Siṃhāchalam there is the reference to Mādhava nāyaka of the community of *komaṭi* who was appointed for the service of supplying a garland daily to the Lakṣmī-Narasiṃha Temple.[30] The *komaṭis* were traders of Telugu country. In Telangana, the term *komaṭi* occurs more frequently than the term *vaiśya*. This community preferred Jainism and it is said that the word *komaṭi* is derived from Gomatha (after the Jaina saint).[31]

The *komaṭis* of the Andhra region were organized into a corporate body called *nakaram*, with eighteen branches and with Penugonda as their headquarters. Subsequently, each *nakaram* emerged as a highly developed and organised distinct social group with well-established *samayas* (socio-religious and economic congregations of the guild) and having *samaya dharma* (code of ethics and conduct prescribed for its members and community).[32]

A very interesting evidence of the son of a *kāyastha nāyaka* being mentioned as a *vaiśya* (in the sense of merchant?) comes from a 11th century inscription from the Madhukeśvara temple during the time of Choḍagaṅga. It is stated that Bhīmanātha, the śrīkaraṇa, *rāja-vidyādhara*, the best of the *vaiśyas* and an officer of Choḍagaṅga, gave a perpetual lamp to the temple. Bhīmanātha's father was *kāyastha* Meḍapanāyaka and his mother Meḍapanāyaka's wife Potama Nāyakāni of Arasavelli.[33] As the father of Bhīmanātha was a *kāyastha*, it is possible that the term *vaiśya* applied to Bhīmanātha indicates not his *varṇa*, but his identity as a trader. In fact an inscription of 1012 Śaka era during the time of Choḍagaṅga from Vishakhapatnam refers to a *vyāparī* or merchant of the maritime trading guild Añjuvaṇṇam named Asāvu who were designated as *nānārājavidyādhara* among other titles. Y. Subbarayalu holds the view that he probably had a connection with the bazaar street called rājavidyādhara at Tañjāvur.[34] There is a fair chance of Bhīmanātha, who was also called 'rāja-vidyādhara', being a very famous merchant (the best of the *vaiśyas*) and associated with Tanjavur in Tamil Nadu. Probably, his inherited profession as a *kāyastha* combined with his expertise as a merchant earned him the post of śrīkaraṇa. However, we cannot be conclusive regarding this. This epigraph also proves that the title *nāyaka* was not a permanent one. There was every possibility of its being changed into some other one in the next generation.

Bhīmanātha was not the only śrīkaraṇa who was the son of a *kāyastha*. Another śrīkaraṇa named Gaṅga-Vidyādhara, son of the *kāyastha* Proli Nāyaka, gifted a perpetual lamp to the temple of Madhukeśvara in the 11th century.[35] He donated another lamp to the temple of Bhīmeśvara at Mukhaliṅgam in the 12th century and from here we are informed that his father Poli Nāyaka (referred to as Proli nāyaka in the earlier epigraph) was the *kāyastha* of Kuppili (in Srikakulam).[36] The 11th century Arasavalli copper plate charter of Vajrahasta III records the grant of Harisavelli (Araṣavalli) village to a *peggaḍa* and its subsequent assignment to Śiriyapanāyaka, Vajjināyaka, Guṇḍamanāyaka and Nuṃkamanāyaka, the sons of

Naḍupananāyaka, a *kāyastha* of the Kāśyapa gotra and his wife Paitapa.[37] Can we assume that the father of the 12th century śrīkaraṇa Bhīmanātha inhabiting Arasavelli was the successor of any of these *kāyasthas*?

In the Srikakulam territory therefore, the inclusion of several *kāyasthas* in the category of *nāyakas* was visible. It is well-known that at present, the *kāyasthas* are regarded as a *jāti*. Probably, these inscriptions show us a transitional phase in between their professional identity as the group of record-keepers and their full-fledged emergence as a *jāti*.

In 13th century, an interesting epigraph from the Lakṣmī-Narasiṃha temple records the gift of lamp and 25 cows to the temple by Kāmaṇḍi-āmmā, mother of Māṅki Nāyaka, son of Surāṇḍi Nāyaka of the Olamaṅgala *gotra*, a śūdra, and belonging to the Drāviḍa (Tāmila) community.[38] This is the only epigraph where there is the evidence of a śūdra nāyaka, but he was from the Tamil region. Whether in the study area the śūdras could and/or did take the title *nāyaka* is open to question. In the 13th century Lakṣmī-Narasiṃha temple inscription we find another donor called Allāla Nāyaka who was the son of Drāviḍa perumal of Viśvāmitra *gotra*.[39] He was definitely from the Tamil territory, though his caste or *varṇa* identity is not given.

The Emergence of the *nāyakas* in Srikakulam-Vishakhapatnam: as individuals

The emergence of the *nāyakas* is seen from the 10th century within our area of study. It is in the 10th century inscriptions that they first started to appear. These are two in number, one of them found from Ponduru of Chipurupalli taluk of Vishakhapatnam referring to the gift of some villages to Itana-nāyaka and Gaṇḍa-nāyaka respectively, the son and grandson of Vali-nāyaka of Kalpapa race. The grant was in fact recognition of the prowess of Vali-nāyaka who saved the life of reigning king in the battle-field.[40] The gift-villages were spread over an expanded territory covering the Srikakulam and Vishakhapatnam areas; the village Gāra located in Srikakulam and Ponduru situated in Vishakhapatnam among them. This epigraph shows that at least the first person identified as a *nāyaka* of this donee-family existed in the 9th century for the inscription is of the 500 Gaṅga era. The second grant from Srikakulam and ascribed to the 10th century records the donation of Vilamvā-*grāma* attached to the Voṅkhāra-bhoga *viṣaya* under Kaliṅga *maṇḍala*. Also, 300 *murayas* to the southern side of Vilamvā was given to Sāvana, the son of Dhavala Nāyaka.[41]

Nanni Nāyaka also was chosen by the king as the donee for his military service. Thus, there is the possibility that Nanni Nāyaka, in the same way as Vali Nāyaka of the earlier mentioned Ponduru plates, achieved the title *nāyaka* by his valour. The names of the sons of Nanni Nāyaka who divided the gift-village into four equal shares have been mentioned as Erama-nāyaka, Chīḍakava, and Revakava. The sons of Erama-nāyaka were Nani and Bhīma Nāyaka, of Chīḍakava as Saṅgramimeru and Nārāyaṇa, and those of Revakava as Dugapa and Chīḍapa.[42] It is fairly clear from the family tree that not all the sons and grandsons of Nanni-nāyaka bore the title *nāyaka*. A very remarkable fact is that Nanni Nāyaka's wife mentioned in this epigraph came from the *gaṇikā-vaṁśa* attached to a Śaiva temple.[43] We do not know if Nanni had other wives. Whether the sons of all the wives coming from different social strata had the equal rights to inherit their father's status-title in this zone cannot be determined.

The number of the *nāyakas* was on increase from the 11th to 13th and again from the 14th to 15th centuries (Table 1). There are a few inscriptions which help us to track the process about how the *nāyakas* achieved prominence to be lifted higher enough in the social ladder and captured some important offices. From the Lakṣmī-Narasiṃha temple of Vishakhapatnam, there is a 13th century inscription which mentions about a person named Narasiṃha Nāyaka, the *karaṇa* of the village of Gannikoṭa, who was well-versed in mathematics, a religious as well as a rich man and who was the son of Surāṇḍi and his wife Guṇḍamāmbā.[44] Narasiṃha's richness reflects in his donation of land and tank to the temple of Siṃhāchalam. It appears that the father of Narasiṃha Nāyaka did not carry this status-title and the son must have acquired it through his wealth and knowledge combined with his office of *karaṇa*. The term *nāyaka* was also applied to imply the chiefhood. From an already mentioned 13th century epigraph from the Kūrmeśvara temple at Śrīkūrmam, we find as donor of lamp a person named Arjjama-seṭṭi who was the *nāyaka* (chief) of Aṃgaḍi. He was the son of Bhīma-seṭṭi and the grandson of Chiṃgama seṭṭi of Ḍaṃkkola *gotra*.[45] Their residence was Oḍḍavāḍi, present Vaddadi in the Chodavaram taluk of Vishakhapatnam. Though we do not know whether Aṃgaḍi was a place or denoted a market (of Śrīkūrmam or Oḍḍavāḍi) as its meaning suggests, it is evident that its headship was given to Arjjama. Thus, the epigraph shows us one of such situations which encouraged a person to address himself as *nāyaka*, though he might or might not carry it as his status-title. Arjjama did continue with the title *seṭṭi* following the footsteps of his father and grandfather, yet his chiefship of Aṃgaḍi helped him to be familiar as a *nāyaka*, though the factor of attaching it to his name instead of (or along with) *seṭṭi* was one of his personal choice. His posterity might or might not carry it with their names. From the 11th century Chikkalavalasa Copper plate of Vajrahasta III we are informed that the village Kuddam in Koluvartani *viṣaya* was given to Mallaya-śreṣthin of the *vaiśya* community who gave a part of the village to 300 brāhmaṇas, headed by Māpaya Nāyaka, son of Karaṇṭamanāyaka from his wife Rekapā and the grandson of Pilliśarman. They were the inhabitants of Jalambura.[46] The question is what inspired the son and grandson of Pilliśarman to change their name-suffix from *śarman* to *nāyaka*. There is a probability that the leadership of these 300 brāhmaṇas was first conferred upon Karaṇṭama Nāyaka and he carried the title instead of śarman and Māpaya Nāyaka also continued it either as a marker of his leadership or inheritance or both. This charter among others led Shishir Kumar Panda to come to the conclusion that "...it seems that the lands in the *agrahāra* villages were donated for the maintenance of the *brāhmaṇas* but assigned to the *nāyakas* as administrators and revenue-collectors." [47] In other words, he assumed that Māpaya nāyaka was an administrator and not to be included in the group of 300 brāhmaṇas. But, the fact that his *gotra* (Aupamanyava) and śākhā or branch of Vedic learning (Bahvṛcha)[48] is mentioned leads us to suggest that he was included in the group of brāhmaṇas.

A 12th century Madhukeśvara temple epigraph shows that Gavarammā (Gaurāmmā), grand-daughter of Gutāṇḍi nāyaka and his wife Ammāṇḍi and their daughter Suramā donated a lamp to temple.[49] S.N. Rajaguru has taken Gutāṇḍi as Gurāṇḍi in the Parlakhimedi taluk of the Ganjam district (now under Gajapati district) and has taken the term *nāyaka* as the headman of the village.[50] From a 13th century Lakṣmī-Narasiṃha temple inscription we find the evidence of a *nāyaka* (...rumāṇḍi) who donated 2 *vāṭis* of land located in the *agrahāra* called Meḍupāka and invested 10 *malla-māḍas* in the temple treasury of the god Narasiṃha for making provisions of food, flowers, incense, and *naivedya* on the festival days of the deity.[51] He probably wielded special power otherwise he would not have the right of alienating parts of *agrahāra*. In 11th century inscription from the Madhukeśvara temple of Mukhaliṅgam there is the reference to brāhmaṇa Daddapanāyaka, the minister of Choḍagaṅgadeva and the son of Ketanāchārya as donor of lamp.[52] His *nāyaka* status and non-use of the suffix āchārya probably resulted from his appointment to the ministerial rank. On the other hand, a 14th century epigraph from the Lakṣmī-Nārāyaṇa temple at Siṃhāchalam speaks about one Madhava *nāyaka* belonging to the community of *komaṭi* (traders) who was appointed for the service of supplying a garland daily to temple, and was granted in return 1 *kuñchā* of *prasādam* per day.[53] It is interesting to note that though he belonged to the *komaṭi* community, he was not heading it. At no point of time therefore, *nāyaka* denoted a *jāti*, which in this case was probably *komaṭi*. The inscriptions give us the impression that within our spatio-chronological context there was a fluid situation in terms of name-suffixes though the fluidity regarding the *jāti* identity was more limited. In modern day Indian scenario, the sensitivities are more about the surnames, at least in first appearance, which probably have replaced the early medieval and medieval name-suffixes. In fact, the history of name-suffixes and *jāti*-identities are not identical but they have parallel (and/or separate) histories though they are not independent to one another either. Little attempt has been done so far to delve into this field.

In the epigraphs of the Srikakulam-Vishakhapatnam zone, we encounter two different conditions: one where *nāyaka* was already a status-title and the other where the chiefhood or leadership was responsible for the gradual attainment of the title. In the second case, *nāyaka* is the marker of status rather than being the definitive evidence of a status-title, though it had the possibility of being carried as a status-title. It was also applicable in the sense of a steward or governor as seen in the 13th century Śrīkūrmam inscription where the *nāyaka* of Kaliṅga, along with the other prominent persons and communities, got the share of *prasādam*.[54] Sometimes, a community could be named after the *nāyakas*. A 14th century Lakṣmī-Nārāyaṇa temple inscription records that a garden was left under the care of some Gaṅgaya who belonged to the community of Megāpa-Chiṅgu Nāyaka.[55] What was Gaṅgaya's own status-title we do not know? And lastly, there were those *nāyakas* who had a military background. From an 11th century epigraph from the Madhukeśvara temple of Mukhaliṅgam we come to know about the donation of lamp by the *senāpati* Siṃhana Nāyaka, son of Meriya *daṇḍanāyaka*.[56] We can cite the 12th century record from the Kūrmeśvara temple at Śrīkūrmam which recorded a donation of two lamps by *mahāsenāpati* Rāmagovinda, son of Kīrttivāsa *gaḍasenāpati*, his son Somīśvara Nāyaka and his son Rāmāṅki Nāyaka.[57] Did the two sons of Rāmagovinda take the title *nāyaka* themselves for their father and grandfather were employed in royal military service? In other words, did they derive the title from the military legacies of their previous generations? It might also be the matter of fact that their grandfather, in his capacity of a *gaḍasenāpati* or the commander in charge of a *gaḍa* or fort was able to create some influence for himself around the fort-area. Could it be that his son and grandson were automatically included in the *nāyaka* category?

Nāyaka as a group and *kula*

In some epigraphs, there is the reference to the *nāyakas* as a group. In the 12th century epigraph from the Hāṭakeśvara temple at Siṅgavaram of the Srikakulam there is the proof of the gift of perpetual lamp and 5 *surabhi-māḍas* for its maintenance to the goddess Koṇḍapatidevī enshrined at Siṃhapura. The money was given at the disposal of the *nāyakas* for the maintenance of the said lamp.[58] It suggests the emergence of the *nāyakas* as a group. The most notable factor was the mention of the Vaiṣṇava Nāyakas of Tirupati. They seemed to belong to the foremost rank of religious personalities attached to the Vaisnavite temple of Tirupati located in the Srikalahasti district of the Andhra region. In the 13th century inscription from the Kūrmeśvara temple at Śrīkūrmam there is the mention of 15 Vaiṣṇava nāyakas who were granted some services. They and the 30 other *nāyakas* constituting a total of 45 brāhmaṇas were jointly to accomplish all the services connected with the god Kūrmanātha. The Vaiṣṇava Nāyakas were selected and appointed by Narahari [tīrtha] Śrīcharaṇa, the old minister of the reigning king Bhānudeva (I). They also got shares in the village of Khonna which Naraharitīrtha gifted in favour of the deity.[59] Their importance thus is self-evident. Next year, the Vaiṣṇava Nāyakas were entrusted with 5 *māḍas* which was given to the temple treasury by Permmāḍi Gopāla for the supply of milk and betel to the deity Prasanna Narasiṃha enshrined in the premises of the temple of Kūrmeśvara.[60]

In the 13th century CE, another donative record from the Kūrmanātha temple informs us that Garuḍa-nārāyaṇadeva paḍirāya gifted a number of articles and also 40 *māḍas* which was entrusted with the council of five (*pañchādi*) of the Vaiṣṇava-nāyakas of Tirupati.[61] Within two decades therefore, the Vaiṣṇava-nāyakas were able to bring an addition to the temple-administration and in lieu of managing the donations together, they gave the responsibility to a council. The 14th century Lakṣmī-Narasiṃha temple inscription from Siṃhāchalam confirms and renews the offerings of Gaṅga-Narasiṃhabhoga and also entrusts it with the five *nāyakas* (association of the Vaiṣṇavas of the temple) as done by the earlier king.[62] Probably, here too they formed a council of five. The endowment was made for meeting the expenditure of the respective services of the *nāyakas*, the Tirupati-vaiṣṇavas, and the *sthānādhipati*. A very interesting 14th century epigraph from the Lakṣmī-Narasiṃha temple records the donation of gold by two royal officials *kaliṅga-parīkṣā* and *bhoga-parīkṣā* for erecting two *maṇḍapas* in the temple of Viṣṇu on the consent (or in the presence) among others, of all the *nāyakas* including the inhabitants of their own village in Kaliṅga.[63] This suggests that not all the *nāyakas* were the inhabitants of their own villages and some of them changed their residences. Also, these *nāyakas*, it may be assumed, included the religious personnel and also the non-religious ones. Our hypothesis can be corroborated by a 13th century Śrīkūrmam inscription.[64] It records the appointment of a judicial tribunal in order to settle a boundary dispute between two villages called Ponnaḍi and Vontalakoṭi. And among the jurors, there were some Nāyaka kulas mentioned below:-

1. the nāyakas of Siṃhapura of Varāhavarttanī with their leader Āditya nāyaka
2. the nāyakas with their head Nārepa nāyaka of Śrīkūrmam
3. the nāyakas under the leadership of Gangama (na) nāyaka of Ippili
4. the nāyakas with their head Viṣṇama-nāyaka of Tāmaracheruvu
5. the nāyakas with their leader Bhīma nāyaka of Kuruviṭi attached to Sammaka-paṃpu
6. the nāyakas with their leader Tollavimallapa nāyaka of Eruḍa-paṃpu
7. the nāyakas with their leader Ennamaṇḍali of Dharmapura

The term *kula* is unlikely to denote family or extended family, where there were many *nāyaka* families and they had to act in unison then they certainly required a leader. We have shown already that even not all the members of one family carried the title *nāyaka*. The manner in which they have been mentioned in this epigraph suggests that here the term *kula* implied social group. So, here the *nāyakas* come from the seven different settlements and they inhabited in their respective localities as groups. Their allegiance to their leaders as well as their solidarity is expressed in this case. The *nāyaka* as a group was prominent as also their leaders who undoubtedly were influential persons. The question is did all the *nāyakas* of all the places have leaders? Or, did they have leaders where they were in large numbers, and regarded as *kula*? Nothing is known about the *varṇa* of individual members of those *nāyaka kulas*. It might be that all of the *varṇas* were included in the *nāyaka* groups recorded in this charter and here the question of *varṇa* was not at all important. Their identity as *nāyaka* was considered prestigious enough. The development of this characteristic exhibits the inclusion of different *varṇas* under the umbrella of nāyaka community and thus, the status-title *nāyaka* was slowly emerging as a social category (and not a *jāti*), and was absorbing different *varṇas* and professions into its fold. Apart from being implied as royal officer, ruling chief, head of a district or general it began to be applied as a *kula*.

Persons with Nāyaka affiliation: their background

Fathers of *Nāyaka* sons

It is undeniable that some of the *nāyakas* whose profession/ office is known from inscription, came from military background. The sons of *daṇḍanāyaka*, *mahāsenāpati* and *gaḍasenāpati* took the status-title *nāyaka* in the Srikakulam district. A 11th century Mukhaliṅgam inscription records the gift of lamp by the *senāpati* Siṃhaṇa nāyaka, son of Meriya *daṇḍanāyaka*.[65] Another interesting 13th century Śrīkūrmam inscription says about the gift of lamp and cash by *mahāsenāpati* Rāmagovinda, son of Kīrtivāsa *gaḍasenāpati*, his son Somīśvara Nāyaka and his son Rāmāṅki Nāyaka.[66] This is already mentioned. They are all from the military background. A 13th century Śrīkūrmam inscription mentions about the gift of Erupota-nāyaka, son of śrīkaraṇa Suru mahāsenāpati.[67]

On the other hand, in the Vishakhapatnam territory, we find Śrīvatsa Nāyaka, son of *mahāsenāpati* Heramba as the donor of garland to the deity Narasiṃha from a 14th century Lakṣmī-Narasiṃha Temple inscription.[68]

The sons of *perumal*, *ṭhakkura* and *paḍirāya* were included in this category. A 13th century Lakṣmī-Narasiṃha temple epigraph speaks about the gift of a permanent lamp by Allāla Nāyaka, son of Drāviḍa perumal of the Viśvāmitra *gotra*, when Vijayadeva paḍirāya was the governor of the Kaliṅga *viṣaya*.[69] Drāviḍa perumal is undoubtedly the person from south. Another 14th century Lakṣmī-Narasiṃha temple epigraph records about Gopinātha nāyaka, son of Chiṃgu (Siṃha) paḍirāya, who got 2 *puṭṭis* of land, located at Teruvapallī for supply of flower garlands to the deity.[70] This *paḍirāya* was certainly a flower-supplier and not of similar status to the governor *paḍirāya* mentioned in the earlier inscription and this suggests that one name-suffix does not denote only one occupation or only one type of status. The only other *paḍirāya* associated with *nāyaka* comes from a 14th century Lakṣmī-Narasiṃha temple. Here Somu *paḍirāya*, son of Prola Nāyaka of the Kāśyapa *gotra* donated cows and one sapphire (*nīla-ratna*) to the deity.[71] A 13th century Lakṣmī-Narasiṃha temple inscription records the donation of flower-garden by Purāi Nāyakāni, mother of Lakṣmaṇa Nāyaka who was the son of Bhavapati Thakkura of the Kauśika *gotra*.[72] These are the only evidences of the existence of *perumal* and *ṭhakkura* within our study-area and study-period as far as the epigraphs are concerned.

Sons of *Nāyaka* Fathers

The sons of the *nāyaka* fathers had more variegated offices, both civil and military. In Srikakulam, the fathers of *leṅkā*[73] (servant, śūdra servant or a writer), *puravari*, *peggaḍa* or *perggaḍa* (superintendent or director), *gajasāhini* (leader of the elephant-force), *pradhānī* (governor, minister, president, noble or executive officer or even a village-headman) and *pasāyata* (fief-holder or official designation) bore the title *nāyaka*.

From the 12th century Madhukeśvara temple epigraph we come to know that the *leṅkā* of Vīrachoḍadeva named Suraya, son of Kannadi Eriyama Nāyaka, gave a perpetual lamp to the deity.[74] Another 12th century Madhukeśvara temple inscription records the donation of perpetual lamp by the *leṅkā* Vellamanāyaka, son of Pañjyaṇḍi Nāyaka and his wife Vimmamā-nāyakāni.[75] A 12th century Nīlakaṇṭheśvara temple inscription from Bobbili of Vishakhapatnam mentions about the gift of perpetual lamp in favour of the god Nīlīśvaradeva at the village of Nāvapallī under Kaliṅga by *leṅkā* Gokana (Gokarṇa), son of Mudali Tāmbika and grandson of ...mara nāyaka of Gumuḍa.[76] In another record of the same year discovered from the same temple, he is mentioned as Gumuḍa-leṅkā-Gokana.[77] Gumuḍa is identified with present Gumuḍā in the Bobbili taluk.

Puravāri sons of *nāyaka* fathers come from the Srikakulam territory. Most of them existed in the 12th century and only one evidence we get in the 13th century. We come to know about: *puravari* Madhukeśvara Gaṅga, son of Narasa Nāyaka and his wife Meḍama Nāyakāni;[78] *puravari* Potaya, son of Tolachi-Proli nāyaka;[79] puravari-karaṇa Māvina, son of Māṅki nāyaka who gave lamp, cash and one *puṭṭi* of land;[80] *puravari* and *rāchapaḍihasta* Surapota, the son of Māliya Nāyaka and his wife Demāḍi Nāyakāni as the donor of 4 *puṭṭis* of land;[81] *puravari* Kāmadeva-peggaḍa, son of Mārtaṇḍa Nāyaka who was a royal officer under the Gaṅga king and belonged to the original astrologers' family (*mūla-ghaṭik-ānvaya*) of the Kauṇḍinya *gotra*;[82] *puravari* Māṅkama, son of Ketana-nāyaka, donor of 2 *puṭṭis* of land;[83] and *puravari* Māṃbi nāyaka, son of Māki nāyaka of the village called Paratala-*grāma*, the donor of 2 jenakolas equivalent to one *puṭṭi* of land located on the north of Nakarapuvāḍa and to the west of Surapotu's land.[84] These persons donated to the Madhukeśvara temple in the 12th century. Another epigraph from the Hāṭakeśvara temple at Siṅgavaram in Srikakulam dated 13th century records the gift of lamp and 5 *surabhi-māḍas* to the god Koṇḍapotidevī of Siṃhapura by *puravari* Mañchi peggaḍa, son of Puruṣottama Nāyaka. The money was given at the disposal of the *nāyakas* for the maintenance of the said gift-lamp.[85] The 12th century Nīlakaṇṭheśvara temple inscription of Nārāyaṇapuram mentions about the donation of lamp by śrīkaraṇa and *rācha puravari* Guṇḍiya (Guṇḍama), son of Kaṇṭhatā Nāyaka.[86] When Guṇḍama's brother Nāgadeva was a *rācha-puravari*, Guṇḍama was not called as *rācha puravari*, as noted from an earlier record.[87] Probably Nāgadeva was his elder brother who held the post before Guṇḍama.

Other persons with different offices are found from inscriptions. A 12th century Kūrmeśvara temple inscription speaks about the donation of [Bhī?]madeva-peggaḍa, son of Keśava Nāyaka to Kūrmasvāmīdeva of Pūrṇakoṭi.[88] Another 12th century Madhukeśvara temple inscription refers to Vaṇapati-peggaḍa of Siṃhapura, and his father Rāyapa Nāyaka and mother Rekama Nāyakāni.[89] Vanapati's wife was Erakama Nāyakāni who was the daughter of Daṇḍama Nāyaka and his wife Sudāma Nāyakāni of Piṣṭapura.[90] In 13th century, Sura-peggaḍa, son of Mādava Nāyaka of the Bhāradvāja *gotra* and a resident of Ḍimila donated 50 cows and 3 *niṣkas* (of gold) for a lamp stand in the temple treasury.[91]

In the 12th century CE, Meḍapota pradhānī, son of brāhmaṇa Erapota-nāyaka of the Vājasaneya *sūtra* (*gotra*) gifted a perpetual lamp and cash to Kūrmasvāmī of Pūrṇakoṭi.[92] In the 13th century, Sura-pradhānī and his brother Puruṣottama, sons of Somi Nāyaka and his wife Māṅkāmā Nāyakāni of Tolachi (Tulasi grāma in Srikakulam taluk?) donated lamp and one *puṭṭi* of land to the deity Madhukeśvara of Nagara.[93] In the 13th century, Vallu pradhāna gifted perpetual lamp to the deity Narasiṃhadeva at Siṃhagiri for accruing religious merit for his father Uttareśvara Nāyaka and his mother Mumbāmbā of the Kaliṅga-*vaṃśa*.[94] We do not know if the point about the mention of his mother's family (as belonging to Kaliṅga as appears from the name of the family) was that his father did not belong to Kaliṅga. From the 13th century Lakṣmī-Narasiṃha temple epigraph we are informed about Savana pradhāna, Dāru pradhāna and Puruṣottama pradhāna who hailed from Raṭṭu *viṣaya* of Cholanāḍu,[95] definitely implying the *nāḍu* or district of the Cholas located in south India. Another 13th century Lakṣmī-Narasiṃha temple record speaks about Nārāyaṇa pradhānī, son of Peddā somayājī and grandson of Nārāyaṇa vājapeyayājī of the Ātreya *gotra*, who was in charge of the temple-treasury.[96]

A 13th century Lakṣmī-Narasiṃha temple record refers to the gift of lamp with stand and land by the general *mahāsenāpati* Bhaggupata (?), son of Proli Nāyaka.[97] A 15th century epigraph from the same temple mentions about Paṭṭanāyaka Gui mahāsenāpati, son of Padma Nāyaka of Poṭnūri as the donor.[98] Another 15th century epigraph from the same temple refers to the provision made by Gāru mahāsenāpati, son of Mārtaṇḍa Nāyaka of Pālakoṇḍa by depositing 5 *veṇḍi-ṭaṅkas* for perpetual lamp.[99]

Persons with the title *senāpati* belonged to this category. A 14th century Lakṣmī-Narasiṃha temple epigraph informs that Koppulakāpi Nāyaka, for a perpetual lamp, donated 50 cows under the care of Rāmaśaṅkara senāpati, son of Kāmi Nāyaka of Poṭṭanūri. In order to grant 2 *puṭṭis* of wetland to this person for his service, the donor invested 20 *gaṇḍa-māḍas* in the temple-treasury.[100] Another 14th century Lakṣmī-Narasiṃha temple epigraph records the gift of perpetual lamp by Padmanābha Nāyaka, the son of Annama Nāyaka of the Ātreya *gotra*. The cows for the maintenance of lamp were given under the care of Anātta senāpati, son of Nārāyaṇa Nāyaka of Oḍḍāḍi, who took the responsibility of supplying 7 *kuñchās* of clarified butter per month to the temple. For this service he was granted 2 *puṭṭis* of wetland, situated at Oḍḍāḍi.[101] This *senāpati* was surely a cowherd one. The cowherd *senāpatis* must be differentiated from the general *senāpatis*. There were the cowherd *konāri* sons of the *nāyakas*. A 14th century Lakṣmī-Narasiṃha temple record mentions about Śivasoma mahānāyaka of Kaliṅga-daṇḍapāṭa as the donor of lamp and cows and along with it about Narisi-konāri, son of Kaliṅga nāyaka who was appointed for their care and for the additional charge of supplying 1 *aḍā* (āḍhaka in Sanskrit) and 7½ *kuñchās* of clarified butter per month.[102]

In a 12th century Madhukeśvara temple inscription, there is the mention of the *gajasāhiṇi* (*gaja-sādhanika* or the officer-in-charge of the war-elephants) Kuppana-vīra, son of Lolepa Araya Nāyaka and Meḍapa Nāyakāni as a donor to the same temple.[103] A 13th century Lakṣmī-Narasiṃha temple epigraph speaks about the gift of 12 *gaṇḍa-māḍas* by sachiva Gaṇeśvara chamūnātha, son of Someśvara nāyaka, who served the king Narasiṃha I.[104]

A 14th century Lakṣmī-Narasiṃha temple record refers to the appointment of a certain Mādhava Nāyaḍu, the son of Saradeva (Sarvadeva) pedināyaka for the service of waving a *chāmara*.[105] A 15th century Lakṣmī-Narasiṃha temple record refers to the donation of a fan by Maḍapali-Naenialli Nāyeḍu, son of Kaḍama Nāyaka of Vīragoṭṭa (Vīrakoṭṭa).[106] It is to be mentioned that all the persons with 'nāyeḍu' as their name-suffix came from the Vishakhapatnam area and donated to the temple of Siṃhāchalam.

Some notable features

The interesting factor is perhaps the evidence of a transitional phase in the emergence of the nāyaka category where the persons carrying other status-titles took the title of *nāyaka* (Table 2):

Table 2: *nāyakas* who carried other status-titles

Date	*Name of Person*	*Find spot of Inscription*
Śaka Year 1015	senāpati Siṃhaṇa nāyaka	Madhukeśvara temple of Mukhaliṅgam
Year 37 of Choḍagaṅga	pasāi Komi nāyaka	-Do-
Śaka Year 1015	senāpati Kuppama nāyaka	-Do-
Śaka Year 1049	pasāita Kommi nāyaka	-Do-
Śaka Year 1060	mudrahasta (designation doubtful) Savvi nāyaka	-Do-
Śaka Year 1062	leṅkā Vellamanāyaka	-Do-
Śaka Year 1063	kāmpus Revi nāyaka and Palli nāyaka	Bhīmeśvara temple of Mukhaliṅgam
Śaka Year 1064	mahā-daṇḍavāsi(mahā-daṇḍapāśika) Vayyapa nāyaka	Kūrmeśvara temple at Śrīkūrmam
Śaka Year 1072	pasāyata Meḍapota nāyaka	Madhukeśvara temple of Mukhaliṅgam
Śaka Year 1085	puravari Māṃbi nāyaka	-Do-
Śaka Year 1206	Arjjama-seṭṭi, the nāyaka of Aṃgaḍi	Kūrmeśvara temple at Śrīkūrmam
Śaka Year 1103	Narasiṃha nāyaka, the karaṇa of the village Gannikoṭa	Lakṣmī-Narasiṃha temple at Siṃhāchalam
Śaka Year 1169	senāpati Dharavṛti nāyaka	-Do-
Śaka Year 1307	Mādhava nāyaka, of the Komaṭi community	-Do-
Year 33 of Kapileśvaradeva	Vīra nāyaka,the koṭhi-karaṇa (koṣṭha-karaṇa or the officer-in-charge of the revenue department or treasury accountant)	-Do-

The titles like *paṭṭanāyaka*, *mahānāyaka*,[107] *puranāyaka*,[108] and *pedināyaka*[109] definitely were some classifications of the official *nāyakas*. Whether these persons or their progeny took the status-title *nāyaka* is open to question.

Another remarkable factor is that the same person, if not referred to in the epigraphs of Srikakulam-Vishakhapatnam area, is not mentioned as *nāyaka*. We can cite the fact by showing the 12th century Nṛsiṁha temple inscription of the time of Choḍagaṅgadeva within the Jagannātha temple complex at Purī where the *gajasādhanika* Lollapa was mentioned only as the son of a minister.[110] But, the same person, when mentioned in the 12th century Madhukeśvara temple inscription as the father of *gajasāhiṇi* Kuppana-vīra, is mentioned as Lolepa Araya Nāyaka.[111] This leads to the question that was there more such persons who did not introduce themselves as *nāyakas* outside our study-area, but were addressed as *nāyakas* within the Srikakulam-Vishakhapatnam territory only? This further leads us to question whether in the Telugu speaking area the custom of using the term *nāyaka* was more prevalent rather than in the Oriya speaking zone. The evidence of the trader Prayāga mentioned as Prayāga upādhyāya in the Kūrmeśvara temple record and being referred as Prayāga Nāyaka in the 15th century Simhachalam temple record is also to be mentioned. Was then the use of the title *nāyaka* more regular if we go towards the south?

Nāyakas in Kakatiya Andhra and *Nāyakas in Srikakulam-Vishakhapatnam: a comparative study*

In *Prataparudra Charitamu*, which reflected the perspective of Telugu warriors of the Vijayanagara Empire of the 16th century, there is the story that Kākatīya Pratāparudra's predecessor gave *nāyaka* status to diverse castes. But, they became corrupted and attacked Warangal's royal temple and the brāhmaṇas during the time of Pratāparudra. As a step, Pratāparudra summoned a group of seventy-seven śūdra padmanāyakas. Thus, he created a class of Telugu warriors, the padmanāyakas.[112] There might be bias in the story, but one point is clear. In the Kākatīya Andhra, caste was not an obstacle to the attainment of *nāyaka* status and the king could confer the *nāyaka* status. But, we do not have the answer to the question whether the king was the sole authority of conferring the title of *nāyaka* in the study area.

The table prepared by Shishir Kumar Panda citing the geographical distribution of the inscriptions (between 1038-1434 CE) mentioning the *nāyakas* shows that the number of related epigraphs found in Puri, Cuttack, Mayurbhanj, Ganjam in Orissa and Godavari in Andhra numbers only eleven in total while those coming from Srikakulam-Vishakhapatnam region are as many as 219 in number.[113] He has also noted that the *nāyakas* in the Kaliṅga territory had 'many other functions than military'[114] and included them in the local administration of the Later Gaṅgas. But, not all the epigraphs suggest that all of the persons holding that title *nāyaka* came from the local level administration. Moreover, the background to which the *nāyakas* belonged differed from region to region, and even from time to time. We can cite the evidence of Śaṅkara-nāyaka, grandson of Gaṇḍa-nāyaka, a *telī* (oilman) found in the Kaijang Plates of Bhānudeva III, dated Śaka 1284, found in Cuttack district.[115] No oilman in the study-area took the title *nāyaka*. Similarly, when Cynthia Talbot had studied the Kākatīya epigraphs, she noticed that the *nāyaka* sons had *bōya* (herder), *chamūpati* (general) and *reḍḍi* (landowning group) fathers. On the other hand, the *nāyaka* fathers had *rāju*, *reḍḍi* and *bōya* sons.[116] But, another important caste-cluster *seṭṭi* in Kākatīya Andhra did not have any connection with the status-title *nāyaka*. And in this regard, it is different from Srikakulam-Vishakhapatnam region where the *vaiśya*, *vyāpārī*, *komaṭi*, *seṭṭi*, *mahājana*, and *vaṇijārā* had the names suffixed by *nāyaka* (Table 2). Therefore, the trading community in Srikakulam-Vishakhapatnam was included in this category, but in Kākatīya Andhra, they were not. However, the proof of the agriculturist (*kāmpu*) and pastoralist communities (*senāpati* and *koṇāri*) acquiring the title *nāyaka* in the area of our study is available, though on a very small scale. Secondly, we can see from Talbot's study that the *chamūpati* fathers had *nāyaka* sons (and not vice versa) , but the *nāyaka* fathers had *rāju* sons (and not vice versa). While the term *chamūpati* implies a general, the term *rāju* has been explained by Talbot as the equivalent of Sanskrit *rāja*. Some of them have been identified with the royal or noble descent and the rest were ministerial or clerical.[117] Though there were some differences between the activities of *rāja* and *rāju* in the pre-Kakatiya Andhra, the difference probably disappeared during the Kākatīya rule. It is clear that *rāja* is higher title than the *chamūpati*. So, it can be concluded that if a *chamūpati*'s son could acquire the title *nāyaka*, he or his son in turn had the scope of rising further to the status of a *rāju*. In fact, evidence is not lacking in this respect. Talbot has shown that a Yādava chief from Addanki used the status-title *mahārāja* and *nāyaka* in two epigraphs found from Ongole in Guntur.[118] Talbot noted that the *nāyakas* moved upwards into the rank of nobility.[119]

Thirdly, we have already seen that in the Srikakulam-Vishakhapatnam region, a number of persons with *nāyaka* affiliation had military background. This is also true in the case of Kākatīya Andhra. Lastly, in Kākatiya period, *nāyaka* was an ambiguous term and encompassed local notables as well as military leaders. The majority of the *nāyaka* men in the corpus of inscriptions mentioned the name of their royal overlords, and roughly one-third of them possessed administrative titles such as *mahāpradhānī* (minister), *sāmanta* and *senāpati*. The *nāyakas* ranked below the kings and princes, to whom they generally owed allegiance.[120] In Kalinga too, the *nāyakas* came from military as well as ministerial or clerical background as we have already seen. *Nāyaḍu*, *nāiḍu* and *nāik* have been considered as the variant versions of *nāyaka*[121] and in the study-area, we find a *nāyaḍu* son of a *pedināyaka* father in the 14th century Lakṣmī-Narasiṃha temple epigraph from Siṃhāchalam in the Vishakhapatnam area.[122]

Several factors mentioned by Talbot are that first, more than any other title in medieval Andhra, *nāyaka* encompassed persons of varied background. Very few of them did not claim to belong to the *kṣatriya varṇa*, nor do they provide many details of their ancestry. And most importantly, like the Rajput, nāyaka was a status that could be acquired, regardless of origin, and move a man up the social ladder. It was essentially an honorific title borne by prominent individuals who participated in military activities.[123] In the present study-area too, the evidence of a *nāyaka* claiming as belonging to the *kṣatriya varṇa* is rare. This could be for the reason that the term began to be used as the substitute of *kṣatriya* which I have mentioned earlier. Both the Nāyaka and Rajput were not *jātis*. But, the difference in between the Nāyaka and Rajput status is that while the Rajput identity involved a claim to kinship, real or imagined, and land-rights, the nāyaka identity did not emphasize on kinship-association, though it was associated with the incorporation into *kulas* which probably were not kinship organisation. Second, Talbot noted that the nāyakas moved upwards into the rank of nobility[124] and it is also partially true in the case of the Srikakulam-Vishakhapatnam region.

Impact of the nāyaka system on society

There are indeed instances where the official status of the *nāyakas* cannot be traced, but that they were donated land by royalty show that they had close connections with the king. The 11th century Ragolu copper plate of Vajrahasta III confirms the donation of two villages named Koṭṭisa (in Palakonda of Srikakulam) and Jampi in favour of Chāmenanāyaka, the son of Śrīdharanāyaka, the resident of Niḍiṃjeruvu. His wife was Maayindaku(ka)va and their two sons were Eriyama and Potaya.[125] The official position of this person we cannot determine, if any. The rise of *nāyakas* as individuals and groups alike and the association of various social groups and administrative posts with *nāyaka* category going through a change over five hundred years indicate that a social aspect is also linked with their origin. Along with the official and religious *nāyakas*, there were the non-official and non-religious persons who took the title *nāyaka*. We do not know whether the political and administrative aspects of the *nāyaka* status encouraged others with some social and economic influence to address themselves as *nāyaka*. The elements of social prestige as well as collective and individual aspirations might be the cause behind that. This situation can be compared with the status title *seṭṭi* which is the variant of śreṣṭhī and denoted very rich merchant and investors involving very high social status. He was the highest among the various kinds of traders. But later, small artisans, shop-keepers and others also started to take the title *seṭṭi*. It is evident from epigraphs, and inscriptions from the study-area also are not the exception. So, it appears that anyone with his quality of leadership and having influence in an area or in his own community, could emerge as a *nāyaka* provided his ancestors had a respectable position in society and/or were related to the administration.

The Nāyakaship was not essentially linked with military capability and probably not always conferred upon by the king. It had an element of social acceptance too. The existence of its female rendering *nāyakāni* further indicates this social aspect. However, the entry into the *nāyaka* category was not easy. But, once a person was recognized as a *nāyaka* in society, his sons and grandsons had the choice of continuing with this title and/or entering into administration, and/or of discontinuing with it. Thus, the emergence of *nāyakas* should be looked as a regional feature and something more than a conscious move on the part of the Gaṅga kings after the initial starting. Probably, after the conscious introduction of this status-title, there was an urge to acquire it among the rest of the population, though the military and administrative officers were always closer to this status as can be seen from inscriptions. (Table 3). Epigraphs inform us about some *nāyakas* whose sons carried over this status-title and about whose position or office, nothing is known from inscriptions. If they actually held any office, they would have made it known probably while donating. There are others with the name-suffix *nāyaka*, whose position was not at all high. In one 15th century Lakṣmī-Narasiṃha temple inscription, a queen of Oḍḍādi gave a perpetual lamp and 50 cows to the temple and also a water pitcher for the sacred bath of the deity for which she gave 5 *māḍas* under the custody of Narasina (Narasiṃha) who was the son of Devaki Nāyaka. Narasina was granted 1 *kuñchā* of *prasādam* daily for fetching water in the pitcher. So, the father of this Narasina, who appears to be a temple-servant, evidently was not included in the rank of official, administrator, or military *nāyakas*.[126]

Table 3: The number of evidences found about the associations of the various social groups, professions, and offices with the category of *nāyaka* in the Srikakulam-Vishakhapatnam region.

	10th century	*11th century*	*12th century*	*13th century*	*14th century*	*15th century*
Vaiśya		1	2			
Vyāpārī		1			1	
Daṇḍanāyaka		1				
Senāpati(general)		1	1	1		
Leṅkā			4			
Gajasāhini			1			
Pradhānī			1			
Pasāyata			4			
Mudrahasta			1			
Kampu			1			
Mahādaṇḍapāśika (Mahādaṇḍavāsi)			1			
Puravari			9	1		
Śrīkaraṇa			4	1		
Perggaḍa			3	1		
Seṭṭi				1		
Karaṇa				1		
Pradhāna				1		
Gaḍasenāpati				1		
Chamūnātha and Sachiva				1		
Perumala				1		
Ṭhakkura				1		
Mahājana (merchant)				1		
Mahāsenāpati				3	1	1
Ghoḍā-vaṇijārā					1	
Paḍirāya					1	
Konāri					1	
Senāpati (cowherd)					2	1

(Contd...)

Nāyaḍu						1
Koṭhi-Karaṇa						1
Paṭṭanāyaka						1
Komaṭi						1

Conclusion: from name-suffixes to surname

In medieval and early modern peninsular India, the title *nāyaka* and its variants were used in different regions in the sense of governor, chief, overlord, military general etc. Commonality of this title in different regions suggests interactions. Authors like R.S. Sharma have noticed that surname like Nayak in Orissa held by landowning families suggests that "...their ancestors were either substantial peasants or rent-receiving landlords."[127] In other words, the author has pointed to the link between the older title and present surname. To what extent the early medieval and medieval *nāyakas* continued with their title into the early modern India and permanently attached the title to their names as surnames in modern Indian context can be a matter of debate, discussion and further research. In an ever-changing environment of community, culture, identity and status, old features constantly give way to new ones, and therefore, the study about the *nāyakas* in Srikakulam-Vishakhapatnam territory from epigraphs spanning several centuries can show only some aspects of the process, not all. In early-medieval India, the *jāti* identity cut across the *varṇa* identity, the status-titles and name-suffixes added another layer the *varṇa-jāti* identity, and some of those status-titles and name-suffixes are still being continued in the forms of surnames. The problem of the identity and origin of the *nāyakas* and the matter of their social acceptance and mobility can be situated within this ever-evolving social process.

References

1. D.C. Sircar, *Indian Epigraphical Glossary*, Motilal Banarsidass, Delhi, 1966, p. 214.
2. Shishir Kumar Panda, *Nāyaka System in Medieval Orissa, Śraddhāñjali Studies in Ancient Indian History: D.C. Sircar Commemoration Volume*, Sundeep Prakashan, Delhi, 1988, pp. 92-107.
3. *Ibid.*, p. 102.
4. Snigdha Tripathy, Naḍagam Copper plate Charter of Vajrahasta III, Śaka Year 979, *Descriptive Topographical Catalogue of Orissan Inscriptions*, Manohar, New Delhi, 2010, no. 56, pp. 651- 652.
5. Shishir Kumar Panda, *op.cit.*, p. 97.

6. Snigdha Tripathy, Srikakulam Copper Plate Charter of Vajrahastadeva, Śaka Year 979, *op.cit.*, no. 55, pp. 650-651.
7. Shishir Kumar Panda, *op.cit.*, p. 94.
8. Snigdha Tripathy, Chikkalavalasa Copper Plate Charter of Vajrahasta III, Śaka Year 982, *op.cit.*, no.62, pp. 659-660.
9. *Ibid.*, Māṭura Copper Plate Charter of Devendravarman Rājarāja I, Śaka Year 995, no. 66, p. 664.
10. *Ibid.*, Mukhaliṅgam Inscription, Śaka Year 1015,no. 25, p. 689.
11. *Ibid.*, Srīkūrmam Inscription of the time of Madhukāmārṇavadeva, Śaka Year 1071, no.145, p. 756.
12. *Ibid.*, Śrīkūrmam Inscription, Śaka Year 1195, no. 227, p. 800.
13. *Ibid.*, Mukhaliṅgam Inscription, Śaka Year 1100, no. 168, p. 769.
14. Probably this Vanapati has been taken by Shishir Kumar Panda in the sense of a forest-chief, Shishir Kumar Panda, *op.cit.*, p. 102.
15. Snigdha Tripathy, Mukhaliṅgam Inscription of the Time of Anantavarman [Rājarāja II], Śaka Year 1097, *op. cit.*, no. 167, pp. 768-769.
16. *Ibid.*, Lakṣmī-Narasiṃha Temple Inscription, Śaka Year 1220, no. 116, pp. 938-939.
17. *Ibid.*, Mukhaliṅgam Inscription of the Time of Anantavarman [Kāmārṇavadeva], Śaka Year 1070, no. 141, p. 754.
18. *Ibid.*, Lakṣmī-Narasiṃha Temple Inscription, Śaka Year 1315, no. 344, p. 1071.
19. *Ibid.*, Lakṣmī-Narasiṃha Temple Inscription, Śaka Year 1337, no. 426, p. 1118.
20. *Ibid.*, Lakṣmī-Narasiṃha Temple Inscription, Śaka Year 1337, no. 427, p. 1119.
21. *Ibid.*, Lakṣmī-Narasiṃha Temple Inscription, Śaka Year 1320, no. 360, pp. 1079-1080.
22. *Ibid.*, Śrīkūrmam Inscription of the Time of Narasiṃhadeva, Śaka Year 1324, no. 295, p. 840.
23. *Ibid.*, Śrīkūrmam Inscription, Śaka Year 1325, Samvat 1459, no. 296, pp. 841-841.
24. *Ibid.*, Chicacole Copper Plate Charter of Madhukāmārṇava, Year 526, no. 51, pp. 646-647.
25. Subrata Kumar Acharya, Maḍgam Plates of Rāṇaka Bhīmakheḍi of the Time of Devendravarman, Ś. 988, *Copper-plate Inscriptions of Odisha-A Descriptive Catalogue-(Circa Fourth Century to Sixteenth Century CE)*, DK Printworld, New Delhi, 2014, pp. 430- 431.
26. Snigdha Tripathy, Mukhaliṅgam Inscription, Śaka Year 1077, *op.cit.*, no. 154, pp. 761.
27. *Ibid.*, Sūryanārāyaṇa Temple Inscription of the Time of Choḍagaṅga, Year 58, no. 76, p. 718.
28. *Ibid.*, Madhukeśvara Temple Inscription, Śaka Year 1130, no. 185, pp. 778-779.

29. *Ibid.*, Śrīkūrmam Inscription, Śaka Year 1206, no. 239, p. 807.
30. *Ibid.*, Lakshmī-Narasimha Temple Inscription, Śaka Year 1307, no.295, p.1042.
31. B.Pramila, 'Society and Economy of Telangana', *Comprehensive History and Culture of Andhra Pradesh, Vol. IV (Medieval Andhradesa AD 1000-1324)*, ed. Somasundara Rao, New Delhi: Tulika Books, 2011, p. 210.
32. Aruna Pariti, 'Society and Economy of Vengidesa', *Comprehensive History and Culture of Andhra Pradesh, vol. IV*, p. 241.
33. Snigdha Tripathy, Mukhaliṅgam Inscription of the Time of Choḍagaṅga, *op. cit.*, no. 84, pp. 722-723.
34. Y. Subbarayalu, *South India under the Cholas*, Oxford University Press, New Delhi, 2012, p. 183.
35. Snigdha Tripathy, Mukhaliṅgam Inscription of the Time of Choḍagaṅga, Śaka Year 1057, *op.cit.*, no. 96, pp. 729-730.
36. *Ibid.*, Mukhaliṅgam Inscription of the Time of Choḍagaṅga, Śaka Year 1063, no. 113, pp. 738-739.
37. *Ibid.*, Arasavalli Copper Plate Charter of Vajrahasta III, Śaka Year 982, no. 60, pp. 656-657.
38. *Ibid.*, Lakṣmī-Narasiṃha Temple Inscription, Śaka Year 1219, no. 112, p. 936.
39. *Ibid.*, Lakṣmī-Narasiṃha Temple Inscription of the Time of Vīra-Bhānudeva, Śaka Year 1200, no. 85, p. 919.
40. Subrata Kumar Acharya, Ponduru Plates of Vajrahasta II, Gaṅga Year 500, *op.cit.*, pp. 426-428.
41. Snigdha Tripathy, Ramapuram Copper Plate Charter of Vajrahasta, Year 495, *op.cit.*, no. 49, pp. 643-644.
42. Subrata Kumar Acharya, Ramapuram Plates of Vajrahasta, Gaṅga Year 495, *op.cit.*, pp. 424-425.
43. Snigdha Tripathy, *op.cit.*, no. 49, pp. 643-644.
44. Snigdha Tripathy, Lakṣmī-Narasiṃha Temple Inscription, Śaka Year 1123, no. 50, pp. 898.
45. *Ibid.*, Śrīkūrmam Inscription, Śaka Year 1206, no. 239, p. 807.
46. *Ibid.*, Chikkalavalasa Copper Plate Charter of Vajrahasta III, Śaka Year 982, no. 62, pp.659-660.
47. Shishir Kumar Panda, *op.cit.*, p. 100.
48. Subrata Kumar Acharya, Chikkalavalasa Plates of Vajrahasta III, Ś. 982, *op.cit.*, pp. 445-446.
49. Snigdha Tripathy, Mukhaliṅgam Inscription of the Time of Coḍagaṅgadeva, Śaka Year 1045, *op.cit.*, no. 50, pp. 703-704.
50. *Ibid.*, no. 538, p. 704.
51. *Ibid.*, Lakṣmī-Narasiṃha Temple Inscription, Śaka Year 1171, no. 70, p. 910.

52. *Ibid.*, Mukhaliṅgam Inscription, Śaka Year 1015, no. 25, p. 689.
53. *Ibid.*, Lakṣmī-Narasiṃha Temple Inscription, Śaka Year 1307, no. 295, p. 1042.
54. *Ibid.*, Śrīkūrmam Inscription, Śaka Year 1219, no. 249, p. 813.
55. *Ibid.*, Lakṣmī-Narasiṃha Temple Inscription, Śaka Year 1309, no. 304, pp. 1047-1048.
56. *Ibid.*, Mukhaliṅgam Inscription, Śaka Year 1015, no. 24, pp. 688-689.
57. *Ibid.*, Śrīkūrmam Inscription of the Time of Naranārasiṃhadeva (I), Śaka Year 1163,no.206, pp. 789-790.
58. *Ibid.*, Hāṭakeśvara Temple Inscription, Śaka Year 1127, no. 173, p. 172.
59. *Ibid.*, Śrīkūrmam Inscription of the Time of Bhānudeva, Śaka Year 1197, no. 229, pp. 801-802.
60. *Ibid.*, Śrīkūrmam Inscription, Śaka Year 1198, no. 230, p. 802.
61. *Ibid.*, Śrīkūrmam Inscription, Śaka Year 1219, no. 249, p. 813.
62. *Ibid.*, Lakṣmī-Narasiṃha Temple Inscription of the Time of Vīra-Bhānudeva, Śaka Year 1275, no. 166, pp. 968-969.
63. *Ibid.*, Lakṣmī-Narasiṃha Temple Inscription of the Time of Narasiṃhadeva (IV), Year 13, no.317, p. 1055.
64. *Ibid.*, Śrīkūrmam Inscription of the Time of Anantavarman (Aniyaṅkabhīma), Śaka Year 1152, no.194, pp. 783-784.
65. *Ibid.*, Mukhaliṅgam Inscription, Śaka Year 1015, no. 24, pp. 688-689.
66. *Ibid.*, Śrīkūrmam Inscription of the Time of Naranārasiṃhadeva (i), Śaka Year 1163, no.206, pp. 789-790.
67. *Ibid.*, Śrīkūrmam Inscription, Śaka Year 1137, no. 188, pp. 780-781.
68. *Ibid.*, Lakṣmī-Narasiṃha Temple Inscription, Śaka Year 1294, no. 216, p. 996.
69. *Ibid.*, Lakṣmī-Narasiṃha Temple Inscription of the Time of Vīra-Bhānudeva, Śaka Year 1200, no. 85, p. 919.
70. *Ibid.*, Lakṣmī-Narasiṃha Temple Inscription, Śaka Year 1278, no. 171, p. 971.
71. *Ibid.*, Lakṣmī-Narasiṃha Temple Inscription, Śaka Year 1265, no. 143, p. 955.
72. *Ibid.*, Lakṣmī-Narasiṃha Temple Inscription, Śaka Year 1220, no. 116, pp. 938-939.
73. It was Gaṅga and Gajapati official designation; also a family surname of Khaṇḍāyat caste, originally belonging to the warrior class. *Ibid.*, no.534, p. 702.
74. *Ibid.*, Mukhaliṅgam Inscription, Śaka Year 1042, no. 46, pp. 701-702.
75. *Ibid.*, Mukhaliṅgam Inscription of the Time of Choḍagaṅga, Śaka Year 1062, no. 111, pp. 737-738.
76. *Ibid.*, Nīlakaṇṭheśvara Temple Inscription, Śaka Year 1053, no. 17, pp. 879-880.

77. *Ibid.*, Nīlakaṇṭheśvara Temple Inscription of the Time of Coḍagaṅgadeva, Śaka Year 1053, no. 15, pp. 878-879.
78. *Ibid.*, Mukhaliṅgam Inscription of the Time of Choḍagaṅga, Śaka Year 1053, no. 74, p. 717.
79. *Ibid.*, Mukhaliṅgam Inscription of the Time of Choḍagaṅga, Year 58, no. 78, pp. 719-720.
80. *Ibid.*, Mukhaliṅgam Inscription, Śaka Year 1054, no. 80, pp. 720-721.
81. *Ibid.*, Mukhaliṅgam Inscription of the Time of Choḍagaṅga, Śaka Year 1056, no. 87, pp. 724-725.
82. *Ibid.*, Mukhaliṅgam Inscription of the Time of Choḍagaṅga, Year 59, no. 88, p. 725.
83. *Ibid.*, Mukhaliṅgam Inscription, Śaka Year 1067, no. 134, p. 750.
84. *Ibid.*, Mukhaliṅgam Inscription, Śaka Year 1085, no. 161, p. 765.
85. *Ibid.*, Hāṭakeśvara Temple Inscription, Śaka Year 1127, no. 173, p. 772.
86. *Ibid.*, Nīlakaṇṭheśvara Temple Inscription, Śaka Year 1073, no. 36, p. 890.
87. *Ibid.*, Nīlakaṇṭheśvara Temple Inscription, Śaka Year 1063, no. 29, p. 886.
88. *Ibid.*, Śrīkūrmam Inscription of the Time of Choḍagaṅga, Śaka Year 1064, no. 127, p. 746.
89. *Ibid.*, Mukhaliṅgam Inscription of the Time of Anantavarman [Rājarāja II], Śaka Year 1097, no. 167, pp. 768-769.
90. *Ibid.*, Mukhaliṅgam Inscription, Śaka Year 1100, no. 168, p. 769.
91. *Ibid.*, Lakṣmī-Narasiṃha Temple Inscription, Śaka Year 1192, no. 79, pp. 915-916.
92. *Ibid.*, Śrīkūrmam Inscription of the Time of Madhukāmārṇavadeva, Śaka Year 1071, no. 145, p. 756.
93. *Ibid.*, Mukhaliṅgam Inscription of the Time of Anantavarman [Rājarāja II], Śaka Year 1109, no. 170, pp. 770-771.
94. *Ibid.*, Lakṣmī-Narasiṃha Temple Inscription, Śaka Year 1129, no. 55, p. 901.
95. *Ibid.*, Lakṣmī-Narasiṃha Temple Inscription of the Time of Rājarājadeva, Śaka Year 1195, no. 82, p. 917.
96. *Ibid.*, No. 110, Lakṣmī-Narasiṃha Temple Inscription of the Time of Narasiṃhadeva (II), Śaka Year 1218, no. 110, pp. 934-935.
97. *Ibid.*, Lakṣmī-Narasiṃha Temple Inscription of the Time of Anantavarma Vīradharadeva, Śaka Year 1141, no. 59, pp. 903-904.
98. *Ibid.*, Lakṣmī-Narasiṃha Temple Inscription, Śaka Year 1335, no. 415, p. 1112.
99. *Ibid.*, Lakṣmī-Narasiṃha Temple Inscription, Śaka Year 1338, no. 436, pp. 1124-1125.
100. *Ibid.*, Laksmī-Narasimha Temple Inscription, Śaka Year 1222, no. 186, p. 979.

101. *Ibid.*, Lakṣmī-Narasiṃha Temple Inscription, Śaka Year 1297, no. 231, pp. 1005-1006.
102. *Ibid.*, Lakṣmī-Narasiṃha Temple Inscription, Śaka Year 1302, no. 273, p. 1030.
103. *Ibid.*, Mukhaliṅgam Inscription of the Time of Coḍagaṅga, Śaka Year 1061, no. 106, p. 735.
104. *Ibid.*, Laksmī-Narasimha Temple Inscription of the Time of Narasimha (I), Śaka Year 1184, no. 71, pp. 910-911.
105. *Ibid.*, Lakṣmī-Narasiṃha Temple Inscription, Śaka Year 1317, no. 355, p. 1077.
106. *Ibid.*, Lakṣmī-Narasiṃha Temple Inscription, Śaka Year 1322, no. 370, p. 1086.
107. *Ibid.*, Lakshmi-Narasimha Temple Inscription, Saka Year 1302, no. 273, p. 1030.
108. *Ibid.*, Lakṣmī-Narasiṃha Temple Inscription, Śaka Year 1346, no. 461, p. 1139.
109. *Ibid.*, Lakṣmī-Narasiṃha Temple Inscription, Śaka Year 1346, no. 36, p. 1077.
110. *Ibid.*, Lakṣmī-Narasiṃha Temple Inscription, Śaka Year 70 (?), no. 36, p. 406.
111. *Ibid.*, Lakṣmī-Narasiṃha Temple Inscription, Śaka Year 1061, no. 36, p. 106, p. 735.
112. Richard M. Eaton, *A Social History of the Deccan, 1300-1761*, Eighth Indian Lives, Vol. I, 2005, p. 28.
113. Shishir Kumar Panda, *The State and the Statecraft in Medieval Orissa under the Later Eastern Gaṅgas (A.D.1038-1434)*, K.P. Bagchi & Company, Calcutta, 1995, p. 78.
114. *Ibid.*, p. 77.
115. Subrata Kumar Acharya, Kaijang Plates of Bhānudeva III, Ś. 1284, *op.cit.*, pp. 501-502.
116. Cynthia Talbot, *Precolonial India in Practice Society, Region, and Identity in Medieval Andhra*, Oxford University Press, New Delhi, 2001, p. 63.
117. Cynthia Talbot, The Society of Kakatiya Andhra, in Upinder Singh (ed.), *Rethinking Early Medieval India A Reader*, Oxford University Press, New Delhi, 2011, p. 177.
118. Cynthia Talbot, *op.cit.*, 2001, p. 62.
119. *Ibid.*, p. 64.
120. *Ibid.*, p.58.
121. *Ibid.*
122. Snigdha Tripathy, Lakṣmī-Narasiṃha Temple Inscription, Śaka Year 1317, *op.cit.*, no. 355, p. 1077.
123. Cynthia Talbot, *op.cit.*, 2001, p. 68.

124. *Ibid.*, p. 64.
125. Snigdha Tripathy, Ragolu Copper Plate Charter of Vajrahasta III, Śaka Year 981, *op.cit.*, no. 58, pp. 654-655.
126. *Ibid.*, Lakṣmī-Narasiṃha Temple Inscription, Śaka Year 1338, no.435, p. 1124.
127. R.S. Sharma, *Early Medieval Indian Society: A Study in Feudalisation*, Orient Longman, edition 2003, (published 2001), Kolkata, p. 9.

Bibliography

Cynthia Talbot, *Precolonial India in Practice Society, Region, and Identity in Medieval Andhra*, Oxford University Press, New Delhi, 2001.

------------------, The Society of Kakatiya Andhra, in Upinder Singh (ed.), *Rethinking Early Medieval India A Reader*, Oxford University Press, New Delhi, 2011.

Pramila, B, 'Society and Economy of Telangana', *Comprehensive History and Culture of Andhra Pradesh, Vol. IV (Medieval Andhradesa AD 1000-1324)*, ed. Somasundara Rao, New Delhi: Tulika Books, 2011.

Richard M. Eaton, *A Social History of the Deccan, 1300-1761*, Eighth Indian Lives, Vol. I, Cambridge University Press, 2005.

Sharma, R.S, *Early Medieval Indian Society: A Study in Feudalisation*, Orient Longman, edition 2003, (published 2001), Kolkata.

Shishir Kumar Panda, Nāyaka System in Medieval Orissa, Śraddhāñjali Studies in Ancient *Indian History: D.C.Sircar Commemoration Volume*, Sundeep Prakashan, Delhi, 1988.

--------------------, *The State and the Statecraft in Medieval Orissa under the Later Eastern Gaṅgas (A.D.1038-1434)*, K.P. Bagchi & Company, Calcutta, 1995.

Sircar, D.C, *Indian Epigraphical Glossary*, Motilal Banarsidass, Delhi, 1966.

Snigdha Tripathy, Naḍagam Copper plate Charter of Vajrahasta III, Śaka Year 979, *Descriptive Topographical Catalogue of Orissan Inscriptions*, Manohar, New Delhi, 2010.

Subbarayalu, Y., *South India under the Cholas*, Oxford University Press, New Delhi, 2012.

Subrata Kumar Acharya, Madgam Plates of Rāṇaka Bhīmakheḍi of the Time of Devendravarman, Ś. 988, *Copper-plate Inscriptions of Odisha-A Descriptive Catalogue-(Circa Fourth Century to Sixteenth Century CE)*, DK Printworld, New Delhi, 2014.

3

The Pudukkottai Princely State: the State and its Subjects, Victims of 'Colonial Diarchy' –An Overview

B.S. Chandrababu

Introduction

There were eleven British Provinces and 562 Princely States in the pre-independence India. Pudukkottai State, one of the smallest Princely States was under the tutelage of the erstwhile Madras Province enjoying quasi-independence status with full powers of administration, that too, subject to the concurrence of the Chief Administrator appointed by the Governor of the Madras Province and also the Diwan of the State's court. The other Princely States in the Madras Province were: Travancore, Cochin, Banganapalli, and Sandur.

Carved out a State comprising the present three taluks of the Pudukkottai District of Tamil Nadu, namely, Kulathur (in the Kirani Taluk), Alangudi and Thirumayam, besides Pudukkottai by the Thondaimans of the Kallar community, the feudal military chiefs, in the midst of political vacuum emerged from the absence of the Sethupathis of Ramanad, the Nayaks of Madurai and the Nawab of the Carnatic, extending help in return for patronage from the East India Company, at the time, nine Thondaiman rulers, beginning from

Ragunatharaya Thondaiman (1686-1730 C.E.) and ending with Raja of Rajagopala Thondaiman (1928-1948 C.E.), ruled the State for more than 260 years.

Irrespective of the big or small in size of the Princely States, both during the hegemony of the East India Company and the British India dispensation from 1858 onwards, the policy of the British in India towards the Princely States was guided and motivated by (i) enforcement of the colonial policy on the Princely States which eventually helped to promote the same policy of the Rajas over their subjects; (ii) strengthen alliances with the rulers of the Princely States and prevent with their help the growing nationalist fervor from spreading against colonialism among the people living in the States. It is likened to a policy of "breakwaters in the storm".

Political Consolidation: The Pudukkottai Princely State and the British in India

Notwithstanding the political rivals' persistent onslaught unleashed on the Pudukkottai territory, whose antiquity dates back to the Megalithic period, by c. 1730 C.E. under the chieftainship of the first ruler Ragunatharaya Tondaiman, the Pudukkottai State comprising three other larger tracts, namely, Alangudi, Thirumayam, and Kulathur, was created. But the State's solid political consolidation had yet to be achieved. Its association with the British East India Company in the Carnatic region, beginning from the 1750's had, however, came in handy, and in the process, both the stakeholders found themselves, the beneficiaries. Participating in the Carnatic war with men and material, as an ally of the British East India Company against the French and Mysore, Vijayaragunatharaya Tondaiman of the Pudukkottai State helped the company to score both a military and political victory over its rivals in the Carnatic region in c. 1753 C.E.

Appreciating the help and support extended by the ruler of the Pudukkottai State in the Carnatic War, the then Governor of Madras, George Piggot wrote a letter to the Tondaiman on 28th September 1755. In the letter, he stated that the Tondaiman of the Pudukkottai State was a sincere friend of the company and therefore the company, in future would ensure the ruler's safety and protection and in return, as usual, he should continue assisting and helping the company. The letter further records that the company would thereafter honour the ruler befitting his status and dignity.[1] This letter of appreciation of the Governor of Madras could be considered as a broad political agreement reached between the ruler of Pudukkottai State and the

British company in Madras. The spirit of the letter was followed with religious faith, in word and deed by the Tondaiman whose support and assistance was sought after by the British Company in Madras in all their battles and wars waged and fought against the French, the Marathas and Hyder Ali and Tippu Sultan of the Mysore as also in all the subjugation and annexation efforts undertaken against the recalcitrant Poligars. This unique service rendered by the Tondaiman of the Pudukkottai State to the British Company in Madras at a crucial time of political uncertainty, in this regard, has been aptly analyzed by K. Rajayyan, in his magnum opus study, *The South Indian Rebellion (1971)* thus: "Tondaiman's long services in particular in putting down "South Indian Rebellion", a widespread and violent struggle of formidable dimension and menacing challenge to the British power raised him high in the opinions of the authorities of the East India Company".[2]

On the other hand, the ruler of Pudukkottai, helped the Nawab of Arcot the ally of the British in all his war efforts in the Carnatic region. Like the British, the Nawab of Arcot in recognition of his service rendered, honoured the ruler and conferred him with the title, "The Raja of Pudukkottai" in c. 1795 C.E.[3]

By 1801 the British East India Company could achieve its political consolidation in the Madras Province and facilitated the Raja of Pudukkottai to rule his territory as a tribute-free State but as an integral part of their political control system and guidance and supervision forever. The Rajas of Pudukkottai too did not hesitate to toe the line of the British East India Company's strategic dominance. The same condition, in their relationships, continued to prevail even after the transfer of power in 1858 till 1948 when the merger of the State with the Madras Province, the "master-subordinate" relationship between them existed with mutual consent and co-operation.

In recognition of the Tondaiman rulers' playing a subordinate role, the British had bestowed upon them rare honours and awards. In 1833, Ragunatha Tondaiman was honoured with the use of the title as prefix "His Excellency", a honour which the rulers retained till 1857.[4] However, this honour was withdrawn by the British on the grounds that the King, due to mismanagement of the affairs of the State had incurred for him a debt of Rs 5.5 lakhs. When a conductive atmosphere prevailed in the State to the liking of the British once again the honour was restored to the King in 1870.[5]

And unlike other States, Pudukkottai was given the independent status by convention by the British due to Tondaiman's loyalty and service to the Raj; the external affairs of the State was however fully under the control of the British.

Without disturbing the status quo in the relations between the British and the Raja of Pudukkottai like in the British Indian States, in Pudukkottai also, in an effort to give participation of the public in the State's administration representative institution had gradually been developed in the State since 1902 with an Assembly of nominated representatives followed by a Representative Assembly and Legislature Advisory Council in 1915 and a Legislative Council whose members were elected by a limited number of eligible voters in 1924. In this new assembly, the elected members were not allowed to discuss matters affecting the Raj and the Raja. But the members were allowed to discuss the general administration of the State without hurting the honour, dignity, and ultimate decisions of the British Resident, Diwan, and the Raja. Though, it seemed to be a good venture towards laying a foundation for representative institutions in the State, under the Raj and Raja administration its scope in addressing grievances of the needy of the State was dismal at the time.

State of Agriculture, Land Revenue Administration and the Plight of the Peasantry

The Pudukkottai Princely State, as per the 1931 Census Report had a population of 3,00,964, and had a less than 2000 sq. Kilometers of area. Broadly the entire State was declared a dry area with hillocks and wild shrubs dotting the territory. About 68% of the working force of the State took to agriculture, which seemed to have been seasonal as it was monsoon-based and largely rain-fed. The agriculture of the State, in the absence of a major and permanent source of water, had to depend on small jungle streams, rivers, ponds, and tanks which were again dependant on rains. The Kaveri River flowing closely near the State had no provision to enter the State.

Having been concerned about the need to develop agriculture in rain-fed State and due to immense distress caused by 1708-09, 1733 and 1837 droughts, Ragunatha Tondaiman, the Raja of the Pudukkottai State recommended the introduction of the waters of the Kaveri in the State in 1838 along with the support extended by the Resident and the Governor of Madras to the court of Directors of the East India Company. The company opinioned that the project would be too costly, hence dropped.[6]

Despite being handicapped by the unfavourable soil and scarcity of rains experienced by the people most of the months in the year, the tillers of the soil and the landless agricultural labourers, labouring either for the absentee landlords or owners of the lands not directly involved in agricultural pursuits, raised both dry and wet crops and of the two the former seemed the option by the farmers mostly.

Since rice is the staple food of the people, it was a privileged crop of the farmers. Other crops raised by them were Ragi, Varagu, Cotton, Gingelly, Millets, Betel-Leaf, Plantain, Chillies, Roots, and Fruits.

Area of cultivation and production aspects of the crops were largely determined by among others the extant land tenure system, the land tax imposed and collected amidst devastation and distress caused by 12 years of floods since 1709 and 25 years of droughts and famines in the State under the rule of the Tondaimans.

The entire land tenure of the State was based on two broad categories i.e. lands alienated and lands un-alienated. The alienated category of land tenure included jaegers to the kith and kin of the royal family, the *Devadayam Inams* (exclusive of *chatrams*), *chatrams*, grants to Brahmins, and *Amarams* and *Ooliums*, minor and life *Umbalams*, whereas the un-alienated land tenure includes both *Amani* or *Varapattu* and *Teervaipattu*. The data furnished below speaks of the distribution of land under the above categories in 1838-39 was according to Bayley's report, dated 7th July 1841.

Sl.No.	*Category*	*Extent Held In Velis*	*% To The Total Extent*
1.	*Devadayam Inams* (exclusive of *Chatrams*)	9594	17.5
2.	*Chatrams*	1641	3.4
3.	Grants to Brahmins	7763	14.1
4.	*Jagirs*	6264	11.4
5.	*Amarams* and *Ooliums*	8935	16.2
6.	Minor and life *Umbalams*	2800	5.1
7.	Non-Alienated lands (both *Amani* and *Teervaipattus*)	17958	32.7
		54955	100[7]

It is clearly understood from the above data that out of the total extent of land that was supposed to have been brought under cultivation at the time of calculation, only 32.7% of lands were in the name of the peasantry and the remainder in the name of the non-agricultural people. Most of the alienated lands were granted free of tax or for a pittance of tax revenue whereas the lands in the name of the peasants were subjected to periodical assessments from time to time, keeping them at tenterhooks with the village administrators.

The land-tenure and the extent of the area either added or brought under cultivation kept changing in the Pudukkottai State. The estimated total extent of land in the State in 1878-79 and its distribution under various categories were:

		Acres
i.	*Poramboke*, waste, etc vested with the govt.	1,29,708
ii.	*Devadayam* and *Dharmadayam Inams*	1,05,239
iii.	*Jagirs*, *Brahmadeyam* and Other *Inams*	2,06,887
iv.	Money Assessment	29028
v.	*Amani* lands	
	(a) Cultivated	74231
	(b) Uncultivated	1,24,255
		6,69,338 [8]

"The items (ii) and (iii) i.e. 3, 12,116 acres, admittedly were in the hands of non-agricultural people or institutions. The items (iv) and (v) 2,27,514 were in the names of the peasants". The above data clearly indicates that there was no perceptible radical change in the pattern of land tenure in the State, even after 40 years of Tondaiman's rule; i.e. in 1878-79.

Sir A. Seshia Satri's role as administrative head and Diwan for sixteen long years from 1878 to 1894, assumes importance in the crucial years of the debt-ridden and corruption-spree Pudukkottai State. His attempts at streamlining the *Jagirdari* and *Inam* system which ate into financial vitals of the State invited strong resistance from the *Jagirdars*, *Amaram* holders, and above all the ruling family themselves. This apart, his attempts at restructuring the land tax system on the *Amani* lands of the peasants during his times and later due to the absence of assessment based on scientific study resulted in the perpetuation of their poverty and a number of peasants either sold out their lands to clear their land tax dues and others suffered imprisonment for their uncleared dues. From the 1890's till 1907-08, there were 1841 land sales, mostly of small landholdings, affected by the Pudukkottai State administration. During the period, out of the land sales, the State could fetch revenue of Rs 43,282, not sufficiently equal to the tax dues of the individual peasants.[9] In the event of non-availability of sufficient landed property of the defaulters equal to the tax dues, out of 7337 convicts suffering imprisonment, in the Pudukkottai Central Jail from 1900-01 to 1946-47, the number of agriculturists and landless agricultural labourers account for 54.23 per cent (3979 persons).[10] Added to the miserable condition of the peasants was the migration of the peasants leaving their own lands, to other districts due to their inability to pay the tax.[11] Thus the system of land tax assessment pursued by the Diwans and the State establishment from the last quarter of the 19th century till 1947 was oppressive and the peasants were not given any benefit of substantial remission in tax in times of bad crops and in times of droughts.[12] In fact, from 1879 to 1945, the Pudukkottai State had suffered immensely due to the outbreak of severe droughts and famines for almost 18 years which put the peasantry, the marginalised section of the society to untold misery and suffering.

Industry, Trade, Commerce and Taxing System

The only industrial tradition of the Pudukkottai Princely State has been its handicrafts. With the exception of Brahmins and Nattukottai Chettiars of the State, the other major caste and community groups, which include Kallar, Maravar, Agamudaiyar, Uppiliar, Koravar, Udayar, Vellalar and also Muslim and Christians, the inhabitants of the State, involved themselves in the following handicrafts production: silk-weaving, dyeing, sari making, perfume preparing, manufacturing musical instruments, bangle making, stone work, wood carving, palm-leaf handiwork and blanket weaving. The textile industry, on a small scale, flourished in Thiruvapur, Parambur, Karambakudi, Ramachandrapuram, and Arimalam villages and towns. Similarly, woollen products at Sellukudi, mat making at Peraiyur and Mirathunilan, match-making at Thirukkokarnam, and bangle making at Vaithur were other occupations of the people.

Small-scale soap manufacturing units in and around Pudukkottai town, hand papermaking industries at Royavaram, and Pudukkottai territory were run on a moderate investment. The Pudukkottai textile mill was only the big industry at Namarasamudram that offered employment to a number of people in the area of its location.

By and large, "as was the case with the rest of India in Pudukkottai State also there were occupational divisions based mostly upon the caste system and employment in different trades was mostly hereditary".[13]

In the Pudukkottai State in about 175 places, the poor Uppiliar community people were involved in the earth salt manufacturing occupation. The salt thus manufactured was cheap and it fetched substantial income to the State when exported to British Indian territories. Since salt manufacture and marketing, it was the one of the main income-generating source for the British in India at the time, since 1817, the Pudukkottai State and the British resident were pressurised by the British to stop manufacturing the earth salt in the State. Succumbing to the pressure the Pudukkottai State imposed a ban on its manufacture with a heavy heart. Thereafter the Pudukkottai State subjects had to buy the salt imported from British India territories by paying more. To make good the loss, the State under the Diwanship of Sir A. Seshia Sastri (1878-1894), could collect Rs 38,000 from the British Indian Government towards the loss of income incurred by the State after banning the money-spinning earth salt in its territory. As a result of this ban, the people involved in its manufacture had to lose the means of their subsistence forever.[14]

During the residentship of Sir William Blackburn (1807-1823) a lucrative business venture was launched in the State along with his brother and the Raja of Pudukkottai State to manufacture a blue coloured dye from the plant available in plenty in the State. The industry was started in 1814 and lasted up to 1841. During the period, the dye manufactured in the State had been exported to England. This had brought in substantial income to the State, besides generating employment to many. The reasons attributed to its closure were not disclosed by the establishment. Thus, the salt and Indigo business were wound up arbitrarily in the State by the British detrimental to the economic interests of the State whose head, the Raja could not resist it then, against the dominant British.

The Pudukkottai Durbar records tell us about the merchandise exported to outside of Pudukkottai State. They were: soap, saffron stones, black stone, groundnut, *Aavarampattai*, saffron, and jackfruit. Salt, paddy, stack, tobacco, bamboo, wooden material, fish, petrol and kerosene were imported from outside of the Pudukkottai State. Since there was a demand for pulses, tamarind, chilies, firewood, and cattle feed in the State, they were not exported to outside of the Princely State freely. The British Government in Madras tried to supply sugar and other food items to the Princely State to an extent.

The goods and commodities produced and marketed at home were taxed and their exports outside of the State as also imported items were taxed. These formed an important source of revenue for the State. The poor economic situation, lack of purchasing power of the people, scarce and inadequate production of essentials for consumption turned the people to rely more on the support of the State which was reeling under corruption, nepotism, and royal extravaganza. A few of the well-intentioned intervention of British residents and Diwans could not prove to be a panacea for the malaise and as a result of it, the peasantry and the small scale producers had to bear the burden of taxation.

The Pudukkottai Durbar Records mention the occurrence of public or popular uprisings against the State and the Raja in 1854, 1862, and 1931. The uprising of 1854 that shook the conscience of the Raja was engineered by the disgruntled Jagirdars and military chiefs whose privileged positions were disturbed with the Raja's financial demands as also the peasantry which included tenants and *pattadars* / landowners who suffered at the hands of the oppressive tax-collectors joined hands and led the uprising for about a year. This was however repulsed with a heavy hand with British military reinforcement which was specifically engaged for the purpose. The Raja's arbitrary decisions and actions that tended to pinch the financial resources of the protestors seemed to have been the principal cause for this public uprising.[15] After this revolt, the Raja and the British resident had abolished the levy of taxes collected as forest tax, small scale irrigation tax, oil crushing tax, bangle tax, indigo tax, oil tax, tax on useless trees, snuff-tax and a tax on indigenous painting.

In order to augment the financial resources of the State, the then British Resident Annasamy Ayyar introduced a new tax system called *Mohdarba* in 1862, which enhanced the house property taxes of the poor and lower middle-class peasants and artisans beyond their reach, hence, the affected people rose in revolt against the Raja and the British resident in 1862. Some of the protesting poor, sat in front of the British residents' quarters for several days until the exorbitant tax rates were withdrawn.[16]

Soon after the severe outbreak of drought and famine that devastated the State for about five years from 1926 to 1930, the Pudukkottai municipality, contrary to the expectations of the poor residents, hiked taxes that affected the rich and the poor alike but the poor in particular certainly ill-afford to pay the taxes. There were taxes on their properties and articles of daily consumption. Eventually, a big public uprising broke out in Pudukkottai town on 15th July 1931 to the total dismay of the Princely State. The protestors were about to attack all the government offices in the town. The State's treasury became the target of attack. In the violent struggle of the people, the prison houses were gate-crashed and the prisoners released. The State-owned properties were destroyed including the government's car. The house of Diwan Bahadur Raghaviah was looted. There were chaos, confusion, and destruction that gripped otherwise peaceful town which was the headquarters of the Raja. To put down this violent revolt of the people, the Punjab Regiment was brought to the town from Tiruchirapplli, and after a day's police crackdown on the protestors; peace was restored in the town. Immediately after this public revolt, the town and the Princely State administration temporarily withdrew the taxes hiked.[17]

A close look at the tax system adopted especially from the 1850s was subject to frequent changes and uniformly, the tax rates imposed on goods and commodities and small ventures of the people including their house properties were on the ascending order and seemed to have catered to the increasing needs and demands of the powers that be. In this systemic failure situation, people's welfare could not found a place for consideration.

Welfare Measures, Tolerance and Cultural Means to Reach People Welfare Measures

Both the Rajas of the Pudukkottai State as well as the British Residents and Diwans of the State administration impacted by the welfare measures of the British Indian States and on their own volition had undertaken efforts at improving the socio-cultural lives of their subjects to an extent.

The Rajas of Pudukkottai State built a number of *Chatrams* or the rest houses at various places in the State for the benefit of traders and other travelling devotees. They were endowed with land grants and a few of them also served as feeding centres for travellers.

In the State, gradually, the judicial administration, trying civil and criminal cases, was put in place since 1814 in Pudukkottai town first and extended to other taluks later.

In 1807, after the death of Rajaragunnatha Tondaiman, his wife practiced *Sati*. Thereafter, when the British and the public opinion being mobilised against this practice, once and for all, this cruel practice being practiced by royal women was done away with.

The hook-swinging a dangerous practice of mutilating the human body performed at the Mariamman temple festivals at Naarthamalai and Konnaiyur by the devotees was banned by the State in 1875.

In 1884, to carry on the distribution of letters, money-order transactions and value payable post services of the public, for the first time in Pudukkottai town, a British-India Post Office was opened.

By the turn of the 20th century, there was a general hospital, a hospital for women and children, and a veterinary hospital in the Pudukkottai town.

To cater to the loan needs of the farmers, the State encouraged setting up of about 134 agricultural co-operative societies by 1948 across the State.

Like in the Madras Province in 1945, the *Devadasi* system was abolished in the State. And it has been noted with pride by the people of the Pudukkottai district whose daughter Dr. Muthulakshmi Reddy was instrumental in bringing out legislation abolishing it in the Madras Province.

In the field of education, the tiny state was Pudukkottai which did not lag behind the British Indian States at the time. Primary education was free and was made compulsory to all children of the State. On the eve of State's merger with the Madras Province, there were 280 primary schools and 22 high schools with a student roll of 20000. Way back in 1883, a High School exclusively for girls was opened in the Pudukkottai town. In all those schools Tamil was taught as the first language. In all the high schools, fee concessions were offered to students belonging to depressed and backward classes. The present Pudukkottai Mannar College was founded by the efforts of the Rajas. There were about fifty libraries in the State and four of them were meant for girls. It is a good attempt at promoting education and fostering knowledge among the needy.

There was a separate school for teaching *Vedas* in Pudukkottai town. Similarly, a number of schools were started both by the State and private lovers of Tamil to teach Tamil. Such of those Tamil schools founded at Melaichivapuri and Koppanampatti are still functioning in the Pudukkottai district.

Tolerance

Right from the founder of the Princely State, almost all the Tondaiman rulers adopted a policy of religious tolerance in spite of their staunch Saivite devotion. Their commitment to foster communal harmony among Hindus, Muslims, and Christians was sincere and total. The Raja Ragunatharaya Tondaiman had done land grants to a mosque at Lakkampatti village in the State.

Endowments to both Saiva and Vaishnava temples were made by the Raja Vijaya Ragunatha Tondaiman at Rameswaram, Palani, Chidambaram, and Tirupati temples. The same Raja had donated expensive jewels to Padmanabaswamy temple at Tiruvananthapuram.

During the 17th and 18th centuries, Aavur in Pudukkottai State was one of the centres of Madurai Christian Mission. The Rajas of Pudukkottai did not prevent them from proselytisation work, and they even provided security against its critics.

The Pudukkottai town became a municipality in 1912. To an extent, in proportion to their population, representations were given in the council to Muslims, Christians, depressed classes and women.

When the temple entry movement gained momentum in favour of depresses classes' entry into Hindu temples in the Madras Province in the late 1930s by 1946-47, the Pudukkottai State also opened temples for the depressed classes in 1946-47.

Cultural Means to Reach People

The Pudukkottai Rajas carved out a name for themselves as patrons of art, men of letters, and music with money presents and land grants. Similarly, tens of Hindu temples across the State were either renovated or buildings added to the existing ones. Liberal land grants were made to the maintenance of temples and for the regular performance of pujas in those temples. From the available land tenure and land grants records, it is found that the land grants made to temples, Brahmins and *Agraharams* far exceeded the lands meant for cultivation by the peasantry in the State.[18]

Dussara festival became the State festival from 1738 onwards. It was celebrated with a lot of pomp and show and religious fervor continuously for ten days by people in Pudukkottai with royal family giving a ceremonious lead. To mark the occasion a new coin called '*Amma Kasu*' was put in circulation, later as legal tender money as well till 1948. It was made of pure copper metal. On the occasion of Dussara festival, for 10 days, the royal family presented every Brahmin of the State with '*Amma Kasus*', and one measure of rice.

The Rajas of Tondaimans strongly believed in the sustenance of *Sanadana Dharma*, but as a policy, they restrained from doing anything against disadvantaged castes and communities in the State.

The Princely State in Opposition to National Movement

Both the Raja's of the Pudukkottai Princely State and the British Residents and Diwans of the State administration were particular about the spirit of nationalism among its subjects not to grow and in this regard, they took efforts to block it from spreading into the State from the British Indian States. The Swadeshi Movement, the Jalianwallabag Massacre, the Home Rule Movement, the Khilafat Movement, and the Non-co-operation Movement that swayed the British Indian States could not impact the Pudukkottai State people until Mahatma Gandhi's visit to southern districts of the Madras province. Thereafter impressed by the leadership of Gandhi on the national front and S. Satyamurthi, the son of the soil on the regional stages, the people of Pudukkottai slowly but steadily began to register their participation in the freedom movement of India.[19]

Having been nurtured by the Home Rule Movement Satyamurthi from 1920 onwards, propagated vigorously the ideals of the Indian National Congress in Pudukkottai State. A modest attempt made by some of the educated elite started a Pudukkottai Mahajana Sabha (Pudukkottai People's conference) in 1920 and it provided a platform for nationalists to campaign in favour of India's freedom. Making use of this organisation, Satyamurthi in 1920 addressed a gathering of few people and urged them to forge their energies towards the people of the State to fight for self-government.[20] Satyamurthi further exhorted the people by pointing out the stark backwardness of the State for which state of affairs lack of national consciousness was also one of the causes.[21] At about the same time, the Tamil Nadu State Congress Committee was formed and it helped to widen the sphere of the people's activity. Fearing that such of those addresses and speeches of Satyamurthi would create hatred among the people against the Raja and the British, the establishment, issued an internment order against Satyamurthi on 2nd February 1921.[22] An appeal made by the people's conference to revoke the order did not fructify. Again in September 1921 when Gandhiji was about to be offered civic reception by the people of the State while visiting Tiruchinopolly and Pudukkottai State the administration issued an order through the State Superintendent of Police, objecting vehemently to the passage of Gandhiji through the State. Sydney Burn, the Superintendent wrote to the Raja and the Diwan on 18th September 1921 thus: "I hope you will agree with my action. We have enough of Gandhi's spirit without having himself here".[23]

Having been disappointed to visit Gandhiji in their State, the members of the State Congress Committee, Municipal Council and Representative Assembly along with several people proceeded to Karaikudi where Gandhi was staying and presented an address along with large sums of money to Gandhiji.[24] Immediately after this incident the State removed those representatives from the Municipal Council.

"The Superintendent, Durbar, and Raja were quite out of step with the tunes. Nationalistic winds had been blowing in Pudukkottai quite strongly since 1920".[25]

Subsequently, in 1924, a core group of nationalists found expression in the form of a Tamil Newspaper *Janmitran* which was started with the support of the Nationalists within the State and outside, notwithstanding the harassment and imprisonment of its editors by the State.[26]

Sensing the mood of the State and outside, the State establishment, seemed to have been little liberal in allowing Gandhiji to visit Pudukkottai and address the meetings. The nationalists of the State presented him at the time, large sums of money and promised to popularise Khaddar, prohibition policy and other constructive programmes of Gandhiji and the Indian National Congress.[27]

K. Arunachalam in his *India Samasthanangal*, a Tamil Work rendered his succinct observation on the post - 1935 Act thus: "The situation after the introduction of the Government of India Act of 1935 had again changed as the Indian National Congress was not satisfied with the reforms of the British government. The new act which advocated the introduction of the federal principle depended on the approval of the princes for the implementation of its central federal provisions. But the absence of princely co-operation had not accomplished its provisions and hence the conciliation of national Forces had been rendered more difficult".[28]

Further, uniformly the Rajas of the Princely States across India were more hostile to the freedom struggles of the people and unleashed a diatribe against the programmes of the Indian National Congress. The Princely State of Pudukkottai was no exception to these phenomena. In October 1936 the State prohibited the entry of Jawaharlal Nehru into the town during his visit to Tamil Nadu[29]. However, the State could not arrest the growing nationalist tendencies of the people for long.

On the other hand, in the absence of a concerted effort on the part of the Indian National Congress in drawing the State to nationalist awakening by mobilising the subjects; notwithstanding the stiff opposition of the Rajas of Pudukkottai State, in the end, did not find any difficulty in roping the State into the national mainstream after independence. Nonetheless, *The Hindu* Newspaper on 4th March 1948, the date on which the State was merged with the Indian Union and the

Madras Presidency pessimistically observed: "Its (Pudukkottai State) economic resources are exceedingly meager, further development and progress are necessarily conditioned by greater resources, which, however, cannot in future, be in the command of the State". But during the post-merger period with the democratic government at the helm, *The Hindu's* fears were to a greater extent allayed.[30]

Conclusion

Pudukkottai, a tiny Princely State with less than 2000 sq. kilometres of area in the Madras Province, was a "dependable choice" of the British East India Company and the British Crown in India and had exercised their predominance over the State with its consent and co-operation. This was done after, successfully enlisting the Rajas' support in subduing the Carnatic region and ensuring in return the political security for the Rajas against their foes in the region. As a result of this arrangement, the Rajas felt themselves in a comfortable position and led a life of luxury and extravaganza with little concern for their subjects and sometimes earning the wrath of the British Residents and Diwans of the Durbar themselves.

The oppressive land tenure system with little scope for the participation of the actual tillers of the soil to the economic development of the State, oppressive tax system, sacrificing the interests of the State in matters of Earth Salt manufacture, wounding up of Indigo Dyeing industry and failure to bring Kaveri waters to the State had produced a telling effect on the rain-fed agriculture and poor or no industrial growth in the State.

The 260 years of Tondaimans' rule in the State had witnessed 12 years of devastating droughts and famines, had added to the agony and distress of the peasant's small manufacturers with little State's support forthcoming. The Pudukkottai Durbar Records bring to light that there were about 7000 poverty-stricken people migrated to Ceylon in search of livelihood after the outbreak of drought in the State in 1945.

The British, the strong ally, and a patron of the 'illusory nature' of the State could not do much towards improving the economic condition of the people. Despite their overwhelming influence and control over the State, they could not prevent the outbreak of public uprisings against the State and its administration in 1854, 1862, and 1931. Their attempts at scuttling the spread of the national movement in the State ended in the increasing participation of the people in the Freedom Movement.

The 'master-subordinate' relationship that existed between the Rajas of Pudukkottai and the British in the Madras Province seemed to have been motivated by the 'survival instinct' of the Rajas on the one hand and the 'imperialist instinct' of the British serving as motivating factor had resulted in denting the State's development and accentuating the sufferings of the marginalised. The fact of the matter is that the needy people of the State had ultimately to succumb themselves to this "colonial diarchy" with its concomitant evils.

Notes and References

1. N.B.No.6. Political, 05-07-1803 and also Military Country correspondence for 1770, letter No. 190.
2. K. Rajayyan, *South Indian Rebellion*, Mysore, 1971, p. 20.
3. J. Raja Muhamad, *Pudukkottai Maavatta Varalaru (Tamil) (History of Pudukkotai District)*, Published by the Director of Government Museum, Tamil Nadu, 2004, p. 96.
4. *Ibid.*, pp. 123, 126.
5. *Ibid.*, p.126.
6. K.R.Venkatarama Ayyar, *A Mannal of the Pudukkottai State*, Vol. II, Part 1, 1940, p. 842.
7. K.R. Venkatarama Ayyar, *A Manual of the Pudukkotai State*, 1921,
   (a) *Devadayam inam*: tax-free land granted to places of worship of all religions for their maintenance.
   (b) *Chatram inam*: tax-free land granted to rest houses for feeding the needy.
   (c) Grants to Brahmins: tax-free land granted; *Brahmadeyam*.
   (d) *Jagirs*: tax-free and taxed lands granted to loyal chiefs mostly of the members close to the royal family.
   (e) *Amarams* and *Ooliams*: tax-free lands granted to those who rendered military service to the Rajas.
   (f) Minor and life *Umpalams*: tax-free lands granted to those who work in the palace.
   (g) *Amani*: this system involved sharing of the land produce of the peasant with the state. *Teervaipattu*: the lands of the peasants whose tax was fixed according to the approximate yield of the land.
8. Gazetteer of India, Tamil Nadu State, *Pudukkottai District*, 1976, p. 546.

9. *Ibid.*, pp. 549-551.
10. *Ibid.*, p. 551.
11. *Ibid.*, p. 548.
12. *Ibid.*, pp. 547-552.
13. *Ibid.*, p. 492.
14. J. Raja Muhamad, *op.cit.*, p. 121.
15. *Ibid.*, pp. 126-127.
16. *Ibid.*, p. 128.
17. *Ibid.*, p. 147.
18. Pudukkottai District Gazetteer, *op.cit.*, pp. 182-185.
19. Subramania Siva, *Sirai Vasam* (Tamil) Prison Life, Undated.
20. S. Kameswara Ayyar, *Sri Rajagopala Vijayam* (Tamil), The Advent of Sri Rajagopala, Pudukkottai, 1939, pp. 32-33.
21. Somale, *Valarum Tamil* (Tamil) Developing Tamil, Madras, 1956, pp. 146-147.
22. S. Kameswara Ayyar, *op.cit.*, pp. 45-46.
23. Gazetteer of India, Tamil Nadu State, *Pudukkottai District*, 1976, pp. 182-183.
24. S.Kameswara Ayyar, *op.cit.*, pp. 57-58.
25. *Pudukkottai District Gazetteer*, *op.cit.*, p. 184.
26. S. Kameswara Ayyar, *op cit.*, pp. 191-202.
27. *Idem.*
28. K.Arunachalam, *India Samasthanangal* (Tamil) (Princely States of India), Madras, 1940, p. 104.
29. *The Hindu*, 16th October, 1936.
30. *The Hindu*, 4th March, 1948.

Bibliography

N.B.No.6. Political, 05-07-1803 and also Military Country correspondence for 1770 letter No. 190.

Arunachalam, K., *India Samasthanangal* (Tamil) (Princely States of India), Madras, 1940.

Gazetteer of India, Tamil Nadu State, *Pudukkottai District*, 1976.

Kameswara Ayyar, S., *Sri Rajagopala Vijayam* (Tamil) The Advent of Sri Rajagopala, Pudukkottai, 1939.

Rajayyan, K., *South Indian Rebellion*, Mysore, 1971.

Raja Muhamad, J., *Pudukkottai Maavatta Varalaru (Tamil) (History of Pudukkotai District)*, Published by the Director of Government Museum, Chennai, 2004.

Somale, *Valarum Tamil* (Tamil) Developing Tamil, Madras, 1956.

Subramania Siva, *Sirai Vāsam* (Tamil) Prison Life, Undated.

The Hindu Newspaper, 16th October, 1936.

The Hindu, 4th March, 1948.

Venkatarama Ayyar, K.R, *A Mannal of the Pudukkotai State*, 1921.

--------------------, *A Mannal of the Pudukkottai State*, Vol. II, Part 1, Pudukkottai, 1940.

4

Tamil-Tulu Linkages: A Historical Narrative

K. Ashok

Kannadamung Kalithelungum Kavinmalaiyālamum Tuluvum
Unnutharat Thēyuthitde

(Kannada, Joyous Telugu, Dainty Malayalam with Thulu! Born of thy lips)

These lines are part of '*Tamizh Thaai Vaazhthu*' an invocation to precede the play Manonmaniam written by Professor P. Sundaram Pillai in 1891 and later it was adopted as the State Anthem of Tamil Nadu in June 1970. These lines refer to the relationship of Tamil with all the South Indian languages including Tulu.

Tamil, the language spoken by the people of Tamil Nadu is one of the earliest languages and it belongs to the Pancha-Drāvida family with other south Indian languages such as Telugu, Kannada, Malayalam, and Tulu as its members. Tulu language is indigenous to the coastal Karnataka region and it is spoken in the districts of Udupi, South Kanara, and Kasaragod taluk of Kerala. When compared to all South Indian languages, Tulu is used by less number of people, despite it, Robert Caldwell, in his monumental work *"A Comparative Grammar of the Dravidian Languages"* records Tulu is, "one of the most highly developed languages of the Dravidian family of languages" and has an equal place among the languages like Tamil, Malayalam, Telugu, Kannada, etc.[1] Since both, Tamil and Tulu belong to the same language family, there is a lot of discourse and engagement between them and with other Dravidian languages. In addition, most of the regions of southern India were ruled by the Tamil kings either directly or through their subordinates during the ancient period. This political hegemony resulted in Tamil cultural assimilation and acculturation of the various regions in Southern India and it enriched the language and culture of each other. This article is a historical narrative of the Tamil-Tulu Linkages through ages.

Tulu Land and People

Tulunād is the place where the natives spoke Tulu and the people living in the region of Tulunād were known as Tuluva. Tuluva denotes the people or area speaking Tulu. A number of theories were put forward to its origin of Tuluvas and it was traced to the legendary ruler called Rama Boja, who is supposed to have made many gifts like Tulu-dāna, Tulu Purusha. So the dynasty was called Tolar and the region called Tulu or Tuluva.[2] Based on the reference from the Tamil classic '*Ahanānūru* and the *Silappadikāram*,' it is noted Tulunādu was a separate province in the early centuries of the Christian era. It is described in *Aham* (294) poem "the Tulunādu is located to the west of the Erumainādu (Skt. *Mahisamandala*) which lay immediately to the north of Tamilakam or the Tamil country proper".[3] Tulu Nadu formed a part of the ancient kingdom which is known as Karunādu of Tamil *Sangam* literature. Tulu Nadu was located at the frontier between Tamilagam and Karunādu. The people of this territory are known as Kosar and Nanmolikkosar in the *Sangam* literature.[4]

V.R. Ramachandra Dikshitar identifies the Satiyaputras of the Asokan Inscription as the Tamil Tribe Kosar. The people were addicted to speaking truth, and hence the attribute Nanmolikkosar.[5] The Second Rock Edict of Asoka mentions five friendly countries in the South of his empire namely, the Choda, the Pandiya, the Keralaputra, the Tambapamni, and the Satiyaputra. K.V. Ramesh was convinced that the Satiyaputra mentioned in the Asokan Edict stood for the Tulu country and the people of the region.[6] It is believed that the Tulus assisted the Mauryans in their southern campaigns that went up to the Tamil region.[7]

If the evidence of *Ahanānūru* (15) and the *Natrrinai* (391) were taken into the note, there is every reason to think that the Tulus were an independent people in the age of Senguttuvan roughly second century C.E., and were brought under the Chera rule by Senguttuvan.[8] This region also finds mention in the Greek accounts and much later, after the Third Mysore War the region was taken by the British and they renamed it as South Kanara, in 1860 and this region remained as a part of Madras Presidency till up to the Linguistic Reorganisation of states.[9]

Linguistic-Linkages

B.A. Saletore, one of the earliest authors on the Tulu history remarks the word '*Tuluva*' can be traced to the Kannada verbal root '*Tulu*' meaning to attack denoting the warlike nature of the people.[10] Some are of the view that the word '*Tulu*' would have come from the Tamil word '*tulir*' which refers to young leaf of tender foliage, based on the meaning softness, mildness.[11] The first inscription in Tulu dates to the 15th century while the literary texts begin in the 18th century.[12] Linguistic scholars are of the opinion that Tulu may well be the first individual language to branch off of Proto-South Dravidian.[13]

The Tamil and Tulu as members of the Pancha-Drāvida had interactions but due to the geographical distance the interaction between Tamil and Tulu went down with the passage of time. The lingual interactions during the *Sangam* Period about the fourth or fifth century CE was limited. However, they were closer to each other culturally in the early centuries of Christian era and prior. The *Sangam* literature has documented the work of Tulu Kings and soldiers. The first epigraph that mentions Tulu comes from Tamil Nadu. The Pattattalmangalam Grant of Nandivaraman II (c. 731-95 C.E.), the Pallava King states that at the gates of the king, there awaited with other rulers of South India the Tulus also.[14]

Mayilai Seeni Venkataswami a renowned Tamil scholar wrote the brief history of the Tulu country under the title '*Tulu Nāttu Varalāru*', which was then a part of the Tamilakam in the earlier centuries of the Christian era. In the Tulu Language, he had traced numerous obsolete old Tamil words even after it moved close to Kannada. He has listed 500 words that are common to Tulu and the old Tamil. He believed that there must be more than 1000 words which can be easily culled from the dictionary of Tulu Language.[15]

The following table gives us the list of some of the common terms present in Tamil and Tulu as found in the Dravidian Comparative Vocabulary, Vol. I edited by R. P. Sethu Pillai, published by the University of Madras in 1959:

Sl. No.	*English*	*Tamil*	*Tulu*
1.	Ray	Katir	Kadir
2.	Moon	Tinkal	Tingol
3.	North	Vatakku	Badekkay
4.	South	Terku	Tenkay
5.	Cloud	Kār (also rainy season)	Kara (rainy Season)
6.	Fire	Kanal	Anal
7.	Water	Nīr	Nir
8.	Earth	Nilam	Nela
9.	Mountain	Malai	Male
10.	Forest	Kātu	Kadu
11.	Sea	Katal	Kadal
12.	Wave	Alai	Ale
13.	Tree	Maram	Mara
14.	Palm Leaf	Ōlai	Oli
15.	Sugarcane	Karumpu	Karmbu
16.	Flower	Pū	Pu
17.	Tamarind	Puli	Puli
18.	Fig	Atti	Atti
19.	Tiger	Puli	Puli
20.	Ape	Konti	Koti
21.	Egg	Muttai	Mutte
22.	Parrot	Kili	Gili
23.	Fish	Mīn	Min
24.	Body	Utal	Udal
25.	Listening	Kelvi	Keli

Literary-Linkages

The *Sangam* literature forms one of the important sources to known about the Tulu region. There are many references in the *Sangam* texts such as *Ahanānūru*, *Puranānūru*, *Natrrinai*, *Kurundthokai*, *Pathitrruppathu*, *Silappadikāram* to testify the fact that the Tulu region was a part of ancient Tamilikam. The people of this region were referred to as Kosars. However, there were 4 Kosar's namely, the eastern, western, northern and southern Kosars and the people of Tulu Nadu were one among the Kosars.[16] "Scholars such as Ramachandra Dikshitar and P.T. Srinivasa Aiyangar tried to identify the Kosar with the inhabitants of Tulu Nadu. Srinivasa Aiyangar argued that the Kosars were *vadugar* or the northerners. The *vadugar* comprised people such as Telugus, Kannada, and those of the Tulu country. According to Ramachandra Dikshitar, the *Ahanānūru* clearly states that the home of the Kosar went by the appellation of Tulunādu. This was the territory lying on the Western Ghats on the Malabar Coast bordering on Mysore, Coimbatore and Coorg".[17]

Māmūlanār in his *Aham* poem No. 36 refers to "*meymmali perumput-chemmar- kosar....... Tulu-nādu*" the Tulu country of the Kosar, who adorned their bodies with golden ornaments. The passage has two important references. It takes the word Tulu referring to the people and the dialect spoke and Kosar were the inhabitants of the Tulu Country.[18] There was a lot of reference to the Kosar in the *Sangam* texts who were known for their valour. *Aham* poem No. 90 remarks "*irumbidam padutta vaduvudai mugattar, karungat-Kosar*" the black-eyed Kosar whose faces bear marks of wounds inflicted by iron arms.[19] Another passage from the *Sangam* text *Puranānūru* reads:[20]

> "..... *ven-vel*
> *ilam-pal-Kosar vilangu padai kanma*
> *rigalinar-erindav-agal-ilai murukkin*
> *perumarak-kambam.......*"
> "Pillars of the *murukku* tress with their wide leaves at
> which many youthful Kosar aim their shining
> spears to find the best marksman in their midst."

The *Maduraikānchi*, another ancient Tamil work, refers to the Kosar as *nānmolik-kosar* i.e. "the four-tongued Kosar". This means the Kosar could speak four languages Tulu, Kannada, Telugu and Tamil.[21] *Aham* 251, lines 6-14, *Aham* 281, lines 4-12 composed by Māmūlanār refers to the invasion of the Tamil country by the Mauryas with the support of the Kosars.[22] The same poet describes Tulu Nadu as a country in whose forest the peacocks peck at the well-grown jack fruits *(pagalarkai paraikkat-pil-ttogai-kkavir-Rulu-nādu)*. He also describes about King Nannan of Tulu Nadu:[23]

> "............*Tulu-nātta-anna*
> *varun-gai vambalaart-tangum panbir-*
> *cherinda cheich-chemmal.........*
> *chuli-yanaich-chudarppun Nannan*"

"Nannan, wearing lustrous ornaments and with his royal elephant the great king of the country which is renowned for its quality of sustaining its indigent neighbours. i.e. the Tulu country". The poet also associates Kosars with Tulu Nadu and King Nannan invaded Tulu Nadu drove the Kosars and made him the ruler of the place.

Geo-referencing Linkages

Foreign notices and *Sangam* works give details of the cities and ports that flourished in the early part of the Christian era in this region. Kōnperungkaanam, Konkana Nadu, and Konkaana Nadu are the other names of Tulu Nadu during the *Sangam* age. Ptolemy, the Greek geographer makes a mention about Tulu Nadu by stating that it is from Tulu Nadu the Damirike i.e., Tamilaham started.[24] The boundaries of Tamilkam as given by the *Sangam* text, on the east, the Tamilnadu is marked by Pulikat, which is the Anglo-Indian corruption of Palaverkkādu (old forest of Vel. trees). The limit on the other side is given as the Tulu land or Konkanam, the territory of the chief Nannan in the first century of the Christian era, which was broken into by a new people Kosar, as a result of a war in which Nannan suffered defeat, and lost his state elephant.[25]

Mayilai Seeni Venkataswami in his work '*Tulu Nāttu Varalāru*' gives information to names of places, mountains, personalities, etc.[26] Towns in the Tulu region as listed by Mayilai Seeni Venkataswami based on the *Sangam* literature:

1. **Cellur** which was situated close to the shore, near to this city towards the east there was a city by the name Niyamam (*Aham:* 90: 9-12). Parasurama did his *Yoga* in this town of Cellur (*Aham:* 220: 3-8). This town was situated close to the shore (*Aham:* 216: 8-15).
2. **Paaram** is another city in Tulu Nadu. The head of the armed forces of King Nannan, Menjiyele resided in this town (*Aham:* 152 :12).
3. **Paazhi** was another town in Tulu Nadu. The town got its name from the neighbouring mountain which was called by the same name Paazhi, which is a part of the Eazhilmalai. The town was surrounded by a fort wall. (*Aham:* 375: 13). From the top of the mountain Paazhi one can see the neighbouring states. (*Aham:* 372: 1-3). King Nannan had accumulated a huge wealth at the fort built on Paazhi (*Aham:* 372: 8-5).
4. **Kodukoor**, a town belongs to Nannan was won and taken over by Cheran Senguttavan (*Pathitrruppathu:* Fifth ten).
5. **Naravu** was a port town in the Tulu Nadu. Traders from Greece and Rome called the city as Navraa. Some scholars identify Naravu with Mangalore.

6. **Viyaloor** is another town in Tulu Nadu located close to the shore which was taken by Cheran Senguttavan (*Aham*: 97: 12-13).
7. **Kadambin Peruvaayil** is another town where Kalangaikanni Naarmudi Cheral won the Nannan. (*Pathitrruppathu*: Fourth Ten).
8. **Vaagai Peruntural** is another town in the south of Tulu Nadu where the commander of Pasumboot Pandian Adiyagaman died in the war field (*Kurunthogai*: 393: 3-5).
9. **Kadal Turuththi** is a group of Islands in the Arabian Sea, which was under the Nannan's control, the chief of the island under the instruction of King Nannan robbed the ships sailed towards the Chera country. Cheran Senguttavan with his navy defeated the chief and trade was improved (*Pathitrruppathu*: Second ten, Fifth Ten).
10. **Mangalore** is another town in the Tulu Nadu (*Silappadikāram* mentions the temple of Mangala Devi and the temple of Kathri).

Eazhilmalai is a mountain located in the southern part of Tulu Nadu. It is also known by Eazhil Neduvarai and Eazhirkuntru (*Aham*: 152: 12-13, 345: 3-7, 349: 6-7). The Portuguese explorer Vasco da Gama when he first arrived in India he saw this mountain from the sea and sailed his ship towards Calicut.

Political-Linkages

Politically the Tulu region was under the Tamil King for a brief period. The *Sangam* literature refers to the rule of three kings known as Nannan who ruled the Tulu region. These three Nannars are known as First Nannar, Second Nannar, and Third Nannar. The First Nannan ruled around the period c. 99 -127 C.E., the Second Nannan ruled around the period c.128 -155 C.E. and the Third Nannan ruled around the period c.155 -185 C.E. Various poets belonging to the *Sangam* age had sung about the praise of Tulu Nadu and Tulu Nannars. The Tulu Nannars had patronised these poets to a very great extend. After the *Sangam* period, the political connections were temporarily shut down.

The Chola Conquest of the Tulu Region

The rise of Chola power during the medieval period reestablished a direct link between the Tamil and the Tulu region and Tulu Nadu became a part of the Tamil country. The Larger-Leiden Plates of Rajaraja I mention his conquest of the Tulu region.[27] In 1012 C.E., a

Tamil general seems to have subdued Tuluva. This is gathered from a record of Rajaraja Chola, who's great general Pancava Maharaya is credited with the conquests of many countries among which Tuluva and Konkan are mentioned. The Balmuri inscription which informs us this is dated 1012 C.E. It further relates that having obtained the rank of Mahadandanayaka for Bengirimandala, and Gangamandala, Pancava Maharaya "seized Tuluva, and Konkan, pursued after Maleya, pushed aside and passed over Chera, Telugu and Ragiga, as if in sport",[28] whether the reference in the above inscription is to an actual invasion of Tuluva by the Cholas, or whether it a temporary occupation is uncertain. The Chola influence was only here and there. The Sōmesvara temple stone inscription found in Mudukeri in Barakuru, refers to a Chola raid and the reestablishment of the Alupa authority by Bankideva Alupendardeva I.[29] The Chola occupation in Tuluva has some traces such as the naming of a street at Barkuru as Colkeri (Chola street). The establishment of the temple Chōlisvara at Bhattakala and the other is a settlement of the Vellala communities in the Tulu region who enjoyed *mirasi* and other rights connected with agriculture. These communities improved to a large extend the cultivation of agricultural crops.[30]

The Pandya Dominance of the Tulu Region

Some scholars are of the opinion that the Pandyas had also conquered the Tuluva. The Velvikkudi copper plates inform us the son of Arikesari Maravarman, Sadaiyan Koccadaiyan Ranadhira had a title Madu-Karnataka, at the great city called Magalapura where the peacock danced with the cuckoo near tanks perfumed with opening flowers attacked and destroyed the Marattas. But the word Marattas confuses whether the Pandyas had really captured the Tulu region.[31] Some scholars believe that Bhutal Pandiya who ruled from Barkur was from the Pandiyan family of Madurai. The Tuluvas were successful in their conflict against the Pandyas, after defeating them the Alupas assumed the title of Pandya Chakravarti.[32] Francis Buchanan remarks that it was they who brought the Bhutagalu or Devils from the Pandava and to have introduced the Aliya Santana rule of inheritance from mother to daughter or from uncle to sister's son.[33] Bhutal Pandiya was the first ruler of Tuluva who levied assessment in rice or its equivalent in money, instead of paddy, thus throwing the cost of husking on the landlords and practically increasing the assessment by about 10 per cent.[34] Bhutalapandya's law of Aliyasantana is another important text that provides information on the history and society of Coastal Karnataka.[35] The central character of the book Bhatula Pandya is a nephew of a merchant Devapandya belonging to the Pandya country of Tamil Nadu.[36]

Religious-Linkages

Tamil-Tulu linkage was later strengthened by the religious discourses. The Dvaita philosophy became prominent in the Tamil region due to the work of Madhvacarya. He was born in Udupi district and was a great exponent of Dvaita. In his spiritual thrust, he made extensive travel in South India from 1256 to 1259 C.E. He visited Kanyakumari and later camped for four months at Rameswaram, many scholars from other disciplines also camped there to try and defeat him. After winning over the scholars Madhvacarya started his journey, crossed the Pandya and Chola country. He stopped for some time at the famous Sri Ranganatha Temple at Srirangam. Somewhere while travelling from Rameswaram to Srirangam he gave to his disciples the famous discourse on the first word *Vishnu* of the *Vishnusahasranama*.[37] Then he travelled through the Kingdom of Tanjore and visited the famous temple of Sri Mushnam dedicated to Bhuvaraha near Chidambaram. The holy pond was created by Sri Madhva's Danda and is known as Danda Theertha.[38] He also addressed many scholars and won their hearts by using logic, Vedas, and *miasma*. Throughout his travels he propagated his philosophy and defeated scholars with incorrect knowledge. Later many scholars were taken by his philosophy and worked for its cause. Notable among them was Sri Raghavendra Swami of Tamil Nadu. The *Bhuta Kola* meaning the spiritual worship of the Tulu region and the *Sudalai Madan* worship of the Tamil region is similar in action and spirit.

Cultural-Linkages

Cultural interactions have been the bedrock of the Tamil-Tulu engagement. This had resulted in the parallels in the cultural aspects of the two regions. The *Jallikattu* and *Manju Virratu* are two sports played in rural Tamil Nadu during the month of January. The reference for the sports is found in *Kalithogai* and it describes it as *ēru thazhuvuthal meaning* embracing the bull or taming the bull. Similarly, there are rural sports in the Coastal Karnataka region known as *Kambala* in which bullocks are used. *Kambala* is a bullock race through muddy waters along a track.

South India has a rich theatrical tradition of both classical and folk forms. *Therukoothu* and *Yakshagana* are folk forms performed in Tamil Nadu and Tulu Nad region. *Theru* means 'street', *koothu* 'play', it is usually performed by the members of the Koodthādi community in Tamil Nadu and is believed the makeup and ornamentation resemble those of *Yakshagana* of Karnataka and the skirts resemble *Kathakali* of Kerala.[39] The *Yakshagana* the best-known form is performed in the south Kanara region, '*yakshagana*' means 'songs of the demigods'.[40] The themes of the two are mythical and are performed in temple festivals. *Puli Āttam* in Tamil Nadu and *Pilivēsha* in the Tulu region is almost similar folk dance. In this dance, the performer paints and costumes himself as a tiger and they dance with the movement and emotions of a tiger. *Kori Katta* in the Tulu region and *Sēval Sandai* in Tamil Nadu were cockfight.

Community- Linkages

It is believed that the Tuluva Vellala community in Tamil Nadu came from the Tulu region. Edgar Thurston in his '*Caste and Tribes of Southern India*' writes, "Tulu, Tuluva or Tuluvan occurs as a name of a sub-caste of the Tamil Vellalas and the Agasas, Billavas, Gaudas, Kumbaras and other castes in South Canara. The equivalent Tulumar is recorded as a sub-caste of Mavilan which speaks Tulu. Concerning the Tuluva Vellalas, A. Stuart writes that these are immigrants from the Tulu country, a part of the modern district of South Canara. Nelson believes that these are the original Vellalas who were invited to *Tondaimandalam* after its conquest by the Chola King Adondai Chakravarthy".[41]

Demarcating- Linkages

From the medieval period with the rise of other dynasties and the transfer of power, the political connection between the two regions came to an end. The Tulu connection with the Tamil country was reestablished during the British rule. In November 1763, Reza Ali Khan, the son of Chand Saheb the former Nawab of Carnatic landed in Canara and got the support from Hyder Ali.[42] His long association with the French was made used by Hyder Ali and he made changes in the army of Hyder according to the European standard.[43] In 1799, the British defeated Tipu Sultan and annexed it with Madras Presidency. They referred the region as South Canara and Captain Munro was appointed as the first Collector of Kanara in June 1799 and it was placed under the control of Madras Board of Revenue.[44] For administrative convince Canara district was divided into North and South, North Canara was transferred to Bombay Presidency in 1862 and South Canara was retained with Madras Presidency. Even after Independence 11 members represented the South Canara in the Madras Legislative Assembly till up to Linguistic Reorganisation of States in 1956. After the reorganisation, it is now a part of the Karnataka State.

Contribution of Tulus to Tamil Nadu

The common man's knowledge of the Tulu region in Tamil Nadu is the Udupi Hotels. Most of the Udupi Hotels which serve vegetarian food was established by the residents of Udupi and Kanara districts. Father Jerome D'Souza who was born in the Moolki town of Mangalore worked as Professor at St. Joseph College Trichy and later served as the Principal at Loyola College, Madras. During the formation of the Constituent Assembly Rajaji proposed D'Souza's name to the Madras Legislative Assembly and he was elected to represent them at the Constituent Assembly.

B. S. Baliga the former Curator of Madras Records Office now the Tamil Nadu Archives had done yeomen service to the field of historical research is from the Tulu region. He served as the Curator for nearly 25 years by preserving and documenting the records. During the Second World War, the Japanese were planning for an attack over Madras. The Government of Madras ordered to transfer the entire document to Chittor, B.S. Baliga carried out the mission successfully for which he was awarded the title Rao Bahadur. Later in 1954, he was assigned to revise and rewrite the District Gazetteers of Tamil Nadu. He personally revised the Tanjore District Gazetteer, Madurai District Gazetteer, Coimbatore District Gazetteer and the South Arcot District Gazetteer and published it in 1957, 1960, 1962, and 1966 respectively. His other important publication is '*Studies in Madras Administration*' in 2 volumes is a basic reference for historical research on Madras Presidency or Tamil Nadu.

Conclusion

Studies in South India are unique, since it is not a single strand but a combination of many to form one. The history of South India exhibits certain common traits in terms of language and culture. The Tamil-Tulu Linkages is a testimony to this fact. The early story of Tulunad is gleaned from Tamil literature and we find there is a lot of socio, cultural and political exchange between the two regions. A nation with diverse cultures can be in prosperity if there is a strong interaction between various cultural groups which is the need of the hour. The linkage between the two regions can be summarised as "*The End, But Not Goodbye*".

References

1. Robert Caldwell, *A Comparative Grammar of the Dravidian Languages*, 3rd reprint, University of Madras, Madras, 1976, p. 32.
2. B. A. Saletore, *The Oriental Series No. 53, Ancient Karnataka, Vol.* I, *History of Tuluva*, Oriental Book Agency, Poona, 1936, p. 3.
3. *Ibid*., p. 48.
4. R. Nagaswamy, (ed.), Prof. V.R. Ramachandra Dikshitar Centenary Volume, *Studies in South Indian History and Culture*, Chennai, 1997, p. 173.
5. *Ibid*., p. 174.
6. K. V. Ramesh, *A History of South Kanara (From the earliest times to the fall of Vijayanagara)*, Karnatak University, Dharwar, 1970, p. 12.
7. S. Srikantha Shastri, *Sources of Karnataka History, Vol. I*, Mysore, 1940, p. 18.
8. R. Nagaswamy, *op.cit*., p. 174.
9. K. V. Ramesh, *op.cit*., p. xviii.
10. K. Abhishanker, *Gazetteer of India, Karnataka State Gazetteer, S. Kanara District*, Bangalore, 1973, p. 1.
11. K. V. Ramesh, *op.cit*., pp. xxiv-v.
12. Sanford B. Steever, *The Dravidian Languages- 2nd edition*, Routledge, 2020, p. 4.
13. *Ibid*., p. 7.
14. P. Gururaja Bhatt, *Studies in Tuluva History and Culture From the pre-historic times upto the modern*, Manipal Power Press, 1975, p. 7.
15. "Mayilai Seeni Venkatasami's Contribution to Tamil Studies", by Bagavathi Jayaraman *Journal of Tamil Studies*, Vol. 18, International Institute for Tamil Studies, Dec. 1980, p. 79.
16. Nagendra Rao, Keynote address at *National Seminar on the History and Culture of South India*, Organised by Mulki Sunder Ram Shetty College, Shirva, Udupi & Mangalore University History Teachers Association on 10/08/2019, p. 4. (https://www.academia.edu/40308963/History_and_Historiography_Making_of_Tulunadus_Identity accessed on 25th February, 2020)
17. *Ibid*., p. 5.
18. K. V. Ramesh, *op.cit*., pp. 12-13.
19. *Ibid*., p. 13.

20. *Ibid*.
21. *Ibid*., p. 14.
22. *Ibid*., pp. 14-15.
23. *Ibid*., p. 18.
24. http://viswamurugu.com/tuluweb1.html accessed on 3rd March, 2020.
25. S. Krishnaswami Aiyangar, *The Beginnings of South Indian History*, The Modern Printing Works, Madras, 1918, p. 86.
26. Mayilai Seeni Venkataswami, *Tamil History Series-6, Tulu Nattu Varalaru*, (in Tamil), Amieltham Publications, Chennai, 2008.
27. P. Gururaja Bhatt, *op.cit*., p. 8.
28. K. A. Nilakanta Sastri, *The Colas*, University of Madras, Madras, 2000, p. 172.
29. B. A. Saletore, *op.cit*., pp. 211-12.
30. R. Nagaswamy, *op.cit*., p. 175.
31. B. A. Saletore, *op.cit*., p. 215.
32. K. V. Ramesh, *op.cit*., pp. 57-9.
33. Madras District Manuals, *South Canara*, Vol. I, compiled by J. Sturrock, Government Press, Madras, 1894, p. 63.
34. *Ibid*., p. 64.
35. Nagendra Rao, *op.cit*., p. 14.
36. *Ibid*., p. 15.
37. B. A. Saltore, *op.cit*,. p. 420.
38. C. M. Padmanabha Char, *The Life and Teachings of Sri Madhvacharayar*, The Modern Printing Works, Madras, 1909, p. 106.
39. James R. Brandon, *The Cambridge Guide to Asian Theatre*, Reprint 2002, Cambridge University Press, UK, pp. 112-13.
40. *Ibid*., p. 115.
41. Edgar Thurston, *Caste and Tribes in Southern India, Vol. VII, T to Z*, Government Press, Madras, 1909, p. 205.
42. Mark Wilks, *Historical Sketches of the South of Indian an attempt to trace the History of Mysoor*, Vol. I. Longman, London, 1820, p. 281.
43. *Ibid*.
44. K. Abhishankar, *op.cit*., p. 65.

Bibliography

Abhishanker, K., *Gazetteer of India, Karnataka State Gazetteer*, S. Kanara District, Bangalore, 1973.

Bagavathi Jayaraman, "Mayilai Seeni Venkatasami's Contribution to Tamil Studies", *Journal of Tamil Studies*, Vol. 18, International Institute for Tamil Studies, Dec. 1980.

Edgar Thurston, *Caste and Tribes in Southern India, Vol. VII, T to Z*, Government Press, Madras, 1909.

Gururaja Bhatt, P., *Studies in Tuluva History and Culture From the pre-historic times upto the modern*, Manipal Power Press, 1975.

http://viswamurugu.com/tuluweb1.html accessed on 3rd March, 2020.

James R. Brandon, *The Cambridge Guide to Asian Theatre*, Reprint 2002, Cambridge University Press, UK.

Krishnaswami Aiyangar, S., *The Beginnings of South Indian History*, The Modern Printing Works, Madras, 1918.

Madras District Manuals, *South Canara*, Vol. I, compiled by J. Sturrock, Government Press, Madras, 1894.

Mark Wilks, *Historical Sketches of the South of Indian an attempt to trace the History of Mysoor*, Vol. I. Longman, London, 1820.

Mayilai Seeni Venkataswami, *Tamil History Series-6, Tulu Nattu Varalaru*, (in Tamil), Amieltham Publications, Chennai, 2008.

Nagaswamy, R., (ed.), *Studies in South Indian History and Culture*, Prof. V.R. Ramachandra Dikshitar Centenary Volume, Chennai, 1997.

Nagendra Rao, Keynote address at *National Seminar on the History and Culture of South India*, Organized by Mulki Sunder Ram Shetty College, Shirva, Udupi & Mangalore University History Teachers Association on 10/08/2019; (https://www.academia.edu/40308963/History_and_Historiography_Making_of_Tulunad us_Identity accessed on 25th February, 2020).

Nilakanta Sastri, K.A., *The Colas*, University of Madras, Madras, 2000.

Padmanabha Char, C.M., *The Life and Teachings of Sri Madhvacharayar*, The Modern Printing Works, Madras, 1909.

Ramesh, K.V., *A History of South Kanara (From the earliest times to the fall of Vijayanagara)*, Karnatak University, Dharwar, 1970.

Robert Caldwell, *A Comparative Grammar of the Dravidian Languages*, 3rd reprint, University of Madras, Madras, 1976.

Saletore, B.A., *The Oriental Series No. 53, Ancient Karnataka, Vol.* I, *History of Tuluva*, Oriental Book Agency, Poona, 1936.

Sanford B. Steever, *The Dravidian Languages- 2nd edition*, Routledge, 2020.

Srikantha Shastri, S., *Sources of Karnataka History*, Mark Wilks *Vol. I*, Mysore, 1940.

PART II

AGRARIAN PATTERNS AND PRACTICES

5

Ecology, Agriculture and Irrigation: Patterns and Practices of Cultivation in Early and Medieval Tamil Country

K. Mavali Rajan

Ecological factors such as climate, water, rainfall, soil conditions, etc. of a region determine the agricultural landscape and irrigation resources. The appearance of the agricultural landscape is the result of interaction between farming activities and natural settings in an established human settlement, which is a form of human habitation in particular geographical settings. The lifestyle of the early inhabitants' in particular ecological zone mostly depends upon the natural resources and agricultural production. The prosperity in agriculture depends on getting the required sunlight, seasonal rains, and the fertility of the soil. Among these elements of nature, sunlight was considered indispensable by the ancient Tamils, because if rains fail other methods of irrigation could be put to use, and if the soil wasn't naturally fertile, artificial manuring would enrich the soil. The early people differentiated the lands based on their fertility and accordingly they cultivated various crops that were best suited for the kind of soil. Of the natural resources, the fertile soil and water sources had provided humans with the ability to produce food crops, through agriculture for their sustenance.

Evidence of Cultivation in Early Epoch

As agriculture is the backbone of the Indian economy, the people of the realm from the earliest times to the present, bestowed maximum attention upon the cultivation of food crops. It was the main occupation of the people and most respected profession too. Initially, before starting the practice of cultivation in river valleys, hunting and gathering was the main lifestyle of the people, existed in many places in south India during the pre-historic age. The pre and proto-historic periods are marked by the rapid expansion of settlements and cultivation of crops in almost all the ecological zones. The available source materials articulate that the cultivation of food crops would have started in the New Stone Age in South India. Attesting the fact Barian Murton observed that in the earliest phase cattle herding was the most important element, but there is indirect evidence of cultivation in the form of rubbing stones for the processing of food. This phase lasted until about 1800 BCE (from 3000 BCE), finds of copper and bronze items in ever-increasing amounts became evident in sites of that era and afterward. This phase involved the dry farming of millets and leguminous crops, which is characterised by low rainfall and is of margins utility for farming, an economy based on millet farming and cattle and sheep/goat pastoral system developed.[1]

The Neolithic culture represents one of the important areas of study in India, particularly in south India. The term Neolithic culture is used for a stage in the growth of human's adaptation for his existence in which the domestication of animals and plants, sedentary lifestyle, and the use of ground stone axes were introduced. The domestication of animals and plants marked a special kind of human interfering in nature and a new stage in the relationship between people, animals, and plants. Archaeological evidence of the recent times reveals that the earliest domestication of plants (crop cultivation) in south India would have started about the late phase of the New Stone Age, which can be dated in the first half of the second millennium BCE.[2] We find sedentary agricultural settlements in several archeological sites of South India. The sedentary agricultural settlements (the practice of cultivation in one place by settled farmers) occurred in Tamil Nadu around the third to first millennium BCE in the Megalithic sites particularly in Kodumanal, which lies in the semi-arid zone on the northern banks of Noyyal river of Erode district. K. Rajan provides a good picture of the nature of the Kodumanal habitation-cum-burial site. According to him at Kodumanal 13 burials in the graveyard and 44 trenches in the habitation were excavated. The Microlithic site Māngudi, which is the earliest cultural deposits located in Tirunelveli district, provide us evidence for black and redware piece containing Tamil Brahmi inscription. The remains from both the sites proved that the sedentary agricultural societies existed there, and the people of the region utilised a variety of stone implements. The elements of sedentary livelihood can be seen among certain hunting-gathering groups, while some farmers and pastoralists retain a migratory lifestyle.[3]

Similarly, the Neolithic sites found at some other sites in Coimbatore and Erode districts yield shreds of evidence of cotton cultivation and use of stone implements. There are several Neolithic settlements that have been excavated at Gollapalli, Barugur, and Tograpalli in Krishnagiri district and at Payampalli and Chandrapuram in North Arcot district. The artifacts of the sites indicate that both permanent agriculture and pastoralism were practiced in the Neolithic period. It is important to note that the Neolithic age is characterised by the introduction of more evolved and developed typo-technological features. In the age, the man of the early period transformed from the "food gathering stage to food-producing stage". The Neolithic stage is generally associated with somewhat self-sufficient village communities with the balance between food production and population. There would also have been a change in the food ethic- hunter gatherers generally collect as much food as they can consume within a particular period. Farmers would have had to products and store the produce for future use.[4]

The distribution of Iron Age culture of the Megalithic period in south India was associated with burial sites. Most of the excavated sites are burial sites except Kunnattur (Chengelpet district) and Paiyampalli (North Arcot district) which are habitation sites as well. The Iron Age urn burial site Ādichanallur,[5] located on the river banks of Tāmiraparani, about 24 km. from Tirunelveli town in southern Tamil Nadu has attracted archaeologists for three important things; an inscription in a rudimentary Tamil-Brahmi script on the inside of an urn containing a full human skeleton; a fragment of broken earthenware and the remains of living quarters close to the sites.[6] Apart from these, the urn burial sites yield several objects which include burial urns (*mutumakkal tāli*) that contain some households implements, husks of rice and millets, grains, rice, charred rice, Neolithic Celts, etc. From the objects, it is very clear that the people of the region practiced agriculture and also perfected in wet crop cultivation and funerary practices.[7] Lot of Iron implements and tools have been found in many places, associated with the Megalithic burials. The iron tools and implements helped in the advancement of agriculture, which in turn leads to the development of civilisation.

Moreover, the establishment of permanent habitation, changes in the settlement pattern and cropping, and major expansion in long-distance trade were the important changes during the Iron Age

(c. 1000-500 BCE) in south India. The people of the Iron Age started the cultivation of crops like rice, barley and wheat and pulses like green gram and horse gram, etc. H.N. Dubey has noticed three phases of the development of agriculture in south India. In the first phase of primitive agriculture, people started making terraces on slopes of hills for cultivation and domestic settlements. The second phase of the development of agriculture started with the introduction of iron technology, characterised by plough agriculture and there was the spread of rice cultivation in south Indian River valleys. In the third phase of agriculture development in south India, the concentration of settlements in the river valleys, harnessing of the bullock to the plough and use of iron ploughshare also gradually developed, which increased in the area of cultivation and unprecedented growth in agricultural productions.[8]

Agriculture in Sangam Age

The agriculture during the early stages of the *Sangam* period was primitive, but it progressively got more efficient during the medieval period with improvement in the cultivation process, irrigation methods, storage, and distribution. The medieval political powers the Pallavas, the Pandyas, and the Cholas took necessary steps to the promotion of agriculture; thereby they developed a number of water sources, through which the country travelled towards the agro-based economy. There are references in early Tamil literature to various agricultural practices, cropping patterns and the domestication and increase of crops. In *Sangam* texts, especially in *Maduraikānchi*,[9] *Perumbānāttruppadai*,[10] and *Malaipadukadām*[11] there are mentions of the wet-land cultivation. The *Perumbānāttruppadai* gives detailed descriptions about the different process of cultivation such as tilling of the land by the use of the plough, sowing of the seeds and harvesting.[12]

In early Tamil society tillers of the soil were respected by the people. They were aware of different soil types, the best crops to grow, and the various irrigation systems suitable for cultivation. The saint-poet Thiruvalluvar has long back highlighted the importance of agriculture and agriculturists. An entire chapter (*Athikāram*: *ulavu:* 104, couplets (*kural*) 1031 to 1040) of in the *Thirukkural* (or *Kural*) [13] extols the glory and greatness of the farmers and their profession. The *Kural* extols agriculture and reflects the existing condition of those times and emphasis the importance of agriculture in the whole section as agriculture had emerged as an important economic activity. This is evident from the following couplets; "the tillers of the soil (*ulavar*) are the axle-pin (*āni*) of the revolving world. On them depends the sustenance of life for those that, unable to take up the plough, follow other occupations".[14] If tillers withdraw their labour, even the serenity, and concentration of spirit of those who have renounced the world will cease to be.[15] Further, it states that many other industries may be taken up, but ultimately the world depends on agriculture. So, despite its troubles, it is the worthiest occupation.[16] Again to show the independence of this occupation, the *Kural* says that "the ploughmen alone live as the freemen of the soil; the rest are mere slaves that batten on their toil".[17] The peasant is one who toils "in the sweat of his brow begs not at other men's doors, but ungrudgingly shares his bread with those that beg for alms".[18] In addition to all this Thiruvalluvar also delineates the agriculture techniques and practices right from ploughing, manuring, weeding, irrigation facilities and guarding of the crops.[19]

In the *Sangam* literature as well as in archaeological sources we also find references to using of iron instruments and new technology of iron ploughshare, etc. with the development of agrarian people of fertile regions, developing minor irrigation facilities like construction of small tanks, wells, and small canals, etc.[20] K.A. Nilakanta Sastri and G. Srinivasachari observed regarding the agriculture in *Tamilakam* in the *Sangam* age. When they discuss the agriculture in the early period they say that 'cultivable land was abundant and the necessities of life plentiful. The fertility of the lands watered by the Kāveri, Pennār, Pālār, Vaigai, Tāmiraparani and other rivers is the recurring theme of descriptions of the early Tamil poets.[21] The river valleys were suitable for wet crop cultivation and people cultivated different food crops in fertile plain lands. The natural forest produces were noticed in the *Sangam* texts that include bamboos, rice, jackfruits, *valli root* and honey, *rāgi*, sugarcane, pepper, turmeric, cotton, etc. Thus, paddy was an important crop cultivated in river valleys and miner millets were produced from the pastoral tracts. The society in the *Sangam* age was organised along with physiographical divisions with habits and traditions of their own, but the population of the large cities and port towns tended to be cosmopolitan'.[22]

Physiographical Divisions and Occupational Pattern

The physiographical divisions of a country such as mountains and rivers, its climate, and natural resources determine the nature of the social and economic life of its people. The choice of occupation of people, their physical and mental competence, their lifestyle as well as customs and manners and institutional practices bear the imprint of the geographical features of the region in which the people inhabited.[23]

Most prominently, it may be said that the geographical features play an important role in determining the history of the particular region. On the other hand, the long history of the trade and commercial relation of Tamil county with overseas countries on either side of the ocean was primarily the result of the geographical location of the Peninsular India.[24]

The *Sangam* texts convey a vivid description of the landscape and cultural pattern of the early period. The core of expression was the categorisation of poems into different modes (*tinai*) depending on nature, location, atmosphere, types of relationship represented by the poem. In *Tolkāppiyam*[25] we find references to four-fold and five-fold physiographical divisions of land and its environment. The descriptions on the four-fold land divisions (*nilapakuppu*) according to *Tolkāppiyam*, are;

māyōn mēya kādurai ulagamunj
sēyōn mēya maivarai ulagamum
vēnthan mēya thīmpuna ulagamum
varunan mēya perumana ulagamum
mullai, kurinji maruta neytalenatch
solliya muraiyār sollavum padumē

In the above passages, we notice the four-fold divisions such as *kādurai ulagam* (forest world), the *maivarai ulagam* (the hilly world), the *thīmpunal ulagam* (the plains or field world) and the *perumanal ulagam* (the littoral or sandy world) as well as the landscape *mullai*, *kurinji*, *marutam* and *neytal*.[26] Here the '*ulagam*' implies each region, which was different from the each other and each unit is considered as a separate component with specific character.[27]

The five-fold landscape division mentioned in the Tamil texts are *kurinji*, *mullai*, *marutam*, *neytal* and *palai*, which is referred to as *aintinai*, (the five *tinais*) and each with its distinct occupational pattern and corresponding forms of worship, customs and manners, and even performance for moods and forms in literature.[28] The *Perumbānāttruppadai* idyll gives detailed descriptions about the five physiographic eco-system or landscape. Ganapathy Subbiah, a historian, in his recent article on "Order of Hierarchy in the Realm of Religion and Society: An Introspective View from Back and Forth in Indian History" state that the Classical Tamil poetry was governed by the concept of *tinai* (genre/type), which were correlated to five eco-zones each of which named after the flora typical to the region. Each of these *tinais* was interrelated to an appropriate mood in love and to a specific heroic deed.[29] Therefore, the five *tinais* reflect the geographical and social characteristics of the early Tamils. It also denotes the distinctive modes of behaviours, social, and moral of the people of each physiographical region.

There are several interpretations among the scholars concerning the concept of *tinai*. K. Rajan, an Archaeologist interprets the *tinai* as an index for people who share homogeneity based either or behavioural or physiographic traits.[30] Radhika Rajamani in her work "*Society in Early Historic Tamilakam*" interpreted that the conception of *tinai* as ecological zones was just a literary convention but a geographical reality.[31] Kamil Zvelebil, an eminent scholar in Indian literature and language, sights that the concept of *tinai* is an evolutionist idea. The five divisions may reflect the historical migration of the pre-Dravidian and Proto-Tamil population from the hills and jungles to the fertile plains and the seaboard or in other words, the development from the Neolithic hunter, through the intermediate stage of the keeper of the flocks to the settled tiller of the soil and fisherman.[32] On the other hand Burton Stein, an American historian attested an interesting view of "ancient and modern Tamil country as a cultural territory is the different kinds of sub-regions with the macro-region of *Tamilakam*. Applying various analytical methods to the extent of literary evidence resulted in the delineation of essentially nodal or functional regions in addition to the formal or uniform regions of the ancient poetic tradition".[33] Accordingly the *tinai*, which consists of a complete poetical landscape- a specific time, place, season in which the poem is set and background elements characteristics of that landscape including flora and fauna, inhabitants, deities and social organisation.

Among the five physiographic divisions, mentioned in the early Tamil literature, the *kurinji* regions (mountainous and hilly regions) were famous for slash and burn cultivation. A typical activity of the inhabitants was gathering honey, digging up edible roots, wandering about the hills, and driving away parrots from millet fields.[34] The main food of the regions was millet, mountain rice (*aivanam*), white paddy (*vennel*), bamboo seeds, honey, and other foods available in the forests. These regions were rich in natural products like pepper, ivory, teak, aromatic woods like sandalwood and *akil*.[35] K.K. Pillai says that in early period cultivation of the soil began in the *kurinji* region, where through nature's gift, the people reared wild forms of paddy and other cereals with minimum effort.[36] Even today the Western Ghats is famous for its pepper.

The next ecological zones the *mullai* (forest pastoral tracts) was pastures, meadows, and scrublands, where shifting agriculture and animal husbandry were found. The inhabitants of the regions were considered pastoralists, cultivating millets called *varagu*, *sāmai*, *tinai*, the pulse horse gram (*kollu*), beans, and other non-specified pulses. Weeding of millet fields, harvesting of millet, threshing of millet, grazing of cowherds, taking of bulls were main activities of the people of the region.[37] From the literary texts of the early *Tamilakam*, we may surmise that these *mụllai* regions were peripheral to the *marutam* lands.[38] The tracts were regions of expanding agricultural activities and we find the slow transition from a pastoral to an agrarian economy. Both the *kurinji* and *mullai* regions had cultivable slopes, where shifting cultivation or slash and burn cultivations were practiced.

The fertile agricultural zone the *marutam* (riverine agrarian region) was the main rice-producing low-lying plains located between the *mullai* and *neytal* regions. The richness of the land, agricultural process, and irrigation facilities in *marutam* landscape are vividly portrayed in the early Tamil literature. P.T. Srinivasa Iyengar noticed that "the domestication of plants, especially the rice, the plantain, the sugarcane and the mango, which probably began in the relatively settled life of the pastoral stage, was completed in this zone".[39] The inhabitants of the tracts were *ulavar* (farmer), *ulumagan* (son of the tiller), *vēlān kudi* (peasants), *kalāmar* (tillers), *toluvar* (tillers or serfs) and their head man. Their main occupation was agriculture and people of the region were mostly involving in tilling, sowing, watering, weeding, reaping, bullfight and other related activities.[40] The significant aspect of the regions is the availability of plenty of water from the natural tanks and rivers, which make the land very fertile.[41] The fertility of the land particularly in the Chola country was due to the river Kāveri, which is constantly referred to in the literary texts. Even today the Kāveri basin (fertile *marutam* region) is one of the richest agricultural landscapes in south India.[42] These fertile tracts were the most productive land and people of other *tinais* depended on livelihood in this area. Rice, plantain, and sugarcane were the most important products of this zone, which were the main stable food of the people of the early Tamil country.

The *neytal* was the coastal region; fishing and salt manufacturing was the main occupation of the people. The *Paratavar/Valainar* was inhabitants of the littoral tracts of *neytal*. These *Paratavar* (fishermen) are portrayed in the Tamil poems as living in small settlements, which are said to be noisy and stinking of fish as the shores of the high areas.[43] The other social groups of the *neytal* tract were the *Umanar* who were manufacturers and traders of salt.[44] The people of *neytal* took pork and liquor. Toddy shops were located near the quarters of the *Paratavar*. It would appear that in the *neytal* there was a greater measure of urbanisation than the other regions.

The *pālai* was a sandy and dry region. According to the literature the *pālai* was not treated as a separate *tinai* as it was a seasonal ecological zone created at times on account of scarcity of rains or hot summer conditions. There are examples in the *Sangam* texts, which show the transformation of *kurinji* and *mullai* in a certain season in to *pālai* lands.[45] Martial groups like *Maravar*, *Malavar* and *Eyinar* were the inhabitants of the region. The *Maravar* or *Malavar* performed diverse activities like robbing, fighting, and killing wayfarers, who passed through their tracts, fighting for chiefs and lifting cattle or recovering stolen cattle.[46] Another martial group mentioned in the early texts is the *Eyinar*, were the warriors who fight bravely with immense strength.[47] The inhabitants of the *pālai* region lived in huts covered with the leaves of the palm tree.

The five ecological zones (*tinais*) are signified by the name of the flower such as *kurinjipū* or *neela kurinjipū* (*Strobilanthes Kunthiana*) in *kurinji* land, *mullaipū* (jasmine, *Jasminium trichotomum*) in *mullai* land, *marutampū* (Indian Laurel, *Terminalia arjuna*) in *marutam* land, *neytalpu* (Indian blue/white water lily, *Nymphaea odorate*) in *neytal* land and *pālaipū* (ivory wood, *Wringhtia tinctoria*) in *pālai* land,[48] which also denoted by three major features namely, *mutal*, *karu* and *uri*.[49] Here *mutal* (primary aspects) indicates space and time, *karu* (organic aspects) refers to the typical features of landscape like flora, fauna, water sources, etc. and *uri* (that one which belongs) refers to behavioural aspects in love (*aham*) and war (*puram*), which is known as *uripporul* in Tamil literature.[50]

The five ecological zones are also identified and named after the trees, shrubs and their blooms which grew abundantly in the respective region. We find several material elements in the five-fold regions such as god, food, flora, occupation, water source, types of habitation, folklore and musical instruments, etc.[52] B.D. Chattopadhyaya has cited the following poem of *Porunarāttruppadai*, (one of the *Pattupāttu* anthology of the *Sangam* literature);

> Those selling honey and roots eatable
> Exchange them for fish's fat and wine

They barter sugarcane and roasted rice
For toddy and deer flesh. The fisher folk
Sing hill men's song, while hill men
Wear garlands of fragrant blooms that grow along the coast.
The dwellers of the deserts sing the songs
Of those in fertile lands, and these in turn
Praise forest lands where grows the *Mullai* blue.
The wild fowl eats rice, while the domestic
Eats millet grain. The hillside monkey rolls
In salty marsh, while cranes that take a bath
In briny sea-waves rest themselves on hills,
From diverse pleasant regions are thus found
Together in a single realm.[51]

The poem ornately narrates the cultural and behavioural pattern and differences of the ecological zones of the early *Tamilakam*. Thus the five ecological regions are identified as a separate cultural zone distinct from each other. Smriti Haricharan and Naresh Keerthi applied the five eco-zones into the modern landscape. The Eastern Ghats and marine landform fell into the categories of *kurinji* and *neytal* respectively. The inland plains and deltaic regions were designated as *marutam tinai*. The Tamil Nadu uplands were categorised as *mullai*.[53]

Apart from the four-fold and five-fold physiographical divisions, the lands in the early *Tamilakam* were broadly classified into *menpulam* and *vanpulam*. The *menpulam* is a wetland plain representing the *marutam* land, the agricultural tracts and the *vanpulam* is a region like *kurinji* and the part of *mullai* tract. The cultivable land was specifically known as *vayal*, *kalani*, and dry and pasture lands were called *kadu* and salty wasteland, which is not suitable for any cultivation was known as *kalari* or *kalar nilam*. In *menpulam* people cultivated rice, betel, plantain, and sugarcane, and in *vanpulam*, people cultivated millets, sorghum, legumes, and cotton. Apart from the wetland farming in core fertile regions, the dryland farming and pastoralism would have continued to be important activities, and various forms of shifting cultivation must have been common in the peripheral regions.[54]

Based on the inhabitants of the five ecological zones, the *marutam* zone was occupied by the agriculturists, the *kurinji* land as semi-agriculturists, and *mullai* people as being pastoral, *neytal* people as mostly fishermen and *pālai* by the robbers and thieves. The soil conditions of the regions were the main determining factor in the process of cultivation, the nature of crops, and the cropping pattern. The red and sandy soil of delta regions was extremely suitable for wet cultivation. The rest of the soils was suitable for dry-crop cultivation.

Consequently, the study of geography and ecology of Tamil country is more important in understanding the social and economic life of the people. The Tamil region is distinctive from any other regions on account of physiographic and ecological differences. The relationship between groups of living things and their environments is closely associated with each other. This geographical region evolved as a cultural unit with a long historical past with certain dominant linguistic, literary, and cultural traditions. The early Tamil tradition was non-Vedic and non-*Sanskritic* in origin. As a distinct geographical unit, it has full of variation that would have influenced the development of potentialities of the different parts of the regions. Subsequently, the development of society and economy in the early historic period of *Tamilakam* was considerably determined and influenced by geographic and ecological variations.

Agricultural Crops

The water source was supposed to be the most important and essential factor for the good production of crops. All the fundamentals of agriculture being well organised, the good production of crops was not possible unless there would be the availability of sufficient sources of water. The Tamils cultivated different food crops in the *Sangam* and post-*Sangam* age. They cultivated paddy, sugarcane, millets, pepper, various pulses, coconuts, beans, corn, cotton, plantain, tamarind, and sandalwood, etc. Of them paddy was the main crop, with different varieties grown in the wetland of *marutam*, such as *vennel* (white variety), *chennel* (red variety), *pudunel* (new variety), *aivananel* (five varieties) and torai.[55] Among them, *chennel* was considered to be superior. *Sāli* is another kind of superior variety of paddy mentioned in Nāladiyār.[56] As understood from the *Puranānūru* and the *Pattinappālai* the *chennel* and *pudunel* were more refined varieties cultivated in the fertile plains. A medieval Tamil inscription mentions that there were two types of cultivation of paddy namely, *kār* and *pāsānam*.[57] The season for the sowing the *kār* began in May or June and the harvest took place about December or January. These references indicate to the point that paddy was the mainstay of the people of Tamil country. The peasants of early *Tamilakam* lived in shady groves of trees close to the farmlands and each house had a jack, coconut, palm, and areca, and plantain trees. The peasants grew turmeric plants in front of their houses and laid flower gardens in between the houses. They believed that ploughing, manuring, weeding, watering and the protection of crops must be done according to a specific method to obtain a good yield.[58]

The inscriptions of medieval Tamil country especially the Pallava records speak of different varieties of the food crops. The Pallankovil copper plate (of the 30 copper plates) grant of the Pallava king Simhavarman (6th century CE) mentions a list of crops grown in the *Tondaimandalam* region.[59] The inscription describes the rice-fields (*sāli*), the rich field of sugarcane (*iksuvana*), the graves of palm trees (*kramukha*), plantains (*rambha*), and others which grew near the river area.[60] The Tamil portion of the copper plate provides elaborate details about the economy, administration, taxation, and educational system of the period. The Udayendiram Copper Plates of Nandivarman II (731-795 CE), issued in his 21st regnal year mentions the different varieties of crops which were grown on the banks of the river Kaveri, such as areca-palms (*kramukha*), coconut trees (*nalikera*), mango trees (*sahakara*), Palmyra (*tala*) and other trees.[61] References to the cultivation of mango, banana, coconut, orange, lime, jack-fruits and grapes are found in the medieval records.[62] Another medieval record contains full of references to the cultivation of dry crops like millet (*varagu*), ragi (*kēlvaragu*), bajra (*kambu)*, maize (*chōlam*), little millet (*sāmai*), black gram (*ulunthu*), pulse (*paruppu*), horse-gram (*kollu*), etc.[63]

The crops were divided into two categories- *van payir* and *pun payir*. Plantains, sugarcane, ginger, turmeric, fruits like mango and jackfruit; cotton seeds and castor seeds are referred to as *van payir* and paddy, millet, and sesame as *pun payir*.[64] The cultivation of both *van payir* and *pun payir* was done both by male and female peasants persistently, with the result, food was produced in abundance in the *Sangam* age. The agricultural products of those days were self-sufficient and we also have references to surplus production. The surplus products of food grain were sent for sale in the markets by bullock carts. We find descriptions of such carts carrying imported goods in the literature of the early *Tamilakam*. The peasants in the early period were living happily because of the surplus production of grain and trades.

Vijaya Ramaswamy, a social historian studied briefly the history of agriculture in south India, covering from the *Sangam* age to the Vijayanagara period. According to her "a major development in the period under the Vijayanagara kingdom and the Deccan Sultanate was the growth in the production and export of spices. The species were produced largely in the Malabar region and consisted of pepper, cloves, ginger, nutmeg, cardamom, and cinnamon. Barbosa writes that these agricultural products were exported to foreign countries where there was a great demand for them. Coconuts and betel were two other major products of south India while coconut groves were to be found along the coast. The betel leaf and betel nuts were produced in all parts of south India".[65] Kathleen D. Morrison examined the land use and agricultural intensification around Vijayanagara with critical attention in her article "Typological Schemes and Agricultural change: Beyond Boserup in pre-colonial South India". The most intensive features of the agricultural landscape date to the early Vijayanagara period have been discussed in a detailed manner. It is necessary to note from her writing that both wet and dry land cultivation was widely practiced in the Vijayanagara period. The dry crops of sorghum (*jōwar* or *chōlam*) and various millets have traditionally been the most important food grains in the region. Cotton was also grown on a large scale during the Vijayanagara period.[66]

Agricultural Implements

The Tamils of the early period used various implements in the process of cultivation. Pieces of evidence are found in archaeological sites in Tamil Nadu. Archaeologists discovered many earthen pots, baked earthenware utensils, several iron weapons, and implements mainly knives, short sword, blades, and a huge number of bones and skulls along with agricultural tools from Ādichanallur excavation.[67] According to Irfan Habib, the plough appeared in the south in the second millennium BCE, basically Neolithic culture; the crops raised were *ragi* millet, wheat, horse gram, and green gram. Rice and the *bajra* millet began to cultivate after the coming of iron. Agriculture of this kind implied the existence of peasantry from the late Neolithic times.[68]

In the process of cultivation, the plough was the main implements. From Vedic literature we get references to plough, it was known as *sira*, *sita* and *tangala*. After discovering the iron materials the iron plough was made for tilling of the soil. But the ploughs during the Vedic period were made of wood and were generally drawn by a team of two bullocks. On the other hand, there are also references to drawing the plough by a team of six, eight, twelve, or even twenty-four oxen. The *Rig-Veda* mentions the use of a team of six to twelve oxen in a plough. There are different opinions among the scholars regarding the reason for the use of more oxen in a plough during the Vedic period. V.B. Rao, Domodar Satavalekar, and others believe that the land shape and heavyweight of the Vedic plough was the main reason behind the use of more than two oxen in a plough.[69]

The use of the plough was very common from the early periods in the Tamil country. *Mēli* and *nānjil* are the two most commonly used terms in the *Sangam* poems for plough and '*ēr* ' for ploughshare. Farmers used a bent plough known as *kodumēli* with a crossbar namely, *kodunugam* or *nugam*.[70] The term '*ēr* ' commonly referred to the act of ploughing, '*ulavu* ', and therefore, the terms '*ērōr* ' and '*ulavar* ' were used for ploughmen.[71] The terms '*ēr*' and '*ērpūttutal* ' stands for a team; yoke of oxen, plough and ploughshare. The term '*uludal*', '*ērattidal*', '*ērōttam*' stand for ploughing or tilling of the soil. The '*kolu*' and '*āni*' refer particularly to the plough point or tip or pointed end of the ploughshare.[72] Interesting information about the agricultural implements used during the period of study comes from Kampar's work of 12th century CE.[73] They are plough (*kalappai*), plough handle (*mēli*), large nail (*urrāni*), the yoke (*nugattadi*), socket (*nugattulai*), iron and wooden rod which holds the yoke in position (*nugattāni*), the rope that ties the yoke to the neck of the bull (*todai*), the plough point (*kolu*), the nail that joins the plough point to plough (*koluvāni*), whip in the hands of the peasant (*tārrukkōl*), the ox or bull that ploughs (*vilavirudu*), a leveler *manvetti* or *mammutti*, etc.[74] In the entire agricultural operation the plough was important, which is used as a main implement for cutting deep furrows in soil and turning it up.

Late medieval Tamil literature especially *Pallu* literatures[75] gives a detailed account of the system of cultivation and kinds of implements used. The implements of agriculture were few and simple. According to *Mukkudal Pallu*, the most important agricultural implement was the plough (*kalappai* or *mēli*).[76] Its construction more or less the same in all the parts of Tamil Nadu. Generally, a branch or a piece of wood was used to make plough with a pointed end, to which a pair of bullocks were yoked by using simple wooden pole and yoke. Buffalos (*erumai*) were also said to been employed in ploughing operation. The *kolu* was often made of iron with a pointed end. One great advantage of the wooden plough was its cheapness both concerning to cost and repair. Generally, village carpenters made and repaired the *kalappai* and other agricultural implements.[77] Harrow (*parambu*) a leveler for ploughed land and a spade (*manvetti*), a tool for scraping the earth for bund making, were also largely used.[78] Apart from these, there were other tools used by the early Tamils. *Tular*, a pickaxe, made of iron was used to dig the land.[79] A knife with wooden handle was also used. They used the sickle called *kaivāl/kathir-aruvāl* for weeding and harvesting paddy crops.[80] Pestle and mortar occupied a significant place among all the common public for removing the husks.[81] These are implements used by the agricultural labourers of the early and medieval Tamil country in the various process of cultivation.

Process of Paddy Cultivation

It appears that during the last three or four thousand years there has not been any basic change in the process and technique of paddy and other dry crops cultivation in the Indian peninsula. In the literary sources, the main agricultural operations have been described and they are ploughing (*uluthal*), sowing (*vitaithal*), reaping (*aruvadai*), threshing (*kathiradittal*), etc. Many of these operations of cultivation and irrigation required the assistance of cattle. The cattle were employed in ploughing, lifting water, threshing, transport of produce, etc.[82] The cattle were then yoked to the plough and a square piece of ground was ploughed. A few furrows were made and care was taken that the plough was dropped towards the right side. Sharat Patil noticed that the agricultural work was done without buffaloes or bullocks it was exclusively in the hands of females; but with the intervention of draught animals, it was taken over by males, soon to be succeeded by male slaves.[83]

Paddy was an important crop cultivated since ancient periods. The Tamils in the early period used both dry and wetland for the cultivation of paddy crops. The dry land cultivation was solely dependent upon local rainfall. Wetlands are those, which were irrigated from river channels or tanks by the natural flow of the water and garden lands, which are irrigated by water artificially, raised from well. On dry lands, the cultivation was simple. Before sowing, the field was ploughed several times in transverse directions. The seed (*vithai*) was generally scattered from the hand (that is known as *vithai-pāval*), but some time a rude bamboo drill was used. The paddy seeds were sown through the scattered in the soil worked up into a semi-liquid state, and sometimes transplanted. Water was supplied as often as it could be obtained, daily if possible; and on each occasion of watering, the land was flooded to the depth of one or two inches. After the crop had been sown, little hoeing or weeding takes place. The harvest was gathered by hand, the labourers being paid in kind.[84]

The ploughing of the land, which is the first process in the cultivation of both wet and dryland crops. Normally, the agricultural labourers or peasants start their work with ploughing on an auspicious day or time and it was known as *nālaridal*.[85] According to Tamil tradition, the Tamil month of *Ādi* (July-August) was considered to be the best time for starting of cultivation.[86] On that particular auspicious day, the peasants started their work of ploughing after their prayers to God for good fortune.[87] On this occasion, the horns of bullocks and the plough were smeared with oil, sandal, and turmeric paste. At every ceremony, god *Ganapathi* was invoked and offerings made to him, after which the master sowed the seed in the furrows already made, the agrarian labourers in the meanwhile praying for a good season, a plentiful harvest and health and prosperity to his landowner and his family. A coconut was then broken on the ploughshare and if it broke into exact halves it was taken as a good omen for a good harvest.[88] The farmers began to plough the four extreme sides of the field first. The Hindus called this practice as *ponnēr pūttutal*, for it would bring wealth ultimately. In certain places, the Pallas/Mallas,[89] the inhabitants of *marutam* land, and the most popular agricultural community in Tamil country was asked to plough first and the others followed them.

Throughout Tamil Nadu, three methods of raising plants could be noticed. They are dry seed, sprouted, and transplanted.[90] In the first method, the seed is sown in the field straightway. In this, the expense is low and the produce correspondingly scanty. For sprouted cultivation, the seeds are sown steeped in water till they germinated and then transferred to the field. According to the last method the seeds are first scattered in well-prepared nursery beds. The sowing of the seeds in the nurseries in an equally scattered manner by the dexterity of hands is called *vitaippāval* or *nāttruppāval*.[91] Of the three methods *Mukkūdal Pallu* describe the last method vividly, which is still in practice largely in Tamil Nadu. After the germination of the seeds, the nurseries are fenced so that the seedlings can escape from being grazed by the cattle.[92] The nurseries are filled up to a certain height of the seedlings in the morning and in the evening the water is filtered out. This practice aims at providing water for budding plants but at the same time preventing growth arrest due to over water stagnation.[93]

The most traditional and productive method of cultivating paddy was through transplantation of seedlings. Before the transplanting of seedlings, the field was made soft and leveled. The field was ploughed four times and three times leveled. The first ploughing was known as *tarissadittal*. The second and third ploughs were *marittadittal* and *muccāladittal*. The fourth plough was the *nālulavu*. The term *toil-ulavu* was the ploughing with water. In between the ploughs the land was leveled three times by a harrow (*parampu*).[94] This custom was known as *parampadittal* in Tamil. Then the seedlings attaining the stage at which it could be transplanted in the already prepared field, which is known as *nāttrusamaital/nāttrunadutal*.[95] The seedlings attain full development within 25 to 30 days. Before transplantation was to be started, the young plants were tied into a bunch and heaped in circles. The transplantation was made at an auspicious time and the planters pray for a good crop, facing all the cardinal directions, by the taking seedlings over their foreheads. Then they transplanted in such a way that crabs could not go and cut the young buds.[96] Mostly women labourers involved in the transplanting the young paddy plant in the field and the womenfolk used to sing song (*nadavuppādal*) when the planting work is going on.

The subsequent operations were generally confined to regular weeding, watering, and occasionally thinning the plants where they appeared too thick by transplanting them elsewhere. Proper manuring is also needed in the growth of the paddy plants. The manures (eruvu/uram) normally prepared from cow dung and other organic matters. Literature speaks of organic manures prepared from the dropping of cows, goats, and sheep, which are nutrients to the crop. When the crops were grown and ready to harvest the agrarian labourers reaped the paddy crop, which is known as *kathir aruttal*. The harvested ripe stalks were tied into bundles with the thread (*kayiru*) of straw. Then the bundled ripe stalks were carried to the threshing floor (*kalattu mēdu*) where the grains were separated from the stalks by beating them on stones.[97] After threshing the paddy, the bunches were spread roundly on the yard. Three or four bulls or buffalos were tied together and driven to go round on bunches, beside each other with some gap, which is known as *thāmpatittal*. This practice (*pinaiyal*) was for separating the sterile chaff car heads and the good paddy from the hay.[98] *Politūrval* was the winnowing of the separated paddy called *poli* after *pinaiyal* by which the remaining chaff car heads are blown away from the fertile grain. The fertile grain was measured after winnowing. This practice was called as *polialattal*.[99] After the winnowing, the paddy was collected through *cākku/kōni* and which were carried to home and stored for future purposes. The following descriptions of *Porunarāttruppatai* give us a picture of the harvest and refer to the surplus production and heaps of paddy stacked up and stored in large bins;

> The farmers with their sickles bend to reap
> Their harvests pile rice sheaf's in immense stacks,
> Heap daily grains threshed out that look like hills,
> And store it in large bins enclosed in straw.[100]

After harvest, the paddy underwent several processes depending upon how it will be used. The steps for preserving the paddy crops are drying and storing. The drying was the process that reduces the grain moisture content to a safe level of storage. Proper storage conditions will ensure minimal loss of paddy rice due to changes in weather and moisture contents, rodents, insects, micro-organisms, etc. The Tamils had a traditional method of storing the food grains in their houses. Mostly *kulumai* (big rice pot made of clay for storage) and *kuthir/kuthuru* (a constructed structure along with the mud wall of the house) were used traditionally for storage.

Irrigation

The life of the people, particularly for those who live on livestock and agriculture, revolves around the water resources. The water is the basic resource for human society and energetic substance for flora and fauna. From the ancient period, human society was able to utilise water for different purposes, primarily for agriculture and animal husbandry. The society also paid much attention to water management, storage, preservation, regulation, maintenance, and distribution of water. Thus, control over water becomes an indispensable component of society. Apart from the society the state also played an important role in the collection and distribution of water resources and constructed several water bodies for the promotion of agriculture. Further, the formation of a new settlement and the emergence of new occupational groups in the water-fed region depended on their control over water. The water is directly related to agricultural production. Therefore, the irrigation system is considered as one of the important mechanism of the agricultural production and growth of rural economy.[101]

In the Indian sub-continent, we find different types of irrigation systems, which are being followed based on its geographical and geological settings. The agricultural production was dominated by the wet-land forming in fertile regions (in the river valley) and dry-land farming in the interior region, though agriculture irrigated from wells was also significant in the garden land cultivation. The *ēttram*, a traditional water lifting device is frequently referred to in inscriptions. Irrigation from rivers and tanks was found along all the streams of the area. A proper irrigation system provides increasing more production to the cultivators (*uluvōr*), profits to the landowner (*uluvittu-unbōr*), and more employment generation for the benefit of the landless agricultural labourers, which also assurances a stable rural economy. So the water resources had become an integral part of the social system through the comprehensive layout of drainage, networks, creation of tank, dam and diversion of river water, the interlinking of tanks, etc.[102]

If we look at the history of early India, we find pieces of evidence on agriculture and water sources during the pre-historic and historic periods. The people of the pre-historic Harappa culture were familiar with agriculture as evidenced by the food grains collected from sites like Mohenjo-dara, Harappa, Lothal, etc. Though no irrigation systems of the period are brought to light, it is evident from their highly advanced drainage and sewerage systems that the Harappa people must have used the water of Indus and other small rivers for irrigating their farmlands by constructing dams and tanks and by digging canals, etc.[103] The people of pre-historic age in Tamil land knew the technique of managing the water. Many water bodies have been discovered from several archaeological sites in Tamil Nadu. In *Thirukkural* it is stated that the world cannot exist without water and rain gives life to all the creation, revives the dying vegetation, restores life to what seems to die.[104] We find a large number of references in inscriptions of the north India and Tamil country, to the irrigation systems. In ancient India, the Sudarsana Lake in Saurashtra, its history from the Mauryas to the Guptas illuminated by epigraphic evidence, marks the beginning of the recorded history of tank and lake irrigation.[105] In Tamil country the construction of the irrigation tanks seems to become well established by the early and medieval Chola times.[106] Historian had earlier perceived that localised peasant agriculture had developed under the Cholas based upon minor irrigation works.

As agriculture depends largely on irrigation, both natural and artificial water resources were utilised by the farmers. Tanks and wells were the main sources of artificial irrigation, which became more popular in south India because of its geographical features, inadequate rainfall, and lack of perennial rivers. From the archaeological sources, we find evidence of artificial means of irrigation such as tanks, wells, channels, etc., that belongs to the Megalithic period in south India. It is interesting to note that the people of the Megalithic period practiced agriculture as their main occupation and knew the importance and value of irrigation.[107] Among the natural water sources all the rivers of the Tamil region like Kāvēri, Pālār, Thenpennai, Vagai, etc. not only provided drinking water to the population but were utilised for irrigation purpose as well. The earliest irrigation attempt was confined mainly to using the flood water of rivers.

Realising the importance of water sources the rulers of early Tamil country took necessary steps to develop the irrigation system to use it for agricultural production. They constructed large reservoirs, tanks, and canals on an extensive scale. The construction of reservoirs and digging of canals were considered as acts of fame to a ruler. One of the celebrated kings of the *Sangam* period, Karikala Cholan (c.150 CE) is accredited with the cleaning of the jungles and introduction of agricultural settlements, construction of embankments on both sides of the Kāveri River, construction of a dam (*Kallanai* now known as Grand Anicut) across the river Kāveri and also digging canals.[108] The dams were an extremely important component of the medieval south Indian agricultural landscape. They were typically placed across valleys or natural drainage to capture monsoon runoff behind an earthen embankment faced with masonry water flowed in the fields below through slab lined tunnels constructed underneath the embankment. The flow of water through the tunnels was controlled by sluices.[109]

In the history of irrigation, tanks are considered as the earliest storage mechanism of water. Many of the Chola inscriptions in the Tamil region refer to the construction of tanks in the area by members of the royal family and their subordinates. There was a rapid increase in the number of tanks constructed from the 10th century onwards. Y. Subbarayalu, an epigraphist says that the reason behind the increase in water bodies due to the special nature of Brahmin settlements, which were naturally created for settling migrant Brahmins by providing equal shares to each Brahmin households. When the *brahmadēya* and *dēvadāna* were established, it seems a regular pattern of canal systems were created newly.[110] Burton Stein noticed that the *brahmadēya* and its *sabha* are response to the organisational needs of settlements on the edges of settled agricultural zones, surrounded by hostile semi-nomadic tribesmen, and meant to bring virgin land under cultivation. He believes that the *brahmadēyas* were supported by the most advanced condition of agriculture, which would place the emergence of the *brahmadēyas* in regions of settled and advanced farming activities.[111]

The establishment of *brahmadēyas* introduced advanced farming methods and irrigation, and was itself a major resource; hence the *brahmadēyas* could be described as reliable and accurate markers of the mature agrarian localities. The most of the *brahmadēyas* had a large reservoir or irrigation tank built at the time of its establishment, which subsequently served the need of many of the hamlets surrounding the *brahmadeya* settlements.[112] For instance in Tribhuvani, a *brahmadēya* village we find six big tanks, eight lakes, and ponds in the Chola times.[113] Noboru Karashima, a Japanese historian studied forty villages including *brahmadēya* and non-*brahmadēya* villages, noticed twenty nine water sources of all sorts like the river, pond, tank, bund, and canal that included the resource for both drinking and irrigational purposes.[114] To a certain extent the land grant inscription of the Chola period mentions about the water management, which was done by the *brahmadēya* to avoid dispute between the agrarian communities.[115]

In medieval Tamil country, the construction of tanks and other irrigational works was taken up as a mission by the ruling classes and all rich sections of the society to promote wet-crop cultivation. The state and temple played a vital role in the promotion of irrigation facilities. It was believed that the construction of water bodies and its maintenance works by the government will increase the virtue and prosperity of the state. Epigraphic evidences are available to understand the state sponsor for the construction of water sources. South Indian inscriptions provide us information about the reclamation which were undertaken by a private agency under the support of the state, village *sabha* and temples.[116] A. Appadorai in his work '*Economic Conditions in Southern India (1000-1500 A.D)*' notes that the state involved reclamation, a large area would come under cultivation thereby the state would get more taxes accordingly. Besides the state, the private agencies like corporate bodies of the village, *sabha*, and the temples involved in maintenance and renovation work of tanks and reservoirs.[117] Among these the *sabha* played an important role in decision making regarding the upkeep, distribution of water, and also regulatory works of water bodies. The *sabha*, tank committee of the village, temple and some landlords gained much power in controlling the water bodies and cultivation of resources produced. The resources produced from various means through proper irrigation, reclamation, and of course through land grants. In the case, without proper irrigation, land could not be cultivated with full potential.[118] The role of the temple also is indispensable in undertaking the control over water bodies. C. Minakshi mentions about the irrigation works done by the ruling authority on behalf of the temple during the Pallava period.[119]

Sources of Water Supply

Evidence for different sources of water supply is noticeable from the literary and archaeological sources. In *Sangam* literature, we find different terms for water bodies such as *aruvi* (waterfalls), *ēri* (reservoir), *kulam* (tank), *āru* (river), *poykai* (pond), *kinaru* (well), *kēni* (well), *samudiram* (sea), etc. Besides these water sources, there are also certain terms associated with water devises namely, *karcirai* (anicut of stone), *kumili* (sluice), *kāl* (channel), *talai-vāy* (head sluice), *tūmpu* (conduit), *madai* (blocking the watercourse) and *madaku* (blocking and diverting the watercourse through canals).[120] The term *madaku/kumili* is releasing point from the *madai*, which controls water in tank or *ēri*. The term *talai-madai* denotes head sluice and *katai-madai* denotes the sluice at the tail end. *Madai-vāy* is the layout. *Tūmbu* (weir), releasing out excess water from tanks, which is usually located at the vantage point.[121] In *Tondaimandalam* region the *tūmbu* was called by the name *kalingu*, even today the term *kalingu* is in vogue concerning to agrarian pursuits.[122] If water is full in a tank/*ēri* there would be a let out in any corner of the tank that is known as *marukāl*, through which the extra water flow out and reach a small *vaykkal* known as *kali-vāykkāl*. Some cultivable lands are irrigating through the *kali-vāykkāl*.

References to the construction of tanks are abundant in medieval south Indian inscriptions from 6th century CE onwards. K. Rajan analyzed the available inscriptional evidence of medieval Tamil country. According to him, there are nearly 1700 published inscriptions relating to irrigation, out of which 160 inscriptions refer to sluice and water distribution technology. Further, he says that more than half of these sluice inscriptions are found in Pudukkottai region, where tank irrigation largely prevailed. The second highest comes from the Pandya country and others are randomly scattered throughout Tamil Nadu.[123] The earliest epigraphic evidence of the construction of irrigation channel in Pandya territory by the initiatives of the state is identified from the Vaigai bed inscription of the fiftieth year of Cētan Arikēsari (c.720 CE). The inscription refers to the construction of a channel (*kāl*) from the Vaigai River of the Pandya territory. We find the term *madagu* in the inscription which is named after the ruler Arikēsariyan.[124] Long canals (*kāl or vāykkāls*) were constructed and used for irrigation to carry water from its origin in a river, lake, or tank through villages and often between villages. Most of the distributory canals of the Kaveri River belong to the Chola period. They are namely, *Uyyakondān* canal, *Rājēndran vāykkāl*, *Sembian Mahādevi vāykkāl*, etc. There was a highly developed efficient system of water management existed in village level.[125]

From a historical point of view, the Cholas and the Pandyas in the south and the Pallavas in the north of peninsular India constructed a good number of big size irrigation tanks with a technical device called *kumili/madai* (sluice). The sluices helped the regulation of water distribution acutely. The tanks of the Pandya and the Pallava territory are called by the term *ēri*, *kulam*, and *tātaka*. The *tātaka* is a common term denoting the irrigation tank in the southern state.[126] The Pallava inscriptions speak of the water bodies after the name of the Pallava king namely, *Tiraiayen-ēri*, *Paramēswara-tātaka*, *Mahēndrat-tātaka*, and *ten-ēri*.[127]

The ē*ris* (lakes) was considered as an important source of irrigation, which we find large in number in the regions where rivers (*ārus)* and tributaries (*sittārus*) were absent. Lakes were mainly constructed to preserve rainwater for future use. In medieval south India, numerous lakes such as *Vairamēgha-tātaka* of Uttiramerur, the *Chōla-varishi* of Sholingur and the *Rājēndra Chōlap-pēriya-ēri* at Punganur were constructed for agricultural expansion.[128] Parantaka I constructed a lake named *Virānamēri* near Kāttumannārkōil in South Arcot district. Other famous lakes of this period are *Madurāntakam-ēri*, *Sundara-chōlapērēri*, *Kundavai-Pērēri* which are named after the Chola kings and other royal members.[129]

There were different terms used for the reservoir system during the Pallava and Pandya periods. The irrigation sources of the Pallava period were referred to as *kulam*, *kuttai*, *ōdai*, *kurangu*, *kurran-vāy*, *ūrani*, *vāyt-talai*. In the Pandya territory, we find the terms like *āru* (river), *kulam* (tank), *vāykkāl* (channel), *peru-vāykkāl* (big-channel), *siru-vāykkāl* (small channel), *karai* (channel bank), *kidangu* (small pond), *kinaru* (well), *kula-vāyl-talai* (water let out from *kulam*), *nīr-nilai* (water-bodies), etc. Different types of *vāykkāl* we find in the Kaveri delta region. The epigraphic evidence speaks of *āttru-vāykkāl*, which is a natural canal leading from the river to the tank.[130] There are also references to *kallina-vāykkāl* (dug out channel),[131] *kula-vāykkāl* (channel originating from the tank),[132] *siru-vāykkāl*, *peru-vāykkāl*, *kali-vāykkāl*, etc. Here *vāykkāl* is the common term which identified for the well-maintained irrigation system in south Indian territories. Technically the *vāykkāls* are differently noticed in inscriptions. In general, the irrigation canal is called *vāykkāl*. The *vāykkāl* is the main distributing channel, is a prominent irrigation system of a village. The water for this channel is diverted from a major river or a tributary river. The *vāykkāls* functioned as feeder channels. There is another term '*vati*' that occurs along with *vāykkāls* which is certainly a branch of the main canal. The *vati* diverts the water from the *vāykkāl* and from the *vati*, the *kannāru* carry water to the filed blocks.[133] There are five different *vati* has been mentioned in Udayārgudi inscription viz. *Vishnu vati*, *Chandrasēkara vati*, *Vīranārāyana vati*, *Kōtantarāma vati*, and *Sridhara vati*. The *vatis* are found in a small locality of wet cultivation in *Vīranārāyana chaturvēdimangalam*.[134] An Uttiramērūr inscription of 1016 CE refers to one *Vikramachōla vati* as *vilakku vāykkāl*, meaning branch canal. And *kannāru* must be a sub-canal of the *vati*, following parallel to the *vāykkāl*.[135] Mostly the *vāykkāls* are named after the royal members of the dynasty; for instance *Parakēsari vāykkāl*, *Kōtandarāma vāykkāl*,[136] *Rājarāja vāykkāl*,[137] *Arumolidēva vāykkāl*,[138] etc.

The *vāykkāl* in the village level is called as *ūr-vāykkāl*,[139] *nādu* level canal is known as *nāttu-vāykkāl*[140] and canal running across more than one village is described as *udaruttup-pōna-vāykkāl*.[141] We also find some other water networks, which are known by the name *ūrunikkulam*, *ūrani* (for drinking water near *ur*), *kalani*, *punnakkulam*, *pulattil-kulangal* (ponds in field), *totti*, *vannāthi-kulam* (pond for washer man community), *siru-kulam* (small pond), *ēmbalā*, etc.[142] The term *kulam* stands for a small water body known as a tank which generally serves a small irrigated area (*āyakattu*). Inscription of Kulottuga Chola I's (1070-1120 CE) phrase '*ivvūr kulattālum ēmbalālum ūrunikalālum n¯irpāyum kor̠r̠i vāykkāl nilam*' indicates the different water bodies namely, *kulam*, *ēmbalā*, *ūruni*, *vāykkāl*, which were mostly utilised for irrigating the agricultural fields.[143]

In other Chola inscriptions, several technical terms indicating the water resources like *vati*, *vāykkāl*, *ut-ciru-vāykkāl*, *talaivāy*, *vāit-talai*, etc.[144] The terms *talai-vāy*, *vāy-talai*, *ut-ciru-vāykkāl* are denoting head-sluice at the vantage points of river or canal. The *vāy-talai* is the head-sluice through which water flows into irrigation canals, which bring water from the river to the land under cultivation. The released water through *vāykkāl* or *peru-vāykkāl* reaches to pond (*kulam*) for storing. The stored water utilised for irrigating the cultivable land. Inscriptions speak of the *talai-vāy* in the names like *enkalūr-vāy-talai*,[145] *Rājēndra-chōlan-vāy-talai*,[146] *Mummudi-chōlamankalattūr-vāy-talai*,[147] *pattāli-vati-enkira-vāy-talai*,[148] etc. which were the important *vāy-talai* found in the *Chōlamandalam* region.

The mechanism of flowing water from a tank, *ēri*, *kulam*, etc. is by gravitation. This is possible through a sluice (*talai-vāy*/*madagu*). Released out water through sluice from the river would flow through *peru-vāykkāl* (feeder channel), *siru-vāykkāl* (supply channel), *ut-ciru-vāykkāl* (sub-channel) and *kannāru* a small canal feed the water to the land.[149] The *kannāru* which is a small channel supply water to the agricultural field. There is a reference to in Uttiramērur inscriptions to *vati-vāykkāl*, which is a type of layout registered in the inscription from *brahmadēya* settlements.[150] This is the layout of canal-based irrigation system in the Kaveri delta region of the *Chōlamandalam*. There was a separate person who looked after the distribution of the water through the *vāykkāl*, who was referred to as *talaivāyar*.

The *kinaru* (well) is another important source of irrigation, mostly used for irrigation in the individual plots of land. The farmers' utilised traditional methods of irrigating the agricultural field in which they used a device called *kavalai* or *kamalai* for lifting out water from deep wells and a manual set up called *ēttram* (mote), for shallow wells were used.[151] The *kamalai* is an animal-drawn device used to lift water from deeper depths. It consists of a leather bucket and discharging spout on one side at the bottom. The bucket has 150-200 liters of capacity and is pulled by pairs of bullocks. Two ropes are attached to the bucket, one at the top for filling the bucket through a pulley, the other at spout vertically as long as the water is lifted. This helps to prevent the water from pouring out while being lifted. As the *ēttram* comes to the surface, the spout becomes horizontal and opens up to pour the water on the channel. A pair of bullocks or buffalos pulls up the bucket by walking alone a slope where they obtain the advantage of their body weight. The animals are trained to climb back up the slope while the bucket is lowered into the well. The mote (*ēttram*) can give a discharge up to 10,000-15,000 liters/hr from a depth of about 4 to 10 m. Cattle were used for cultivation and irrigation purposes. They were employed in ploughing, lifting water, threshing, etc.[152] Wells were connected to fields mainly to supplement irrigation from the lakes and tanks. In some areas, wells became an important source of artificial irrigation.

Maintenance and Management of Irrigation

The maintenance and management of water sources are another important part of the irrigation system. The construction and renovation work of all major water bodies like a tank, channel, and reservoir were the responsibility of the ruler, while the maintenance work fell with the village bodies of landlords, temple as well as rich merchants. Many inscriptions in medieval Tamil country speak of the irrigation sources and their management system. For illustration, a Chola inscription of the 10th century CE refers to the dredging arrangement made for a tank by the assembly of *Nayadhira-mangalam*.[153] The maintenance work is known as *maramat*, which was done regularly. The *maramat* works mostly done by the temple authorities, private individuals, mercantile community, village assembly, minister of the state, and the royal government.[154] In the village level the local assembly was given the responsibility to deepen the tank and to repair the pond regularly. In most of the Chola villages *ēri-vāriyam* the tank supervision committee looked after the maintenance and repair works of the tank. The well-known Uttiramērur inscription of Parantaka Chola I (907-955 CE) gives an elaborate description of the rules regarding the composition of this committee. There were six members called *ēri-vāriyap-perumakkal* forming the tank maintenance committee to represent 6 out of 30 *kudumbus*. The committee was in the main, concerned with expanding of water resources and their utilisation for the maintenance of irrigation works.[155]

In medieval Tamil country there were a group of people were in-charge of managing the water bodies. A Tiruvaduturai inscription speaks of a committee known as *vāyttalai-kulai-araiyarkal*, who was in-charge of head-sluice and banks of the canal.[156] In Karandai plates of Rajendra Chola I (issued during his 8th regnal year in 1019 CE), the in-charge of *ēri* are registered as *ēri-araiyarkal* and *kulattār*. The *ēri-araiyarkal* was the manager of the tank *Tri-bhuvana-mahādēvi-pērēri* and the *kulattār*, also known as *talai-vāyar* was in-charge of releasing out the water from the *ēri* through a sluice (*madagu*). The inscription also refers to a land grant called *vettappēru*, which was given to the *ēri-araiyarkal*, who maintained the big *ēri*.[157]

In the Pandya country, there was a separate community known as *madaiyar*, who was in-charge of releasing water through *madai*.[158] And *nīrpāytchi* or *nīrkatti/thannikatti* is an employee directly involved in watering the land. They received mostly some share or *karukka nel* as their remuneration from the landlord. Similarly, a Pandya inscription mentions the certain local bodies were functioning under the *sabha* or *ūr* primarily for the maintenance purpose. An inscription of Vira Pandya found at Srivilliputhur (c. 879 CE) records the existence of an assembly called *ēri-vāriyap-perumakkal*,[159] who looked after the maintenance of the *ēri* (tank). The main function of the committee was to store water full-fledged for the upcoming years, to get the slit removed from the tanks. For the maintenance activities, special endowments were made by the king. In some times a special tax called '*ēri-āyam*' was collected from the peasants of the village for its maintenance.[160]

In the village level, the *sabha* and its member *sabhaiyār* had the right to control water bodies especially head sluice, *vāy-talai*.[161] There were also different people involved in the control of water bodies in rural areas. *Kulattār*, *madaiyar*, *talaivāyar*, and *talai-vāy-chchānrōr* are in-charge of water sources, who involved in control and distribution of water. Of them, *talai-vay-chchānrōr* was in-charge of operating head sluice to regulate water from the river to supply channel.[162] *Vēttappēru* was a sum offered to the individual who was in-charge maintained the head sluice.[163] Y. Subbarayalu views that the term *vettappēru* is the land set apart for the use of the *talaivāy* people, those who looked after head sluice. An inscription from Tiruchirappalli district refers to the *vettappēru* land given to the *talaivāyar* by the local *sabha*. Another inscription from the same district refers to the sale of their *vettappēru* land by the *talaivāy* group consisting of eleven members.[164] In every aspect of irrigation the private individuals had their share and it applied even to the maintenance of sluices.[165] The early Tamils had a considerable skill, experienced not only in constructing new tanks, canals, and new water bodies but also in the continuous maintenance and repair works of water sources.

Water Tax

The water taxes are differently recorded in inscriptions. The Pallava records mention about different water taxes such as *nīrkkirai*, *nīrk-kūli*, *nīr-vilai*, *nīr-nilaikkāsu*, *nīr-vilaik-kāsu*, *nīr-amanji*, *cennīr-vetti*, etc.[166] We also find terms like *vetti*, *amanji* and other taxes in the Pandya inscriptions. These taxes were collected according to the fertility of the soil. The revenue for wetlands includes *ēri-pāttam*, *ēri-vari*, etc.[167] and water tax for dry land were called *puncey-kadamai*, *puncey-vāram*, *nīrani*, *olukku nīr* and *olukku-nīr-pāttam*.[168] There was a separate fund created by the villagers to meet the expenses of maintaining tanks and lakes in medieval Tamil country that is known as *ēri-mutal*. The special watch and ward staff to supervise and report breaches was called as *ēri-kāval*, *vettiyāns*, etc.[169] K. Rajan has noticed two kinds of taxes namely, *pāsi-pāttam* and *mīn-pāttam*, which were levied for having fishing rights in tanks of the villages.[170] The lease for fishing right and various charges brought the income from tanks to be used for their maintenance, repairs, and other works.

The Chola inscriptions speak of *nīrk-kūli*, which was the only registered tax as water levy. *Āttrup-pāttam*, was a special tax levied on water taken from the river for irrigation.[171] The *ēri-āyam*, the tax which was collected by village assembly from peasants to maintain and upkeep of irrigation tank.[172] The *vetti*, a term used for compulsory labour in the Chola territory who involved in repair the banks of river and tank. The epigraphical phrase '*nīr-pāya-kulamum karaiyum akki*'[173] clearly describes that the tank with the bank was created intentionally to flow the water into the tank.

Conclusion

From the foregoing account, it is discernible that agriculture is the foundation of the economy of Tamil country since very early times. Most of the pastoral population in Tamil country was largely dependent on agriculture for their subsistence. The agriculturists were an important social group, played a vital role in the growth of the agrarian economy. They were aware of different soil types, the best crops to grow, and the various irrigation systems suitable for the cultivation of different food crops. They had attempted to study all aspects of agriculture relating to seeds, their storage, and vigour. In the five geographical divisions of the Sangam age, the *marutam* region was the fertile zone fit for all cultivation, as it had more water resources. During the medieval period, the land was classified, according to its fertility, as *menpulam* (fertile land), *pinpulam* (dry land), *vanpulam* (hard land), and *kalarnilam* or *uvarnilam* (salty land). The *menpulam* yielded rich produce on a variety of crops, but *pinpulam* was cultivated only with dry crops due to limited irrigation facilities. The yield from *vanpulam* was limited, while *kalarnilam* was unfit for cultivation.

The early Tamils cultivated a variety of food crops, domesticated cattle for farm use, and developed suitable farming implements. They took measures to protect the crops carefully knowing that each crop exhausted nutrients of the soil they applied manures to the field before raising the next crops or adopted rotation of crops. These practices were improved and refined by successive generations of farmers and handed down to posterity as a traditional system of agriculture. The traditional system of cultivation performed by both male and female peasants' laboriously; with the result, food was produced in abundance in the early period. In the harvest operation, both men and women and even children were engaged. The removal of weeds and transplantation of seedlings was done almost exclusively by women. When the sown seeds had begun to sprout care was taken by women by maintaining watch and ward. Numerous references are in the *Aham* works of the *Sangam* literature to girls engaged in watering the fields entering into remain adventures.

The agriculturists in the early and medieval Tamil country were given much importance to the use of specific kinds of agricultural implements or tools in their agricultural operations. Many tools were needed for agriculture, from ploughing to harvesting, were manufactured. The basic device for tilling of soil was the plough which was variously known as *ēr*, *kalappai*, *mēli*, *nānjil*, etc. Due to their technical skill and knowledge, the farmers preferred a bend plough, which would assist a good harvest. They adopted certain traditional techniques such as planning the plough in a vertical position. Such an age-old ancient traditional custom continues to exist even today in the rural areas of Tamil Nadu. Ancient implements are still in vogue.

In the irrigation of agricultural fields, both natural and artificial water resources were used by the farmers in the process of cultivation. The earliest irrigation attempt was confined mainly to using the floodwaters of rivers. Since the rivers of the region were not perennial in all seasons, several irrigation techniques were developed to ensure an adequate and continuous supply of water. They constructed several water bodies like dam, tank, and lake, which were used as water storage systems and the people regulated and distributed the water from the different water bodies using sluices and shutters. They had also adopted tank irrigation as the main source of water for their lands and whenever the monsoon failed and tank got dried up, they led dug wells for tapping sub-soil water. The early Tamils started construction of a lot of sluices and shutters during the medieval period. They used traditional methods of watering the field in which the farmers used a bullock-propelled device for bailing out water from deep wells.

Thus, the agricultural activities in south India date back to the Neolithic period and have undergone numerous changes and developments during the long history from the early historic period to the present times. The natural fertility and richness of the soil supported the early Tamils to engage themselves in agriculture in almost every part of the land which was more valuable in the delta areas than elsewhere. The Tamils of early and medieval Tamil country were well aware of the fact that a pamper harvest and rich agriculture yield will keep the state away from famine. As a consequence agriculture was the noble profession of the state surpassed and dominates all the other activities. The agriculture was linked with the different aspects of the life of the early Tamil society. The relationship, which existed between agriculture and other aspects such as politics, religion, society, and nature, too suggests the importance of agriculture pursuits.

Notes and References

1. Brain Murton, 'The Emergence of Sedentary Agriculture in Interior Tamilnadu in the Thirteenth Century', in Kenneth R.Hall (ed.), *Structure and Society in Early South India: Essays in Honour of Noboru Karashima*, New Delhi, 2004, p. 160.
2. H.N. Dubey, 'Agriculture in the Age of Sangam', in Lalanji Gopal and V.C. Srivastava (eds.), *History of Agriculture in India (up to 1200 A.D.*), Vol. V, Part. I, New Delhi, 2008, p. 415.
3. For more details about Kodumanal see K.Rajan and V.P. Yatheeskumar, 'Cultural Transformation from Iron Age to Early Historic Times: A case Study of the Vaigai River Valley, Tamil Nadu', in Appasamy Murugaiyan (ed.), *New Dimensions in Tamil Epigraphy*, Cre-A, Chennai, 2012, p.177; for details of Māngudi site see Dorian Q Fuller, *Archaeobotany of Early Historic Sites in South India*, Institute of Archaeology, University College of London, London, 2005, pp.1-3; see webpage http://www.ucl.ac.uk./archaeology/staff/profiles/fuller/tamil.htm
4. K.S. Ramachandran, *Archaeology in South India*: *Tamil Nadu*, Delhi, 1980, p. 207; also see K. Rajan, "Situating Early Historic Times of Tamil Nadu", *Presidential Address delivered at Sixty-eighth Session of Indian History Congress*, Delhi University, Delhi, 28-30 December, 2007, pp. 3-7; Upinder Singh, *A History of Ancient and Early Medieval India*, New Delhi, 2009, p. 128.
5. Alexander Rea, British Archaeologist, himself had done a detailed investigation of the sites during the period between 1899-1905 and discovered several artefacts, which was on time catalogued and documented in his book titled "*Catalogue of the Prehistoric Antiquities from Ādichanallur and Perembair*" in 1915.
6. B. Sasisekaran, *et.al*. "Adichanallur: A Prehistoric Mining Site", *Indian Journal of History of Science*, 45.3 (2010), pp. 373-375.
7. T.M. Srinivasan, "Agricultural Practices as gleaned from the Tamil Literature of the Sangam age", *Indian Journal of History of Science*, 51.2.1 (2016), pp.167, 168.
8. H.N.Dubey, *op.cit*., pp.415, 416.
9. *Maduraikānchi*, written by Mānkuti Marutanār, is the longest poem in the *Pattupāttu* collection, consisting of 792 lines mainly in the *akavel metre*. It gives a good description about the city of Madurai and the achievements of the Pandya king Nedunceliyan.
10. *Perumbānāttruppadai* (guide for bards with a large lute), written by Uruttirankannanar in the praise of the ruler of Kanchi Tondaiman,

Ilantiraiyan, consisting of 500 lines, provides a graphic account of the five ecological *tinais*.

11. *Malaipatukadām*, is one of the collection in the *Pattupattu* literature, authored by Perunkunrūr Perunkancikana. It consists of 583 lines that describe the nature scenes, the people and the culture of mountain countryside under the king Nannan.
12. Cited by Vijaya Ramaswamy 'The History of Agriculture in South India', in Lalanji Gopal and V.C. Srivastava, *op.cit.*, p. 619.
13. *Thirukkural*, written by Thiruvalluvar, is one of the oldest of extant Tamil books and generally accepted as belonging to the second century CE. *Thirukkural's* approach to moral doctrine is marked by a very thorough knowledge of human psychology and a desire to help imperfect men with practical hints in the struggle against evil. It is a poetic composition of great antiquity in the Tamil literature; see K.Mavali Rajan, "Agriculture in Early Tamil Country", *Central India Journal of Historical and Archaeological Research*, Vol. 2, No. 7, July-September 2013.
14. *Thirukkuaral*: *Kural*: 1032; C. Rajagopalachari, *Kural, the Great Book of Tiru-Valluvar*, Mumbai, 2005, pp.108-110; the kural '*ulavōr ulakattārkku āniagthāt trāthu eluvārai ellām poruttu*'.
15. *Kural*: 1036; '*uluvinār kaimataṅgin illai vilaivathūvum vittem en pārkkum nilai*'.
16. *Kural*: 1031; '*sulantrrum ērp pinnathu ulagam athaaāl ulanthum ulavē thalai*'.
17. *Kural*: 1033; '*uluthundu vālvāre vālvarmat trellām tholuthundu pincel pavar*'.
18. *Kural*: 1035; '*iravār irappārkondru ēvār karavāthu kaiseithoon mālai yavar*'.
19. *Kural*: 1038; '*eārinum nantrāl eruviduthe kattapin neerinum nandrathan kāppu*'.
20. H.N. Dubey, *op.cit.*, p. 416.
21. K.A. Nilakanta Sastri and G. Srinivasachari, *Advanced History of India*, Madras, 1957, p. 179.
22. K. Mavali Rajan, "Agriculture in Early Tamil Country", *Central India Journal of Historical and Archaeological Research*, Vol. 2, No. 7, July-September 2013, p. 17.
23. K.K. Pillay, *A Social History of Tamils*, Vol. I, 2nd edn., University of Madras, 1975, p. 13.
24. K.Mavali Rajan, "Geographical Features of Early Tamilakam as Portrayed by Tamil Literary Texts", *Journal of Modern Thamizh Research*, Vol.6, No.3, July-September 2018, pp. 599-605.
25. *Tolkāppiyam*, written by Tolkāppiyar, is the most ancient Tamil grammar text and the oldest surviving work of Tamil literature. It consists of three books (*athikāram*) namely the *eluttathikāram* (letter), *sollathikāram* (word) and *porulathikāram* (subject matter) i.e. prosody, rhetoric,

poetics. The each book consists of nine chapters (*iyal*) with a cumulative total of 1612 sutras in the *nūrpa* meter. It is a comprehensive text on grammar and includes sutras on orthography, phonology, etymology, morphology, semantics, prosody, sentence structure and the significance of context in language. For further reading see D. Albert, *Tolkāppiyar Tolkāppiyam Phonology and Morphology*, International Institute of Tamil Studies, Chennai, 1985.

26. *Tolkāppiyam, Porulathikāram*: 5; Part I published by N.Ponnaiah, Tirumakal Press, Chunnakam, 1948, p.16.
27. K. Sivathamby, "Early South Indian Society and Economy: The Tinai Concept", *Social Scientist*, Vol.3, No.5 (December 1974), p. 28; for more details see T.M. Srinivasan, *op.cit*., p.170.
28. *Ibid*., p. 35.
29. Ganapathy Subbiah, 'Order of Hierarchy in the Realm of Religion and Society: An Introspective view from Back and Forth in Indian History', in K.Mavali Rajan, et.al. (eds.), *Facets of Temple Culture: Perspectives on Religious and Social Traditions in Early Medieval India*, New Delhi, 2018, p. 7.
30. K. Rajan, 'Archaeology of Tamil Nadu: Early Historic period', in Domodaran *et.al*. (eds.), Tamil Nadu: Archaeological Perspectives, Chennai, 1999; cited by Smriti Haricharan and Naresh Keerthi, "Can the *tinai* help to Understand the Iron age Early Historic Landscape of Tamil Nadu?", *World Archaeology*, 2004, pp. 641-660. For more information see the website http://dx.doi.org/DDI:10.1080/00438243.2014.953709).
31. Radhika Rajamani, *Society in Early Historic Tamilakam*, Delhi, 2009, p. 31; see also B.D. Chattopadhyaya, *The Concept of Bharatavarsha and other Essays*, State University of New York Press (first published by Permanent Black), Albany, 2018, p. 41.
32. Kamil Zvelebil, "Tamil Poetry 2000 years ago", *Tamil Culture*, Vol.10, Madras, 1963, p. 39.
33. Burton Stein, "Cultural and the Historical Geography of Tamil Country", *The Journal of Asian Studies*, Vol. 37, No. 1 (November 1977), p. 9.
34. Kamil Zvelebil, *The Smile of Murugan on Tamil Literature of South India*, Leiden, 1973, p. 97.
35. *Ahanānūru:* 172: 6-13 and *Pattinappālai:* 1188 mentions the sandalwood and *akil* of the Chera country arriving in Kaverippattinam.
36. K.K. Pillai, *op.cit*., p.13.
37. Kamil Zvelebil, *The Smile of Murugan on Tamil Literature of South India*, p. 99.
38. Radhika Rajamani, *op.cit*., p. 32.
39. P.T. Srinivasa Iyengar, *History of Tamils: From the Earliest times to 600 A.D.*, Madras, 1926, p. 2.
40. *Puranānūru*: 13:11; *Ainkurunūru*: 3: 8.
41. T.M. Srinivasan, *op.cit*., p.171.

42. Radhika Rajamani, *op.cit.*, p.32.
43. *Ahanānūru*: 180:1-2; 60:1-3.
44. *Puranānūru*: 313:5.
45. K. Sivathamby, *op.cit.*, p.26; *Silappadikāram* speak of;
    mullaiyum kurinjiyum muramaiyir trinthu
    nalliyal palittu nadunkkuthuya kuruttup
    pālai yenpothōr padivang kollum (*Silappadikāram: kādukānkathai*: 64-66).
46. *Ahanānūru*: 121:11; 337:11.
47. *Puranānūru*: 219:2.
48. T.M. Srinivasan, *op.cit.*, pp.170-172.
49. *Tolkappiyam: Porulathikāram, Akattinai Iyal*: 3.
50. Kamil Zvelebil, *The Smile of Murugan on Tamil Literature of South India*, p. 97.
51. K.A.Nilakanta Sastri, *Sangam Literature: Its Cults and Culture*, Madras, 1972, pp. 28-30; also see T.M. Srinivasan, *op.cit.*, pp.169-173.
52. B.D.Chattopadhyaya, *The Concept of Bharatavarsha and other Essays*, State University of New York Press (first published by Permanent Black), Albany, 2018, pp.41-43. For more information see J.V. Chelliah, *Pattupattu: Ten Tamil Idylls*, 2nd edn. Tirunelveli South India Saiva Siddanta works Publishing Society, Madras, 1962, pp. 73-75.
53. Smriti Haricharan and Naresh Keerthi, "Can the *tinai* help to Understand the Iron age Early Historic Landscape of Tamil Nadu?", *World Archaeology*, 2004, pp. 645-647.
54. Brain Murton, *op.cit.*, pp.179, 180.
55. T.K.Venkata Subramanian, *Environment and Urbanization in early Tamilakam*, Thanjavur, 1988, p.7.
56. *Nāladiyār*: 367; composed by Jain monks, is a Tamil poetic work of didactic nature, belonging to *Patinenkeelkanakku* work of Tamil literature, deals with morals and ethics, extolling righteous behaviour. This text belongs to post-*Sangam* period corresponding to between first and fifth century CE.
57. *S.I.I.*, Vol. II section I, nos. 9 and 22; Vol. II, p.117.
58. T.K.Venkata Subramanian, *op.cit.*, p.7.
59. T.N.Subramaniam, "Pallankovil Jaina Copper-plate Grant of Early Pallava Period", *Transactions of the Archaeological Society of South India* (TASSI), Vol. 5, 1958-59, p. 76.
60. Chithra Madhavan, *History and Culture of Tamil Nadu- As Gleaned from the Sanskrit Inscriptions*, Vol. I, New Delhi, 2005, pp. 104-105.
61. *S.I.I.*, Vol. II, nos. 74, 1, 37, p. 367.
62. *A.R.E.*, no. 17 of 1908.
63. *A.R.E.*, nos. 62 and 66 of 1916.

64. Vijay Ramaswamy, *op.cit.*, p. 622.
65. *Ibid.*, p. 630.
66. Kathleen D.Morrison, et.al., "Typological Schemes and Agricultural Change: Beyond Boserup in pre-colonial South India", *Current Anthropology*, Vol. 37, No. 4, August – October 1996, p.592.
67. L.S. Leshnik, *The South India Megalithic Burials: the Pandukal Complex*, Wiesbaden, 1974, p. 63.
68. Irfan Habib, *Essays in Indian History- towards a Marxist Perception*, New Delhi, 2001, p.127.
69. *Rig-Veda*: IV, 58.8; VI, 91.1 cited by A.L.Yadav, 'Some Materials for the study of Agriculture in Vedic India: Problems and Perspectives', in Lalanji Gopal and V.C. Srivastava, *op.cit.*, p. 237.
70. *Ahanānūru*: 224: 4.
71. Rajan Gurukkal, *Social Formations of Early South India*, New Delhi, 2010, p.142.
72. T.M. Srinivasan, *op.cit.*, p.174.
73. *Kambar, erelupadu*, verses 3 to 14, 35, 55, 63, 64, and 65.
74. *Pattinappālai*: II. 205-207; A. Appadorai, *Economic Conditions in South India (1000-1500 A.D.)*, Vol. I (reprint), University of Madras, Madras, 1990, pp. 234-235.
75. *Pallu* works of the 17th century gives details of paddy cultivation. There are many *pallu* literatures in late medieval Tamilnadu. The *Mukkūdal Pallu* occupies the first and foremost place. The *Mukkūdal Pallu*, documented in 1670, and *Sengōttu Pallu* in 1850 which collectively mention 90 rice varieties. So far, around, 270-300 traditional rice varieties and 110 Bullocks types have been documented by the authors in these books. Still now, some of the songs are sung by the Pallas of Tamil Nadu.
76. *Mukkūdal Pallu*, V.110.
77. A.Sarada Raju, *Economic Conditions in the Madras Presidency (1800-1850)*, University of Madras, Madras, 1941, p.55.
78. *Ibid*.
79. *Perumbānāttruppadai*: 201.
80. *Puranānūru*: 316:6.
81. *Ahanānūru* : 393: 12.
82. A.Sarada Raju, *op.cit.*, p.102.
83. Sharad Patil, *Dasa-Sudra Slavery*, New Delhi, 1982, p. 251.
84. W.W. Hunter, *The Imperial Gazetteer of India*, Vol. IX, 1886, p.29.
85. *Mukkūdal Pallu*, V.34.
86. *Ibid*. VV.77.109; There is a popular saying in Tamil that '*Ādi pattam thēdi vithai*' meaning the Tamil month *Ādi* is the best month for sowing the seeds.
87. *Ibid.*, V. 34.
88. K.P. Padmanaba Menon, *History of Kerala*, Vol. I, Ernakulum, 1924, pp. 98-99.

89. The Pallas also known as *Mallar* is a class of Agricultural labourers, believed to be one of the earliest inhabitants of Tamil country. For centuries together they were the cultivators of the land. Tilling of the soil and cultivation of paddy has been down the ages mainly in the hands of Palla community. The following poem (seyyul-104) of *Thiruvēttainallur Ayyanār Pallu*, composed in 1882 CE by Subramaniya Nāvalar, narrates beautifully the greatness of the *ulavu* (forming) and the involvement of the Mallar community in different forming activities; (see P.V.Nagarajan, *Thiruvēttainallur Ayyanār Pallu*,1992, p.168)

    ulavumallar thirandu sañsuvang kondu
    ulungkālai kal-anaittum paṭṭrik kondupōi
    pulavartamil manakkum nallūrt dharman
    pillaiyar kulappuravil utkitaich cheyyal
    valavaradi yilninra setiyum vetti
    varampil udaiuyarttip punal niruttik
    kulavu kanakkan ōrai rāsatha vēlaiyum vanthu
    kūdum kadikaiyil nālēraip pūttinārē

90. Francis Buchanan, *A Journey from Madras, Through the Countries of Mysore, Canara and Malabar*, Vo.II, New Delhi, 1988, pp. 57-58.
91. *Mukkūdal Pallu*, V. 121.
92. *Ibid.*, VV. 122.
93. N.V. Jeyaraman, *Tamil Ilakkiyattil Vēlānamai Ariviyal* (Tamil), Madras, 1978, p.16.
94. *Mukkūdal Pallu*, V.110; *Thirumalai Murugan Pallu*, V. 143.
95. *Mukkūdal Pallu*, V.108.
96. *Kannudaiyamman Pallu*, V.89.
97. *Mukkūdal Pallu*, V.138.
98. *Ibid.*
99. *Ibid.*, VV.138-141.
100. *Porunarāttruppatai*: 291-95 (translated by J.V.Chelliah); cited by M.Arokiaswami, *The Classical Age of Tamils*, University of Madras, Madras, 1972, p.69.
101. K. Rajan, *Ancient Irrigation Technology: Sluice Technology in Tamil Nadu*, Thanjavur, 2008, p. .
102. *Ibid.*, pp. 1, 2.
103. Gugulothu Ravi and B. Babu Rao, "Irrigation as a Social Responsibility: A case study of Kakatiya Period", *South Indian History Congress Thirty Ninth Annual Session Proceedings*, Hyderabad, 2019, p. 323.
104. T.M.Srinivasan, *Irrigation and Water Supply, South India, 200 BC- 1600 AD*, Madras, 1991, p. 1.
105. Irfan Habib, *op.cit.*, p. 127.

106. Burton Stein, *Peasant State and Society in Medieval South India*, Delhi, 1985, pp. 24-25.
107. K.R. Srinivasan and N.R. Banerjee, "A Survey of South Indian Megalithic", *Ancient India*, No. IX, Delhi, 1953, pp.103-105.
108. K.V. Raman, 'Irrigation in South India (up to 1300 A.D.): Techniques and Management' in Lallanji Gopal and V.C.Srivastava, *op.cit.*, pp.500, 501.
109. Kathleen D. Morrison, et.al., *op.cit.*, p. 594.
110. Y. Subbarayalu, *South India under the Cholas*, New Delhi, 2012; see N.Kathiravan and N.Athiyaman, 'Irrigation System of Kaveri Delta region: A case Study of Cembian Madevi Village', in S.Rajavelu et.al. (eds.), *Amaravati: Felicitation Volume for Professor P.Shanmugam*, Chennai, 2017, p. 271.
111. Burton Stein, *op.cit.*, p. 151.
112. R.Champakalakshmi, 'Reappraisal of a Brahmanical Institution: The *Brahmadeya* and its Ramification in Early Medieval South India' in Kenneth R. Hall (ed.), *op.cit.*, pp. 61, 75.
113. S.Chandni Bi, *Urban Centres of Pondicherry- through the Ages*, New Delhi, 2006, p. 91.
114. Noboru Karashima, *South Indian History and Society, Studies from Inscriptions (850-1800 CE)*, New Delhi, 1984, pp.44-49.
115. S.Chandni Bi, '*Brahmadēyas* verses *Vellanvagai*: Socio Cultural Hierarchy in Medieval South India', in K.Mavali Rajan, et.al. (eds.), *Facets of Temple Culture*, p.44.
116. Hinduja Ramesh "Aspects of Irrigation System of Pallava and Pandya dynasty: A Comparative Study from the Inscriptions (7-10th century CE)", *South Indian History Congress Thirty Eighth Session Proceedings*, Calicut, 2018, p.515.
117. A. Appadorai, *op.cit.*, pp.194 and 195.
118. Hinduja Ramesh, *op.cit.*, p.517.
119. C. Minakshi, *Administration and Social Life under the Pallavas*, University of Madras, Madras, 1938, pp.102-106.
120. K.Rajan, *Ancient Irrigation Technology*, p.18.
121. K.Mavali Rajan and Suman Saha, "Sources of Water Supply and Water Management during the Chola period", *Indian Historical Studies*, Vol. XI, No.1, October 2014, p. 89.
122. *A.R.E.*, no. 417 of 1912.
123. K.Rajan, *Ancient Irrigation Technology*, p. 5.
124. Rajan Gurukkal, "Aspects of Reservoir System of Irrigation in early Pandya State", *Studies in History*, Vol.2, New Delhi, 1986, pp. 155-156.
125. K.Mavali Rajan and Suman Saha, *op.cit.*, p. 90.
126. P. Shanmugam, *The Revenue System of the Cholas, 850-1259*, Chennai, 1987, p. 48.
127. *S.I.I.*, Vol. II, no. 342 and Vol. I, no. 151.

128. S. Jeyaseela Stephen, (ed.), *The Land, Peasantry and Peasant Life in India*, New Delhi, 2008, p. 114.
129. K.V. Raman, *op.cit.*, p. 501.
130. *S.I.I.*, Vol. VIII, no. 241.
131. *S.I.I.*, Vol. XXVI, no. 16.
132. *S.I.I.*, Vol. XXII, no. 27.
133. N. Kathiravan and N. Athiyaman, *op.cit.*, p. 272.
134. *S.I.I.*, Vol. XIII, no.146; see Y.Subbarayalu, 'Conception and Understanding of Some Technical Terms in Tamil Inscriptions' in Appasamy Murugaiyan (ed.), *New Dimensions in Tamil Epigraphy*, Cre-A, Chennai, 2012, p. 36.
135. *S.I.I.*, Vol. VI, no.316.
136. *S.I.I.*, Vol. XIX, no.66.
137. *A.R.E.*, no.123 of 1927.
138. *A.R.E.*, no. 294 of 1927.
139. *S.I.I.*, Vol. III, no.310.
140. *S.I.I.*, Vol. X, no.568.
141. *S.I.I.*, Vol. III, no.151.
142. Hinduja Ramesh, *op.cit.*, p.515.
143. *I.P.S.*, no.124, p.121. The inscription located on the wall of north prakara of Sundararajaperumal temple, Irumbanadu, Tirumayam Taluk.
144. K.R.Sankaran, "Water Right and Irrigation under the Chola State (Preliminary Survey)", *South Indian History Congress Thirty Eighth Annual Session Proceedings*, Calicut, 2018, p. 568.
145. *S.I.I.*, Vol. XIII, no. 151.
146. *S.I.I.*, Vol. XIX, no. 105.
147. *A.R.E.*, no. 276 of 1927.
148. *A.R.E.*, no. 434 of 1908.
149. K. R. Sankaran, *op.cit.*, p. 568.
150. *Ibid.*, p. 569.
151. W.W.Hunter, *op.cit.*, p.29.
152. K. Mavali Rajan, *Medieval Tamil Society and Agrarian Slavery*, Kolkata, 2014, p. 129.
153. *Annual Report on Indian Epigraphy (A.R.I.E.)*, 1945-46, Introduction part, p. 4.
154. James Heitzman, *Gift of Power, Lordship in an Early Indian State*, New Delhi, 1997, p. 39.
155. K.Mavali Rajan and Suman Saha, *op.cit.*, pp. 87, 88; K.Rajan, *Ancient Irrigation Technology*, pp. 41, 63.
156. *S.I.I.*, Vol. I, no. 151.
157. Y.Subbarayalu, 'Cila ariya corrkal (some rare terms)' in Y.Subbarayalu and S.Raju (eds.), *Tamilakak Kalvettiyalum Varalarum* (Tamil), Tamil University, Thanjavur, 2001, pp.102-103.

158. K.R.Sankaran, *op.cit.*, p. 569.
159. *S.I.I.*, Vol. VI, no. 359.
160. K.A.Nilakanta Sastri, *The Colas*, University of Madras, Madras, 1955, p.531.
161. *S.I.I.*, Vol. XIII, no.151.
162. Noboru Karashima, *op.cit.*, p.44.
163. *E.I.*, Vol. XXII, p. 140.
164. *S.I.I.*, Vol. XIII, no.240; Vol. VIII, no.689; cited by Y.Subbarayalu, 'Conception and Understanding of Some Technical Terms in Tamil Inscriptions', p. 39.
165. *A.R.E.*, nos. 68 of 1908; 419 of 1923.
166. P. Shanmugam, *op.cit.*, pp. 50, 51.
167. Noboru Karashima, *op.cit.*, p. 109.
168. P.Shanmugam, *op.cit.*, p. 111.
169. K.V. Raman, *op.cit.*, p. 503.
170. K. Rajan, *Ancient Irrigation Technology*, p.40.
171. P.Shanmugam, *op.cit.*, p. 48.
172. *S.I.I.*, Vol. VII, no. 805.
173. *A.R.E.*, no. 64 of 1913.

Bibliography

Ahanānūru: Published by the South India Saiva Siddhanta Publishing Society, Tinnevelly, 1966.

Ainkurunūru: Edited with Tamil commentary by U.Ve. Swaminatha Iyer, U. Ve. Swaminatha Iyer Publication, 6th edn., Madras, 1980.

Annual Report on Epigraphy (A.R.E), 1908, 1912, 1913, 1916, 1923, 1927.

Annual Report on Indian Epigraphy (A.R.I.E.), 1945-46.

Appadorai, A., *Economic Conditions in Southern India (1000-1500 AD)*, Vol. I, University of Madras, Madras, reprint, 1990.

Appasamy Murugaiyan (ed.), *New Dimensions in Tamil Epigraphy*, Cre-A, Chennai, 2012.

Arokiaswami, M., *The Classical Age of Tamils*, University of Madras, Madras, 1972.

Burton Stein, "Cultural and the Historical Geography of Tamil Country", *The Journal of Asian Studies*, Vol. 37, No. 1 (November 1977).

---------------, *Peasant State and Society in Medieval South India*, Oxford University Press, Delhi, 1985.

Chandni Bi, S., *Urban Centres of Pondicherry- through the Ages*, Icon Publishers, New Delhi, 2006.

Chattopadhyaya, B.D., *The Concept of Bharatavarsha and other Essays*, State University of New York Press (first published by Permanent Black), Albany, 2018.

Chithra Madhavan, *History and Culture of Tamil Nadu- As Gleaned from the Sanskrit Inscriptions*, Vol. I, D.K. Printworld, New Delhi, 2005.

Epigraphia Indica, Vol. XXII, 1933-34, edited by N.P. Chakravarti, Archaeological Survey of India, Delhi, 1938.

Francis Buchanan, *A Journey from Madras, Through the Countries of Mysore, Canara and Malabar*, Vol. II, Asian Educational Service, New Delhi, 1988.

Fuller, D.Q., *Archaeobotany of Early Historic Sites in South India*, Institute of Archaeology, University College of London, London, 2005.

Gugulothu Ravi and B. Babu Rao, "Irrigation as a Social Responsibility: A case study of Kakatiya Period", *South Indian History Congress Thirty Ninth Annual Session Proceedings*, Hyderabad, 2019.

Hinduja, Ramesh "Aspects of Irrigation System of Pallava and Pandya dynasty: A comparative study from the Inscriptions (7-10th century CE)", *South Indian History Congress Thirty Eighth Session Proceedings*, Calicut, 2018.

Hunter, W.W., *The Imperial Gazetteer of India*, Vol. IX, Government of India, Delhi, 1886.

Inscription of the Pudukkottai State (*I.P.S.*), Part I, Arranged according to dynasties, published by the Government Museum, Chennai, 2002.

Irfan Habib, *Essays in Indian History- towards a Marxist Perception*, Anthem Press, New Delhi, 2002.

James Heitzman, *Gift of Power, Lordship in an Early Indian State*, Oxford University Press, New Delhi, 1997.

Jeyaraman, N.V., *Tamil Ilakkiyattil Vēlānamai Ariviyal* (Tamil), New Century Book House, Madras, 1978.

Jeyaseela Stephen, S. (ed.), *The Land, Peasantry and Peasant Life in India*, Manohar Publishers, New Delhi, 2008.

Kamil Zvelebil, "Tamil Poetry 2000 years ago", *Tamil Culture*, Vol. 10, Madras, 1963.

----------------, *The Smile of Murugan on Tamil Literature of South India*, E.J. Brill, Leiden, 1973.

Kannudaiyamman Pallu, Published by Nagarattar Publishers, Nattarasankottai, 1938.

Kathleen D.Morrison, et.al., "Typological Schemes and Agricultural Change: Beyond Boserup in pre-colonial South India", *Current Anthropology*, Vol.37, No.4, August – October 1996.

Kenneth, R. Hall (ed.), *Structure and Society in Early South India: Essays in Honour of Noboru Karashima*, Oxford University Press, New Delhi, 2004.

Lalanji Gopal and V.C.Srivastava (eds.), *History of Agriculture in India (up to 1200 A.D.)*, Vol. V, Part. I, Concept Publishing Company, New Delhi, 2008.

Leshnik, L.S., *The South India Megalithic Burials: the Pandukal Complex*, Franz Steiner Velag Gmbh, Wiesbaden, 1974.

Maduraikānchi, edited by U.Ve. Swaminatha Iyer, Chennai, 1931.

Malaipatukadām, see J.V. Chellaiah, *Pattupattu-Ten Tamil Idylls*, 2nd edn. Tirunelveli South India Saiva Siddanta Publishing Society, Madras, 1962.

Mavali Rajan K. et.al. (eds.), *Facets of Temple Culture: Perspectives on Religious and Social Traditions in Early Medieval India*, Kaveri Books, New Delhi, 2018.

Mavali Rajan K. and Suman Saha, "Sources of Water Supply and Water Management during the Chola period", *Indian Historical Studies*, Vol. XI, No.1, October 2014.

Mavali Rajan K., "Geographical Features of Early Tamilakam as Portrayed by Tamil Literary Texts", *Journal of Modern Thamizh Research*, Vol.6, No.3, July-September 2018.

-----------------, "Agriculture in Early Tamil Country", *Central India Journal of Historical and Archaeological Research*, Vol.2, No.7, July-September 2013.

---------------, *Medieval Tamil Society and Agrarian Slavery*, Maha Bodhi Book Agency, Kolkata, 2014.

Minakshi, C., *Administration and Social Life under the Pallavas*, University of Madras, Madras, 1938.

Mukkudal Pallu, edited by M. Arunachalam, 2nd edn., Madras, 1949.

Nāladiyār: Published by the South India Saiva Siddhanta Publishing Society, Tinnevelly, 1958.

Nilakanta Sastri K.A., *Sangam Literature: Its Cults and Culture*, Swathi Publications, Madras, 1972.

------------------, *The Colas*, University of Madras, Madras, 1955.

Nilakanta Sastri, K.A. and G.Srinivasachari, *Advanced History of India*, Allied Publishers, Madras, 1957.

Noboru Karashima, *South Indian History and Society, Studies from Inscriptions (850-1800 CE)*, Oxford University Press, New Delhi, 1984.

Padmanaba Menon, K.P., *History of Kerala*, Vol. I, Ernakulum, 1924.

Pattinappālai: see J.V. Chellaiah, *Pattupattu-Ten Tamil Idylls*, 2nd edn. Tirunelveli South India Saiva Siddanta Publishing Society, Madras, 1962.

Perumbānāttruppadai: edited by P.V.Somasuntaranar, South India Saiva Siddhanta Publishing Society, Tirunelveli, 1967.

Pillay, K.K., *A Social History of Tamils*, Vol. I, 2nd edn., University of Madras, Madras, 1975.

Porunarāttruppatai: edited by P.V.Somasuntaranar, South India Saiva Siddhanta Publishing Society, Tirunelveli, 1970.

Puranānūru: edited with commentary by Auvai Duraisami Pillai, South India Saiva Siddhanta Publishing Society, Tirunelveli (3rd edn.), 1956.

Radhika Rajamani, *Society in Early Historic Tamilakam*, Bharatiya Kala Prakashan, Delhi, 2009.

Rajan Gurukkal, "Aspects of Reservoir System of Irrigation in early Pandya State", *Studies in History*, Vol. 2, New Delhi, 1986.

---------------, *Social Formations of Early South India*, Oxford University Press, New Delhi, 2010.

Rajan, K., *Ancient Irrigation Technology: Sluice Technology in Tamil Nadu*, Heritage India Trust, Thanjavur, 2008.

---------------, "Situating Early Historic Times of Tamil Nadu", *Presidential Address delivered at Sixty-eighth Session of Indian History Congress*, Delhi University, Delhi, 28-30 December, 2007.

Rajavelu, S., et.al. (eds.), *Amaravati: Felicitation Volume for Professor P.Shanmugam*, Chennai, 2017.

Ramachandran, K.S., *Archaeology in South India*: *Tamil Nadu*, Sandeep Prakashan, Delhi, 1980.

Rig-Veda: IV, 58.8; VI, 91.1.

Sankaran, K.R., "Water Right and Irrigation under the Chola State (Preliminary Survey)", *South Indian History Congress Thirty Eighth Annual Session Proceedings*, Calicut, 2018.

Sasisekaran, B., *et.al.* "Adichanallur: A Prehistoric Mining Site", *Indian Journal of History of Science*, 45.3 (2010).

Sarada Raju, A., *Economic Conditions in the Madras Presidency (1800-1850)*, University of Madras, Madras, 1941.

Shanmugam, P., *The Revenue System of the Cholas, 850-1259*, New Era Publications, Madras, 1987.

Sharad Patil, *Dasa-Sudra Slavery*, Allied Publishers, New Delhi, 1982.

Sivathamby, K., "Early South Indian Society and Economy: The Tinai Concept", *Social Scientist*, Vol.3, No.5 (December 1974).

Smriti Haricharan and Naresh Keerthi, "Can the *tinai* help to understand the Iron Age Early Historic landscape of Tamilnadu?", *World Archaeology*, 2004.

South Indian Inscriptions, Vols. II, III, VI, VII, VIII, X, XIII, XIX, XXII, XXVI.

Srinivasa Iyengar P.T., *History of Tamils: From the Earliest times to 600 A.D.*, Asian Educational Services, Madras, 1926.

Srinivasan, K.R. and N.R.Banerjee, "A Survey of South Indian Megalithic", in *Ancient India*, No. IX, Delhi, 1953.

Srinivasan, T.M., "Agricultural Practices as Gleaned from the Tamil Literature of the Sangam Age", *Indian Journal of History of Science*, 51.2.1 (2016).

---------------, *Irrigation and Water Supply, South India, 200 BC-1600 AD*, New Era Publications, Madras, 1991.

Subbarayalu, Y., '*Cila ariya corrkal* (some rare terms)' in Y.Subbarayalu and S.Raju (eds.), *Tamilakak Kalvettiyalum Varalarum* (Tamil), Tamil University, Thanjavur, 2001.

-------------------, *South India under the Cholas*, Oxford University Press, New Delhi, 2012.

Subramaniam, T.N., "Pallankovil Jaina Copper-plate Grant of Early Pallava Period", *Transactions of the Archaeological Society of South India* (TASSI), Vol.5, 1958-59.

Thirukkuaral: C.Rajagopalachari, *Kural, the Great Book of Tiru-Valluvar*, Bharatiya Vidya Bhavan, Mumbai, 2005.

Thirumalaimurugan Pallu, edited by Periyavan Kavirayar, 3rd edn., Madras, 1964.

Tolkāppiyam: Porulatikāram, Akattinai Iyal, Part I published by N.Ponnaiah, Tirumakal Press, Chunnakam, 1948.

Upinder Singh, *A History of Ancient and Early Medieval India*, Pearson Publishers, New Delhi, 2009.

Venkata Subramanian T.K., *Environment and Urbanization in early Tamilakam*, Tamil University, Thanjavur, 1988.

6

Agrarian Conditions in the Kaveri Delta during the Later Cholas

V. Palanichamy

The Kaveri delta region, the fertile agricultural tract, is the core area of the Chola dynasty called Cholamandalam, which attracted human settlement from very ancient times. The Kaveri delta is lies between 10° 8' and 11° 25' North latitude and 78° 47' and 97° 52' East longitude and contains an area of 3,259 square miles. The delta is roughly triangular in shape. It is comprised of the present districts of Thanjavur, Tiruvarur and Nagapattinam districts.[1] The people of the region mostly involved in agrarian activities since agriculture was one of the main occupations of the locality, as it is in modern times; and from time immemorial irrigation has been one of the chief needs in developing agriculture. In understanding the agrarian conditions of the Kaveri delta region there are several sources available in the works of literatures and inscriptions. The inscriptional sources present the most valuable picture of agrarian conditions such as land system, land survey, land revenue assessment, cropping pattern, irrigation method, etc. during the period characterised by the presence of the Cholas in *Cholamandalam*. The present endeavor is intended to study the agrarian conditions in the Kaveri delta region during the later Cholas rule, which has been an important aspect of study in medieval south India.

In medieval agrarian society, the Brahmins and the Vellalas were the dominant landowning community, who legitimised the political power for their control over land. But the landless agricultural peasants were involved in agrarian activities in the Kaveri delta region for the development of the state economy. There is a poetic proverb among Tamils, '*chōzhanādu chōrudaithu*' which means Chola country that is a micro-region of the Kaveri delta (Thanjavur) was the "granary of South India". It consisted of numerous distinctive localities and different ecological conditions, which formed the foundation for the peasants' society. Y. Subbarayalu's book "*Political Geography of the Chola Country*", deals about the macro unit *Cholamandalam* which was divided into *nādus* (micro-regions), was considered to be a very important unit of the agrarian society.[2] After analyzing the inscriptions of the Cholas Y. Subbarayalu has identified nearly 140 *nādus* and 1070 *ūr* (villages) in *Cholamandalam*, the heartland of the Chola country. Nearly, 1300 villages are identified by Subbarayalu as the total number of villages within the micro-region that came under Cholas. It evidences that the delta region had relatively a large number of villages that were inhabited by the agrarian community. The agrarian unit the *nādus* was varied by the availability of water resources in that particular delta region.

The distribution of peasant villages in the *nādus* was also shaped by the availability of reliable irrigation sources. This is revealed by the overall density of villages in part of the Kaveri delta. Medieval south Indian Historians have estimated that there was one village per two square miles in irrigated eco-regions. In *Cholamandalam*, most of the *nādus* with reasonable boundaries fell within the range of fifteen to thirty square miles.[3] There were artisans, merchants, labourers apart from Brahmins, Vellalas, and Nāttārs who altogether formed the consistency of *nādus* with great economic stability by interacting with each other in all kinds of land relations. Kinship ties, cult practices, and defensive arrangements that the agrarian and artisan groups had with the resulted in common interests in the management of land relations.

Historians in the recent field of sequential research have been studied the agrarian conditions of medieval south India. Very recent work on agrarian society is K. Mavali Rajan's[4] '*Medieval Tamil Society and Agrarian Slavery*', which highlights the social setting of the agrarian slaves and their economic behaviours by reflecting upon the aspects of an agrarian society. Further the work spotlight the Brahmins of the medieval Tamil country, who occupied the highest position in the social hierarchy. They were not only top in social life but also the most powerful in terms of economic resources. They have engaged the peasants in the Kaveri basin, as elsewhere in Tamil country specialised in fieldwork such as ploughing, transplanting, seedlings, harvesting, and threshing the crops and other works related to agriculture. In the process of paddy cultivation, the slaves and perhaps the ordinary peasants were engaged, and sometimes they were forced by the state to build and repair irrigation tanks in the dry season. K.A. Nilakanta Sastri's[5] monumental work "*The Colas*", deals with the agricultural production and irrigation methods and also land revenue system during the medieval period of Tamil country. T.V. Sadasiva Pandarattar, [6] who wrote the book "*Pirkkālachchōlar Charittiram*" in Tamil which discusses some aspects of the Chola revenue system. The American historian Burton Stein's (1985) magnum opus "*Peasant State and Society in Medieval South India*",[7] analysis the Brahmin and non-Brahmin settlements and the peasant's conditions in medieval south India. During the medieval period in the river valleys under the 'alliance' between Brahmins and Vellalas- a high-ranking, non-Brahmin 'peasant' caste developed as 'high-caste landowners' brought under their control land, labour, and water; established their status in the agrarian system as a whole; and developed technical skills to expand the irrigation economy. All the changes took place in medieval society in a particular period.[8]

The Japanese historian Noboru Karashima[9] discusses a new agrarian order, landholding community, and assessment of land revenues and also cataloged the revenue terms during the Chola and Pandya times. R. Tirumalai[10] has written a book in the field of agrarian history, which deals with the problem connected with the land grants and agrarian practices in South India, especially in Chola and Pandya Times. It gives a clear explanation of many abstruse terms occurring in the inscriptions such as *Kudi*, *Kudinīkki*, *Kilkudi*, *Kudimai*, *Ulukudimakkal*, etc. The agrarian community was in distress, and some regulatory measures were adopted by the townships and the *Nāttār* in the heartland of the Chola and Pandya country. A. Appadorai[11] studied the agrarian society of medieval south India by examining inscriptions in Tamil and other languages, in his '*Economic Conditions in Southern India* 1000-1500 AD'. He also discussed the landholding pattern in villages and the revenue system of the Cholas based on the original inscriptions found in the Kaveri delta region. Therefore the present study carried out based on the available source materials in understanding the agrarian condition in the Kaveri delta region.

The early empires of this part of South India played a crucial role in the establishment and expansion of an agrarian order through a vast network of the agricultural village spread across the Kaveri delta. Thanjavur seems to have a collection of small villages controlled by *Muttaraiyars*, the local was based in nearby Sendalai.[12] It was during the Chola tenure at Thanjavur that the agrarian structure of the Kaveri delta took definitive form especially about the development of irrigation and technology. The agrarian expansion evidenced the prosperity of the rural economy led to the establishment of temple towns. The growth and development of the Chola State were primarily backed by the temple economy. *Nādu* unit had the priority to build more temples to strengthen the state economy as well as the extension of *nagaram* adjoined to the peasant village.

Thus, the *nādu* was identified as the basic peasant and governing unit of the Chola age. The notable feature in the Chola Kingdom at Kaveri delta region was the production of all the arable land, which was divided into two main parts *Mēlvāram* which belonged to the state and the '*Kīlvāram*' belonging to the cultivators. The majority of villages under the system called *Vellān-Vagai* (peasant tenant) had kinship communities together with specialised and kinship groups of village artisan and village servants like common irrigators.

Agrarian Order

An agrarian system is a social arrangement, involving in the use of land and its products; and its employment. In the case of medieval South India, the core of social relationships, involving the land was that between landholders and the employers. Particularly, the landholding authorities were Vellalar, Nattar and the employees were a few Sudra groups. The Japanese historian Noboru Karashima[13] has understood and analyzed some aspects of agrarian conditions viz.: (i) land, (ii) community; (iii) agriculture; and (iv) revenue in their chronological setting; with some sub-divisions under each head, for example, irrigation, cultivation, cultivator and crops being grouped under the head of agriculture. In general, the agrarian order was maintained and managed by landholders (*kāniyatchikārars*) and dominant peasant groups (*ulukudi*), chiefs, and prestigious communities. He also discussed the transactions of land properties in seven common villages on the northern bank of the Kaveri River near Tiruchirappalli, which were regarded in some sixteen inscriptions of the later Chola period. These inscriptions have survived in the Jabhukesvaram temple at Tiruvanaikkaval.[14] The purpose of the analysis is to elucidate the stage of landholding in the later Chola period, it seems that land transfers were prevalent among individuals in the lower Kaveri valley during the later of the Chola rule. This is supported by a similar analysis made on the inscriptions of the Vedaranyam temple in Thanjavur district and those of the temples in Lalgudi taluk in the Tiruchirappalli district.[15] This may have some important change occurred in the agrarian order towards the end of the Chola period.

Since the majority of people lived in rural areas, agriculture was their principal occupation. Land ownership meant a prestigious social value and dignity in medieval times and the independent land proprietor became the backbone of social life as well as the agrarian economy. The village was primarily a settlement of peasants,[16] around whom the village assembly was tied. Part of the land surrounding the village was held in common and some of the lands were subject to periodical redistribution. The periodical redistribution of common land appears to have survived in the villages of Thanjavur. Chola records confirm that there was strong evidence of communal ownership of land, namely, *sabhamanjikkam*,[17] *ūr-manjikkam*,[18] and *ūrppodu*.[19] *Sabha-vilai* is another term used in the inscription of Sundarachola from Madhurantakam records, meant for sale of an appropriated common land of the village by *sabha*.[20] Individual ownership of land was recognized. Numerous examples of alienation by sale or gift of the absolute proprietorship of the land by individuals and of the inheritance of such property from fathers to son, which has been noticed in the inscriptions of the Cholas.

The change must have taken place as a result of the economic development of the Kaveri delta during the Chola period was seems to have prepared the way of the emergence of a new mode of production in the succeeding period. *Brahmadēya* was also a mode of agrarian integration in which several settlements were brought together under the management of Brahmins. It was Brahmans who became the major beneficiaries of the production of the land despite their minority strength among the peasant population. It was also Brahmans who made crucial decisions about the utilisation of resources within the settlement of villages. In all cases, the establishment of *brahmadēya* created a comprehensive integration among a circle of established and productive villages under the central direction of a group of Brahmins.

The *periyanādu* assembly was the other core component of the nuclear area, which posed importance in agrarian life. The functioning methods of *periyanādu* assemblies differed from the *brahmadēyas* in that they were not essentially management bodies over a circle of neighbouring settlement but a legislative body for what appears to be the entire nuclear area. The *periyanādu* assemblies dominated by respectable cultivating castes, the style of these assemblies were very nearly the same as that of Brahmans and itinerant merchant associations. This is quite clear the language of the inscriptions which were ordered by the *periyanādu*, examples of such arrangements as follows:

> "Hail, Prosperity, We [are] the *chitramēli-periyanāttār*, who have the great fame for best justice, resplendent in all quarters, of the eighteen lands in the four quarters, the local merchants [and other named merchant groups] being subordinate to us. We, the above bodies having met in fall quorum..... With unanimity made this arrangement on [a date in 1235 A.D.]...."[21]

The composition of the *periyanādu* varied according to the problem with which the assembly dealt. In some inscriptions, the assembly appeared to be comprised only of agriculturists; in other, it seems the assembly-included members of local artisans and merchant associations, who were specifically mentioned as subordinate to the *periyanādu*. Finally, some of the *periyanādu* inscriptions were placed on the walls of temples in *brahmadēyas*, in which the assembly had met to confer their support and production upon the settlement of priests and the temple in which they officiated. These integrated areas were normally dominated by the high caste warriors of peasants especially various branches of the Vellala castes, artisans and merchant groups, and by the dual divisions of right-hand (*valangai*) and left-hand (*idangai*) castes.

Categories of Land

The contemporary inscriptions of the Cholas reveal that land was categorised into various types. They were: wetlands (*nañjai*), dry land (*puñjai*), garden (*nandavanam*), and riverside land (*padugai*, also called *āttrupadugai*). These lands were categorised based on the soil condition and availability of water resources. The Chola inscriptions refer to *nañjai*[22] lands easily irrigated by river waters. They were also called by various indigenous names such as *nīrnilam* (irrigated lands), *vilainilam* (productive lands), and *payirnilam*, croplands. Another inscription[23] state that an individual converted a fallow land into a wetland, which yielded two seasonal crops (*irupūvilaiyum-nilam*). *Kuruvai* lands referred to monsoon paddy land and *pāsanam* to winter paddy lands. Drylands, known as *puñjai*, were entirely dependent upon the monsoon.

The inscription of Thanjavur refer to dry lands as *kollai*,[24] some non-subsistent grains such as *cholam*, *kambu*, pulses, and oilseeds were cultivated in *kollainilam*. Another land is garden (*thōttam*) was horticultural land dependent on well water for cultivation. *Nandavanam* (flower garden) and *tōppu* (fruit garden) are mentioned in epigraphs. Sembian Irukkuvel, made a gift of the land after purchase, to the temple of Tiruvalandurai to rear garden. In an instance[25] a gift of the garden was made to the temple at Tirukkurukkutturai. The gardens were donated to the temple to ensure the supply of flowers for worship to deity. *Padugai* were silt land in river beds. The changing geographical conditions brought this new type of very fertile soil commercial and value crops such as sugarcane and betel were generally grown in Kumbhakonam nine and a half *vēli* of *padugai* land were cultivated.[26] Forest lands (*kādu*) were used for cultivation during the Cholas period. The term *kādu* is also to denote the semi-dry land under cultivation.

Land Grants

The development of lands was one of the economic activities that medieval south Indian temples carryout. American historian Burton Stein[27] has pointed out that the temple-directed regional agricultural development grew out of the nature of the endowments which temples received. Endowments were made to provide income for temple maintenance, for festivals, honouring the deities, and for good offerings to the deities. The endowment typically involved the provision of a perpetual service for the merit of the donor or someone designated by the donor. To provide for these services, permanent earning resources had to be established, the proceeds from which would pay for the specified service. Besides he explains that the land endowments were two kinds: land and money. Village or land endowments usually gave the temple the major share of income (*mēlvāram*) while the cultivators retained the minor share (*kudivāram*).[28] The temple, thus, did not have ownership over the endowed land but command over a share of its income.

There were important responsibilities towards the endowed lands. During the Chola period, for example, a series of Srirangam temple inscriptions from the reign of Kulottunga I (1070-1118 CE) describe a massive process of redevelopment of a large portion of temple lands buried under sand by floods of the Kaveri River. Under the auspices of the temple, these ruined lands were leased on a new basis for reclamation and ultimate re-cultivation.[29] Rajaraja I gave extensive lands as *dēvadāna* to the temple of Rajarajesvaram from all over his empire for the expenses required for the supreme lord (*Paramasivam*) of the sacred stone temple (*karrali*). In the medieval period, we can see inscriptional records that show the most part those took the form of gifts of land to gods. Some inscription reveals that the king Rajaraja donated land to priests (*brahmadēyam)* on behalf of the service of the Brahmins in the temple of Thanjavur and charitable institutions. The revenue from these villages was settled orally and then engraved on stone in the temple of Thanjavur.

In 918 CE Sembian Irrukkuvel appealed to the Chola King Parantaka I[30] to grant 3 *velis* of wetland to be denoted as tenant-free (*kudinīnkiya dēvadāna*) land in the holdings of Andavanallur. Accordingly, he was granted 3 *vēlis* of land with the stipulation that he had to measure out 360 *kalams* of paddy to the local temple in the village. Seven years later, the King, however, directed that Arayan Vira Cholan should be inducted as an inextinguishable occupant '*Kudinīkka dēvadānam'* into the land. Consequently, Sembian Irukkuvel directed his revenue officer of Urattur Kurram to give effect to the royal command. Vira Cholan was, however, to measure out 300 *kalams*.[31] The customary irrigation rights were to be enjoyed, but no obligations to render free labour were to be demanded;[32] perhaps, sixty *kalams* were to be appropriated by Vira Cholan. Some years later Arayan Vira Cholan re-inducted the *ūrar* of Andavanallur as the occupants into 3 *vēlis* of land on the same terms as he had been granted. This has been enjoying and released the lands from his possession (*vittukkudutten*).[33] Another instance at Tillaiccangadu in Thanjavur a sum of 100 *kāsu*, was raised from the professional and religious groups of the locality for making certain necessary endowments in the local temples in the reign of Rajaraja I.[34] All lands held under service tenures were subject to the usual imposts, central and local, those were levied on land. The king appoints any tenant who has willing to cultivate temple land and after harvest season the king to measure the produce on its terms to his service.

Ownership of Land

Agriculture was the most important economic activity in the medieval Tamil country. The relationship of the social structure and land-control in an essentially agrarian society is elaborated by Burton Stein as follows: "The reduction of forest and expansion of regularly cultivated land was a continuous process. This may be regarded as the ecological concomitant of the social displacement and co-simulation of tribal people." This was a perpetual profess from early times.[35] Inheritance right overland from father to son, land grants, and transactions of community land holdings into independent individual land holdings, decided the factors of actual ownership of land. After the post-Sangam period, land ownership was drastically changed from the people of *Samana* and *Buddhist* tradition to the people of *Saiva* and *Vaishnava* tradition as there was state policy for designing of temple economy introduced during the later Cholas.

The principle of ownership of land has been much disputed. Some holding that the King was the ultimate owner of all land, and others that individual ownership existed alongside the obligation to pay tax to the King. The ownership of land was, by a large source of social and economic power in that dominant agricultural policy, and Burton Stein states with conviction that "dependence of power, livelihood, and status on control of land is manifest".[36] Though generally speaking, the above analysis of power may be correct the political and economic power. *Vēli*, *Mā*, and *Kuli* were standard units of land. After measuring the land it was fenced mainly for two reasons: (1) to prevent damage from the cattle and (2) to avoid boundary disputes. Boundaries were marked by stones and shrubbery.[37] By royal order the entire cultivable land in the Chola kingdom was periodically surveyed in the reigns of Rajaraja I, Rajendra I, and Kulottunga I. There were residential and non-residential land-holders. The Karandai plates of Rajendra I mention two bits of land in two different villages held by the Brahmin. So he had to be non-owner of one of the two bits. Persons who were unwilling to cultivate their lands and migrated, had their lands confiscated by the king, who granted them to others who undertook to cultivate them.[38] Therefore, land being an important economic entity should be possessed by the members of the community or collectively were left to improve the village by their efforts.

Land Tenure

The economic life of the people during this period largely depended on the lands, which was the primary source of wealth. The land was held under a variety of tenures such as private sole ownership, joint tenure, and special tenure like service and tax-free, and lease-holding. A. Appadorai has pointed out that most of the village land was held by the Brahmin community. This Brahmin community was a landlord body of a class of tenants, who were bound to pay certain shares of the yield to their masters. This landlord body might hold all the land collectively, sharing the yield, or might hold individual allotments, with or without periodical redistribution, with some portion of the village land hold in common.[39] The practice of making gifts of land for religious merit and also for the maintenance of various professionals was the order of the day. This practice gave rise to what may be called special tenures. Lease tenancy was a common form of the agricultural holding. It is recorded[40] in one instance, that the lessee or tenant should enjoy the lands after repairing the tanks in disuse and bringing under cultivation such of the lands as were covered with jungle and that while the lands were being enjoyed. But he should pay to the temple a *mēlvāram* of one out of three. In the case of lands which had been brought under cultivation by clearing jungles, he should pay one-tenth in the first year, one-ninth in the second year, one-eighth in the third, and so on for all subsequent years. A permanent *mēlvāram* of 1:3 should be paid. A similar record gives different rates of *mēlvāram* for certain other crops, but it is stipulated that the lessee must keep the land fallow. *Kuttahai* was the payment was paid to the emperor or the state by the chieftains, and this was also in the form of a lease-hold. When lessee did not keep to the terms of the lease, the lease was transferred to others.[41]

Reclamation of Land

An important and interesting aspect of the economy of the period was the reclamation of lands. There is no means to assess exactly the extent of land under cultivation during this period. A. Appadorai[42] deals with the extent of land under cultivation in the medieval period, land reclamation was practiced in south India since time immemorial to bring more fresh land under the plough and thus to promote the cause of agricultural production. In 924 CE[43], the *ūrar* (the villagers) of Āllur donated lands as *dēvadāna*. The lands have never been yielding in the previous year. They were ālkaline (*kalar*) and perhaps had been infested with termites (*karaiyān-kolli*). The *ūrar* donated these lands to the temple so that the lands could be reclaimed into wetland. Reclamation of land had two distinct advantages; firstly, it provided the means for the community to cope with the pressure of population in the form of new settlement that was founded on the tracts reclaimed. And secondly, larger areas of uncultivated land were brought under the plough as a result of which the state's revenue also increased. The land was thus reclaimed by cutting down forests for the village as also for the founding of new settlements and for constructing tanks and temples.[44]

Indirectly reclamation of land also provided avenues of employment to many people. A promise of production, assurance of facilities, like exemption of taxes might have also induced the charity-minded persons to take up reclamation. It was the social, which was benefited as the product could be consumed by the society through the temple. The efforts to settle on reclaimed and cultivated land on the part of the enterprising individual was encouraged by the local administration, for it is already noted that the permitted an individual to reclaim a wasteland. Reclamation led to the expansion of agricultural activities and also the accumulation of lands by the temples which ultimately became a big landholding authority.[45]

Sale of Land

An inscription[46] of 1117 CE records a sale of land by the assembly of Pavaikkudi alias *Nittavinoda-chaturvedimangalam* to the temple of *Kailasamudaiya-mahādevā* at Tirunallam, which called *brahmadēya* in *Vennādu* a sub-division of *Uyyakkondar-Valanādu*. In 1006 CE, one *vēli* of land was sold for 100 *kalañjus* of gold at Tiruvaiyaru of Thanjavur district.[47] Two years later, in the same district, 2 *vēlis* and 8 *mās* of wetland including a tank together with dry land of the same extent were sold for the low amount of 10 *kāsus*, though the *irai-kāval* on it 190 *kāsu*.[48] Land of the extent of three and a half *veils* and two mās was sold for 50 *kāsus* and an equal amount provided for bringing it under the plough at Tiruvarur in the eighth year of Rajendra II.[49] A private sale of land registered in the year 1156 A.D., by a person called Govinda Bhattan to Tiruvaruangam Udaiyan Nambi, both the persons were lived in the place at Tirutturai.[50] R. Tirumalai states that the *Mahāsabhā* of Kulottunga Cholamangalam had become separated from Keralantaka Chaturvēdimangalam. They had some lands, 12 *vēli* and 8 *mā* in extent which could not be cultivated all the previous years. None could root out the shrubs, and cultivate the land which was lying waste. Nevertheless, the king's land revenue and *antarāyam* were demanded. Hence, in the 8th year of Kulottunga-II (1141-42 CE), the *Mahāsabhayār* sold the lands to one Vāmanan Anparkaraisan alias Tirunaraiyur Nattukōn of Tandantōttam (a township near Kumbhakonam). The village assemblies were held responsible for land revenue due to the central government from the lands in the village. A record from Kalappal[51] in Thanjavur district dated 1274 CE describes the sale of land by an executive body of the village assembly that land belonging to a certain person who emigrated to the Pandya country and died there without paid dues on his land for ten years. Those arrears of revenue were allowed to accumulate for so many years gives us incidentally a measure of the difference of the method of collection between now and then.

System of Agricultural Production

The economic conditions of medieval Tamil country were responsible for the emergence of the Chola Empire in the 9th century CE. In the Kaveri delta region agriculture was established predominantly by the

Chola rulers essentially peasant-based. Paddy was the main cultivation in this region. The basic unit of production was peasant family, settled in villages clustering the fertile tracts in the Kaveri deltas, and enjoying customary rights of the land. The backbone of the state was the village and cultivation was the primary activity. The rich soil and plentiful water made paddy cultivation as main agriculture production in the riverine deltas could certain multi-cropping, whether if rice itself, or of rice and other crops. These tracts were thus sources of abundant surplus produce, and we could see the surplus production in agriculture throughout the medieval and early modern periods.

The available contemporary sources are extremely insufficient to understand agricultural production. The level of development and the special characteristics of agricultural production in the period were developing first of all based on utilising the natural features of the land. The most important these were: (i) the tropical climate, allowing in principle, provided the was enough moisture, some kind of agriculture all through the year; (ii) more even distribution of rains than in northern India (the combination of south-western, south-eastern monsoon), which to an extent made it possible to vary dates of sowing and harvesting of some crops; (iii) large quantity of unoccupied lands, absence of land-starvation, and on the contrary, a shortage of labour; and (iv) the greatest expenditure of labour for bringing into cultivation the new lands.[52]

Agriculture was the mainstay of the people of the Chola country. The majority of the people lived in villages where they led an energetic communal life. The *Cholamandalam* was noted for its fertility because of the flow of the Kaveri, its tributaries and branches. The prosperity of the owners depended on the fertility was known from the peasant cultivation of two or more crops a year.[53] The soil of the Kaveri delta is entirely alluvial but various, greatly in high-quality. The best soil of the delta is found in the west of the district, and the quality slowly deteriorates as we pass further east. The limits of high quality soil coinciding approximately with the north and the south lines on the Thanjavur district. East of this region has heavy black soil, less fertile and sometimes waterlogged, is met with, and there is a fairly extensive area of really bed saline land at Tirutturaippundi and Nagapattinam taluks were drainage is notoriously defective to certain rivers failing to get a free discharge into the Nagapattinam and Vedaranyam canal.[54]

The most intensive and productive method of paddy cultivation was based on the transplantation of seedlings. The cultivation of virgin black soil demanded first of all the clearing forests and bushes.

Then the part of the land was ploughed several times in mutually perpendicular directions. The hard black soil was cultivated with heavy plough, each drawn by two to three pairs of bullocks or buffaloes. The unusually heavy plough drawn by four or five pairs of bullocks was used. For less hard land the medium-size plough was used. The plough used on wetland was the smallest. The ploughs were made of certain kinds of hardwood. For the light sandy soil, a wooden ploughshare was sometimes used, but as a rule, the ploughshare was of iron. Peasants were involved in the work of ploughing, transplanting, seedlings, harvesting, and threshing the crops and other works related to agriculture.[55] Vellalas were utilised additional labour for the harvest season. Each householder, even the marginal peasant, had use additional labour (Paraiyar) in these seasons. Noboru Karashima has discussed that this additional labour was sometimes provided in the form of peasant cooperation but also in the form of labourers from untouchable castes, whose locality called *parai-chēri*. We can find references to the existence of the residential quarters of the untouchable community in the Chola region. There is a direct reference in the inscription of Rajaraja I, mentioned '*tindā-chēri*', which was the residential place of untouchables.[56]

Generally, the main cultivation on the wetlands was paddy in the delta region, besides, the people were cultivated sugarcane and betel-leaves particularly in Kumbhakonam taluks and also cotton cultivation was in practice both wet and drylands. The *Ulās* mention a special variety of paddy called *chenchalli* or channel, the red paddy. Rice was called *valsi* and the cooked rice.[57] Dry cultivation was less in the Kaveri delta region compare with other parts of the medieval Tamil country. The dry crop's cultivation was *varagu*, *tinai*, green-grams, black-grams, horse grams, and gingili etc.[58] the cultivation of these crops was usually good in the rainy season.

Irrigation System

In India, early civilization flourished on the riverbanks, where water was available in plenty. Agriculture depended upon irrigation. Irrigation works may be divided into three main types i.e., '*ēri*' (tank) irrigation, river, and canal irrigation. The canal and tank irrigation come under the artificial irrigational sources and river irrigation is the natural flow of water. Each village of the Chola period had to have part of land artificially irrigated to reduce the risk of crop failure and starvation. Therefore, the canal system of irrigation had been an important source of water in wet crop cultivation during the time of the later Cholas. Storing rainwater and high-flood water in special reservoirs or with the help of dams (*anicuts*) became the main method of irrigation. Lands with good irrigation were used mainly for fruit trees and vegetables and were called 'garden lands' (*tōtakkāl*). The construction of an irrigation system usually was beyond the labour resources of a single household hence undertaken by a village or a group of villages.[59] Irrigation was considered a work of religious merit, with the result that during all the known history of South India. The state in medieval south India had taken all the steps to construct ēri, (big water storage) and '*kulam*' (small storage of water) and stored rainwater for irrigation purposes during the dry season.[60] The use of stored water was connected with the village committee (*ērivāriya-perumakkal*) which was necessary to control the water level and distributing water for irrigation in the field through the channel up to crops harvest season.

The construction of 'ēri' was limited in the Kaveri delta region but it considered in later times as a meritorious work as gleaned from inscriptions. The problem of containing the flood-waters of large rivers like the Kaveri was faced by Karikala Cholan.[61] According to Tamil literature '*Kalingattupparani*'[62], the early Chola ruler Karikala Cholan, who realised the necessity of providing facilities for irrigation, who constructed '*vella karai*' (embankments) on both sides of the river Kaveri and turned its irrigation channels which crisscrossed the delta area into fertile land. The bank of Kaveri was also known as *karikalak-karai* during the time of Aditya I and Parantaka I.[63] Karikala Chola ordered his enemies captured in the battlefield to provide labour for this great undertaking. Another reference to Parakesari Karikala Chola who raised the banks is made in the Tiruvaduturai inscription. In the reign of Kolottunga III, some lands damaged by Kaveri floods were reclaimed.[64]

The existence of *ēri* (tanks), *ōtai* (streams), āru (river), *kulam* (small water tank) and the common drinking water called 'ūruni' is found in the inscription of temple wall at Thanjavur. The frequent references to the term '*vāykkāl*' in Chola inscriptions can be taken as a testimony of the existence of a well-developed irrigation system in Chola times. Another frequent mention of the term '*mayakki*' or '*tirutti*' in Chola inscriptions in the sections of kind of land and cultivation may well be taken as indicating the extension of the area of intensive cultivation in the Chola times.[65] The Kaveri river lent itself to the excavation of an elaborate trellis work of irrigation canal, like the Virachola *vāykkal* and Uyyakondan *vāykkal*, which have now become regular distributaries channel.[66] When the fresh channels had to be dug, they were so done as to admit of the easy flow of water. The flow of water in the channel passing through the villages is evidenced to irrigate the lands of other areas.

Water Management

Maintenance of irrigation works was important as their construction and many endowments of land and paddy were made for the maintenance of lakes and tanks. Their maintenance was one of the primary concerns of local administration; it was the main source that provided water for agriculture. Sometimes it also served as drinking water (ūruni). The works of conservation and preservation such as preventing damages to irrigation works, repairing the damaged ones, raising tank bunds, removing silt, and such other works are the responsibility of the village assembly. Any deliberate attempt to damage irrigational tanks was considered a crime. Inscriptions swear curses on those who destroyed or caused any damage to tanks.[67]

In the management of water the village and its *sabha*, the smallest administrative unit under the Cholas, which was a local self-governing organisation, looked after the maintenance works of the water bodies in the community level. The village sabhā consisted of all the male inhabitants of the area. They had complete control of the rural administration and acted independently without intervention of kings. K.A. Nilakanta Sastri's work on '*Studies in Cola History and Administration*',[68] clarified the functions of the *sabha* formed by Brahmin landholders in Brahmin village. The *sabhā* managed village affairs, including cultivation, through various committees (*vāriam*) formed under it, including those for garden land (*tōttam*), tank (*ēri*), wet field (*kalani*), taxation (*pañchavāram*) and accounts (*kanakku*). There was a committee called 'ēri-*vāriyam*' that looked after the management of *ēri*. The committee appears to have changed its members annually. The king, nobleman, or the villagers made endowments in the form of gold or land for the maintenance of tanks. The ēri-vāriam took up the responsibility of regular maintenance of *ēri* and opening the sluice (*madaku* in Tamil), failing which the members of the assembly were liable for fine and punishment. The leadership of the village was in the hands of farmers. Rajendra I (1012-1044) dug a large lake (*Chōlagangam*) near his new capital Gangaikondacholapuram and this was used for irrigation purposes.[69] The *Chōlagangam* Lake is now called as *Ponneri*.

The traditional irrigation management systems, which prevailed in Tamil Nadu, reflected very well, the rights enjoyed by the village societies over water and other natural resources. The village community had complete control and access over water and other natural resources within their jurisdiction. The system was functioning well and there existed well laid out rules and regulations to undertake all critical functions of water management such as system maintenance, water sharing during times of scarcity, conflict resolution, and collection of penalty for non-participation in the maintenance work and so on. There existed a hierarchy of functionaries to undertake all these activities. The caste structure played a crucial role in preserving and in allocating responsibilities among various functionaries. For instance, a farmer invariably held the position of a canal manager from a high caste only and the people held the position of irrigation workers (*menials*) from low castes. Nevertheless, the traditional irrigation body had an enforcement mechanism, which facilitated the smooth functioning of water control systems.

Historically, the community of water users undertook all essential functions of water management including the construction of small diversion weirs and central networks. Such water user communities were called '*samudhayam*', in the case of central irrigated villages and '*nādu*' for the tank and dry villages. The water rights enjoyed by upper communities that are the landholder of Brahmins and Vellalas. The organisational structure for carrying out the responsibilities of traditional water institutions operated at two levels. The first is supervisory called *kāval-māniyam* or *kāvalkārar*, who performed the role of an enforcing authority of rules and regulations concerning water management. The second one is who were locally called *neerkātti* or *neerpaichi*, was more of a *menial* nature, former is an honorary position, and the community at the end of every season or yearly paid the latter category in kind. In many parts of the country, these positions were held on a hereditary base. They were collected water tax (*nīrkuli*) and entered in the *variputthakam*. Water rates are usually associated with land revenue. The assessment was mostly demanded in the form of services and some times in the form of kind or cash. On what basis the cess on water used for irrigation was made is not clear. The epigraphs mention a phrase, *innilattal-vanta-nirk-kirai*[70] *by* which one may infer that the cess was fixed on a unit of the land which used the water for irrigation.

Condition of Peasantry

The peasantry is a wider economic sector in agrarian countries like India. The peasantry could be defined in socio-economic history as the major area where a set of rural communities, comprising, landowner, land-tenants, landless-labourers were involved in agricultural production for subsistence as well as for market. It also means the pros and cons of the rural communities who had nexus with the traders and other economic groups. Peasant villages have never existed in isolation, for peasants' farm their land also in large-scale, complex-societies. As a result those villagers never move from day to day in simple, homogeneous harmony, modern romances to the country.[71] The power, order, legitimacy within the locality world of the South Indian peasantry was mediated by Brahmins. The feudal model must see the religious grants as part of a more generalized alienation of power over land from rulers to local power holders, and then link evidence of the subjugation body of feudal complex in distinction to earlier state power.

It was truer in those localities of wealth and prosperous agriculture and trade than in those peripheral tracts where people survived on hazardous, rain-dependent agriculture.[72] The evaluation of statesmanship and the polity of Chola, basically started from the land. The small peasants to produce agricultural surpluses tilled the land provided with the availability of water resources. But the produce was appropriated by elites emerging from the peasant economy and eventually standing about it. The most commonly used in the Chola period to describe ritually impure, were *purakudi* people who lost their land due to their degradation in the social hierarchy and became landless labouring groups. The segregated settlements of these people adjoined many villages in Cholamandalam.

The economic position of labouring groups is clear in one record, which serves as a classic summary of hierarchy in the Chola period. It seems likely, based on observations of more recent practices that are arrangement of production[73] was most common in the areas that supported irrigated agriculture. In the Kaveri delta region larger concentrations of Brahmins and other non-cultivating groups lived in their settlements. The Vellalas remained strong cultivating groups in this region. But other landowners cultivated the land relying on an extended network of the family labour force, which was a very similar system of slavery available in European countries; it existed during the Chola period. Smaller holdings especially, or those that yielded a lower annual surplus, required less outside labour.

James Heitzman has stated that the peasants associated with low-status agricultural labour indeed, were forced to become cultivators and they handled almost all production within kinship networks. In border areas of Cholamandalam, irrigation was a problem and cultivation was in trouble. About the level of agricultural labourers, but below the level of the *kāniyalar* was the stratum of cultivating people (*kudimakkal*).[74] The terminology *kudimakkal* that appears in Chola inscriptions suggests that the cultivating people personally tilled the fields. The crucial question, and that one has the most bearing on Stein's concept of a 'peasant state', is whether the process of cultivation was typically separated through tenancy arrangements from the status of land ownership (*kāniyātchi-kārar*), or whether both categories were typically folded into one large stratum of peasant cultivators without superiors who simply paid taxes to the state.[75] As peasant colonists opened new tracts of land, those who had formerly occupied the land either fled more deeply into the forests and hills to find a place in the new order. Places had to be found for the later within the expanding peasant tracts of Coromandal because the conversion of dry tracts of forest to wet field cultivation required the number of new labours. Coromandal plain, north of the Kaveri delta was a distinctive, old and dense region of peasant agriculture and settlement in the region. Numerous and scattered peasant localities separated by large and small tracts of inhospitable land were quite prevalent. The cover of the slope, forest, and other factors reduced the suitability of these tracts for peasant agriculture. In such tracts, only non-agrarian people adopted to live.[76] By the ninth century, peasant society gradually shifting and pastoral peoples, peasants, was not possible for them and they continued to deal cautiously with non-peasant people even after peasantry became the primary economic institution in South India.

Agricultural Slavery

There was no slave system in the history of medieval South India before the Pallavas rule. Generally, those who involved in agricultural activities were mostly called as son of the soils. They had land property more or less for their potential intention. We consider that slavery was caused in two reasons, they are: (i) during the Chola period, the rulers and the elite communities were forced small landholders to endow their lands for the development of religious consideration, charitable purpose, and to the services of Brahmins, and (ii) they may sell their lands to the elite landholding communities in the case of economic deprivation. Therefore, they became a landless community. The dominant landholding communities were engaged landless labourers to work in their lands for the development of agricultural activities. Later they were attached permanently with their soils as '*adimai*' (slave) and the slave master served meals every day for their work; hence, they were called agricultural slaves. This has predominantly existed in Vijayanagara rule and it has been extended up to the first half of the 19th century of British rule. The agricultural labourers were not directly worked under the Brahmins, but they involved agricultural activities under the supervision of non-Brahmin communities of Vellalas in the Kaveri delta region.[77] Regarding the condition of the agricultural slaves, K. Mavali Rajan has emphasised that the marginalised communities and agrarian slaves of medieval Tamil country were mostly landless labourers and agricultural serfs. They worked in the field of caste-Hindus and got very little wages for their work, most of them were in a condition of slavery.[78] They received their wages mostly in kind as paddy or grain. Though, the grain component of the wage was higher *at kuruni* and 4 *nāli* per head. Sometimes, they were forced to do even free labour (*vetti*). The landowners provided two sets of cloths annually for their labours.[79] Sometimes to keep a watch over the river bund (*kulaikāppu, kāval*) and also to contribute labour for strengthening the earthwork embankment for Kavery river and for clearing the channels (removing silt) at the time of freshens of water. Besides, they put up a *korombo* work across the river to divert water into the supply channel.[80] Later, a decision taken by a certain village assembly prohibited the labourers from keeping slaves.[81]

Land Measurement

The survey of all lands in Cholamandalam was undertaken during the reign of Rajaraja I, Kulottunga I, and Kulottunga III. Measuring rods of various lengths were used. In the same manner, different land measures were adopted in different regions. The proper measurement of lands and lying of the boundary stones denote the keen interest shown by the Chola rulers and the local authorities on the agricultural lands. An inscription from Tiruchchengattangudi in the Thanjavur district, mentions a revenue survey in the 17th year of Rajaraja I in 1002 CE. The two other inscriptions one from Kuhur in Kumbhakonam taluk dated 1007 CE. and the other from Tiruvisalur in the same taluk dated 1009 CE. mention revenue survey in the same region.[82]

In the 16th year of Rajaraja I (1001 CE) followed by many such surveys at intermittent intervals of unequal lengths of time. The standard unit of land was *vēli* (6.6517 acres) which was divided into *mā* and *kuli*.[83] It is commonly known that 20 *mā* made up a *vēli* and 100 *kuli* made up an *mā*. These land measures were popular in Cholamandalam. The basic units of linear measurements used in the Chola state were *jān* (one span=approximately 9 inches), *ati* (one human foot=10.46 inches) and *piti* (one first=4.5 inches).[84] The measuring rods used for revenue survey were formed by the multiples of such units of length. The rods are mentioned as *nilamavu-kōl* measuring rods of *ati* units vary from 9 *ati* units (7′ 8′ to 22 *ati* units (19′ 1′) in length.[85] A *panniratik-kōl* (rod of 12 *ati*) was used in the revenue surveys of 1112 and 1156 CE. at Tiruvidaimarudur in Thanjavur district.[86] Another measurement the 16 *jān-kōl* was used in the same district, and 9 *ati-kōl* used at Tiruchirappalli district in the year of 1122 C.E.[87] The measurement was made by a rod measuring 28 spans which were perhaps the standard rod of Prantaka's times.

Land Revenue System

The Chola rulers strengthened their state economy through the collection of different taxes from the people. The Cholas have collected eleven types of taxes, but the main tax was land revenue. It can be broadly classified into two; the first one based on the local rights to produce and the other based on the right of produce by authorities. The former includes the payment to labourers, cultivator's dues, irrigation labour dues, local cess, and commercial and occupational cess, while the latter refers to the appropriation of produce by authorities connected with Chola state or its agents. Land taxes were collected in two categories viz., in-kind, and money. Payment to labourers includes payment for 'manual cultivation', wages for digging generally paid in kind. *Iraikāniyōkam*[88] was a payment demanded the dispatch and delivery of the royal order to the party concerned.

The cultivators (*kudi*) of agricultural land had to perform personal service called *Kudimai*. R. Tirumalai cited the Mannargudi inscription which explicit that "no part of the *Kudimai* shall be collected from the Brahmins and the Vellalas".[89] the term '*kudi* ' is used in a variety of meanings; it has to be understood only regarding the context in which it occurs. The term, in its generic sense, could mean a tenant and more particularly, an occupant. It is also used to denote a cultivating tenant, a service holder, or a tenant-at-will or a mere cultivator hired for labour. K.A. Nilakanta Sastri[90] has mentioned in his book '*The Cōlas* ', that the *kudi* should himself be the 'actual' cultivator of the land. The close association of the term *kudimai* of rice and animals (for ploughing), indicate that the cultivator dues. Irrigation labour dues, necessary for the provision of water to agricultural fields, were the additional duties of the cultivator. In Cholamandalam, *nīrkuli* was the only term used for water tax. A special tax levied on water drawn from river sources known as āttrup-pāttam.[91] A canal tax called '*vāikkāl-pāttam* ' was one of the taxes which was collected for the maintenance of the irrigation sources. Certain officials were deputed to look after the *anicuts* and sluices which controlled the floodwaters.[92] Another instance is known from Tiruverumbur in the Tiruchirappalli district. The *sabhā* at its meeting (*perrunkuri*) imposed a levy for desilting of the village irrigation tanks on the cultivators (*ulukudikal*).[93]

The most important source of royal revenue was land. It was called *Kadamai or Kanikkadan or Irai*. The terms often used for these taxes are *kadamai* or *irai*, which indicates in the vast majority of cases the specific duty of paying on the thrusting floor.[94] It is a duty to pay *kadamai* which becomes effective only on the induction of an occupant. It is payable in kind (usually in Paddy) or cash or both, in the case of irrigated crops. It is the primary charge on the land and its occupant.[95] The state collected several dues from the landowners. The dues from the land property are known as *kāni-kadan*. The entire range of action of the land revenue department resolved around the schedules of land taxes based on soil type, availability of irrigation, land measurement, and a scale of land grades (*taram*).[96] The Chola kings were attempted to standardise the tax rates from rice-growing land to 100 *kalams* of paddy per *vēli* of land, a rate applicable in some locations for 200 years.[97] The early Chola epigraphs show that they were frequently used the terms '*puravu*' and '*puravu vari*' in the sense of land tax. The land tax levied based on *taram* or different types of soil conditions of the land. The prosperity of the owner depended on the fertility of the soil. The fertility of the land was known from the cultivation of two or more crops a year. If the land was fertile, it was taxed more. There were fallow lands and substandard lands. Forest and wastelands were reclaimed and concession in taxes and favourable terms of the lease in the initial years were given to the cultivators. In *Cholamandalam* no such term has been used to denote the wetland tax, however, the term *nañjai-puravu* meaning tax on the drylands was also used.[98]

There was a tax collected from landholder called *Vetti* which means 'free labour' for communal service.[99] Even the *mahāsabhā* of Uttiramerur in Chengalpattu district which was granted a good portion of tax-free land not titled for using *vetti* labour.[100] This service was demanded maintenance of watercourses in general, ārrukkāl-vetti was a service demanded the proper upkeep of channels branching from the rivers.[101] A special tax called *kāveri-kulai* was commended for maintaining the banks of the river Kaveri.[102] An inscription of Kulottunga III dated in his 31st regnal year (1209 CE) from Tirupappuram states about a tax called *kāverikkarai-viniyōgam*, collected from the people to raise the banks of Kaveri and her branches during floods.[103] This record shows in the interest of the local authorities in caring for the banks of rivers and safeguarding the same in times of danger. Another tax was collected by the village *sabhā* called *ūr-kil iraiyili*, tax-free under the *ūr*, employed of some lands also implies that such lands were exempted from all dues because the residents of the village had undertaken to pay these dues in the ration of their holdings in the village.[104]

Land Revenue Assessment

During the Chola period, the assessment of land revenue depended upon a seemingly accurate land measurement. The rulers and officials have followed a well-established mode of tax collection and maintained land records in an appropriate method. The revenue surveys conducted to assess the quantum of tax on land are known from the Tiruchirappalli and Thanjavur district,[105] which in fact could indicate a somewhat localised nature of the revenue survey. R. Tirumalai has analyzed the land assessment modes of the Chola and Pandya periods. The *olugu* was the register of occupancy and enjoyment. *Vari* or *varipottagam* was the register of assessment of land showing the tenure of the land, the occupants from whom the land-dues in respect of each holding had to be collected.[106] Whenever changes in tenure occurred they were promptly ordered to be entered in the *vari*, and the authenticated extract of the mutation (*ulvari*) made by the *variyilar*. The authorities' in-charge of the land-tax register was conveyed to the grantees. The land register showing lands assessed to full demand. Besides, there was a *tarapottagam*[107] maintained. This showed such of those lands classified based on the assessment rate charged for it. Land revenue accounts at the village level were maintained by local officials. In the *ūr* the village accountant called ūrk-kanakku or ūrk-karnam is mentioned. The village accountants had binding responsibility for the collection of taxes. In some cases, the village accountant was punished for misappropriation of temple funds. Sometimes *ūrk-kanakku* is seen attesting documents on behalf of the *ūr*.

Kāniyālar had an inextinguishable right over the land which is his holding (*kāni*) and had to bear the obligation fastened on the land (*kāni-kadan*). The Thanjavur inscription records the royal order issued by Rajaraja I in his 29th regnal year that the particular of the assessment of 100 *kalams* of paddy is mentioned (*kāni-kadan*)[108] due to the Thanjavur temple from the villages granted by him as *dēvadāna* to the Thanjavur temple should be engraved on stone.

The inscription also notices the description of forty villages granted in *Cholamandalam*. An analysis of epigraphs of Chola State clearly states the assessment of land revenue system, where the rate fixed for wetland (*nīr-nilam*) may be considered first. A piece of wetland belonging to the *dēvadāna* category was assessed at an annual rate of 120 *kalams* of per *veli* in 926 CE at Andavanallur in Tiruchirappalli district.[109] At Gangaikonda-cholapuram in the same district, 100, 102, 105 *kalams* of paddy were assessed on different lands situated at various places on a *veli* in 1068 CE.[110]

Noboru Karashima[111] has also expressed this view in his critical analysis of land revenue assessment as seen in the inscriptions of Thanjavur and Gangaikonda-cholapuram. The Chola rulers were maintained the different rate structure with a limited area was due to both the nature and the productivity of taxable land. These assessments were made on lands cultivating two crops per year. There are two categories of taxable land i.e., *irupū-vilaiyum-nilam* (two cropsland) and *orupū-vilaiyum-nilam* (one cropland). Karashima also identified more villages in the Kaveri delta region, all the taxable land was *nīr-nilam* (wet paddy fields) and another one *punjai-nilam* (dry land).[112] He has stated that the assessment rate in all these taxable land was *nīr-nilam* (*irupū-vilaiyum-nilam*). It is exactly one hundred *kalam* per *veli* and another group of villagers cultivated in *punjai-nilam* or lands. Though the number of instances is small, it may suggest that the rate for *nir-nilam* or *irupū-vilaiyum nililam* is just one hundred and the decrease from one hundred in rate seen in many villages may be attributed to the fact that less fertile land such as *orupū-vilaiyum-nilam*, *punjai-nilam*, or land of some other category, is included in the taxable land of those villages. The dry land assessment was also made in terms of paddy. The different rate structures for both wet and dry lands could be due to the different rates of productivity. More instances of *dēvadāna* grants made by Chola kings would yield on close examination, more substantial knowledge of revenue assessment in Chola times.

Remission of Taxes

R. Rajalakshmi has been discussed in very detailed manner about the remission of taxes in Tamil country, particularly during the later Cholas. The exemption was granted to particular groups and for special reasons, and on particular occasions, to individual cases. The Brahmins were the prime social group enjoying most tax-exemption. Learned Brahmins were settled in tax-free villages, which they collectively enjoyed.[113] The Brahmins who did *pooja* in temples were given grants called *archanabhōgam*. *Sālabhōgam* and *Brahmadēyas*, were other tax-free provisions for Brahmins. These exemptions were called *bhōgam*, *kāni* and *vritti* if perpetual, and *jīvita*, if an annuity. This *sālabhōgam* was an exemption granted to lands owned by *sālas* or schools.[114] Another form of tax remission was granted by local bodies. The *sabhā*, *ūr*, and *nādu* effected these remissions. The *ūr* assembly also granted remission known as *uruk-kil-iraiyili* (the *iraiyli* remission granted by the ūr). In one instance in 1090 CE at Tiruppugalur of Thanjavur district, an exemption of taxes on a piece of land to a village accountant was granted for his meritorious services.[115] Tamil literature *Kulottunga Cholan Ulas* speaks on tax system during the reign of Kulottunga I. Kulottunga I abolished certain tolls called *suṅgam*, so he was called as *Suṅgam Tavirtta Cholan*'.[116] The abolition of the toll was represented his kindness of the people under his rule. *Taraku* seems to be a local cess, probably a variant of *suṅgam*. An epigraph from Kudumiyanmalai (1106 CE) refers to *taraku* imposed on betel-leaves brought into the locality (*innāttil-vantirankiya-verrilaikku-taraku*-kontu).[117] From this it may be understood that *taraku* was levied on the merchandise brought into a locality from outside.

Conclusion

In medieval Tamil country, however, we have observed from the inscriptional evidence, the Brahmins and other rich landlords had political and economic power in the social hierarchy during the Chola rule. Through their control over land, the landowning community legitimised the political power and controlled the temple economy. There is no doubt that most of the Brahmins were settled in fertile areas of Kaveri delta, where the productivity of land was very high and served to the temples. The existence of a large difference in productivity between the northern and southern banks of Kaveri in Chola times is attested in certain inscriptions. Some people accumulated larger amounts of land and became locally influential big landlords, others lost possession of their *kāni* lands and must have slipped into the position of tenants or landless cultivators due to donating their land to the temple or the Brahmins. This indicates the emergence of a new agrarian order in the Kaveri delta areas in the thirteenth century. The landless agrarian communities were worked as a slave labourer in the lands of the big landlords. The agrarian slaves were landless, whose labour was fully exploited by their master. The master had full power over his slaves. They were treated as moveable properties when the land was sold the slaves also were transferred with the land. Besides, these landless labourers were worked menial labouring works such as digging canals and removing the silt from channels and distributing water to the wet field. The landless labourers were socially pushed down in society and forced them to serve to the top of the society, though their life was miserable and worked for hand to mouth during that time.

Acknowledgment

I would like to express my earnest gratitude to my brother Dr. K. Mavali Rajan, Assistant Professor, Department of Ancient Indian History, Culture and Archaeology, Visva-Bharati Central University, Santiniketan for his constant support and encouragement in completing the task of my article preparation. We discussed several times regarding the theme and content of the article and I got benefited from the discussion that I had with him in framing the subject matter of the present endeavor.

Notes and References

1. F.R. Hemingway, *Madras District Gazetteer: Tanjore*, Vol. 1, Government Press, Madras, 1915, p. 1.
2. Y. Subbarayalu, *Political Geography of the Chola Country*, University of Madras, Madras, 1973, pp. 21-22.
3. F.R. Hemingway, *op.cit.*, p. 22.
4. K. Mavali Rajan, *Medieval Tamil Society and Agrarian Slavery*, Maha Bodhi Book Agency, Kolkata, 2014, pp. 39 and 97.
5. K.A. Nilakanta Sastri, *The Cōlas*, University of Madras, Madras, 1937, pp. 520-545.
6. T.V. Sadasiva Pandarattar, *Pirkkālachchōlar Charittiram* (in Tamil), Annamalai University, Annamalai Nagar, 1974, pp. 13-15; 52-67, 68-73.
7. Burton Stein, *Peasant State and Society in Medieval South India*, Oxford University Press, 1980, p. 85.
8. David Ludden, *Peasants History of South India*, Princeton University Press, Princeton, 1985, p. 12.
9. Noboru Karashima, *South Indian History and Society: Studies from Inscription A.D. 850-1800*, Oxford University Press, Delhi, 1984, pp. 15-31, 94-99.
10. R. Tirumalai, *Land Grants and Agrarian Reactions in Cōla and Pandya Times*, University of Madras, Madras, 1987, pp. 41-47, 88-94, 135.
11. A. Appadurai, *Economic Conditions in Southern India (1000-1500 A.D)*, 2. vols., University of Madras, Madras, 1936, pp. 671-700, 728-729.
12. George Micheal, *Eternal Kaveri*, Mumbai, 1999, p. 90.

13. Noboru Karashima, *op.cit.*, p. 129.
14. *Ibid.*, p. 15.
15. *Ibid.*, p. 17.
16. K.A. Nilakanta Sastri, *The Cōlas*, University of Madras, Reprint, 1984, p. 569.
17. *South Indian Inscription* (hereafter *S.I.I.*), Vol.III, Nos. 156 and 181.
18. *Annual Report on Epigraphy* (hereafter *A.R.E.*) No.4 of 1890; *A.R.E.*, No. 266 of 1901.
19. *A.R.E.*, No. 42 of 1903.
20. *A.R.E.*, No. 396 of 1922.
21. *A.R.E.*, No. 601 of 1902, Tiruchirappalli District, dated 1235 CE.
22. *A.R.E.*, No. 341 of 1902.
23. *A.R.E.*, No. 386 of 1924.
24. *South Indian Temple Inscription* (hereafter *S.I.T.I.*), Vol. I, pp. 40-41.
25. *S.I.I.*, Vol. XVII, No. 641.
26. *A.R.E.*, No. 259 of 1927.
27. Burton Stein, *All the Kings Mana: Papers on Medieval South Indian History*, New Era Publication, Madras, 1984, p. 162.
28. *Ibid.*, p.162.
29. *A.R.E.*, 1947-48, p. 3.
30. *S.I.I.*, Vol. VIII, Nos. 668 and 669.
31. *S.I.I.*, Vol. VIII No. 668-669, cited in T. Tirumalai, *op.cit.*, pp. 42-43.
32. *S.I.I.*, Vol. VIII, No. 668.
33. *Ibid.*
34. *A.R.E.*, No.90 of 1931-1932.
35. *'Kādu Konru Nādakki', 'Kulam tottu Valam Perukki'* – *Pattinappalai*.
36. Burton Stein, 'Agrarian Integration in South India', quoted in R. Rajalakshmi, *Tamil Polity*, (A.D.600-A.D. 1300), Ennes Publication, Madurai, 1983, p. 196.
37. *A.R.E.*, No. 28 of 1919.
38. *A.R.E.*, No. 531 of 1931; also see R. Rajalakshmi, *op.cit.*, p. 197.
39. A. Appadorai, 'The Committee System of Village Administration in Cōla times-An Interpretation' in S. *Krishnaswami Aiyangar Commemoration Volume*, Published by the Committee, Madras, 1936, pp. 148-154.
40. *Madras Epigraphical Report* (hereafter *M.E.R.*), No. 66 of 1916
41. *M.E.R.*, No. 410 of 1918; and also see R. Rajalakshmi., *op.cit.*, p. 199.

42. A. Appadorai, *op.cit.*, p. 187.
43. *S.I.I.*, Vol. III, No. 641.
44. *S.I.I.*, Vol. III, No. 695.
45. S. Swaminathan, *The Early Cholas: History, Art and Culture*, Sharada Publishing House, Delhi, 1998, p. 166.
46. *A.R.E.*, No. 653 of 1909.
47. *A.R.E.*, No. 219 of 1894.
48. *A.R.E.*, No. 102 of 1925.
49. *A.R.E.*, No. 677 of 1919.
50. *A.R.E.*, No. 431 of 1925.
51. *A.R.E.*, No. 336 of 1925, also see K.A.Nilakanta Sastri, *The Cōlas*, Vol. II, Part I, 1937, pp. 320-321.
52. A.L. Alave, 'South India', in Tapan Raychaudhuri and Irfan Habib (eds.), *The Cambridge Economic History of India*, Orient Longman, Delhi, 1982, p. 226.
53. *A.R.E.*, No. 271 of 1915.
54. S.Y. Krishnaswamy, *Report on the Development of Irrigation under the Cauvery- Mettur Project*, Government Press, Madras, 1941, p. 22.
55. A.L. Alave, *op.cit.*, p. 226; K. Mavali Rajan, *Medieval Tamil Society and Agrarian Slavery*, p. 97.
56. Noboru Karashima, 'The Untouchables in Tamil Inscriptions and other Historical Sources in Tamil Nadu', in H. Kotani (ed.), Caste *System: Untouchability and the Depressed*, Manohar, New Delhi, 1977, p. 21.
57. 'Sankara Cholan Ula', k.111, cited in G. Thirumavalavan, *Political, Social and Cultural History of the Cholas as Gleaned from Ula Literature*, Ezhilagam Publisher, Cheyyar, 1991, p. 154.
58. A. Appadorai, *Economic Conditions in Southern India (1000-1500 A.D)*, p. 331.
59. *A.R.E.*, No.364 of 1906; *A.R.E.*, No. 304 of 1907.
60. *A.R.E.*, Nos. 262 and 264 of 1906; *A.R.E.*, No. 394 of 1907.
61. R. Rajalakshmi, *op.cit.*, p. 197.
62. Jayankondar, '*Kalingathupparani*' edited by Palanivel Pillai, published by South Indian Saiva Siddhantha Work Publishing Society, Madras, 1950, p. 54.
63. *S.I.I.*, Vol. V, No. 693.
64. *M.E.R.*, No. 113 of 1927.
65. *A.R.E.*, No. 206 of 1921 and *A.R.E.*, No. 66 of 1937.
66. Noboru Karashima, *op.cit.*, p. 129.

67. On visualize over the meticulous attention, which the Chola bureaucracy had devoted to irrigation. One gets a clear idea of this if one studies the various stipulations that had been laid down, for instance in the Leyden Grant, calling upon the *nattam* to ensure that, in respect of the Anaimangalam lands gifted to the *Chulamani Vihara Palli*, 'water passing in the existing channels for irrigating the lands of this village shall be allowed to do so as usual and the excess water was flowing down on its way. No one shall be permitted to cut any branch channels from them to dam them across, to put up small picottahs, or to bail out their water in baskets. Thus, the donees, in this case, were given the sale right to the use of the existing irrigation channels for irrigation in a way that did not hold up the water but let it flow down easily. also see B. Venkataraman, *Rajesvaram: The Pinnacle of Chola Art*, Madras, p. 63, fn.1.
68. K.A. Nilakanta Sastri, *Studies in Cōla History and Administration*, University of Madras, Madras,1932, pp. 108 - 113.
69. V. Balambal., *Studies in Chola History*, Delhi, 1998, p. 187.
70. *S.I.I.*, Vol. VIII. No. 67.
71. David Ludden, *op.cit.*, p. 8.
72. Burton Stein, *Peasant State and Society in Medieval South India*, p. 9.
73. The arrangement of production in Kaveri delta was purely a Brahmin-Vellala joint venture. These two groups controlled the employment, production, and assessment of Kaveri delta. *Kadamai* was obligatory is rendered to the tax-free landholdings like *Brahmadēya*. Vellala groups had land ownership and some of the Sudra communities became strong labour forces instead of the *purakudi* people due to their ritual pollution.
74. James Heitzman, *Gifts of Power: Lordship in an Early Indian State*, Oxford University Press, New Delhi, 1997, p. 10.
75. *Ibid.*, p. 10.
76. The general distribution of plains and forest and upland tracts in Tamil country; see K.Ramamurthy, 'Some Aspects of the Regional Geography of Tamilnad', *Indian Geographical Journal*, Vol. 23, Nos. 3 and 3 (1948); *Inscription of Madras Presidency*, Vol. II, p. 1287.
77. James Heitzmen, *op.cit.*, p. 10.
78. K. Mavali Rajan, *op.cit.*, p.51.
79. K. Mavali Rajan and T. Chandrasekaran, "Marginalished Communities and Agrarian Slavery in Medieval Tamil Country", *Proceedings of the Thirty Second Annual Session of South Indian History Congress*, Chennai, 2012, pp. 286-289.
80. R. Tirumalai, "Land Reclamation and Flood-Damaged and Sand-cast Lands- A Study in Prices, Rentals and Wages in Later Chola Times (from A.D.1070-A.D.1210)- Based on Srirangam Inscriptions", *Journal of Epigraphical Society of India*",Vol.11, 1985, pp. 65-87.

81. *A.R.E.*, No. 538 of 1918.
82. Y. Subbarayalu, *op.cit.*, pp. 67-68.
83. P. Shanmugam, *The Revenue System of the Cholas, 850-1279 A.D*, University of Madras, Madras, 1987, p. 70.
84. *Ibid.*
85. *Inscriptions of Pudukkottai State* (hereafter *I.P.S.*), No. 175 and *A.R.E.*, No.104 of 1927-28.
86. *S.I.I.*, Vol. V. No.702.
87. *I.P.S.*, No.175.
88. P. Shanmugam, *op.cit.*, p. 57.
89. *S.I.I.*, Vol.VI, Nos.48, 50, 58 cited in R. Tirumalai, *Land Grants and Agrarian Reactions in Cōla and Pandya Times*, p. 90.
90. K.A. Nilakanta Sastri, *The Colas*, Vol. II, Madras, 1937, Vol. II, Part I, p. 402.
91. P. Shanmugam, *op.cit.*, p. 49.
92. *A.R.E.*, 1909; Part II, para 26.
93. *S.I.I.*, Vol. XIII, No. 165.
94. *S.I.I.*, Vol. XXIV, No.53 An inscription from Srirangam includes eleven taxes under the heading *kadamai* used in the generic sense of duty; *irai* taxes the place of *kadamai* at times in Kumbhakonam taluk.
95. R. Tirumalai cited the phrase "*Kadamai kola kadan parramayil*"- appended to "Rajendra Vinnagar" published by Tamilnadu State Department of Archaeology, 1980; quoted in R. Tirumalai (1987), op.cit., p. 88. fn. 14.
96. *S.I.I.*, Vol. III, No. 577.
97. James Heitzman, *op.cit.*, p. 166.
98. *A.R.E.*, No. 357 of 1925.
99. R. Tirumalai, *Land Grants and Agrarian Reactions in Cōla and Pandya Times*, p. 91.
100. *S.I.I.*, Vol. VI, p. 297; This inscription speaks of:
    "Kudiyilar Vettiyum, amañjiyum, Iraiyum
    Eppērpattanum kollaperādār āgavum".
101. P. Shanmugam, *op.cit.*, p. 50.
102. *Ibid.*, p. 50.
103. V. Balambal, *op.cit.*, p. 186.
104. *AR.E.*, Nos. 109 of 1911; 224 of 1917. From Korkkai, Thanjavur district, dated 1169 CE, furnishes an example of the *sabhā* taking 160 *kasus* from the temple treasury and agreeing to pay the taxes due on half a *nilam* which, after years of neglect was brought under cultivation to provide for the supply of a flower garden every night to the temple; the *sabha* agreed to continue to pay the taxes on the land irrespective of any changes in ownership. Also see K.A. Nilakanta Sastry, *The Cōlas*, (1937), Vol. II, Part I, p. 318.

105. P. Shanmugam, *op.cit.*, p.140.
106. R. Tirumalai, *Land Grants and Agrarian Reactions in Cōla and Pandya Times*,pp.103-115.
107. *S.I.I.*, Vol. XIV, No.245, in Ambasamudram.
108. *S.I.I.*, Vol. II. No. 4.
109. *S.I.I.*, Vol. VIII, No. 688.
110. *S.I.I.*, Vol. IV, No. 528.
111. Noboru Karashima, *op.cit.*, pp. 94 and 105.
112. *Ibid.*, p. 96.
113. R. Rajalakshmi, *op.cit.*, p. 152.
114. *Ibid.*
115. *A.R.E.*, No.89 of 1927-28, p. 63
116. *Kulottunga Cholan Ula: line 51-52*, also see K.A. Nilakanta Sastri, *The Cōlas*, p. 599; R. Rajalakshmi, *Tamil Polity*, p. 153.
117. *I.P.S.*, No. 125, Vol. II, 9-10.

Bibliography

Annual Report on Epigraphy, (in various years), 1890, 1894, 1901, 1902, 1903, 1907, 1909, 1915, 1918, 1919, 1922, 1924, 1925, 1931.

Annual Report on South Indian Epigraphy, 1927-28, 1931-32, 1947-48.

Appadorai, A, *Economic Conditions in Southern India (1000-1500 A.D)*, 2 vols, University of Madras, Madras, 1936.

Balambal, V, *Studies in Chola History*, Kalinga Publication, Delhi, 1998.

Burton Stein, *Peasant State and Society in Medieval South India*, Oxford University Press, 1980.

___________, *All the Kings Mana: Papers on Medieval South Indian History*, New Era Publication, Madras, 1984.

David Ludden, *Peasants History of South India*, Princeton University Press, Princeton, 1985.

George Micheal, *Eternal Kaveri*, Mumbai, 1999.

Hemingway, F.R, *Madras District Gazetteer: Tanjore*, Vol.1, Government Press, Madras, 1915.

Inscription of Pudukkottai State, (Translated into English by K.R. Srinivasan), Part I (Early Pallava and Chola Inscriptions), Pudukkottai, Reprint, 2002.

James Heitzman, *Gifts of Power: Lordship in an Early Indian State*, Oxford University Press, New Delhi, 1997.

Krishnaswami Aiyangar, S, *Commemoration Volume*, Published by the Committee, Madras, 1936.

Krishnaswamy, S.Y, *Report on the Development of Irrigation under the Cauvery-Mettur Project*, Government Press, Madras, 1941.

Kotani, H, Caste *System: Untouchability and the Depressed*, Manohar, New Delhi, 1977.

Madras Epigraphical Report, 1916, 1918, 1927.

Mavali Rajan, K, *Medieval Tamil Society and Agrarian Slavery*, Maha Bodhi Book Agency, Kolkata, 2014.

Nilakanta Sastri, K.A, *The Cōlas*, University of Madras, Madras, 1937.

____________, K.A, *Studies in Cōla History and Administration*, University of Madras, Madras, 1932.

Noboru Karashima, *South Indian History and Society: Studies from Inscription A.D.850-1800*, Oxford University Press, Delhi, 1984.

Rajalakshmi, R, *Tamil Polity*, (A.D.600-A.D. 1300), Ennes Publication, Madurai, 1983.

Ramamurthy, K, 'Some Aspects of the Regional Geography of Tamilnad', *Indian Geographical Journal*, Vol. 23, Nos. 3 and 3 (1948).

Sadasiva Pandarattar, T.V, *Pirkkālachōlar Charittiram* (in Tamil), Annamalai University, Annamalai Nagar, 1972.

Shanmugam, P, *The Revenue System of the Cholas, 850-1279 A.D*, University of Madras, Madras, 1987

South Indian Inscriptions, Vols. II, III, IV, V, VI, VII, VIII, XIII, XIV, XVII, XXIV. Archaeological Survey of India.

South Indian Temple Inscription, Subramanian, T.N, Vol. I

Subbarayalu, Y, *Political Geography of the Chola Country*, University of Madras, Madras, 1973.

Swaminathan, S, *The Early Cholas: History, Art and Culture*, Sharada Publishing House, Delhi, 1998.

Tapan Raychaudhuri and Irfan Habib (eds.), *The Cambridge Economic History of India*, Cambridge University Press, Cambridge, Reprint, 1987.

Thirumavalavan, G, *Political, Social and Cultural History of the Cholas as Gleaned from Ula Literature*, Ezhilagam Publisher, Cheyyar, 1991.

Tirumalai, R, *Land Grants and Agrarian Reactions in Cōla and Pandya Times*, University of Madras, Madras, 1987.

7

Water Resources in Early Medieval Tamil Country: The Kāveri Delta Valley during the Imperial Chōḷa Period

Sudip Narayan Maitra *and* **Suman Saha**

The Indian subcontinent is well recognised for its natural resources, and economic stability. It is measured as the land of the river. The river has made land fertile and has paved the way for agrarian development which has been the foundation of India's economy from very early times. The majority of the Indian population adopted agriculture for their sustenance. To promote surplus agriculture, many substantive steps were taken by the state. Among them, one of the most important initiatives on behalf of the state was the construction of various irrigational projects in the form of dams, tank, canals, sluices etc. In south Indian history, a major portion of the economic activities is centred on around the agriculture and the use of water bodies as irrigational resources. Though irrigational projects were started during the *Sangam* period, it reached its organised form by the Pallava period. Historical evidence related to irrigation system suggests that an organised water management planning was introduced by the Pallava rulers of Kāñci, *Toṇḍaimaṇḍalam* and then by the Chōḷas of the Kaveri delta region. Contemporary literary sources have described this area as a drought-prone area and agriculture was badly affected by frequent famines.

The Pallava rulers and their feudatories developed an efficient water management system to store rainwater to overcome the scarcity of the water. They got water from the Pālaru and Kāveri rivers for irrigation. They also irrigated their fields with the help of tanks, inundation canals and channels as well as wells. *Vāriya Perumakkals* were appointed for the maintenance and repair of irrigation projects. An important feature of the irrigation system of this period was that most of the projects were initiated and funded by the state. The fact that the state patronage encouraged the irrigation projects is proved by the references of the royal tanks called '*Rājatāṭaka*' and these were prefixed by the name of the king or queen who had commissioned them. It indicates the direct initiative of the state to the development of an irrigation system.

With regards to successful protection, circulation of water, we cannot ignore the contribution of King Karikala Chōḷa, who assembled the Grand Anaicut crosswise over River Kāveri. There are a few chronicled confirmations to demonstrate that old Tamil rulers had knowledge on eater management, and water board frameworks set up in their core regions.

The Pāndya rulers built dams across the River Vaigai. The Pandya king Maravarman Arikesari, otherwise called Koon Pāndyan, who ruled Madurai amid seventh century CE made-up a check dam crosswise over Vaigai and named it after him. It is close to the Kuruvikaran Salai Street and archeologists have discovered a stone engraving there. Similarly, the king Parakrama Pāndya built a small dam called *Sitranai* in Kuruvithurai close to Madurai. He additionally removed the rock from the close-by slope *Kuruvikāl* and assembled a stone quarry. Stone engravings in Kuruvithurai Perumal Temple record this.

In the early days, leading communities were comprised for the upkeep of the water bodies. These were the *ēri vāriyam* (lake board) and *kalingu vāriyam* (floodgate board). Sri Vallabha Pāndya, architects of '*Vaiyai Thadam Thēdi*', is recollected even today.

The act of making a water body to help individuals has been there for a long time. Rulers made water bodies and gathered land charges from individuals. Pallavas developed lakes over their kingdom and named the lakes after them. There were likewise a few lakes like the *Thoosi Māmandoor Yēri* close to Kānchipuram. They named engaged keepers to prevent individuals from contaminating water bodies. The *ēri-vāriyam* utilised the collected taxes to de-silt the lake and to maintain sustenance from floods. They likewise let the lake on contract for fishing and shipping "for viable passage, there are distinct sorts of floodgate doors like *Pulikan madai* (which has three outlets)". Depending upon the capacity the water is discharged through these outlets. The one with seven outlets is situated close to Srivilliputhur. It is built by the Koon Pandyan, the hunch-backed Pandyan was the nickname of a king who ruled Madurai around 7th century CE, and to control the stream a column is raised at the focal point of the primary conduit door.

Water is always the primary need in human society. Human existence owes with the effective use of water resources. Its importance emphatically described in the *Tirukkural* thus: "the world cannot exist without water; there will be no ceaseless supply of rainfall".[1] It is further replicated as "rain gives life to all creation, revives the dining vegetation, and restores life to what seems dead".[2] Water considered as liquid gold or the elixir of human immortality. It is also an important medium for transportation as well as a source of irrigation and drainage.

Insufficient rainfall drove the human mind towards the artificial application of natural water resources as irrigation. Earlier civilisations are the gifts of great rivers and largely dependent on them for their evolutions. Further, largely with the help of river water agriculture developed. This laid to organise dense population and to organise society and other commercial activities.

An interesting fact emerged from the South Indian economic history that agriculture could only be possible or originated and practiced largely with the construction of artificial tank irrigation. The majority of the megalithic sites in South India are in close proximity to large reservoirs or river banks. Most scholars of south Indian history, therefore, ascribed the authorship of the "artificial tank irrigation system" in South India image with this megalithic culture.[3] Thiruvaḷḷvar emphatically puts stresses on agriculture by saying "the yoke and the plough where the true emblems of freedom, honour and virtue". Agriculture depends mainly on water from above (rain) or below (rivers and springs).[4]

In between the *Sangam* age and the Pallavas the Kāveri Delta region did not suffer from the neglect of irrigation facilities. After the decline of these two powers, Pallavas, and the Pāndyas, the Imperial Chōḷa rulers seized the Chōḷa country in the second half of 9th century C.E. They shifted their homeland from Urāiur to the banks of the Kāveri. They also followed the tradition set by the *Sangam* ruler Kārikāla Cholan. They built-up a well-organised network of canals and branch channels from the Kāveri River. With the expansion of the Chōḷa Empire irrigation facilities increased from time to time under their patronage. Parāntaka I, also known as Vīranārāyaṇa, founded the *Vīranārāyaṇa-Chaturvēdimangalam*. Further, he constructed the famous *Virānm-ēri* [5] near the place. Several tanks constructed near *Chōḷa-varidhi*.[6]

Construction and Maintenance of Tanks

Due to the inadequate rainfall, the construction of tanks (*ēri* or *kulam*) mainly accelerated. With three sides' embankment, a central sluice on the fourth side of these tanks constructed for the distribution of water. The main function of these sluice equipped tanks was to irrigate agricultural lands known *āyacut*. Various literary and inscriptional records of the medieval Tamil country emphatically uphold the construction of a tank and erection of a sluice as a noble task. Generally, the institutions responsible for the construction and maintenance of these tanks were the state, the village communities, trade guilds, temple authorities, and sometimes private individuals.

The state's share in this construction was often large. In place of providing water to its subjects state increases its income as taxes. The royals who initiate such activities receive appreciation in the literary works of their times. Kārikāla, the most famous *Sangam* Chōḷa king, claims of controlling the river *Kāveri* by raising the banks with earthen embankments and introducing the technique of cutting inundation channels.[7] The *Puttēri* reservoir was built by Āditya Chōḷa.[8]

Kavirkuḷam and *Paramēśvara Pērēri* were built by Rājarāja I.[9] Inscriptional evidence further shows that between sixth to ninth centuries C.E. the construction of numerous tanks increased in number. Besides the kings', officials, chieftains, local rulers, and also the private individuals contributed greatly. Along with the construction of new irrigational tanks later inscriptions carry evidence on the maintenance, repair, and construction of additional sluices where being done extensively.

The big tank at Madurāntakam and another at Tribhuvani were constructed by Uttama Chōḷa (970-985 C.E.). Sundara Chōḷa (956-970 C.E.) in his reign constructed two big tanks *Sundara-Chōḷappērēri* and *Kundavai-ppērēri* to establish his name with his sister.[10] Inscriptions of Rājarāja I, mentions the construction of three tanks; the *kavirkulam*,[11] or *kavir nāḍu* tank, the big tank at Bahur (Pondicherry), and the *Arikesarimangalam* tank.[12] *Rājarāja* I was also associated with the construction of the *Uyyakoṇḍān* channel. This channel connects Tiruchirapalli with Kāveri River and finally falls into a village tank named *Vālavandānkoṭṭai*.[13]

Among the Chōḷa rulers Rājendra I alone raised his name of prominence in the Chōḷa irrigational history. He constructed a large irrigational tank called *Chōḷa-Gangam* in his new capital *Gangaikoṇḍachōḷapuram*. Famous Tiruvālangāḍu plate refers to this tank as a "liquid pillar of victory", *ganga-jalamayam jayasthambam*.[14] It further states that this Lord constructed in his old dominion as a pillar of victory (the tank) known by repute as *Chōḷa-gangam* which was composed of the waters of the Ganges.[15] This tank was about 16 miles long and facilitated with all necessary sluices and channels for the irrigation over larger cultivation land. At present, the tank is useless and mostly ruined but shows the might of skills of Chōḷa engineers and the good wishers of the rulers for the benefit of their subjects. Usually victorious Kings in the past erect pillar of victory or *Jayastambha* rather than the liquid-pillar of victory or *jalastambha*. This appears to be an act of service ruler offer for the benefit of his subjects. Rājendra Chōḷa also built a lake named *mēkhalachampapalle*, in Andhra, in his fourth regnal year.[16]

The accession of Kuloṭṭunga Chōḷa further accelerates the excavation and administrative measures regarding the construction of water bodies. Records testify by associating him with the construction of several reservoirs. The *Rājendra Chōḷa ppērēri* at Kunganur, Andhra Pradesh, and *Madurāntaka ppērēri* dig out in the third and thirty seventh years of his reign.[17]

An inscription of Tacasamuttiram in Omalur taluk of Dharmapuri district issued in the 11th regnal year of Rājarāja I, clearly describes the active involvement of the village community.[18] The transaction of the land regarding the maintenance of tanks found in the Tiruvilankuḍi record issued in 1013 C.E. of Rājarāja I. It clearly describes that the village *Mahāsabhā* sold some land named *nurruvēli* to the temple for renovation work of the damage of the tank. It illustrates that the preservation or repair work of the water tanks considered a collective social action.

The maintenance work of the tanks emerged as the utmost necessity for the village assembly. They often assigned some adjacent lands for this purpose. The incomes from these lands spent fully on the maintenance work. These lands were known as *kuḷappuram*, *kuḷappaṭṭi*, and *ērippaṭṭi*.[19]

Another different but effective way of collecting funds for the maintenance of tanks was by levying the taxes. These taxes were known as *pācipaṭṭam* or *mīnpaṭṭam*. The *mīnpaṭṭam* generally denotes the fishing rights over the tank area. Sometimes by assigning fishing rights temple asked some individuals to carry out the de-silting work.[20]

The existence of small groups or committee for the maintenance of water bodies is also found in Chōḷa inscriptional records. These committees are well organised and structured efficiently. In the *Uttiramērur* inscription, we find the existence of five important communities, especially in the village administration. *ērivariyam* is one such committee responsible for the tank supervision. The existence of another such committee known as *vāyttalai-kulaiyaraiyarkal* mentioned in the inscription at Thiruvāḍuthurai.[21]

Royal Initiative and Agrarian Expansion

From the early time irrigation had been measured as one of the chief requirements in having an advanced form of agriculture. The development of agriculture was possible only based on the obtain-ability of irrigation conveniences. Tamil people were mostly depended on irrigation upon natural water. Thus, the importance of rains in their proper seasons was considered auspicious. According to *Tirukkuṛaḷ*, the constituents of a kingdom are the two-modes of water sources from above (rains) and below (springs). The building of reservoirs and digging of canals were considered as acts of reputation to a ruler by the *Sangam* poets. So the ruling kings and chieftains in the early period always engaged themselves to undertake irrigational schemes to contribute to the agricultural wealth and increase water resources for the general welfare of the country.

Depending upon the land tenancy lands were separated into three categories, i.e. '*Vellanvagai*', '*jivitham*', and '*vāram*'.[22] The irrigated land was divided into wet, dry, and garden lands. In Chōḷa Inscriptions these lands are mentioned as '*nanjai*' (wetland), '*punjai*, (dry land), and '*thōttakal*' (garden land).[23] The term *nanjai*, derived from the Tamil word '*nal*' (good) and '*shai*' (cultivation), refers to land suitable for rice farming through irrigation. The term '*punjai*', derived from the Tamil word '*pun*' for '*pul*'(deficient, inferior), refers to land incapable of irrigated rice cultivation but suitable for minor crop cultivation. The '*thōttakal*' land, watered from wells, was set aside for the cultivation of vegetables and fruits. The *nanjai* and *punjai* lands were known as '*nīrnilam*' or '*nērraramban*' and '*kollainilam*' or '*kattāramban*' respectively.

Dry lands were those which exclusively depending upon local rainfall. Wetlands were irrigated from river channels or tanks by the natural flow of water and garden lands were flooded by water artificially, lifted from well, etc. In the process of wetland rice cultivation water was supplied as often as it could be obtained, daily if possible and on each occasion of watering, the land was flooded to the depth of 1 or 2 inches. On the orchard, lands irrigation was done on a sumptuous scale. Three methods of raising the water were adopted, according to the height of the field from the source of supply. For the low lifts, a bucket was used swung on a rope, this was raised and lowered by two men, while the third lift it over the field. For the high lifts, the *picottah* (*ēatrram*) was used. A horizontal pole was balanced upon an upright post; on one end the bucket was suspended; the counterbalancing weight at the other end was usually supplied by a man who walks along the pole, but sometimes by a lump of clay. The third from the lift, the *kamalai*, will raise water from wells 40 feet rope, which runs over a roller and was worked by a pair of oxen moving up and down an inclined plane.[24]

The primary cause behind the regal endeavor for the augmentation of the water system was to give conveniences to his subjects as an end-result of the duties gathered and somewhat to fulfill his own craving to acquire justify. Rulers knew about the way that to run an express a very much prepared treasury is constantly required. Kautilya in his *Arthaśāstra* has requested the King to keep his treasury in every case full. In pre-current India, a lion's bit of the state's pay originated from land income which was gathered as assessment. Land income turned into the consistent, enduring wellspring of income for any kingdom in the post-Gupta period. To anchor the persistent stream of income and to keep power over land income state took activities for the development of horticulture through appropriate water system offices. In such a way, a significant decent number of uncultivated terrains were brought under development. Additionally, lands were legitimately studied, estimated, arranged, and recorded by the state apparatus.

The rulers focused on gathering land incomes as well as in the meantime they were likewise worried to acquire social union. Indian culture has dependably been a pluralistic culture. Different classes of individuals whether it is proprietors of land, merchants, labourers of land, warriors, individuals having a place with different customs (*sampradāya*) or talking distinctive dialects, and so forth lived respectively in the general public. To control such a pluralistic culture and to keep up harmony in the general public social union was required. Lords attempted to acquire social attachment the agrarian culture through the development of agribusiness, explicitly by making *Brahmadēya* and *Devadāna* settlements.

As Brahmins were the ordering specialist of the *Dharmaśāstras* laws, kings gave them lands to build up the *Dharmaśāstras* ruled stratified social structure and division of work which allocate obligation and status in the general public. In this way, the appropriation of social riches and its offer among classes were set up in an agrarian culture. The general population was sorted by their callings and they had their own bit of offer in the generation. With the development of surplus generation began to develop. Brahmins settled the proportion of offer for every specific class to dodge any question. In this way, through the Brahmins and sanctuary organisations, the rulers endeavored to keep harmony in the general public which at last aided in agrarian extension.

A large number of inscriptional references prove the king's concern to provide maximum irrigation facilities to the farmers. The thoughtful attempts of the kings for the extension of cultivation are further attested by the remains of old and extant irrigation works. From the early period, a large number of water tanks, canals, sluices, etc. were constructed in the Tamil country by the royal officials, state authorities, nobles, and private individuals. Even with the creation of *Brahmadēya* and *Dēvadāna* settlements irrigation facilities were extensively extended, maintained, and controlled. Kings of this period issued orders to dig new tanks and to make the extension of the existing channels to provide water to the *Brahmadēya* and *Dēvadāna* settlements.[25]

Our concern here is to go through the Chōḷa rulers efforts, who founded an enormous empire centered on the Kāveri delta region. They properly diverted river water from the Kāveri to cultivate a huge area and also developed the artificial way of the water management system. They were able to collect a large amount of land taxes which was the main source of the exchequer. Their contribution to the water management system, land reclamation process, and land measurement system is the matter of our concern. The *Chōḷa* State's role to the extension of irrigation facilities can be classified under two categories: construction and maintenance of irrigation work by the state and remission of taxes on water and land.

Water Supply and Management

The fertile valley of the *Kāveri* River and proper organisation of its water was the key source of agricultural prosperity in Tamil land. As the Kāveri River contains one-fourth of all the riverine water in Tamil Nadu, benefitting from both the south-west and north-east monsoon rains in the Western Ghats. The Chōḷa Empire which grown on the bank of the Kāveri River properly used its water by channelising it throughout their kingdom. To cultivate the fertile lands of Kāveri delta the Chōḷa kings sponsored irrigation facilities which led towards unprecedented growth in crop production. During the Chōḷa period agriculture became a well-advanced profession of the people of Tamil Nadu. A large portion of uncultivated land was brought under cultivation with the help of state efforts. Through the proper study of the Chōḷa inscriptions, it can be viewed that history of the Chōḷa Empire was closely attached with the state-sponsored irrigation on the Kāveri River.

Medieval South India is known for its frequent failure of monsoons which in turn affected crop cultivation badly and brought drought.[26] Various sources of the Chōḷa period provide shreds of evidence regarding the periodical failure of monsoons. For instance, an inscription of the Chōḷa king Kuloṭṭunga III (c.1178-1218 CE) speaks about the failure of monsoons. On the other hand, heavy rainfall which ultimately caused flood situations also affected crop cultivation. Because of overwhelming floods, a lot of lands wound up uncultivable under sand sediment tossed by the over-flooding of stream Kaveri. It made significant harm to the rice fields and products for a broad time span. During the reign of Rājendra Chōḷa I lands were damaged, in the villages of Allur and Isanamangalam located on the southern bank of the river Kaveri, by the flood.[27] The Kaveri delta region came to be called the 'land of floods' (*Punalnadu*) and continuous efforts were made to regulate and tame it by digging canal networks for the distribution of its water to irrigate the lands.[28]

Substantial precipitation and floods represented a major issue to the potential farming area lost because of soil disintegration. A few tons of soil had likewise been lost because of water disintegration. In this manner corrupted land represented a significant issue. This best layer of the dirt contained indispensable parts since every one of the supplements required by plants had been available in this layer. This top layer of soil is considered as the feeding zone of plants. This fertile soil was the most valuable natural resource and it usually lied at some depth (of 15-20 cm.) over the face of the soil. Because of the frequent failure of monsoons and unprecedented rains people realised the importance of water and its storage. Therefore, people tried to solve the water problem by establishing man-made sources of water supply like dams, tanks, lakes, etc and planned to manage the water efficiently.

The policy of the tank construction can be said to be the innovative involvement of the Chōḷas to irrigation technology. Their construction of tanks essentially elaborates the idea that a river is best controlled at the head of its delta.[29] 'Tank' in Tamil country is variously known as '*tātaka*', '*ēri*', '*pērēri* ', '*kulam* ', etc. Other sources of irrigation in South India were wells or '*kinarus* ', ponds or '*kuttai* ', lakes or '*ēris* ', etc. According to *Sangam* literature, the construction of reservoirs and digging of canals were considered as one of the seven meritorious acts- *saptasantana* and ensured one's happiness in the next world.

Among the *Sangam* Chōḷa kings, Karikala Cholan (c.150 C.E.) was the first who tried to a great extent to harness the natural sources of water. The '*Pattinappālai*' anthology contains a poem by Uruttiram Kannanar, who lauds Karikala for his contributions to the construction of irrigation tanks.[30] He controlled the over the flow of the banks of the river Kaveri. He is credited with the construction of embankments on both sides of the Kaveri River and constructed a dam, popularly known as '*Kallanai Dam*' or Grand Dam across the Kaveri near Tiruchirapalli as well as dug many canals. As an honour of this pious work, he was granted the title '*Peruvalattān* ', the great benefactor or fertiliser. It is known from an inscription that after a victorious expedition at Ceylon, Karikala Cholan brought 1200 slaves as war captives who were employed as labour to complete the dam.[31] In effect; his pioneering activity successfully prevented the annual inundations for nearly fifteen centuries.[32]

The Imperial Chōḷa kings also constructed a large number of dams as well as tanks and also channelised water to the agricultural fields through various canals. There was a rapid increase in the number of tanks constructed from the 10th century onwards due to the increase of royal patronage.

The Chōḷa king *Āditya Chōḷa* constructed the *Puttēri* reservoir. Parāntaka I, who was entitled as *Virnārāyana*, constructed a large lake called '*Virānam-ēri* ' near *Kāttumannārkoil in* South Arcot district which even today seems an important source of irrigation.[33] According to Karandai Copper Plates, Parantaka I excavated thousands of deep streams to make the earth fertile. He is credited with the construction of the *Chōḷavaridhi* tank near Sholingur, *Vinnamangalam* tank at Ambur, the *Sodiyambakkam* tank near Ukkal, the *Virasōlanvadavāru* running to the north of Tanjavur and the *Madurantakam-vadavāru* branching off from the grand anicut on Coleroon north of Tiruppanandal. Further, he was responsible for diverting the Kaveri waters along the Mannai River which was called *Kunjaramallan* after him. It seems that Parantaka-I was not only a great warrior but also he was conscious about the welfare of his subjects. The Sholinghur inscription records that Parantaka's subordinate, Prithvipati II donated a paddy land named *mūngilvari* for the maintenance of the tank, *Cholavaridhi*.[34] In 909 C.E. Parantaka I granted the entire collection of royal revenue derived from the *mūngilvari* land to the above-stated tank for its improvement. An official of Parantaka-I stationed in the Pandyan country donated 12 *kasu* as a deposit for securing payment of taxes in the land to the assembly of *Narasingamangalam*. In return, he obtained the land to be converted into a tank *Urudaiyankulam* alias *Kalyanēri*.[35] Another tank called *Rajadhirajan perun-kulam* was dug at *Kulottunga-cōlanallur*.[36]

Gandrāditya, son of *Parāntaka-I*, is associated with a tank called *Gandarāditya-pereri*.[37] His Queen, Sembiyān Mahādevi, donated some funds to dig a tank at Tirumalapadi. In the memory of this Queen, a tank at Tiruchirapalli had been designated as *Sembiyan-mahadēvi-ppērēri*. One of the canals in the same region is known as *Sembiyan-mahadevi-vaykkal* after the name of the Queen *Sembiyan Mahadevi*.[38] Uttama Chōḷa (970-985 C.E) constructed the 'Big Tank' at Madurantakam and another one at Tribhuvani (Pondicherry). In order to establish his name and to perpetuate the memory of his daughter the Chola King Sundarachola Parantaka II (956-970 C.E) dug two tanks namely, *Sundara-cōlappērēri* and *Kundavai-ppērēri*.[39]

Rajaraja I built three tanks, which already stated in the previous pages.[40] Among them the *Bahur* tank was constructed by Rajaraja I and maintained by the tank supervision committee. He constructed the *Uyyakondan vāykkāl* which is still serving the district of Tiruchirapalli.[41] This channel branches off from the river Kaveri near the Vettuvayttalai Railway station[42] and falls into a tank in the village of Valavandankottai, about 10 miles to the east of Tiruchirappalli, an ancient irrigation tank in that district.[43] During the Chola rule initiatives were taken by the state for the peaceful regulation of the irrigation system. For instance, the Larger Leiden plates of Rājarāja I speak of peaceful methods adopted by the state to secure peace and harmony among the people of the adjacent villages and to safeguard their rights.[44] The two clauses specially mentioned in the plates are as follows:

(i) The irrigation channel passing through the lands of this village to other villages in the outskirts shall be permitted to flow without any impediment of the done, and

(ii) The channels passing through outside villages to irrigate the lands of this village shall be allowed to flow uninterrupted by the people of the out-lying villages.[45]

Rājendra Chōḷa I (1012-1044 C.E.) constructed the sixteen-mile-long tank (reservoir) called '*Chōlagangam*' with substantial sluices at his capital town *Gangaikonda Cholapuram*. Water from the *Chōlagangam* was channelised to a large area north of the *Kollidam* River, including the capital city, through its connecting sluices and canals.[46] The tank was partly filled by a channel from the Kollidam River which enters at its southern end and partly by a smaller channel from the Vellar River on the northern end. It represents the solitude of the ruler for the welfare of the subjects and its immense economic profit to the people in that part of the Chola country. As a result, there was tremendous agrarian expansion during the rule of the Imperial Chōḷas (c. 850-1270 C.E). Rājendra Chōḷa constructed this tank after returning from his victorious march to the north up to the river Ganga and by bringing from there symbolically several pots of water to be emptied into that big tank to mark and celebrate that glorious and victorious event and to add sanctity to thus stored water which was thenceforth called as *Chōlagangam*. It is also known that in the fourth year of his reign he made a lake at Mekhalachampalle (Chittoor, Andhra Pradesh).[47] According to a Copper Plate grant of the 11th century, Rajendra Chola directed the people of the village Thiruvalangadu to undertake the digging of minor channels wherever necessary from the main canals to ensure proper utilising of the water for irrigation purposes.[48]

The accession of Kulottunga Chola I (1070-1120 C.E) marks the beginning of a new era in the history of the *Cholas*. He is credited for excavating several reservoirs. The *Rājendrachōlappērēri* at Kunganur (Punganur, Andhra Pradesh) and the *Madurāntakappērēri* located to the east of *Alinjanēri* at Idaiyur (Eduru) were constructed. The *Kulōttungasōlappērēri* at Muniyur and the *Sindhuvalli* tank (Mysore) were also built by him.[49] The *Chola* Kings not only constructed tank and canals but also paid great attention to the maintenance of water sources. For example, it is stated in an inscription of king

Kuloṭṭunga that every year from the 12th year of his reign the tank of *Somangalam* alias *Pañcanadivanaca-caturvēdimangalam* breached at various places due to heavy rains. Seeing this perennial problem, in his 14th regnal year Kulottunga donated forty *palankasu* (a kind of coin) as an endowment for repairing the channels and the tank bunds.[50] One Masavaipettai Nayaka, an officer under the king Kulottunga, donated the tank named *Pedda-samudra* to god *Sithavatesvara* and at the same time, the three Vellalas who laboured in the construction of that tank were granted land irrigated by the water from the same tank.[51]

The Cellur plate of Virachola, son of Kulottunga I, mentions a great lake (*Mahasaras*) in Vengimandalam. During the rule of Rajaraja III a large reservoir, known as *Sembarambākkam*, was constructed.[52] It is regarded as one of the biggest irrigation tanks in the Chingleput district. In his ruling period in the *Pēriya Vāykkāl* (great channel) at Musiri the head sluice was built of stone in 1219 C.E.[53] It is known that in the thirty-third year of his reign a piece of land was endowed for digging a channel to feed the tank in the *dēvadāna* village Tiruccirremam.[54] A few records belonging to the time of Kulottunga III speaks of a large seized *madagu* (sluice) and other channels connected to the reservoirs for conveying water to nearby tanks. During his rule, a royal order was issued to the village authorities of Tiraiyanur to make a tax-free gift of three *vēli* of land to one individual who closed the breaches in the tank at Tenneri. This incident proves that the state apart from its direct involvements also encouraged private initiatives for the maintenance of irrigation projects.

Land Reclamation

Another vital part of the economy of the concerned period was the recovery of terrains. Land recovery was drilled in South India since time immemorial with the end goal of bringing all the more new land under the furrow and therefore to advance the reason for a farming generation. In a roundabout way recovery of terrains likewise given roads of work to numerous individuals. Development of tanks and burrowing of channels brought not just the dry land under the water system framework yet, in addition, squander lands, sandy grounds, and backwoods lands were brought under development. Because of land recovery, numerous timberlands were tidied up woods and numerous sandy regions were cleaned up sand which was till now lying unused. Engravings notice the recovery of the place that is known for various classes.

The *Sangam* Chōḷa king Kārikāla Chōḷan is credited for deforesting a large tract of Chola country and made them fit for cultivation and human habitation.[55] The Karaṇḍai Tamil *Sangam* Plates of king Rājendra Chōḷa mentions that fresh lands were reclaimed.[56] Another inscription states that land reclamation was done for laying a garden in the 25th year of Kuloṭṭunga Chōḷa.[57] Two more inscriptions refer to the clearing of sand dunes as an act of reclamation for agricultural purposes. An inscription from Tirumayanam of Rājādhirāja's period records the gift of twenty-three *vēli* of land to the temple. It states that the land was obtained after its reclamation from the sandy mounds. It appears that the state through the *ūr* and *sabha* of the concerned place got the land for donation.[58] These instances prove that state initiative was quite impressive for bringing new lands under cultivation through the land reclamation process.

Land Measurement

The Chōḷa economy was mainly dependent on land. The bulk of the government revenues as stated above came from the land tax. In order to register the land rights and to fix the land tax a unique form of the measurement system was implemented by the Chola rulers. They even tried to introduce a standard system of land measurement in the whole kingdom.[59] The land was measured by different units called *ma*, *vēli*, *kāni*, *patti*, *patakam* and *kuli*. Among these *patti* was used in the northern districts of Chengalpattu, North Arcot and South Arcot and the adjoining districts in Andhra Pradesh. But after the early eleventh century, this unit was possibly out of use. The unit *patakam* was used in few *brahmadēya* villages. On the other hand, *kuli* and *vēli* were the most popular land units. Usually, *kuli* was the smallest basic unit of measurement, the other units like *vēli*, *patti* and *patakam* were expressed in multiples of this unit. It is proved by the Tamil literary evidence (first-third centuries C.E) that the largest standard unit, *vēli*, was in use from the early times.[60]

The basic land measuring instrument that we have literary and inscriptional reference is to *adi-kōl* which means a rod or *kōl* of *adi* (probably equal to the present day one foot). The foot is mentioned in the inscription as equal to the length of the foot (*shri-pāda*) which invariably refers to the foot of king Kulottunga. The length of the king's foot (approximately twelve inches) was taken as the standard unit in the beginning as the length of the *kol*.[61] An inscription mentions the name *Panniradikkōl* that is rod of twelve feet length (12 x 12= 144 inches).[62] One square of *Panniradikkōl*, i.e.144 square inches

(12 square feet) formed one *kuli* and hundred *kuli* formed one *mā* (possibly '*mā*' is an abbreviation of the form of *mattara*, a kind of land measurement).

The above discussion proves that the state played a key role to the agrarian expansion during the study period. Though the state's primary concern was to collect a large amount of taxes from the land but in this process other issues, like the establishment of *Dharmashastra* laws and maintenance of social cohesion, were also settled down through the agrarian expansion. *Brahmins* and temple institutions were the key instrument in this process who was appointed by the state not only to achieve religious merits but also to establish the *Dharmashastra* dominated stratified society. The direct intervention of the state to the agricultural activities gave an impetus to the agrarian expansion. The Chola kings appropriately utilised water of the Kaveri River to irrigate a large number of agricultural lands and due to their constant efforts, many uncultivable lands were brought under cultivation.

Water-right is another significant feature of irrigation. The supply of water was generally according to water rights. A water right may either be hereditary in nature or be purchased. Sometimes participation in the construction of irrigational tanks along with landholders may generate some water rights. After the fields of the water right holders are irrigated the excess water generally sold which intern accumulates a fund for the maintenance of water bodies. Inscriptional evidence regarding water right show disputes and rights were resolved amicably within the *āyacut* itself. Normative water rights belong to the landholders and land donees. In some cases, the direct interference themes for higher authority took place when two rival groups quarreled to hold the tank right. This clearly shows that the supreme right on the water management lies with the state. From the time of the *Pallavas*, the king has the sole right to give permission to dig river channels. State directives were also issued related to the neighbouring village dwellers. It restricts the neighbouring villagers from misusing water in the channels by using a basket or by cutting out branches from the main channel.

During the Chōḷa rule, these regulations further improved and enforced strictly. The copper plate inscription of Tiruvālangāḍu, belongs to 6th regnal year of Rājendra Chōḷa I, emerged as the best examples related to the water management.[63] In clear terms, the grant described the prevalent water rights. This order took the utmost care to avoid any water dispute in the future. And also try to denote the equitable distribution of water to all fields in a village. What assigned to a particular village community shall not be wasted.[64] By these well accounted royal orders, rulers were to ensure a full supply of water to all individuals, small and big landowners.

The management of the *Chōḷa* Empire was more unified than that of the Deccan rulers. The well-known local self-government authorities like *sabha*, the *ūr*, the *nāḍu* and the *nagaram* enjoyed more autonomy during the *Chōḷa* age.

Earlier practices of land revenue scrutiny and tax calculations of the Pallava and Pāndya age were continuous with more intensity from the days of Rājarāja I.[65] According to inscriptions; the land revenue service was mostly done in the core area of Chōḷa Empire. The village assemblies generally collect several types of taxes. According to P. Shanmugam there were at least 66 types of taxes connected with land.[66] Other than this, he mentioned thirty-two types of taxes associated with water found in records from *Chōḷamandalam* the *Pāṇḍiamaṇḍalam*, and the *Toṇḍaimaṇḍalam*. They were collected from the tenants and the landowners as service charges for the maintenance of irrigation works.

From the above brief explanation, it may be concluded that the prudent and practical royal policies of the early medieval south Indian rulers the problems like seasonal drought and famine like the situation could easily be checked and brought under control. It was due to the creation of an adequate number of irrigation facilities and reclamation of wasteland by bringing under the plough. All these efforts intern increased the revenue and facilitate the state exchequer. The present irrigation system prevalent in *Kāveri* delta certainly owes its inception from these early efforts of kings with their experience and expertise in the entire length and breadth of South India.

Discussion

The South-Eastern part of India which includes the southern Andhra and northern Tamil Nadu includes a mixture of diverse climatic and psychological settings. It is a combination of rivers, mountains, and sea and largely depends upon the rainfall patterns for the evolution of this region. Here the centre of the problem was to provide an adequate supply of water for irrigation. Of Peninsular India which is mainly agriculture and most of the rivers are not perennial and heavily depends upon rainfall which interns uncertain.

The mention of *Mahēndra tātaka*, *Chitramēgha tātaka*, *Paramēsvara tātaka*, shows that several times were named after the ruling authority of the period along with their feudatories. The Pallava tanks and wells, several of which function even today, were the lifeline of the Pallava villages. Although tanks, referred to as *tātaka* and *ēri* in Pallava irrigation, and wells seem to be the widely prevalent and preferred forms of artificial irrigation under the *Pallavas*. Other useful methods where spring channels or *urrukkāl*, sluices or *tumbu*.

In the case of large tanks, reservoirs, and canals, which required a greater amount of resources, were mostly constructed by the state. Sluices, wells, and other such irrigational devices required comparatively less sponsorship who are constructed by the well the reasons or local village bodies. Construction and maintenance of all these means of water supply were strictly under administrative control. Even initiatives of the private individuals were levied by the village authorities. Despite of administrative control over the machinery of water supply, the state encouragement was given to private individuals to construct works of irrigation mostly *brahmadēya* and *dēvadānas* villages easily got permission to construction works free of charge, even the arrangement of lands and financial help.

The keenness behind the state in encouraging the establishment of artificial irrigation techniques is mainly two folded. Primarily to motivate cultivators for more production of crops and to raise new varieties of crops, this practice gradually helps the state to bring more and more wastelands under the domain of agricultural land, which intern generate more wealth for the state in the form of tax.

In agrarian state water is the basic resource for agricultural production. Frequent monsoon failures lead to the development of various irrigational methods for agrarian production. Irrigation is the artificial application or process of supplying water to crops where either rainfall is insufficient or rain comes in the wrong season. The ancient civilisations, situated in the riverside, of the Near East, were the first to apply irrigation on a large scale as they had a lack of water and also hot summer was another cause to move towards an artificial water management system. In these regions irrigation was not a compliment but rather a supplement of farming. Thus, it is true that irrigation, as practised in the ancient civilisations was the result or fruit of an evolution of many generations. The oldest civilisations of the world are off-springs of the great rivers and had a great dependency on them for their evolution. Rivers helped them to grow agricultural products and also helped those to maintain commercial intercourse with the distant lands to fulfil their desires. In the early days, river acted as a great agent to enrich the soil by its seasonal inundation and providing irrigational facilities for growing up crops as well as a highway by which the produce of the land could be sent into the cities. In the early civilisations like Egypt, Mesopotamia, India and China highest importance was given to irrigation; it is attributed that irrigation is one of the strongest agencies in promoting civilisation, encouraging providence and care and fostering communal existence and co-operation, without which progress is impossible.

To trace the antiquity of irrigation in India, it is essential to look at the dawn of civilisation. In India, people from food gathers became food producers during the Neolithic period. In the Indus Valley Civilisation people practised agriculture is proved from the archaeological evidence in the form of food products like rice, wheat, barley, peas, sesame, etc. In Lothal existence of charred rice from a storage jar kept in mud-brick house points to the cultivation of rice which relates the importance of irrigation. The existence of water reservoir has been disclosed from *Dholavira* which is direct evidence of irrigation work during the ancient period. Since the river Indus was perennial, it became unnecessary for the Harappan's to practice artificial tank irrigation. Such a civilisation, technically highly skilled must have had a thorough knowledge of irrigation by moulding the nature blessed sources like the rivers and streams. The use of irrigation is recognised in the Vedas and in the *Brāhmaṇas*, mention is made of wells, canals and dams.

India is known as the agricultural country and the biggest part of its economy was depended on agriculture during the early days. India gets uneven rainfall. The seasonal rainfall was seldom normal in the subcontinent. Sometimes there was the failure of monsoon which caused famine and sometimes due to heavy rain flood disturbed the agricultural production. Thus, due to inadequate rainfall people moved their attention towards the artificial irrigation system. In India, sources of irrigation are mainly canals, wells and tanks. Organised irrigation system was started in South India and gradually it spread to the whole country. It is important to note down that half of the irrigational resources are situated in south India, especially in the states of Tamil Nadu and Andhra Pradesh. The historical record proves that kings and princes of South India gave great attention to the development and promotion of the water management system. They constructed dams, tanks, and canals. Actually in the southern part of the sub-continent failure of monsoon, the uneven rainfall, its scarcity, and excess led the rulers to restrain and regulate these natural resources. One of the most interesting and important parts of the economic history of south India is attached to the agriculture and promotion of the water management system which was the ultimate priority for them. It is predicted that the history of the irrigation system in south India is related to the Megalithic period. As most of the Megalithic sites of South India are in close proximity to large reservoirs or river banks. Most of the sites are situated in such a place where excellent water supply is provided by a tank or water resources.

Being an agricultural country people recognised the importance of irrigation from the dawn of the civilisations. Besides the archaeological sources there is also literary evidence which discloses the fact that people were too serious regarding the water management system. It is from the literary source of south India that we find a large number of references regarding irrigation. In the *Sangam* literature and also in the contemporary literature consciousness about water management is evident. In *Tirukkural*, author Tiruvā̤ḷvār has praised the people for solving the puzzle of food problems by properly utilising water resources and also has paid attention to the storage of rainwater. In the *Puram* literature, it is stated that by constructing large reservoirs and canals people emphasised the importance of irrigation and encouraged artificial irrigation of the soil on an extensive scale. Even it is said in the literature that one who has taken the burden to turn the low land into the reservoir has established his or her name in the world. It has always been given preference to settle down near the river as it will provide drinking water and also cultivation works will be continued smoothly. According to ancient literature, the digging of a tank is regarded as the greatest of the seven meritorious acts of a man. In the inscriptions creation of irrigational resources has been attached to the religious and social significance. Even construction of a tank has been considered as an act of charity that attributed religious merit. Thus, from this point of view kings, queens, officials and private individuals took initiative to the construction of various irrigation projects. Whenever new settlements were formed it became customary to connect them with proper water resources which will help people to fulfil their needs of drinking water as well as agricultural needs. The material traces of irrigation works bear witness to the enterprise and devoted attention to the people of south India in promoting irrigation projects.

Material evidence found from Ādichchanallūr on the banks of the *Tāmaraparani* River in Tamil Nadu leads our knowledge about the practice of farming in south India during the early Iron Age. Evidence of rice cultivation has been explored here. They cultivated rice with the help of iron implements and had limited available irrigation facilities.

The ecosystem as depicted in the Sangam literature of the *Sangam* age is known as *Tinai*. The five-fold divisions or regions or five types of terrains as classified by the poets were the *Kurunji* or the mountain region, the *Mullai* or the forest or pastoral tract, the *Marutam* or the agricultural region, the *Neithal* or the sandy coastal tract and the *Palai* or the desert tract. Each tract has its own peculiar flora and fauna and other economic aspects. In the *Sangam* literature, it is mentioned that in the *Marutam* or *Menpulam* or the agrarian region the villages were invariably surrounded by green fields. At the same time this land had many tanks (*ayam*), minor dams (*sirai*), and fresh water ponds (*ūruni*) in the villages. Similarly, it has been noticed in the literary sources that people of this land used deep sunk wells. There were many rivers and branch channels with well-connected sluices. The people of this tract were called *kalāmars*. It is documented in the literature that people of this land were well acquainted with cultivation.

The role of irrigation in the agricultural economy need hardly be stressed. An agricultural country like India, mainly dependent on the rural economy, has from ancient times made provision for the storage of water in big tanks, reservoirs, and dams to meet the requirements of the agriculturists and artisans in different seasons.

The importance of irrigation was realised in southern India from early times. Dams were erected across streams and channels took off from them at convenient points. In the absence of natural streams, large tanks were constructed. In south India particularly during the Chola rule special facilities and tax concessions were granted for specified periods to people who reclaimed land and brought it under cultivation. The main feature of the irrigational system was the existence of a network of tanks or reservoirs in which rain water was brought and stored for utilisation. There were also channels for drawing water from large rivers. Most of the fields derived water from the storage tanks and wells sunk deep in the earth. Each village had one or two or more tanks- known as *cheruvo* or *keri* in Kannada. The Eastern *Chālukyas* inscriptions present some information on their irrigation system. An inscription refers to an additional tax of one *visa* as service tax to the state (of a *paṇa*) on each load of betel. The *tãmbuligas* (*tàmbulikas*) were expected to pay this surcharge in addition to the one imposed by the local authority. Certain specified incomes from taxes and fines were set apart for digging a tank called *Rattasamudra* in 1041 C.E. A *Kadamba* prince presented the *mahājanas* of *Nirili (Niralgiin Dharwar*), the entire house tax of the place for the maintenance of the *Periyakara* the big tank in it. Sometimes the land was specially allotted for the maintenance of a big tank, or endowment especially made for the building of a new tank. Stress was thus laid on minor irrigation projects rather than on the construction of big dams.

The *Chōḷas* paid much attention on the development of irrigation sources. An inscription refers to the raising of the banks of the Kāveri, for the prosperity of the Chōḷa country. Tanks were properly maintained. A large number of irrigational tanks are noticed in inscriptions, some dating from the Pallava times. These tanks were under the care of the village assemblies to get silt removed before the rains set in, and secure the proper depth needed to store the full supply for the next year. Special endowments were often created, and where the annual repairs were not provided for a special cess, the *ēri-āyam*, was earmarked for this purpose and collected from the *rayots* in the village. The *Kākatiyas* also took a special interest in irrigational projects. They realised the utility of the storage of water, and so they constructed large tanks and dams, but not as part of the state activity. The construction of water bodies such as *ēri*, *kulam* and *vāykkāl* was regarded as an act of charity that would confer great religious merit.

References

1. *Tirukkural*, ch. 2:10, tr. V. R. Ramachandra Dikshitar, p. 5.
2. *Ibid.*
3. T.M. Srinivasan, *Irrigation and Water Supply*, New Era Publications, Madras, 1991, p. 4.
4. *Indian Antiquity*, IX, p. 199; *ASI Annual Report*, 1903-04, p. 202.
5. *A.R.E*, No. 615 of 1920; *Gazetteer of the South Arcot District*, 1906, p. 132.
6. *E.I.*, VI. No. 32, pp. 221-25.
7. K. A. Nilakanta Sastri, *The Colas*, Madras, 1955, p. 583.
8. *A.R.E.*, 1935-36, p. 62.
9. *S.I.I.*, Vol. XVII, No. 336.
10. *A.R.E.*, No. 264 of 1915.
11. *A.R.E.*, No. 307 of 1904.
12. *A.R.E.*, No. 160 of 1895.

13. K. Mavali Rajan and Suman Saha, "Sources of Water Supply and Water Management during the Chola Period", *Indian Historical Studies*, St. Joseph's College, Tiruchirapalli, Vol. XI, No. 1, October, 2014, p. 90.
14. *S.I.I.*, Vol. III, Part III, p. 425, Verse 24.
15. T.M. Srinivasan, *op.cit.*, p. 28.
16. *A.R.E.*, No. 190 of 1931-32.
17. *A.R.E.*, Nos. 540 of 1906; 202 of 1931-32.
18. K. Shanmugam, *Lithic Documents in Tanks*, an International Institute of Tamil Studies, Chennai, pp. 29-43.
19. *I.P.S.*, Nos.776 and 301.
20. *I.P.S.*, No. 351.
21. *S.I.I.*, Vol. I, No. 151.
22. *A.R.E.*, No. 176 of 1926; also see *Annual Reports on South Indian Epigraphy*, No.119 of 1926-27.
23. *A.R.E.*, No. 91 of 1918.
24. K. Mavali Rajan, *Medieval Tamil Society and Agrarian Slavery*, Maha Bodhi Book Agency, Kolkata, 2014, pp. 128-129.
25. P. Chandrasekharan, *Agrarian System of Tamilnadu from A.D 850-1300'* Manju Publication, Rajapalayam, 2004, pp. 38-39.
26. K. Karuppiah, *A Social-cultural History of the Later Cholas: As Gleaned through Epigraphy*, Sharada Publishing House, Delhi, 2010, p. 76.
27. R. Tirumalai, "Allur and Isanamangalam Revisited" in K.V. Ramesh, et.al., *Svasti Sri (Dr. B.Ch. Chhabra Felicitation Volume)*, Agam Kala Prakashan, Delhi, 1984, pp. 25-55.
28. K. V. Raman, "Irrigation in South India (up to 1300 A.D) Techniques and Management", in Lallanji Gopal and V. C. Srivastava (eds.), *History of Agriculture in India (up to 1200 AD)*, New Delhi, 2008, p. 500.
29. *Ibid.*, p. 624.
30. *Ibid.*, p. 619.
31. K. Mavali Rajan and Suman Saha, *op.cit.*, p. 85.
32. T. M. Srinivasan, "Irrigation and Irrigation Works" in *History of Technology in India from Antiquity to c. 1200 A.D.*, Indian National Science Academy, New Delhi, 2008, p. 558.
33. K. V. Raman, *op.cit.*, p.501.
34. K. Mavali Rajan and Suman Saha, *op.cit.*, p. 86.
35. S. Swaminathan, *The Early Cholas: History, Art and Culture*, Sharada Publishing House, Delhi, 1998, p. 68.
36. K. Karuppiah, *op.cit.*, p. 78.
37. T.M. Srinivasan, *Irrigation and Water Supply: South India, 200 B.C-1600 A.D.*, New Era Publication, Madras, 1991, p. 27.
38. *S.I.I.*, Vol. XIII, p. 151.
39. *A.R.E.*, No. 264 of 1915.

40. *A.R.E.*, Nos. 307 of 1914, 178 of 1902, 160 of 1895.
41. T.M. Srinivasan, "Irrigation and Irrigation Works" p. 571.
42. T.M. Srinivasan, *Irrigation and Water Supply: South India, 200 B.C-1600 A.D.*, p. 175.
43. *Ibid.*, p. 28.
44. *Ibid.*, p. 159.
45. *E.I.*, Vol. XXII, p. 234.
46. K. V. Raman, *op.cit.*, p.501.
47. T. M. Srinivasan, *Irrigation and Water supply: South India, 200 B.C-1600 A.D.*, p. 28.
48. C.T.M. Kotraiah, *Irrigation System under Vijayanagara Rule*, Directorate of Archaeology and Museums, Mysore, 1995, p. 15.
49. T. M. Srinivasan, *Irrigation and Water supply: South India, 200 B.C-1600 A.D.*, p. 28.
50. K. Mavali Rajan and Suman Saha, *op.cit.*, p. 88.
51. C.T.M. Kotraiah, *op.cit.*, p. 12.
52. T.M. Srinivasan, *Irrigation and Water supply: South India, 200 B.C-1600 A.D.*, p. 29.
53. K. Mavali Rajan and Suman Saha, *op.cit.*, p. 90.
54. T.M. Srinivasan, *Irrigation and Water supply: South India, 200 B.C-1600 A.D.*, p. 69.
55. S. Swaminathan, *op.cit.*, pp.165-166.
56. K. Karuppiah, *op.cit.*, p. 80.
57. *S.I.I.*, Vol. XXII, Part I, No. 56 of 1906.
58. *S.I.I.*, Vol. XXII, Part II, No. 55 of 1906.
59. K.A. Nilakanta Sastri, *op.cit.*, p. 622.
60. Y. Subbarayalu, *South India under the Cholas*, Oxford University Press, New Delhi, 2012, pp. 77-78.
61. K. Karuppiah, *op.cit.*, p. 80.
62. *A.R.E.* No. 214 of 1911.
63. *S.I.I.*, Vol. III, No. 205.
64. *I.P.S.*, Nos. 283, 285, 405.
65. K.A. Nilakanta Sastri, *A History of South India: From Prehistoric Times to the Fall of Vijayanagar*, Oxford University Press, New Delhi, 1997, p.195.
66. P. Shanmugam., *The Revenue System of The Chōḷas, 850-1259*, New Era Publication, Madras, 1987, pp. 45-49.

Bibliography

Annual Report on Epigraphy, 1895, 1902, 1904, 1906, 1911, 1914, 1915, 1918, 1920, 1926, 1931-32, 1935-36.

Annual Reports on South Indian Epigraphy, 1926-27.

Chandrasekharan, P., *Agrarian System of Tamilnadu from A.D 850-1300'* Manju Publication, Rajapalayam, 2004.

Epigrphia Indica, Vols. VI, XXII.

Gazetteer of the South Arcot District, 1906.

Indian Antiquity, IX, p. 199; *ASI Annual Report*, 1903-04.

Inscriptions of Pudukottai State, Nos.776, 351, 301. 283, 285, 405.

Karuppiah, K., A Social-cultural History of the Later Cholas: As Gleaned through Epigraphy, Sharada Publishing House, Delhi, 2010.

Kotraiah, C.T.M., *Irrigation System under Vijayanagara Rule*, Directorate of Archaeology and Museums, Mysore, 1995.

Mavali Rajan, K. and Suman Saha, "Sources of Water Supply and Water Management during the Chola Period", *Indian Historical Studies*, St. Joseph's College, Tiruchirapalli, Vol. XI, No. 1, October, 2014.

Mavali Rajan, K., *Medieval Tamil Society and Agrarian Slavery*, Maha Bodhi Book Agency, Kolkata, 2014.

Nilakanta Sastri, K.A., *The Colas*, University of Madras, Madras, 1955.

----------------, *A History of South India: From Prehistoric Times to the Fall of Vijayanagar*, Oxford University Press, New Delhi, 1997.

Raman, K.V., "Irrigation in South India (up to 1300 A.D) Techniques and Management", in Lallanji Gopal and V. C. Srivastava (eds.), *History of Agriculture in India (up to 1200 AD)*, New Delhi, 2008.

Shanmugam, K., *Lithic Documents in Tanks*, an International Institute of Tamil Studies, Chennai.

Shanmugam, P., *The Revenue System of The Chōḷas, 850-1259*, New Era Publication, Madras, 1987.

South Indian Inscriptions, Vols. I, III, XIII, XVII, XXII.

Srinivasan, T.M., "Irrigation and Irrigation Works" in *History of Technology in India from Antiquity to c. 1200 A.D.*, Indian National Science Academy, New Delhi, 2008.

------------------, *Irrigation and Water Supply*: *South India, 200 B.C-1600 A.D.*, New Era Publication, Madras, 1991.

Subbarayalu, Y., *South India under the Cholas*, Oxford University Press, New Delhi, 2012.

Swaminathan, S., *The Early Cholas: History, Art and Culture*, Sharada Publishing House, Delhi, 1998.

Tirukkural, ch. 2:10, tr. V. R. Ramachandra Dikshitar.

Tirumalai, R., "Allur and Isanamangalam Revisited" in K.V. Ramesh, et.al., *Svasti Sri (Dr. B.Ch. Chhabra Felicitation Volume)*, Agam Kala Prakashan, Delhi, 1984.

8

Water Right and Irrigation in the Chola Country

K.R. Sankaran

In the historiography of South India, the history of the *Cholas* of Vijayalaya line (846-881 C.E.) has its own significance in terms of the complex texture of Chola polity and society. A series of research work has been going on dealing with the above said factors by way of utilising the epigraphs *en masse*. They are being used for different sorts of research.[1] Here, an attempt was made to know the practice of water rights that prevailed during the Chola period. It is known that ecology and environment are the determining factors to plan the irrigation system in the past as at present. In the Kaveri delta, which is our study area, the predominant mode of irrigation is based on the canals. A combined pattern of tank irrigation and canal irrigation has been the norm in *Tondaimandalam* and *Pāndiamandalam* whereas in *Konku* upland well irrigation system is in practice till now. In Pudukkottai and Ramanathapuram regions which lie in the semi-wet and semi-dry zone, the prime mode of irrigation system is relying upon the stored water in tanks.[2] Here, the present study area covers the Chola *Nādu* which is corresponding to the eastern portion of Tiruchirappalli district, the southern portion of *South Arcot* district, and the entire area of composite Thanjavur district. Epigraphical evidence from this area demonstrates that even before the emergence of the *Cholas*, canal irrigation system had been in practice in this region. So, our objective here was to know the exercise of water right during the Chola period in this region. As said earlier, the environment is seen the determining factor for the emergence of the state. The nature of the environment would cause the model of the state. In Tamil country, the state first emerged in the semi-wet and semi-dry zones viz., *Tondaimandalam* and *Pāndiamandalam*. The effect of the ecology and the nature of water resources on society are explained in detail. Despite the fertile territory with water affluence, Kaveri delta had the state emerged very later. What could be the reason for it? This could be seen easy to control and distribute the water in tanks found in the dry zones whereas, in plain land of Kaveri delta, this could not be done so. With this point, the present study attempted to know the water right during the Chola period.

Historical Background

The Chola country has an unbreakable historical continuum from the *Sangam* Age, coeval to the Iron Age. This is covered with a water grid by the rivers, their branches, and their supply channels. As the entire surface land was reclaimed for cultivation at different phases in Chola country, some scholar claims that pre-historical evidence cannot be traced back in this region.[3] But, strikingly prehistory antiquities have been unearthed in different places which are historically important. By taking into account the references given by the *Dēvāram*, we would presume that all along the bank of the river Kaveri habitation sites were created by the autochthonous groups.[4] Unearthed Roman coins from Karur and Uraiyur and the archaeological antiquities collected from *Kāvēripukum-pattinam* (Kāvēripattinam) and other places explain the historicity of these settlements.[5] Significant battles taken place on the banks of the rivers across the Chola country have been the bloodshed for water historically.[6] What for such historical events took place by the rivers? In the past, rivers and canals were treated as the boundaries of ethnic groups of the concerned territories.[7] They are the markers to determine the power and boundaries of the state. Holding the right on water resources and their catchment areas had been the pre-requisite assets for any dynasty to establish the state. Following this principle, the Cholas as the feudatories of the Pandyas and the Pallavas, often changed their alliance and got hold of the river Kaveri. Subsequently, scheme by scheme, the entire Chola territory, and its rivers were brought under their control. To control the river Kaveri from its mouth to tail end Cholas followed two main schemes: (1) war (2) matrimonial alliance. The Chola dynasty had a matrimonial alliance for three generations with the royal families of the border territories wherein originated many of the rivers running across the

Tamil country.[8] By the second scheme series of war was waged to all directions from Parantaka I to Rajendra II. The creation of the Chola-Pandya dynasty, which is a collateral family of the Cholas, is the explicit illustration of the war exercise and the occupation of the conquered territory.

Epigraphical Evidences

Epigraphical evidences were taken as the primary sources to do this work. In the beginning, inscriptions do not speak of the matters relating to irrigation affairs and water right.[9] From the last quarter of the 9th century C.E. onwards, we have the evidences in the inscriptions relating to water rights. Many such evidences are found in the contexts dealing with the land transaction, repairing work of the water resources, and the references concerned with canals and the sluices. Many of those inscriptions are from the settlements viz., *Kulit-talai*, *Tiruch-chenturai*, *Vayalūr*, *Tiru-verumpūr*, *Thanjavūr*, *Kuta-mukku*, *Kuttālam*, *Tiruk-kataiyūr* and *Chidamparam* and others. Mostly, all these places are oriented with the *Bhakti* Movement. A few Pandya inscriptions from this area also yielded references to the water rights. Besides them, Karantai copper plates and Leiden copper plate inscriptions are taken into account.

To begin with, inscriptions speak of a group of people called *Talai-vāyar* who were in charge of controlling the head of the canals branching-off from the rivers. The local bodies such as *Ūr*, *Sabhā*, and *Nagaram* played vital role in assigning the water right to the individuals, temples, officials, and others, which are clearly spoken of in the inscriptions. Later on, as the political scenario changed, the landholders started to entail the water right in purchasing the lands. In the next stage, the land holders got not only the right on the water but also earned the right on water resources. In the beginning, private parties and village bodies appeared as the major landholders, but in due course, the temple got that place. Flooding the relief works carried on by the private parties and others are referred to in the evidence. Generally, the water right holders were seen exempted from the taxes to be collected for repairing the water resources.

Significance of the Chola Period

The middle of the 9th century C.E. may be seen as the harbingering of socio-economic changes in Tamil country: *Jainism* got considerably declined, a widespread trade network built by *Ticai-āyirattu-ainūrruvar* became well developed, the epic works *Kampa-Rāmāyanam* and *Civakacintāmani* came up. The social mobile sped up because of surplus production and political expansion. All the factors are because of changes in the mode of production and relations of production. During this period, literary works are bigger in pages and temples are massive in sizes- they are many in number. Royal families got extended; women were overweighed with chastity. Local authorities became unpopular. *Utaiyān* and *Arayan* title holders turned out to be the locality chiefs. Another striking feature of this period was development in arts viz., paintings, dance, music, and metallurgy. The reduaction of *Bhakti* hymns happened to be an unearthing of Tamil music. An enormous number of people appeared enrolled in martial groups for political expansion. For all the above said process, the food production would be more essential. To do so, land and water resources are inevitably much more important. So, to know how far the water was socially shared would be the focal point of this study.

Methodology

The epigraphs of the Chola period describing the water right are scrutinised and the factors culled out of them have been analyzed. By way of analysis, the following points were collected. In the beginning, village bodies, temple officials particularly the *Pat-tutaiyārkal*, *Can-tēswarar*, and *Ōlai* officials were the pre-dominant water right holders. There has been a great scope to research the above said groups. But, here with a linear version we aimed to deal with how the water right in the Chola country got an important place over the centuries and to identify the technical terms dealing with water rights. Barring the land right, we could not visualise the water right. Inscriptions which directly speak of water right are rather few when compared with those of land right. The *vāt-talai, talai-vāy, kumil and madai* that are referred to in the inscriptions could not rightly be traced *in situ*. It can be done in a separate work. In days to come, an attempt will be made to locate them. Some village names ending (*Kulit-talai, Pettai-vāit-talai* and others in Tiruchirappalli district) in the suffix *talai* would recall the term *talai-vāy* as those villages are found at the vantage points where feeder canals started branching-off from the river Kaveri.

Historiography

Though the writing the history of the Cholas was started as early as from the second quarter of the 20th century C.E., it began to be critical with a methodology introduced by Burton Stein.[10] But till now,

K.A. Nilakanta Sastri's *The Colas* holds the field. He says that the inscriptions speaking of the land right would yield the matters relating to water rights. He further says that in the erratic season, peasants bailed the water by native technical devices such as picotah and basket made of leather. He establishes a view that the Cholas stood as a role model in the irrigation system. This technical practice adopted may be correlated with centralised Chola administrative system.[11] Some scholars held a view that branched-off channels leading from the river Kaveri appeared to have been excavated by the Chola rulers.[12] This point does not go along with a view expressed by C.N. Subramaniam.[13] Though G.W. Spencer's view that plundered wealth by the Cholas was pumped into agrarian expansion is acceptable, the population might also have been the factor as described by A. Appadorai.[14] It is a known fact that the traders got involved in agriculture also from the time of the Pallavas. Here, a view expressed by Kenneth R. Hall may be taken into account that in every *nādu* division there had been one *nagaram* settlement functioning during the Chola period.[15] In Pudukkottai region, the peasants who were engaged in trade are referred to as *Vellala-cetti* in the inscriptions.[16] Some traders in a *nagaram* settlement called *Telinga-kula-kala-puram* of the same region purchased some water resources.[17] This factor confirms the different roles of the traders. To maintain the rivers and channels running criss-cross in the Kaveri delta, particularly during the flooding, some taxes were collected from the people. This aspect is statistically studied by P. Shanmugam.[18] Some other scholars and epigraphers with empirical data studied the dry zones like Pudukkottai.

Water Right

As said earlier, the matters related to water rights are available in the inscriptions, speaking of land transactions in terms of sales and donation. As elsewhere in the medieval Tamil country, in the Chola region also land right entailed the water right. In some cases, the land right with water rights entailed the right on water resources, right on increasing the water level in water resources. In the study area, village bodies (*ūrār* and *sabhaiyār*), locality chiefs, the *nāttar*, and the *Brahmadēya-kilavar* (the prominent stature of *Brahmadēyam* settlement) were in charge of assigning the water rights. They possessed the right of increasing the water level in the water resources by way of raising the banks of the supply channels. The *sabha* in due course shared its water right with temples. The earliest reference speaking of water right in the inscription is available from 894 C.E.[19] It says that an individual called *Puti-aticca-pitariyar*, who was the daughter of a local chief, donated to a temple some land with sufficient amount of water.[20] This is described in the inscription as *nīr-kollak-katava-takavum* (let the water for irrigation). But this land was exempted from the taxes: *eccoru*, *kulai-vetti*, *kurappu-vetti* and others. These were the taxes to be paid in service by the water user. So, they are categorised as service taxes. From this above given factor, we could get the following points: women from the royal family owned the land with water rights; the river water was under the control of the regional chiefly families; the service taxes were necessary to maintain the water resources. In this case, the temple got an exemption from paying the taxes. But, it would be borne out by some other else. If the donor and donee used not to render the service taxes, their tenants were expected to render the same. In c. 900 C.E., a private party called *Mayavak-kirama-vittan*, a native of *Marincikai- Chaturvēdimangalam* exclaimed and repaired some wetland and dry land.[21] In turn; he was given the land of 3 *mā* with the right of bailing the water from the river for cultivation. The bailing of water is described in the evidence as *nīr-iraittu* (*water to be bailed out*). In 911 C.E., the *ūrār* of an agricultural settlement called *Allūr* transacted some lands in terms of *Talai-marru* (exchange of lands) to a group of people known as *Talai-vāyar*, who were in charge of controlling the head channel of the river Kaveri.[22] This land was subsequently donated as *Dēvadānam* tax-free land to a temple in the same village. But, the cultivation right on that land was given to a *Talai-vāyan*. The other members of *Talai-vāyar* group were declared as the *kudi* (tenants) of that temple land. This meant they were socially brought down from the position of independent water controller to that of the tenants. This process was exercised by the *nāttar* and the *brahmadēya-kilavar* of *Urattur-kūrram* at the instance of *Ōlai* official according to the royal order. This land was given the right of getting water at the time of scarcity and got an exemption from paying the service tax *cennīr-vetti*. If so, who would be responsible to render such service? The tenants- *Talai-vāyar*. A remarkable point that we get from this instance is the benevolent obedience shown to the royal order by the officials, locality chiefs, and others in the irrigation affair. This was the dynamism to make an independent *Talai-vāyar* group lose their right and they became subject to the temple. This can be seen as an aspect of social change. In the same way, in 937 C.E. a group[23] of *Talai-vāyar* of 11 members of *Allūr* sold their land *vettap-peru*[24] in an auction to a private party called *Ciriyan-pullan* who made it as *dēvadāna* land to a temple in the same settlement. Why was this land sold? It was left barren for some years because of the breach of the river Kaveri. We do not know the reason for which the *Talai-vāyar* left the land uncultivated even though they were in charge of controlling the river water. This shows that the empowerment of *Talai-vāyar* over the water was shattered in the emergence of the Cholas through the temples. In 946 C.E. an inscription from *Kuta-mukku* (the modern Kumbhakonam) which is located in the core part of the Chola country speaks of water right.[25] The inscription says that a royal attendant (*pentātti*)[26] purchased some *Kāni* land from an *utaiyan* and it was given to the temple authorities called *Parutai-yārkal*. She permitted the *Parutai-yarkal* to make a tank on that land. Here also, we can see that the temple authorities had some role in irrigation affairs.

In one of the previous cases, we saw that the *Talai-vāyar* are of a different group from the *ūrār*.[27] But in 961 C.E., the *sabhaiyār* of *Virasimha- Chaturvēdimangalam* in *Chola nādu* themselves were the *talai-vāyar* of their settlement.[28] They described their head channel as *enkal vāt-talai* (our's head channel). That was why, as it were, the water was allotted to the land owned by the temple in that settlement. The allotted water is described as *pantu-nīr-pāyum-parice-pāyap-peruvatakavum* (let the water as it were). The water was let from the river Kaveri. In this case, we saw that *talai-vāyar*, *ūrār*, and *sabhaiyār* were exercising their right in water distribution. In another instance, in a village called *Erumpiyur*, a group of people called *Kulattār* was in charge of controlling the water in the tank. Comparatively, *Erumpiyur* is located in the dry-zone. The *ūrār* of this village and the *sabhaiyār* of *Sri-kanta-Chaturvēdimangalam* concurrently sold some lands to the *Utaiyan* of a village called *Ciru-tavvur* in *Kiliyur-nādu*.[29] *Sabhaiyār* and *ūrār* concurrently permitted the *Kulattār* to release the proportionate water from the village tank and it would flow through the sluice.[30] In 987 C.E., the *sabhaiyār* of *Tiruk-kannapuram* claimed their right on the water in the village tank.[31] But, it was known created by an individual who had the title *enāti*. It is a striking feature that the tank was created individually but owned commonly. This point has to be seen sociologically.

In another instance, in 992 C.E., an *Utaiyān* of *Tiru-verumpur* purchased some land from the *sabhaiyār* of *Peru-venkur* and gave it to the deity.[32] To that land, the *sabhaiyār* of another village called *Sri-kanta-mankalam* gave the water. It establishes a view that in the agrarian production co-ordination among the settlements would be needful scrupulously in sharing the water. From it, we can infer a fact that such co-ordination seemed to work out at a higher level. In 992 C.E., the *sabhaiyār* claimed the right on that tank. Not only that, the *sabhaiyār* got the right to install the sluice across the channel and broaden it. This can be seen as a kind of social change in irrigation affair. In 993 C.E., the *sabhaiyār* who were the *ūrār* as well of a village called *Tiru-netunkalam*[33] with the concurrence of a group of temple authorities called *Dēva-kanmikal* sold some *kuti-nīnka-dēvadāna* land to the *Kilavan* of a village called *Curalur*.[34] But, the *sabhaiyār* and *ūrār* collectively sought permission from the temple authorities to give the water to that land. It shows that the temple authorities as elsewhere in the Chola country held the right on the water in the rivers. In 993 C.E. to a god in *Tiruc-cirampalattu-Chaturvēdimangalam* in *Mērkka-Nādu*, land was sold by 5 members. Of the 5, 4 were divided into two groups.[35] The first group is of uterine brothers as the second group. The 5th one is single. All the 5 had *kāni* right with *utaiyān* title. From the commonly owned village tank, they allotted water to the sold land. Here a question would arise why did the elder brother concurrently with the younger brother sold the land with water? It has to be responded from the anthropological point of view. The representation of elder brother and younger brother in the land deed can be viewed as that of higher share and lower share of the concerned lineage/family.

In 995 C.E., a private party called *Cavanti-nārayanan-centan* of *Brahmadēyam* in a village called *Ciru-paluvur* sold some land to a deity.[36] The land is described as *Acciru-paluvurin-mēlaik-karunkulattu-kulic-cey*. In the same year, a private party called *Nakkan-cakantan* of a village called *Alayyūr* in the name of his wife gave some land irrigated by sluice in a tank called Cenkulam.[37] An individual of *Tiru-vicalūr* to the deity of the same village gave the land being irrigated by the tank called *Mar-ppituku-ēri*.[38]

In one of the above said cases, we saw that the collective ownership of land was established by way of making donation by a group of some brothers. In other words, we can say that it would suggest the division of lineage/family which meant collective ownership was divided into individual ownership. If so, that could be a horizontal division. In another instance, in 995 C.E., in a village called *Ciru-paluvūr*, land right with water was held jointly by two individuals. These two were father and son. We may assume that this meant the anthropologically higher share was held by the father; the lower share was held by the son.[39] We can see it as a vertical division in owning the land. Accordingly, *Cavanti-nīlakantan* and his son *Nakkan* of *Ciru-paluvūr* jointly sold the land to the deity of *Tiru-valanturai*. They said we sold (*nānkal virru*) the land being irrigated by the tank *Ayyan-kulam*. This shows that a father and his son had the right on the same tank. In addition, a tank under repair was given. In the same year, to the same deity, one more private party gave the land being irrigated through sluice from a tank.[40] What we learned from this instance is: land right entailed the right on the water in the tank and its sluice. This trend has happened in the peripheral area of the core territory wherein the tanks are the prominent water resources. In the core area, the scenario would be entirely different.

In 997 C.E., an *utaiyān* of *Ciru-kāttur in Mērkka-Nādu* for the deity purchased some land from the *sabha* of *Kanna-mankalam*.[41] The temple authorities called *Kōyil-utaiyārkal* accepted to give the water to that land from the river Kaveri. In the same year, a group of people called *Talip-pat-tutayārkal* who were in charge of the temple in a village called *Avani-kanta-īsvara-mankalam* permitted an individual to repair one tank. Further, he was permitted to save the surplus amount of water from that tank into another tank called *Ponnan-kulam*.[42] Both the tanks were in the same village. This instance shows the paramount of temple over the water resources. In 999 C.E., an *araiyan* titleholder, who was known as a military authority, took an effort to sponsor some *nivantam* to the deity of temple in a village called *Tiruk-katavūr in Ampar-Nādu*.[43] One half of the water in some tank was given to that land. That military authority is referred to as *Parivāram*.[44]

We have seen earlier the collective function of *Talai-vāyar* and *Kulattār* in irrigation affair. In 998 C.E., a single member of *Talai-vāyar* group was assigned a half *ma* of land as *vēttapperu*.[45] Singularly, he was referred to as *Talai-vāyan*. It was enforcement of private ownership into *Talaivāyar* group. They lost their collective ownership on such land when they sold it in 937 C.E.[46] At an instance in 1009 C.E., some land was sold with concerned well by a group of some individuals.[47]

In history, it is known that primitive communism was changed into communal ownership which in turn turned out to be into private ownership. This was happened not only in land rights but also in the water right. Such change would happen vertically in the community and family horizontally. As such, the younger generation of particular families would not neglect to refer to the elder generation in the land deed. Thus, one younger seller had to involve his elder brother in the land transaction. This is a feature of male chauvinism. Accordingly, in 1012 C.E., an individual called *Tiruk-kukaip-piran*, son of *Tirup-parkatal-dāsar* of Pullur sold some land with water to a trader who was further permitted to get water according to the level of the water in the canal.[48]

In 1019 C.E., two *Ōlai* officials who were also the traders repaired some land damaged in flooding in *Sri-rankam* and rebuilt the banks of the Kaveri.[49] This establishes a view that there had been a network among the state officials, traders, and temples in irrigation affairs.[50] In 1042 C.E., an individual called *Madurāntakan-Brahmarāyan* made a figurine of a female counterpart to the deity of a temple in *Tirumala-pati* and repaired the land given for *nivantam* to the same deity. The land was given water from *Cempiyan-mādevip-pērēri*. Further, the *Brahmarāyan* deposited 50 *kalanju* of *kāsu* at the hands of temple officials *Dēva-kanmikal* for deepening and embankment of the *eri*. To the deity of another temple, a private party called *Sana-nāyakan-kōyil-perun-taccan* who had the *kāni* right in 1078 C.E. purchased some land with water in the canal from three Brahmin.[51] They were the brothers. Here, the land right entailed the right on the tank. The *nagarattār* of a village called *Tiru-venni* in *Sutta-malli-Nādu* to meet out the interest for some amount of *Panam* from the treasury of temple assigned some land. It happened sometimes earlier. But in 1079 C.E., they made the donated land tax-free. Further, to the land, they gave water according to turn systems from the *ūr* tank.[52] The temple was permitted to bail out the water from the tank at the time of scarcity. From this point of time, references to turn system are available in the inscriptions. This could be seen as a sort of the change in the irrigation system. But, it is registered in the records in different ways. Around 1070 C.E., a dramatic change appeared to take place in Chola regime.[53]

In 1113 C.E., the *sabhaiyār* of *Putuk-kuti-ūr*, a *Brahmadēyam* in *Tiruvārur-Kūrram* sold some land with water to an official called *Panimakan* for 24 *kalanju* of *pon*.[54] The water was to be released out by the existing system from the concerned canal. It was made tax-free land. Further, it was permitted to bail out the water at the time of scarcity. In 1122 C.E., the *sabhaiyār* of *Puloka-mānicka-Chaturvēdimangalam* to an *Ati-can-tēsvarar* officer sold some land as tax-free.[55] It was permitted to get water from the sluices: one at the higher level; another at the lower level. In another case, in the same year *sabhaiyār*[56] of *Tirunallur in Vēla-*

Nādu, sold a tank to the temple authority known as *Can-tēswarar* in *Tiruvarūr-Kūrram*. In the next year,[57] *Sabhaiyār* of *Uttama-chōla- Chaturvēdimangalam* in *Tiruveluntūr-Nādu* sold some land as tax-free to an individual who held the title *Vilup-paraiyan*. The land was, in addition, given water from two resources: well and river. In 1132 C.E., a *Mūvēntavēlan* for *nivantam* to the temple in *Tirup-painneli* assigned land with water as tax-free.[58] In the declining phase of the Chola, the Pandya rulers took interest in the temple affairs sentimentally and they started donating the lands to them. Accordingly, the Pandya ruler *Māravarman-parakkiraman* (1143-1166 C.E.) created an *Akaram* settlement for the priests who settled in *Kō-danta-rama-Chaturvēdimangalam* of Tiruvarankam.[59] Additionally, the ruler donated three irrigation tanks found in three different villages. They were found in peripheral areas of the Chola core territory. How was it possible for the Pandyas while the Cholas were in the rule? To the rulers and the priests, territories are not the target; temples are crucial media for their politics. It is said that during the Chola regime, the tribal groups slowly started setting to agriculture.[60] In this changing process, such tribal groups would ape the culture of their masters. As far as Tamil country is concerned, the motto was to patronise the temples. So, in 1203 C.E., the chief of a hunting community of *Puvani-Nādu* deposited 3 *kalanju* of *pon* in the treasury of the village called *Muti-valanku-Chōlapuram*.[61] That *pon* was given to the *ūrār* of *Tattaiyūr*. In turn, the *ūrār* gave that chief *Tiru-nāmattuk-kāni* land with water as *Patikāval* right. In other areas of the Tamil country also, during the medieval period hunting community turned to agriculture.[62]

In 1209 C.E., *Tiru-nāmattuk-kāni* land was given to an individual, who was an *olai* official, trader as well with *utaiyān* title.[63] The sellers are temple authorities and military chiefs. From this evidence, we can infer the view that the state official *ōlai* being a trader engaged in agricultural production also. It shows how the individuals at the power structure exploited the wealth of the state. Another *olai* official in 1211 C.E., instructed some temple authorities of *Tiruvarankam* to repair the water resources.[64] Accordingly, the temple officials called *Sri-vaishnavarkal*, *Data-nampi-mārkal* repaired the land along the river course and repaired the water resources of a different sort. In 1214 C.E. *Tennavan-brahmarāyan* , an *ōlai* official in accordance with an individual was called *Madurānrtakan-vilup-paraiyan* sought permission from the authorities of the temple in *Tillai* to attach the cultivating tenants to the temple.[65] The cultivating tenants are referred to as *Tōppuk-kutikal* (literally the tenants to be attached to the garden). They may be taken as *corvee*. To them, 100 *ma* of land had to be given with water from *ūr-ēri*. It exhibits the interaction between the state officials and the temple officials. It is a general perception that at the declining phase of any kingdom, chiefly feudatories or their counterparts would imbibe some traits of the polity of the ruling kings. Following this principle, at the declining phase of the Cholas, *Māravarman-sundara-pāndyan* in 1245 C.E. made an inscription in *Tiruvarankam*.[66] This evidence speaks of horse-trading *cetti* who purchased from a private party some asset of the temple. It is described in the inscription as *kōyil nilay cottu* (immovable property of the temple) i.e., *Panankulam*. It was comprised of a tank, wetland, dry land, habitation site, garden, and others.

As said earlier, the emergence of the local chiefs at the decline of the ruling dynasty is the historical phenomenon. Similarly, in the declining phase of the Cholas, Kopperunchinkan in 1246 C.E. engraved an inscription on the wall of the temple dedicated to the goddess called *Tillayamman*. This says that the members of Brahmin families of *Kasusika-gotra* sold some land to a private party called *Sivan-cirrampala-mutaiyān* of the same *gotra*.[67] Additionally, he was given one-half of the water in a tank. He could take the water by way of bailing. This would say that irrespective of dynastic rule and chiefly order, land transactions with water had been carried out. In the same year, the same parties engaged themselves again in a land transaction.[68] Here, the purchaser was permitted to install the devices for *picotah* to bail out the water. Another one individual called *Vikramachōla-brahmata-rāyan* of *Sri-vīranārāyan- Chaturvēdimangalam* in the same year sold some land to the temple officials.[69] They were permitted to get water as per the existing distributive system.

It has already been established that at the emerging phase of the Chola rule, the chiefly families wielded enormous power with water rights. In due course when the Cholas consolidated their rule, such right slipped into the hands of the ruling kings. *Karantai* plates, *Leiden* plates attest to this view. Such changes had at least taken place in the core territory of the Chola country.

It is to be noted that at the declining phase of the Cholas, land transaction and water distribution had to take place within the *Brahmin* community. It was not seen widespread, absolutely taken place in an independent *Brahmin* settlement called *taniyūr*. Such a transaction was carried on between the individuals.

Not only the above said group, but the artists also were known through inscriptions enjoying the water-right. In 1254 C.E., a dance master called *Alaccan-ponnmpalak-kuttan-nirutta-rajan* of *Perumparrap-puliyūr*, a *taniyūr* settlement, with the consent of the temple officer *can-tēswarar* sold some land to the temple officials viz., *Sri-Mahēswarar*, *Kankāni-ceyvār*, *Sri-kāriyam-ceyvār*, *Dēva-kanmi*, and *Kōyil-kanakku*.[70] They were permitted to get the water by three modes: water to be flown through the canals; water to be bailed out by *picotah*; water to be fetched by other devices. They were permitted to install the poles of *picotah* threshold and make a pit for bailing the water.

After the emergence of the Second Pandyan Empire, Virapandya I in 1266 C.E. engraved an inscription on the wall of the temple in *Tiruk-katavur* in order to register his legitimacy in the Chola country.[71] The inscription says that the king gave the water right in a tank called *Tāmaraik-kulam* to the temple officials of the village.

Water Right and State

Studies dealing with state and irrigation have been going on for more than a hundred years. In the discussion on Indian history, Karl Marx (1818-1883) and Frederick Angels (1820-1895) exchanged their views through letters about the relationship between the state and irrigation. In 1853, Karl Marx registered that as far as India is concerned British state neglected the traditional irrigation system and it resulted in reducing agricultural production.[72] Karl A. Wittfogel, who studied almost all the past Asian states, tried to correlate the role of state and irrigation system.[73] His view cannot be fully applied to India. His theory that water resources in Oriental countries were under the ruler's control does not get wide acknowledgment. His views are testified in a combined work of inscriptional study and field survey by R.A.L.H. Gunawardana.[74] He came to establish a view that the state did not have a major role in irrigation technology; local chiefs had a vital role in irrigation technique and water right in peripheral areas of pre-modern Sri Lanka. With this backdrop, we can see the relationship between state and irrigation. According to Karl A. Wittfogel, Oriental rulers were expected to create the water resources and they must have direct involvement in irrigation affairs. Has it happened in Chola country? The answer could possibly be *YES*. In *Pattinappālai* which is one of the ten *Idylls* of Tamil Literature, we have a reference to it. This says that the Chola king *Karikālan* destroyed the forest in terms of land reclamation and created the irrigation sources.[75] The same work to be done by the rulers is advocated in one of the Tamil didactic works, *Nālatiyār* of c. 8th century C.E. This refers to a *Muttarayar* chief Suvaran Maran (704-745 C.E.).[76] Villages in the Muttarayar territory from where references relating to *Talaivāy* are available endured with original names till now. It is said that from the *Muttarayas*, the Cholas confiscated the river Kaveri.[77]

In his statistical study of the Chola society, Noboru Karashima does not point to the interaction between the state and irrigation, though the importance of *nattār-vāykkāl* was brought to our notice.[78] In his research on the mode of production in Chola country, James Heitzman does not see rulers' direct role in water rights and water resources.[79] Contrarily, factors described in the inscription of *Karantai* plates and *Leiden* plates,[80] kings appeared to have direct role in irrigation affairs and water rights. According to Karantai plates, while staying in a house in a settlement called *Perumparrap-puliyur* Rajendra - I (1012-1044 C.E.) issued an order.[81] Here it is to be mentioned that another traditional name of Chidambaram is Perumparrap-puliyur. This settlement was located in between the rivers Kaveri and Vellar. The royal order was to the people of the following groups in *Venni-Kūrram* and *Virachōla-Valanādu*: The groups were: *Nāttār*, *Brahmatāya-kilavar*, the holders of *Pallic-candam*, *Pacana-bōgam*, *Ūrār*, *Nagarattār*, and others. The *Nadu*, *Nagaram*, and *ūrs* described in the inscriptions are located in the area covering present Thanjavur, Kumbhakonam, Mannarkudi, Papanasam, and others. These are of the core part of the Chola country. The royal order goes on saying that the *Arayyarkal* who were in charge of the tank called *Tirubhuvana-mādēvip-pērēri* had been given the land *vēttap-peru*. But, they got only *karānmai* and *miyātchi* rights; the tenants (*kudi*) attached to that land were evicted. It is described in the evidence as *kudi-nīkki* which meant the *Arayyarkal* would work on the land. This group of *Arayarkal* can be compared with their counterparts *Talai-vāyarkal* and *Talaivāyc-cānrōrkal* of Allur in Tiruchirappalli. All these groups of people at the beginning appeared to have right on the land independently. But in 911 C.E., the right on the land by *Talai-vāyar* had been removed by the official at the issue of royal order. Their land was exchanged by way of *Talai-maru*. We can say that it was the starting point of direct interaction between state and irrigation. Similarly, according to *Karantai* plates, *Arayyarkal* of *Tirubhuvanamādēvip-pērēri* were conferred on merely *karānmai* and *miyātchi* rights. This meant, really the right on that land lay in state's hand i.e., kingly role. The role of *Arayyarkal* had been an important one in the history of irrigation in Tamil country. In a recent study, it is said that how the *Arayyarkal* exercised their power in the dry zone to control the water right which in due course brought to them the right to rule.[82] In the dry zone, the *Arayyarkal* were of the martial group. Similarly, in Chola country *Arayarkal* might be of a martial group. The martial character could be the pre-requisite qualification to protect the water resources.

In *Karantai* plates, 15 channels are referred to after the respective villages. They are called as *Ūr-vāykkāls*. 8 branched-off *vāykkāls* are spoken of. In donating the land, the ruler in the plates specifically mentioned the respective irrigation channels. This confirms his interest in water rights and water resources. In the same evidence at another instance, the ruler donated a tax-free land with water proportionate. Additionally, he gave the right of deepening the channels.

In brief, we can say that Karantai plates speak of different kinds of water rights.

(1) Water may/can be bailed at the time when water is low in the channel.

(2) Water can be stored in the time of scarcity.

(3) The donee should protect the channel; diverting the channel is prohibited. Water can be bailed out by the donee by way of using a basket and small *picotah*. Other than the donee is not to be allowed to use such devices.

All these are the privileges conferred on the donee. Such kind of privileges has already been referred to in the *Leiden* plates of Rajaraja I (985-1012 C.E.). From these copper plates, we would come to know the state's interest in irrigation affair. And all the factors are attesting the state's role in irrigation and water right.

Irrigation Techniques

The application of irrigation techniques in the undulating country would be rather cumbersome especially during the rainy seasons. So, ecological and geographical features and contour should be taken into account viably to preserve the water in tanks and lakes. In plain areas like Kaveri fed Chola Nadu the use of water for irrigation is to be easy on the one hand and the maintenance of water resources would be rather difficult on the other hand. So, in the historical period to control the water running through the river Kaveri and its branches, the water users devised a canal based irrigation system. By way of this grid pattern, the speed of the water is contained. The criss-cross set-up of the canals acutely irrigates the lands. This grid pattern can be visualised as given below.

River Kaveri =>Branch river =>Feeder canal =>canal =>sub-channel=>supply channel=> land

(Kāveriyāru=> Kilaiyāru => Peruvāykkāl => Vāykkāl => Ut-ciruvāykkāl => Kannāru => Nilam)

Kannāru has been the supply channel or the water terminus. This criss-cross set-up of the channels maintains the gradient of the running water. Though the Chola country is known for canal irrigation, inscriptional evidence speaks of tank irrigation system practiced in this region. The epigraphical terminology *pāyccal* and *pāyccutal* demonstrate the canal irrigation. Contrarily, the word *irayttal* explains the bailing of water from the wells.

Well Irrigation and Tank Irrigation

The epigraphical terms referring to the well in use for irrigation are *Kinaru* and *Turavu*.[83] Mostly, the river and canals feed the tanks in Chola country. Till today, *picotah* are found lifting the water from the tanks.[84]

Canal Irrigation

As aforesaid, the canal irrigation system is rather strenuous in maintaining the flow of water on the earth's surface. The head canals branching-off from the river is described as *talai-vāykkāl*, *vāittalay*, *and vāikkāl-talai*. The canal branching-off from the above said is described as *uvari vāykkal*[85] from which also sub-channels are branched-off. Some epigraphical phrases explain how the rivers are feeding the canals. Not only that, but they also feed the tanks.[86]

Vati-Vāyukkāl-Kannāru-Catiram

Some scholars acknowledging the significance of this system say that this description is purposely recorded in the inscriptions for periodical revenue assessment.[87] It could not practically function as described in the inscriptions. Such descriptions are recorded in the epigraphs from a semi-dry zone like *Tondai Nādu* also. In the field work, the clear idea of this system could not be earned from the users of the water. The agricultural engineers may find its unique feature in further research.

Kurampu and Kulai

A temporary structure called *Kurampu* is elsewhere found across the river Kaveri diverting the water at wanted points.[88] Inscriptions from the study area explain the work done by the peasants to make such bunds. The damaged portions of the river banks due to flooding are repaired.[89] It is described as *ārru-anai*. Some service taxes like *kulai-vetti*, *ārruk-kulai*, *ārran-karait-tēvai* and others were rendered by the water utilisers to repair the damaged river banks.[90]

Kumili and *Madai*

Kumili and *Madai* are the technical devices releasing out the water or blocking the water stored in the tanks/lakes. It is technically distinct from the canal system and such devices are epigraphically referred to in the dry-zones like Pudukkottai and Ramanathapuram areas. Regarding the Chola country such evidences are found from the peripheral settlements like Tirukkovilur, Tiruverumpur, Ariyalur, Pudukkottai, and others.[91] As early as from 994 C.E. references to sluices are recorded in the inscriptions. Such complex and intricate devices are more essential in tank based irrigation system. In canal irrigation, diverting the water from one channel into another one is technically easy. But in Chola territory, *Kumili* and *Madai* are spoken of in the epigraphs dealing with land transactions. We can say such devices as an empowering tool in the mechanism of water management over the water resources. Sources say that individuals built some sluices; some others repaired them.[92] Though some sluices in the dry zone are researched from the technical point of view, those in other zones remain untouched. R.A.L.H. Gunawardana examined and studied a kind of cistern sluice found nearby Gangai-Konda-Cholapuram. He made a theory that South India and Sri Lanka might have shared some traits of hydraulic techniques against the backdrop of South Asia. The writer of this article examined a few numbers of epigraphically referred to sluices found in use till today in Pudukkottai region. He is indebted to Karu. Rajendran who published some epigraphs found on the sluices from the same area. Almost all are of granite structures. Some of the components are laterites. Though there is a good number of granite temples found in Kaveri fed area, stone sluices are so far not found.

Notes and References

1. Prof. K.A. Nilakanta Sastri was first to utilise the epigraphs *en masse* to study the history of the Cholas. To understand the political geography of the Chola country from the point of administrative institutions such as *nādu*,*valanādu* and *ūr*, etc., Y. Subbarayalu studied almost all the published and unpublished Chola inscriptions. A team headed by Noboru Karashima with the assistance of computer, analysed the Chola

inscriptions for the study of the personal names. Kenneth R. Hall used such data to know the role of Nagaram settlement during the Chola period while George W. Spencer with that material attempted at knowing the political expansion of the Chola country. P. Shanmugam for his study on the Chola revenue system used enormously the Chola inscriptions. By way of using inscriptions, the women names also were studied. To know the political ideology of the Cholas R. Champakalakhsmi used the epigraphs. K.A. Nilakanta Sastri, *The Colas*, (reprint), University of Madras, Madras,1984; Y. Subbarayalu, *Political Geography of the Chola Country*, The State Department of Archaeology, Government of Tamil Nadu, Madras,1973; idem, 'The Chola State', *Studies in History*, Vol. 5:2, 1982; Noboru Karashima, *South Indian History and Society : Studies from the Inscriptions AD 850 to 1800 AD*, OUP, New Delhi, 1984; Kenneth R. Hall, *Trade and State Craft in the Age of the Cholas*, Abhinav Publications, Delhi,1980; George W. Spencer, *The Politics of Expansion: The Chola conquest of Sri Lanka and Sri Vijaya*, New Era Publications, Chennai,1983; P. Shanmugam, *The Revenue System of the Cholas 850 -1259*, New Era Publications, Chennai 1987; Leslie C. Orr, 'Women in the Temple, the Palace, and the Family: The Construction of Women's Identities in the Pre-colonial Tamil Nadu' in Kenneth R. Hall (ed.), *Structure and Society in Early South India: Essays in Honour of Noboru Karashima*, OUP, New Delhi, 2001; K. R. Sankaran, *'Thanjavur Peruvudaiyar Koyilin Taliccerippendukal'* in *Arivottam*, Mayiladuthurai, 2003; R. Champakalakshmi, *Trade Ideology and Urbanisation: South India 300 BC to AD 1300*, OUP, New Delhi, 1996.

2. K. Rajan, *Ancient Irrigation Technology: Sluice Technology in Tamil Nadu*, Heritage India Trust, Thanjavur, 2008, pp. 6-7.
3. C.N. Subramaniam, *Aspects of the History of Agriculture in the Kaveri Delta c. 850 AD to c. 1600 A D*, Unpublished M. Phil. Dissertation submitted to JNU, New Delhi, 1983, p. 23.
4. See M. Rajamanickanar, *Periya Purana Araychi* (research on Grand epic), 3rd edition, Pari Nilayyam, Chennai, 1978. In this work the author attempted at correlating the birth places of Nayanmars to the *Saiva Bakthi* centres with the help of epigraphs. See his another work on *Caiva Camaya Valarchi* (growth of Saiva religion).
5. Natana Kasinathan, Undersea Exploration off the Shore of Poompukar, State Department of Archaeology, Government of Tamil Nadu, Chennai, 1991; In Kaveri-Pukum-Pattinam, recently a potsherd with Sinhala-Brahmi inscription was found. S. Rajavelu, *Poompukaril Sinhala-Brahmi Poritta Matkalattundu* in *Avanam*, Vol. No. 10, p.154.
6. Pallava king Nandhi-varman III (846-869 C.E.) won his Pandya counterpart Sri-maran-Sri-vallabhan by the river Tellaru. By the same river, in 13th century C.E. Kopperunchinkan II (1243-1279 C.E.) won Rajaraja III (1246-1279 C.E.). Nirupatunga-varman (859-899 C.E.) won his Pandya counterpart by the river *Aricil-aru*.

7. The victory over *Vatapi* by the Pallavas and the spread over of their valour up to the river *Krishna* can be seen from the point of occupying the water resources. The Chalukya territories are the originating places of the river *Palar*, *Kaveri*, *Pennai* and others. Water resources were treated as the boundaries of the Nadu (Y. Subbarayalu, Political Geography of the Chola Country, 1973, p. 22).
8. In the first phase (850-985 C.E.) the Kaveri-fed area was confiscated by the Chola from the *Muttarayyas*. The Cholas had matrimonial alliance with the chiefly family of Pudukkottai region where the river *Vellar* runs, and with *Milatutaiyarkal* chiefly family which seemed to have controlled the rivers *Amaravati* and *Ten-pennai*. This kind of blood bond directly helped the Cholas to consolidate their position in the core territory. Parantaka I by marrying the princess of Kerala territory expanded the Chola power westwards. He is also known as the conqueror of Madurai area. This is the core part of Pandymandalam. By expanding the Chola country westwards, the Chola rulers got hold of the originating places of the rivers running across the Tamil country. Rajaraja I (985-1016 C.E.), Rajendra I (1012-1044 C.E.) had matrimonial alliance with western Chalukyas by which the originating points of the rivers in Karnataka region came to the hands of the Cholas. Such kind of kin relationship was based on cross-cousin marriage which is a typical *Dravidian* feature.
9. At the beginning, in the inscriptions names of the rulers are not properly referred to. We can identify them with their epithets and regnal years. Mostly, the rulers donated the live-stock to the temples.
10. Studies on the Cholas were first started by K.A. Nilakanta Sastri. After that, Noboru Karashima and his team members studied the Chola society and polity by using statistics as a tool. Burton Stein applied anthropological theory to understand the role of peasant community under the Cholas. He made an attempt to say that Chola state was not centralised one. In fact, its polity was of segmentary state. With the publication of his works, Chola study had a great fillip. Noboru Karashima says he had useful discussion with him to work on Chola society. Y. Subbarayalu highlights the enlightening role of Burton Stein in studying the history of South India (*Kalachchuvadu*, Vol. 5, 2004).
11. K.A. Nilakanta Sastri, *The Colas*, (reprinted) University of Madras, Madras, 1984, pp. 583, 451.
12. The rivers *Kollitam*, *Manni*, *Venni*, *Katuvay* and others are referred to in *Bhakti* literature. T.V. Sadasiva Bhandarathar says that from 10th century C.E. onwards the Chola rulers created many rivers. Branched rivers and channels with royal names misled him to have that view. They were called after the royal members but they did not create them. T.V. Sadasiva Bhandarathar, *Pirkalachcholar Carittiram*, Annamalai University, Annamalai Nagar, 1946.
13. The rivers enumerated by T.V. Sadasiva Bhandarathar are found running in the northern portion of Kaveri delta wherein as C.N. Subramaniam says we can see most of the *Saiva* centres. He says that this is the area where came up the settlements earlier. To support this view, he says that

some names of the settlements end in suffix *kadu* (forest) in southern portion of Kavery delta. But, we can see such settlements in the delta region. *Tiru-venkadu*, *Tiru-vlankadu* and *Saya-vanam* are the names of the villages found in the northern portion of Kaveri delta.

14. A. Appadorai, *Economic Conditions in Southern India (1000-1500 AD)*, Vol. I (reprint), University of Madras, 1900, p. 205.
15. Kenneth R. Hall, *Trade and State Craft in the Age of the Cholas*, Abhinav Publications, New Delhi, 1980.
16. Burton Stein, *Peasant State and Society in Medieval South India*, OUP, New Delhi, 1982, p.302; A.V. Perumal, "Trade in Pudukkottai – A Study" in *Arivottam*, Vol.1, Mayiladuthurai, pp.15-24. In this article, the author says that agricultural groups called *Vellalar* engaged themselves in trade also. In other words, we can understand that trade group called *Cettiyars* engaged themselves in agriculture. This could be vice-versa.
17. From the inscriptional evidences, we know that the *Nagarattar* of *Telinga-kula-kalapuram* had *utaiyan* title and they purchased land with water resource.
18. P. Shanmugam, *The Revenue System of the Cholas 850-1279 AD*, New Era Publications, Madras, 1987.
19. *S.I.I.*, Vol. VIII, No. 63.
20. *Puti-aticca-pitariiyar*, the daughter of *Irukkuvel* chief called *Maturantakan-Irukkuvel*, was married to the Chola prince *Arincayan* (956-957 C.E.). Her name is referred to in the inscriptions of Aditya I and Parantaka I. By way of maintaining matrimonial alliance with *Velir* family, the Cholas put them at the bay from the conflict.
21. *S.I.I.*, Vol. VIII, No. 640.
22. *S.I.I.*, Vol. VIII, No. 692.
23. *S.I.I.*, Vol. VIII, No. 689.
24. Of late, this term is interpreted and analyzed; see Y. Subbarayalu, *'Camuka varalrru nokkil vettiyum muttalum'* in *Moli Mukakankal* (felicitation volume to Prof. Ki. Arankan), Thanjavur, 2003, pp. 148-155.
25. *S.I.I.*, Vol. III, Part 3, 4, No. 110.
26. The word *pentatti* refers to royal lady attendant. Concordance of Tamil Epigraphical Terms, Santi Satana, 2003, p. 449; This term is well treated by some scholars, Leslie C. Orr, 'Women in the Temple, the Palace, and the Family: The Construction of Women's Identities in the Pre-colonial Tamil Nadu' in Kenneth R. Hall (ed.), *Structure and Society in Early South India: Essays in Honour of Noboru Karashima*, OUP, New Delhi, 2001, p. 213.
27. *S.I.I.*, Vol. VIII, No. 692.
28. *S.I.I.*, Vol. XIII, No. 151.
29. *S.I.I.*, Vol. XIII-A, No. 50.
30. Rajan Gurukkal, "Aspects of Reservoir System: Irrigation in Early Pandya State" *Studies in History*, Vol. 1, No. 1, New Delhi, 1986;

R.A.L.H. Gunawardana, "*Inter-societal Transfer of Hydraulic Technology in Pre-colonial South Asia: Some Reflections based on a Preliminary Investigation*" *South Asian Studies*, Vol. XXII, No. 2, Kyoto, 1984, pp. 115-142; K.R. Sankaran, "*Irrigation in Medieval Tamil Country with special reference to Pudukkottai Region*", Article Submitted to *INSA* New Delhi, 2005.

31. *S.I.I.*, Vol. XIII, No. 65.
32. *S.I.I.*, Vol. XIII, No. 163.
33. *S.I.I.*, Vol. XIII, No. 182.
34. *S.I.I.*, Vol. III, Part 3, 4, No. 110.
35. *S.I.I.*, Vol. VIII, No. 289.
36. *A.R.E.*, No. 248 of 1926.
37. *A.R.E.*, No 234 of 1926.
38. *S.I.I.*, Vol. XIII, No. 222.
39. *S.I.I.*, Vol. V, No. 668.
40. *S.I.I.*, Vol. V, No. 669.
41. *S.I.I.*, Vol. XIII, No. 231.
42. *S.I.I.*, Vol. XIII, No. 227.
43. *S.I.I.*, Vol. XXII-1, No. 22.
44. The term *parivaram* denotes the ethnic groups *Maravar* and *Akampatiyar* as well. They were of martial groups. Tamil Lexicon, p. 2519. A sub-division of *Maravar* and *Akampatiyar* castes. Probably, the same meaning is given in Concordance of Tamil Epigraphical Terms, 2001, p.405.
45. *E.I.*, Vol. XXII, 1929-30.
46. *S.I.I.*, Vol. VIII, No. 689.
47. *A.R.E.*, No. 243 of 1926.
48. *S.I.I.*, Vol. IV, No. 512.
49. *S.I.I.*, Vol. IV, No. 511.
50. *S.I.I.*, Vol. V, No. 638.
51. *S.I.I.*, Vol. V, No. 983.
52. *S.I.I.*, Vol. VII, No. 1031.
53. To understand the Chola polity and society, the scholars divided the Chola regime into four sub-periods: (1) 850-985; (2) 985-1070; (3) 1071-1120; (4) 1120-1279. The scholars say that the third sub-period witnessed the consolidation of the Chola power. In his critical vision of the Chola ideology K. Kailasapathy says that the period from 850 C.E. to 975 C.E. is the emerging phase of the Chola country. He sees that the Rajajara I's regime attested to the development of Chola administration. K.A. Nilakanta Sastri sees his regime the formation period of the Chola state.
54. *S.I.I.*, Vol. XVII, No. 585; *Panimakan* was identified with *Natuvakai* official; P. Shanmugam, *The Revenue System of the Cholas*, 850-1279, p. 129.

55. *S.I.I.*, Vol. XXIII, No. 490.
56. *S.I.I.*, Vol. XVII, No. 608.
57. *S.I.I.*, Vol. XXIII, No. 489.
58. *A.R.E.*, No.164 of 1938-39.
59. *S.I.I.*, Vol. XXIV, No. 277.
60. Y. Subbarayalu says that some martial and pastoral groups in Tamil country turned out to be in the caste conclave. *Palli*, *Srutiman*, *Nattaman* and *Sri-gopala* are the conferred caste names on the tribes. With this point, we have to visualise the role of the chief of hunting community on water right; Y. Subbarayalu, 'The Chola State', in S. Rajagopal (ed.), *Kaveri: Studies in Epigraphy*, *Archaeology and History (Prof. Y. Subbarayalu Felicitation Volume*, Chennai, 2001, p. 97; see also Y. Subbarayalu, 'Some Aspects of Social Changes during the Chola Period' in S. Krishnamurthy et.al. *Tamiliology: Prof. R.M. Sundaram Felicitation Volume*, Chennai, p. 121.
61. *S.I.I.*, Vol. III, Part 1, 2, No.24.
62. In Pudukkottai region an individual called *Muvan-katappillai* from hunting community (*Valaiyar*) earned the *Patikaval* right; K.R. Sankaran, *Aspects of the History of Pudukkottai Region*, 2003, p. 27; *I.P.S.*, No. 439.
63. *S.I.I.*, Vol. XXIV, No. 146.
64. *S.I.I.*, Vol. XXIV, No. 147.
65. *S.I.I.*, Vol. VIII, No. 53.
66. *S.I.I.*, Vol. XXIV, No. 193.
67. *S.I.I.*, Vol. VIII, No. 707.
68. *S.I.I.*, Vol. XXII, No. 709.
69. *S.I.I.*, Vol. XXII, No. 179.
70. *S.I.I.*, Vol. XXII, No. 166.
71. *S.I.I.*, Vol. XXIV, No. 45.
72. Karl Marx, Frederick Angels, *Collected Works*, Vol.12, Moscow, 1979, p.127.
73. Karl A. Wittfogel, *Oriental Despotism: A Comparative Study of Total Power*, New Haven, Yale University, 1957.
74. R.A.L.H. Gunawardana, "Total Power or Shared Power? A Study of the Hydraulic State and its Transformations in Sri Lanka from the third to the ninth century AD" *Indian Historical Review*, New Delhi, 1982; idem, "*Function and Political Power : A Case Study of State Formation in Irrigation Society*" *Indian Historical Review*, Vol. 6, 1978, pp. 1-2.
75. J.V. Chellaih, *Pattuppattu*, Tamil University, Thanjavur, 1986.
76. *Nalatiyar*: 200, 206; The chiefly name *Peru-Muttarayyan* referred to in this literature is identified with *Suvaran-Maran* by M.S. Govindasamy in his work. M.S. Govindasamy, *The Role of Feudatories in Pallava History*, Annamalai University, 1965, p. 62.

77. K.A. Nilakanta Sastri, *The Colas*, (reprint), University of Madras, Madras, 1984, p. 112.
78. Noboru Karashima, *South Indian History and Society: Studies from the Inscriptions from 850 AD to 1800 AD*, OUP, New Delhi, 1984.
79. James Heitzman, *Gifts of Power: Lordship in an Early Indian State*, OUP, New Delhi, 1997.
80. K.R. Sankaran, *Some Historical Trends as Gleaned from the Nomenclature of the Canals (vaykkals) in the Chola Inscriptions,Dr. C.R. Srinivasan Commemoration Volume*, Bharatiya Kala Prakasam, New Delhi, 2004.
81. K.G. Krishnan, *Karantai Tamil Sangam Plates of Rajendra I*, Archaeological Survey of India, 1984; *E.I.*, Vol. XXII, No.34, *Larger Leiden Plates of Rajaraja I.*
82. K.R. Sankaran, *Aspects of the History of Pudukkottai Region, Pudukkottai*, 2003; V. Manickam, *Pudukkottai History up to 1600 A D*, (in Tamil), 2004.
83. *A.R.E.*, No.259 of 1923; *A.R.E.*, No.227 of 1917; *S.I.I.*, Vol. XIX, No.139 - *manaykalail-vata-talayvil-kitanta-kinarrril-ettam-irayk-kavum*; *A.R.E.*, No.16 of 1925- *melayt-tottattu-munpu-iraytttu-varukira-turavil.*, fn. no. 3 in ch. IV. in C.N. Subramaniam, *op.cit*.
84. *A.R.E.*, No. 263 of 1922, 1151 C.E.- Sayavanam/ Sirkali Tk :*tiruk-kulattile-nir-iraikkavum*; *A.R.E.*, No.671 of 1919, 1094 C.E. Tiruvarur/ Nagappattinam Tk: etta-mirayt-takulam; *A.R.E.*, No.5 of 1911, 1249 C.E. Nallur/ Papanasam Tk – *ik-kulattil-oru-nirk-kovaikku-iraikkalam-nilam. fn*. no. 8-10 inch; C.N. Subramaniam, *op.cit*.
85. *A.R.E.*, No.113 of 1938-39. Srirankam/ Tiruchirappalli--*talai*, *vaitttaly*, *vaykkaltalay*; *S.I.I.*, Vol. XXIV, No. 142 Sivapuram / Kumbakonam Tk; *A.R.E.*, No. 276 of 1927, 1126 C.E. Tiruvicalur/ Kumbakonam Tk; *A.R.E.*, No. 14 of 1907, 1194 C.E.; *S.I.I.*, Vol. XXIII, No. 14 Tiruvenkatu/ Mayiladuthurai Tk; *S.I.I.*, Vol. III, No.151. 972 C.E. Anaimankalam/ Nagappattinam Tk; *S.I.I.*, Vol. VIII, No. 521 *vattalaykkum-uvanrikkum*; *A.R.E.*, No. 245 of 1894, 888 C.E. -Tiruvaiyaru/ Thanjavur Tk; *S.I.I.*, Vol. II, No. 99 *kurranvay-mite-uvanryceytu; A.R.E.*, No. 296 of 1917, 1019 C.E. Kukur / Kumbakonam Tk, fn.no. 17-18 inch. IV in C.N. Subramaniam, *op.cit*.
86. *S.I.I.*, Vol. XXVI, No. 769; *S.I.I.*, Vol. V, No. 649; *S.I.I.*, Vol. VII, Nos. 1015, 141, 137, 840; *S.I.I.*, Vol. VI, No. 678; *S.I.I.*, Vol. XXII, No. 287; *S.I.I.*, Vol. XXIV, Nos. 981, 97; *S.I.I.*, Vol. VI, No. 879; *I.P.S.*, Nos. 109, 161.

    Ut-Ciruvaykkal

    S.I.I., Vol. VIII, No. 641 Nangavaram/ Tiruchirappalli Tk; *S.I.I.*, Vol. VIII, No. 184 Anbil/ Tiruchirappalli Tk; *S.I.I.*, Vol. XIII, No. 102 Tirukkotikaval/Kumbakonam Tk; *S.I.I.*, Vol. XIX, No.55 Tirumalapadi/ Tiruchrappalli Tk; *S.I.I.*, Vol. XIX, No. 138-Pullamangalam/ Thanjavur Tk; *S.I.I.*, Vol. XIX, No. 29 Tiruvilakkuti/ Thanjavur Tk; *S.I.I.*, Vol. XIII, No. 65 Tirukkannapuram/ Thanjavur Tk; I.P.S., No. 30 Nirpalani/ Kulattur

Tk; *S.I.I.*, Vol. III, Part 3, 4, No. 154 Uttaramallur/ Kanchipuram Tk; *S.I.I.*, Vol. III, No. 109 Kamarasavalli/ Tiruchirappalli Tk; *S.I.I.*, Vol. V, No. 612 Tirucatturai/ Thanjavur Tk; *S.I.I.*, Vol. XIX, No. 352 Utaiyarkuti/ Southarcot Tk; *S.I.I.*, Vol. XXVI, No.996 Konerirajapuram/ Mayiladuturai Tk; *S.I.I.*, Vol. XVII, No. 614 Thiruvarur; *S.I.I.*, Vol. V, No. 702 Tiruvitaymarutur/ Thanjavur; *S.I.I.*, Vol. XIX, No. 404 Tirukkolampiyur/ Thanjavur.

Kannaru:

S.I.I., Vol. XIII, Nos.67, 68 Koildevarayanpettai/ Thanjavur; *S.I.I.*, Vol. XIII, No. 169 Muniyur/ Thanjavur; *S.I.I.*, Vol. XIX, No.211 Kilappaluvur/ Tiruchirappalli; *S.I.I.*, Vol. XIX, No. 137 Viruthacalam/ Southarcot; *S.I.I.*, Vol. VI, No. 317 Uttaramallur/ Kanchipuram; *S.I.I.*, Vol. XIII, Nos. 138, 163, 164 Tiruverumpur/ Tiruchirappalli; *S.I.I.*, Vol. V, No. 1409 Karuntattankudi/ Thanjavur; *S.I.I.*, Vol. XXII, No. 143 Tirukkoyilur/ Southarcot; *S.I.I.*, Vol. VI, No. 339 Tirupulivalam/ Kanchipuram; *S.I.I.*, Vol. XXIII, No. 485 Kuttalam/ Thanjavur; *S.I.I.*, Vol. VII, No. 416 Kavantantalam/ Kanchipuram; *S.I.I.*, Vol. XIII, Nos. 48, 99; *S.I.I.*, Vol. XIX, Nos. 452, 371.

87. C.N. Subramaniam, *op.cit.*, p. 112; Subbarayalu, Y., '*Cila ariya corrkal* (some rare terms)' in Y. Subbarayalu and S. Raju (eds.), *Tamilakak Kalvettiyalum Varalarum* (Tamil), Tamil University, Thanjavur, 2001.

88. *A.R.E.*, No. 219 of 1899, 1006 C.E. Tiruvayyaru/ Thanjavur; *S.I.I.*, Vol. V, No. 518; *A.R.E.*, No. 509 of 1920, 1917 C.E. -Alankud I /Papanasam Tk; *A.R.E.*, No. 126 of 1938, 1113 C.E. Srirangam/ Tiruchirappalli Tk; *S.I.I.*, Vol. XXIV, No. 99; *A.R.E.*, No. 293 of 1908, 1021 C.E. Tirukkalittaittai/ kumbakonam Tk-*kulayym-kurappum-vetti*.

89. *S.I.I.*, Vol. XXIV, No.148; *A.R.E.*, No. 113 of 1927; *S.I.I.*, Vol. V, No. 572; *A.R.E.*, No. 17 of 1895 *anai-vaykkal-arru-anaiku-mankonta-nilam*.

90. This kind of taxes was statistically studied; see P.Shanmugam, *op.cit.*, p. 50.

91. *S.I.I.*, Vol. VIII, No.739, 907 C.E. Tiruvamattur/ Viluppuram Tk--*tumpininrupontavaykkal*; *S.I.I.*, Vol. XIII, No. 31. 988 C.E. Tirumalpuram/ Valajapettai--*kumilkkal*; *S.I.I.*, Vol. III, Part 1-2, No. 50, 992 C.E.--Tiruvallam--*tumpinintumerkku nokkippona kuruvanpattikkpayntavaykkal*; *S.I.I.*, Vol. XXVI, No. 739, 992 C.E. Tirunedunkalam/ Lalkuti Tk—*ten-narrininru-paynta-vaykkalin-kumiliyal-nirkintava*; *S.I.I.*, Vol. VII, No. 1015, 1002 C.E. Tirukkovilur—*tumpininrum-ponta-peru-vaykkal*; *S.I.I.*, Vol. VII, No. 440, 1004 C.E. Siyamankalam/ Valajapettai--*perei perun-tumpi-ninru-ponta ampalattati-vaykkal*; *S.I.I.*, Vol. III, Part 1-2, No. 84, 1070 C.E. *Perampalur—ivveri-ninrum-ampalattu-tumpi-ninrum ten-merku-nokkip-pona-vaykkal*; *S.I.I.*, Vol. XXIV, No. 97, 1112 C.E. Sri Rangam/ *manavalan-kumili-ninrum-vatakku nokki-pona-vaykkal*.

92. *A.R.E.*, No. 68 of 1908, 865 C.E. -Kamarasavalli koil/ Valuvur; *A.R.E.*, No. 417 of 1912, 871 C.E.-Marutadu (the *ūrār* of Marutadu village sold

some land being irrigated through a *madai*). *A.R.E.*, No. 62 of 1935-36, 1087 C.E. -Paranur/ Tirukkovilur (in this case a private party sold some quantum of paddy to repair the *madai*). In the same year an individual made one *kumili*, *A.R.E.*, No. 67 of 1935-36.

Bibliography

Annual Report on Epigraphy, 1894, 1895, 1899, 1907, 1908, 1911, 1912, 1917, 1920, 1922, 1923, 1926, 1927, 1935, 1935-36, 1938, 1938-39, 1969.

Appadorai, A., *Economic Conditions in Southern India (1000-1500 A.D.)*. Vol. I (reprint), University of Madras, 1900.

Burton Stein, *Peasant State and Society in Medieval South India*, Oxford University Press, New Delhi, 1982.

Champakalakshmi, R., *Trade Ideology and Urbanization: South India 300 BC to AD 1300*, Oxford University Press, New Delhi, 1996.

Chellaih, J.V., *Pattuppattu*, Tamil University, Thanjavur, 1986.

Epigraphia Indica, Vol. 22, Year 1929-30.

George W. Spencer, *The Politics of Expansion: The Chola conquest of Sri Lanka and Sri Vijaya*, New Era Publications, Chennai, 1983.

Govindasamy, S., *The Role of Feudatories in Pallava History*, Annamalai University, 1965.

Gunawardana, R.A.L.H., "Function and Political Power: A Case Study of State Formation in Irrigation Society" *Indian Historical Review*, 1978, Vol. 6.

---------------------, "Inter-societal Transfer of Hydraulic Technology in Pre-colonial South Asia: Some Reflections based on a Preliminary Investigation" *South Asian Studies*, Vol. XXII, No. 2, Kyoto, 1984.

----------------------, "Total Power or Shared Power? A Study of the Hydraulic State and its Transformations in Sri Lanka from the third to the ninth century AD" *Indian Historical Review*, New Delhi, 1982.

Inscriptions of Pudukkottai State, Nos. 30, 109, 161, 439.

James Heitzman, *Gifts of Power: Lordship in an Early Indian State*, Oxford University Press, New Delhi, 1997.

Karl A. Wittfogel, *Oriental Despotism: A Comparative Study of Total Power*, New Haven, Yale University, 1957.

Karl Marx, *Frederick Angels*, Collected Works, Vol.12, Moscow, 1979.

Kenneth R. Hall, *Trade and State Craft in the Age of the Cholas*, Abhinav Publications, New Delhi, 1980.

Krishnan, K.G., *Karantai Tamil Sangam Plates of Rajendra I*, Archaeological Survey of India, 1984.

Leslie C. Orr, 'Women in the Temple, the Palace, and the Family: The Construction of Women's Identities in the Pre-colonial Tamil Nadu' in Kenneth R. Hall (ed.), *Structure and Society in Early South*

India: Essays in Honour of Noboru Karashima, Oxford University Press, New Delhi, 2001.

Manickam, V., *Pudukkottai History up to 1600 A D* (in Tamil), 2004.

Nalatiyar: 200.

Natana Kasinathan, Undersea Exploration of the Shore of Poompukar, State Department of Archaeology, Government of Tamil Nadu, Chennai, 1991.

Nilakanta Sastri, K.A., *The Colas*, (reprint) University of Madras, Madras, 1984.

Noboru Karashima, *South Indian History and Society: Studies from the Inscriptions AD 850 to 1800 A.D*, Oxford University Press, New Delhi, 1984.

Perumal, A.V., "Trade in Pudukkottai- A Study" in *Arivottam*, Vol. 1, Mayiladuthurai.

Rajamanickanar, M., *Periya Purana Araychi* (research on *Periyapuranam*), 3rd edition, Pari Nilayyam, Chennai, 1978.

Rajan Gurukkal, "Aspects of Reservoir System: Irrigation in Early Pandya State" *Studies in History*, Vol.1, No.1, New Delhi, 1986.

Rajan, K., *Ancient Irrigation Technology: Sluice Technology in Tamil Nadu*, Heritage India Trust, Thanjavur, 2008.

Rajavelu, S., "Poompukaril Sinhala-Brahmi Poritta Matkalattundu" in *Avanam*, Vol. 10, p.154.

Sadasiva Bhandarattar, T.V., *Pirkalachcholar Carittiram*, Annamalai University, 1946.

Sankaran, K.R., *Some Historical Trends as Gleaned from the Nomenclature of the Canals (vaykkals) in the Chola Inscriptions*, Dr. C.R. Srinivasan Commemoration Volume, Bharatiya Kala Prakasam, New Delhi, 2004.

--------------------, *'Thanjavur Peruvudaiyar Koyilin Taliccerippendukal'* in *Arivottam*, Mayiladuthurai, 2003.

--------------------, *Aspects of the History of Pudukkottai Region*, Pudukkottai, 2003.

--------------------, *Irrigation in Medieval Tamil Country with special reference to Pudukkottai Region*, Article Submitted to INSA, New Delhi, 2005.

Shanmugam, P., *The Revenue System of the Cholas 850-1279 AD*, New Era Publications, Madras, 1987.

South Indian Inscriptions, Various Volumes, Vols. II, III, IV, V, VI, VII, VIII, XIII, XVII, XIX, XXII, XXIII, XXIV, XXVI.

Subbarayalu, Y., '*Cila ariya corrkal* (some rare terms)' in Y. Subbarayalu and S.Raju (eds.), *Tamilakak Kalvettiyalum Varalarum* (Tamil), Tamil University, Thanjavur, 2001.

--------------------, *'Some Aspects of Social Changes During the Chola Period'* in S. Krishnamurthy et.al. (eds.), *Tamiliology: Prof. R.M. Sundaram Felicitation Volume*, Chennai.

--------------------, *'The Chola State'*, in S. Rajagopal (ed.), *Kaveri: Studies in Epigraphy, Archaeology and History (Prof. Y. Subbarayalu Felicitation Volume*, Chennai, 2001.

--------------------, *"Camuka varalrru nokkil vettiyum muttalum"* in *Moli Mukakankal* (felicitation volume to Prof. Ki. Arankan), Thanjavur, 2003.

--------------------, *Political Geography of the Chola Country*, The State Department of Archaeology, Government of Tamil Nadu, Madras, 1973.

--------------------, *The Chola State*, Studies in History, Vol. 5:2, 1982.

Subramaniam, C.N., *Aspects of the History of Agriculture in the Kaveri Delta c. 850 AD to c. 1600 AD*, Unpublished M.Phil. Dissertation submitted to JNU, New Delhi, 1983.

9

Agriculture and Land Revenue Policies of the Second Pandyan Empire

K. Thangapandian

Agriculture was the main occupation for the majority of Tamil people and land tax was the principal source of revenue for the state. The king, being an absolute owner of the land, had to take special care in the distribution and development of the land in the state. The Pāṇḍya rulers took the effort to bring large tracts of lands under cultivation, which remained uncultivated for long periods. In the medieval period, villages were inhabited by the farmers. The status of land and agriculture indicates the economic condition of the people of Tamil country.

Types of Land

In the medieval Tamil country, various types of lands were present in a village and were determined by the administrative convenience of the state, besides others. The lands of the village that existed in the medieval Tamil country could be classified as wet lands (*naṉcey*), dry lands (*puṉcey*) and garden lands (*tōṭṭam*).[1]

Wet Land

The west lands were most important cultivable tracts of land which were denoted in the medieval inscriptions as *nancey*.[2] In the wet land cultivation, there were generally two harvests, the *kār*, and *pāsānam*. The season for the sowing of *kār* season had to begin in June and harvest took place around December. The crop was raised for a six month period. The number of crops raised each year on paddy land was two, sometimes three, occasionally in the inscriptions there was a mention of fields that bore three crops.[3] Similarly, the terms *orupū*[4] (single crop), *irupū*[5] (two crops a year) and *kaḍaipū*[6] (literally the last) being applied to the several harvests.[7]

The inscription from Poṉṉamarāvathi, Thiruchirapaḷḷi district, issued in the reign of Māṟavarmaṉ Kulasēkhara dated 1283 C.E., records a sale of wet lands (*nīrnilam*) as *sēnāpathi-peruvari* by residents of Pulaṅkuṟichi of Puramalināḍu to the servants of the temple.[8] Yet another thirteenth-century epigraph from Tirchchōpuram, South Ārcot district; issued in the reign of an unidentified Sundara Pāṇḍya, records the gift of wet lands (*naṉcey*) in the village of the Tyagavaḷḷi in the eastern division of Mērku-nāḍu by the king as an offering and for undertaking certain repairs in the temple.[9]

Dry Land

Dry lands were commonly known as *puṉcey*. The dry lands were called *kaḻaṉi puṉcey* and *kāṭṭupuṉcey*.[10] Dry lands cultivation mostly depended on the monsoon rains and sometimes the well water. An inscription from Jambai, South Ārcot district, dated 1301 C.E. and issued in the reign of Māṟavarma Kulasēkhara I records the alienation of 900 *kuḻi* of dry lands (*puṉcey*) at Maṉḍuyyaperumal-nāṭṭur, a tax-free *dēvadāṉa* village, in favour of a Brāhmaṉa of Manalūr for his services by the temple authorities.[11]

Garden Lands (*Tōttam*)

Garden lands were called as *tōṭṭam*.[12] The fruit trees were grown in the garden lands (*tōṭṭanilam*) such as *mā* (mango), *palā* (Jack fruit) and *vāḻai* (plantain). A thirteenth-century epigraph found at Perumal temple, Sēvūr, Coimbatore district and issued in the reign of Jaṭāvarmaṉ Sundara Pāṇḍya, records a sale of puṉcey *tōṭṭam* for a 300 *anṟāḍu-varagaṉ-paṇam* by Siṟuvaṉ Āṇḍān to the deity of the place.[13] An inscription found at Śivatokanātha temple in Grāmam, South Ārcot district, dated 1269 C.E. and issued in the reign of Jaṭāvarmaṉ Sundara Pāṇḍya I, registers an endowment of land to the temple made by the king for the improvement of gardens (*tirutōppu*).[14]

Main Crops and Crop Pattern

The major *kār* crops were rice, *karnol*, and the paddy cultivated during the time *pāsān* was called *passan* crop. Apart from paddy, varagu pulses, gingelli, castor (āmaṇakku) were cultivated in the dry (*puṉcey*) lands. The crops cultivated with the expectation of rainfall was called *vāṉpayir*.[15] The dry crops were called *puṉpayir*.[16] The two different dry lands were called as *kaḻaṉipuṉcey* and *kāṭṭupuṉcey*.[17]

Crops to some extent determined agricultural practice, an understanding of principal crops that were grown in the medieval Tamil country. But, we do not have a comprehensive account from which we could compile the evidence scattered through some inscriptions which record rates of landlords share in various crops,[18] the revenue assessment of land[19] and tolls on goods which enter internal trade. Traveller's account also supply some interesting information on the subject.[20]

The study of several inscriptions and foreign accounts leaves us with the impression that the medieval Tamil country produced almost all the crops that are cultivated at present. References are available to the cultivation of dry crops like varagu, ragi, kambu, black gram, sāmai, millet, horse gram, dhall, pulse etc. These crops are frequently mentioned in the inscriptions. The crops cultivated in the Tamil country seem to have comprised the following categories. A near exhaustive list of crops cultivated in all *naṉcey*, *puṉcey*, *tōṭṭam* and *kollai* lands in the Pāṇḍya country has been furnished below:

(i) cereals - rice, wheat, and barley
(ii) millets - millet (grain) millet (the sticky variety)
(iii) pulses - peas, gram - green, black, Bengal gram, red beans
(iv) oil seeds - gingili, sesame, castor
(v) sugarcane
(vi) fibers - Hemp, cotton
(vii) dyes - Indigo
(viii) drugs - lac, sandal wood
(ix) spices - pepper, ginger, cinnamon, cumin, mustard, cloves nutmeg, cardamom, coriander
(x) garden crops - melon, gourd, turnip, bottle, guard, tamarind, brinjal, turmeric.[21]

Land Revenue – Tax Policy of the State

The land tax was probably the oldest form of taxation. Essentially a tax on the yield of the land, in its primitive form was assessed based on area. It is more developed form, which was a tax collected from the annual revenue derived from land or on the capital value of the land.

Land revenue was an important source of income of any state, as before as and even after and during the medieval period of the Tamil country. The economy of medieval states depended on land and the bulk of the revenue was generated through land tax.

The later Pāṇḍyas collected different kinds of taxes. For the convenient handling, the taxes are classified as under:

(i) Taxes on land

(ii) Taxes on property

(iii) Commercial taxes

(iv) Professional taxes, and

(v) Miscellaneous items of income.

Taxes on Land

The most important item of revenue was undoubtedly the land tax which was commonly denoted by the term *kaḍamai*. The other terms used to denote the tax on and productions are *iṟaikāśu*, *nelkaḍamai*, *nelvari*, and puṉcey *varam*. The tax on wet land was known as *naṉceykaḍamai*. The tax collected from the dry land was known as *puṉcey kaḍamai* or *puṉpayir kaḍamai*.[22]

Taxes on Property

As in many modern countries, a tax was levied in the later Pāṇḍya kingdom on all property, movable and immovable. But one difference between the levying of taxes in the later Pāṇḍya period and in the modern period is that, while in modern India, the annual income or the rental value of the property is the basis for assessment but in the later Pāṇḍya kingdom, the whole property itself, irrespective of the income from it, was taken into consideration for fixing the tax.

Taxes were collected on properties such as, houses,[23] house-sites,[24] gardens,[25] animals,[26] trees,[27] etc. Marco Polo in his travel account states that the cultivators in the area of St. Thomas mount (Mylapore) paid a tax of six goats per annum for each coconut tree.[28] The rate of taxes on properties must have varied from place to place.

Assessment of Taxes

From the many available epigraphs belonging to the medieval period, it could be assumed that the assessment and levy of tax were based on types of land, irrigation facilities, and the nature of crops they cultivated. Permanent and progressive assessments were the other two methods of collecting land tax from the land owners. They were also assessed according to the grades (*taram*) of land. The assessed lands were known as *taramiḍu* and non-assessed lands were called *taramili* which indicates that only land of a good grade or quality is taken into account for assessment purpose.[29] The land assessment also varied from track to track and from time to time. The wet land was assessed at the rate of 3 *kaḷam pēr vēli* per annum.

It varied according to the classification of lands based on grade; for example:

1st *taram* - per mā 8 *kaḷams*.

2nd *taram* - per mā 4 *kaḷams*

3rd *taram* - per mā 3 *kaḷams*

4th *taram* - per mā 4 *kaḷams*[30]

In the epigraph of Jaṭāvarmaṉ Sundara Pāṇḍya it is mentioned that some lands were assessed at the rate of 7 *kaḷam*, 1 *kuṟuṇi* per mā.[31] The *pāsaṉam* (wet land) crop was fixed with highest of levy. Especially the *mā* in crop of *Kuṟuvai* was levied mostly at the rate of 3/4.[32]

The land assessment varied from territory to territory. It is stated in the inscription of Kāḷaiyarkōil region that the land tax was at the rate of 1 *kaḷam* 1 *kuṟuṇi* per mā and antarāyam 3 *paṇam* during the reign of Jaṭāvarmaṉ Sundara Pāṇḍya. But they have also assessed at 7 *kaḷam* 1 *kuṟuṇi* per mā and some bore cash assessment of 18 *paṇams* in the 14th year of Māṟavarmaṉ Vikrama's rule.[33]

Other Commodities

A record from Vīra Pāṇḍyapaṭṭiṉam (Tiruchendur) on the east coast refers to the assessment of Khadhi *(kadar)* which was at the rate of 1/4 *paṇam* per 100 *kaḷam* on the goods imported and exported from the roadstead.[34] The trans-regional merchant community from Western Ghats transported their products especially spices, areca nut, camphor, pepper, turmeric, cotton cloth, and dried ginger from west to eastwards. The following rates were assessed for the above commodities.[35]

(a) Spices and camphor - 1 *kalam* or 1/20 *paṇam*

(b) Cotton fabrics - *kāśu*

(c) Areca nut, pepper, turmeric -1 *kāśu* (nārppu).

Another record (1283 C.E.) states that the merchandise levies were assessed at the rate of 1/2 *mā or* 1/40 *paṇam*, on areca nut (cattle load) 1 *mā* or 1/10 *paṇam* or pepper and rice cattle load 1/20 *paṇam*.[36]

Collection of Tax

Revenue administration was one of the most important responsibility of the kings and the most convenient and lawful means of acquiring revenue was the imposition of taxes on the people. The ideal king in the Indian tradition was one who was moderate in tax-collection. The *Dharmasaśtras* permitted the rulers to collect the taxes from the people in a just manner. According to *Manu*, "just as the leech, the half and the bee taken their food little by little, even so much the king draw from his realm moderate annual taxes".[37]

Oppression by the rulers has also been condemned in the *Tirukkuṟaḷ*.[38] The types of taxes levied by the rulers on different sections of the society can be understood from the numerous Sanskrit epigraphs issued during the periods. Tax remissions were granted by the kings in many instances.

The numerous dues were levied upon cultivated lands, *kaḍamai*, *antarāyam*, *viniyōgam*, *accu-vari*, *kāriyavaram*, *vaṭṭi-paṭṭam*, *pañjupili*, *sandiviggirahapēru*, *vāsal pēru*, *iṭaciṉaippēru*, *uḻudāṉkudi*, *paḍikkāval*, *poṉvari* and others during the period.[39]

Occasionally we get an idea of the rates of those dues especially in connection with a *dēvadāṉa* lands. We learn, for instance, from an inscription dated in the eleventh year of a certain Sundara Pāṇḍya that the *Kaḍamai*[40] on some temple lands[41] was fixed at three *kaḷams* on each *mā* of land or one-half of what prevailed among other *dēvadāṉa* lands and that for the assessment, crops of full yields alone were taken into consideration, those that had suffered damage or failed altogether being left out of the account.

The Thiruchirappalli and Pudukottai inscriptions[42] shed light on the 31 taxes levied by the Pāṇḍyas. They were:

1. *Achchuvari* - tax in *Achchu* coins.
2. *Iḷañjiṉai pēru* - tax for the service person who keeps the royal seal.
3. *Kariya-aratchi* - tax for the service of government officers.
4. *Santiviggraha* - tax for the service of the king's messenger or mediator.

5. *Taṭṭōli* – a tax on drummers.
6. *Pañju-pili* – a tax on cotton.
7. *Antarāyam* - which means 'inner āyam (tax)' tends towards decreasing use.
8. *Idaiyar - vari* - tax on the Idaiyar (shepherd) community.
9. *Ina- vari* – a tax on some community.
10. *Iṟai vari* - The most general term for tax in Chōḻa inscriptions continued to appear in the Pāṇḍya period also.
11. *Echchōru* - which means the supply of meals to public servants or forced labourers.
12. *Kaḍamai* - Another term for land tax.[43]
13. *Kaṇikkai* - which means gift.
14. *Karthigai pachchai* – a gift of new crops in the month of *Karthigai* (November- December).
15. *Kiḻ-iṟai* - which means 'mirror tax' appears.
16. *Kuḍimai* – a tax on *kuḍi* (cultivator).[44]
17. *Kuṟṟu - arisi* - rice for the service of *kuṟṟu* officer.
18. *Sil-vari* – a small tax.
19. *Sekku - iṟai* – a tax on oil mills.
20. *Taṭṭar - paṭṭam* – a tax on goldsmith.
21. *Tari - rai* – a tax on looms.
22. *Nadenra-vari* - Tax collected for the Nāḍu.
23. *Nāṭṭu - viniyōgam* - Tax fort the Nāḍu's expenditure.
24. *Pāsi - paṭṭam* – a tax on fishing.[45]
25. *Pēru - vari* - big tax.
26. *Poṉ vari* - tax in money.
27. *Muṭṭa-al-* continuous free labour.
28. *vari* - one of the most general terms for tax.
29. *Vāsal pēru* - tax for the palace.
30. *Viniyōgam* - expenditure.
31. *Veṭṭi* - free labour for public works.

Property tax was also collected from the land owners. The rate of taxes on properties varied from place to place. Commercial taxes were collected for commercial goods like salt, paddy, rice, green-gram, cotton and chamber oil, etc. The rate of taxation on salt and paddy was uniform.

Tari-iṟai tax is a common term that would refer to a tax on a loom. *Ulai*, *ulai -paṭṭam* and *kollar-ulai paṭṭam*[46] were levied on weavers during the period of later Pāṇḍyas. *Iḍaiyar-vari* was a popular term found in use, was levied on shepherds. Various miscellaneous taxes were also collected from government officers, kings' messengers or mediators and other servants.

Uḻavukkāśu was levied at the rate of 2 *kaḷam* per vēli (plough fee) on cultivators as cultivator levy. *Maṉai-iṟai* was collected from residential lands in the Pāṇḍya period. The assessment of Khādi (Khadar) was *mā* de at the rate of 1/4 *paṇam* per *paṇam* on the goods imported and exported from the roadstead. A tax of *paṇam* per annum was levied on looms of the Kaikkōlas, Sāliyar, and oil mongers. Ūr Viniyōgam was collected at the rate of 3 iṟai *paṇam* per annum during the later Pāṇḍyas.

Economic Status of Peasants

Agriculture formed the principal source of livelihood of the people of the medieval Tamil country. The land and taxes represented the major source of revenue of the state. Though agriculture during the medieval period under the Pāṇḍyas was monsoon-based, there were attempts made by imperial Pāṇḍyas to provide irrigation facilities to the people for the development of agriculture.

Many crops like paddy, oilseeds, sugar and millets were raised in the agricultural sector. The surplus agricultural produce was sold for a price on the value both at home and overseas. During the period of natural calamities and especially, when the monsoon failed, the price of products got very high and that the peasants couldn't afford them. Many agricultural products had been sold in the domestic market. In the overseas trade, the products sold internally were exchanged for other products.

The temple was the biggest landlord during the Pāṇḍya times. The temple authorities formed *Sabhā* which had exclusive rights over the village administration and management of the temple.

During the Pandya time kings offered tax exemption to temple lands which were called dēvadāṉa *iṟaiyili* land. In the tenure of *agrahāra* or *chaturvēdimaṅgalam*, Brahmins who had a whole village as *brahmadēya* or *chaturvēdimaṅgalam* looked after the cultivation.[47] Some inscriptions of Pāṇḍyas are very well supporting the fact of creation of *Brahmadēyas*, *chaturvēdimaṅgalam* and *agrahārams*. *Tiruviḍaiyāṭṭam* lands were given to Vishnu temple and they were exempted from the payment of tax hence it is known as *iṟayili tiruviḍaiyāṭṭam*.

The two major perennial rivers Vaigai and Tāmirabarani made the Pandya country rich and prosperous, provided water for cultivation as well as drinking purpose. The prosperity of an agricultural country depends on the facilities provided for irrigation and securing an adequate water supply; it was recognized in South India from very early times. Natural streams and dependable channels and canals were the first sources of water supply. The agricultural development in the Pāṇḍya country owed much to the Vaigai and its tributaries. The *veṭṭiyāḻ* the village servant had to repair the dam on receiving the information from the watchman. Ērivari,[48] *pāsipaṭṭam*,[49] *nīranai*,[50] ērimin-paṭṭam, vāyakkal- paṭṭam[51] were collected for the maintenance of irrigation. The taxes such as *vāyakal-paṭṭam*, *pāsi-paṭṭam*, a duty collected by local assembly from the tenants.

Impact of Land Revenue Administration

In the medieval Pāṇḍya Tamil country, the taxing system on cultivated lands was somehow complicated due to the prevalence of different kinds of land tenures, varied tax structures on different lands, numerous grants to various sections of society with varying immunity, introduction of frequent fresh levies and so on. Besides the land dues, several taxes were collected which was not uniform over the whole country.

The state made the village assemblies responsible for the tax collection from the landowners, both private and communal and the cultivators.[52] Also the village assemblies were authorised to sell the defaulter's lands in a public auction to realise the land tax defaults.[53] An inscription from Kuḍumiyāṉmalai dated 1267 C.E. and issued in the reign of Jaṭāvarmaṉ Vīra Pāṇḍya, registers a sale of *puravū* (tax-paying) land by the ūrār as they had been at default for a long period in the payment of *kaḍamai-kiḻiṟai*.[54] Another inscription from the same place and of the same king records a sale of 3 *vēli* of land by the ūrārs of Visalūr to the Tirunalakkuṉram-uḍaiya-nāyanār for some *kāśus*, as they were otherwise unable to pay the taxes due from their village when demanded by Dēvar Vaṉadirayar and Uḍaiyār Kaṅgeyarāyar.[55] A fourteenth century inscriptions of later Pāṇḍyas found at Kīramaṅgalam,[56] Kūḍalur,[57] Piṉṉaguḍi,[58] and Tēṉṉāṅguḍi,[59] also record similar sale of the village lands in public auction by the ūrārs as they found themselves to pay the *kaḍamai* dues when demanded from them.

Scattered evidence referring to the oppressive actions of revenue officials and chiefs in the collection of land revenue from the ryots is recorded in the inscriptions of the second Pāṇḍyan Empire. The landowners and tenants were suffering because of the heavy land taxes imposed on them during the later Pāṇḍya times. The rate of taxes due on the lands was high owing to some severities of the old system under which they were suffering. People of Siruperuchichiyūr and Kaṉrapūr were very much reduced in circumstances and began to feel that life in woods and would be preferable.[60] An inscription from Iḍaiyattūr, dated 1236 C.E. and issued in the reign of Māṟavarmaṉ Sundara Pāṇḍya I, records a sale of wet land by the Maṟavars and the ūrārs of Ollaiyūr to Tiruttantoniriśvaramuḍaiya-nāyanār temple for 8,000 aṉṟadunārkāśu under the distressing circumstances. They had no means of discharging their revenue dues to the government. Evidently, the taxation was heavy and the people were much oppressed by the revenue collectors (*achchupperṟaporuḷar*).[61] The other inscriptions of the 13th century from Irumbanāḍu, [62] Karaiyūr, [63] Tirukkalakkuḍi,[64] Mēlattanaiyam[65] also attest to the sufferings of the communal landholders and individual landowners due to the oppressive methods exercised by the tax collecting officials.

Agriculture formed the principal source of livelihood of the people of the Pāṇḍya country. In medieval times lands were broadly classified into cultivated lands, uncultivated waste lands, barren lands, pasture lands forest lands, and common lands. Cultivated lands were having paramount importance and it was classified mainly into wet lands, dry lands and garden lands. The cultivated lands in the villages were held under various tenures and hence there was a spectrum of ownership patterns. The landownership that existed in the medieval Pāṇḍya times followed a definite pattern, namely, *veḷḷāṉvagai*, *brahmadēya*, *dēvadāṉa*, service tenures, private ownership and crow ownership. The land taxes represented the major source of revenue of the state.

References

1. N. Alagappan, *Economic Conditions in the Medieval Tamil Country*, Chidambaram, 1998, pp. 9-10.
2. *S.I.I.*, Vol. II, No. 22, p. 116.
3. A. Appadorai, *Economic Condition in South India (1000-1500)*, Vol. I, Madras, 1990, p. 237; K.A. Nilakanta Sastri, *The Cōlas*, Madras, Second Edition, 1955, p. 585.
4. *S.I.I.*, Vol. XIV, No. 144.
5. *S.I.I.*, Vol. VIII, Nos. 217 & 222; *S.I.I.*, Vol. XIV, No. 305.
6. *S.I.I.*, Vol. XXIV, Nos. 206 & 223.

7. *S.I.I.*, Vol. II, No. 22; Vol. XXII, p. 117; Vol. II, p. xii.
8. *S.I.I.*, Vol. XXVI, No. 21.
9. *S.I.I.*, Vol. XVII, No. 127.
10. *A.R.E.*, No. 66 of 1919.
11. *S.I.I.*, Vol. XII, No. 98.
12. *S.I.I.*, Vol. XII, No. 450.
13. *A.R.E.*, No. 119 of 1987-1988, p. 39.
14. *S.I.I.*, Vol. XXII, No. 196.
15. *A.R.E.*, No. 59 of 1914, Part-II, Para 44.
16. *S.I.I.*, Vol. II, No. 61.
17. *A.R.E.*, No. 66 of 1919.
18. *A.R.E.*, Nos. 62 and 66 of 1916.
19. *A.R.E.*, 1916, Para 28.
20. *S.I.I.*, Vol. VII, No. 442.
21. N.Alagappan, *op.cit.*, p. 10.
22. *Ibid.*, pp. 56-57.
23. *A.R.E.*, No.357 of 1922
24. *A.R.E.*, No.107 of 1924.
25. *S.I.I.*, Vol. XXIV, No. 223.
26. *A.R.E.*, No.261 of 1940-1941.
27. *S.I.I.*, Vol. XXIV, No. 223.
28. *S.I.I.*, Vol. XXIV, No. 228.
29. T.V.Mahalingam, *South Indian Polity*, University of Madras, Madras, 1967, p. 153.
30. *A.R.E.*, No. 196 of 1981-1982.
31. *S.I.I.*, Vol. VIII, No. 170.
32. *A.R.E.*, Nos. 34 & 35 of 1931-1932.
33. R.Thirumalai, *Land Grants and Agrarian Reactions in Cola and Pandya Times*, University of Madras, 1987, p. 235.
34. *A.R.E.*, No. 311 of 1963-1964.
35. *S.I.I.*, Vol. XXII, Nos.430 & 434.
36. *Ibid*
37. Chitra Madhavan, *History and Culture of Tamil Nadu*, Vol. I, New Delhi, 2005, p. 64.
38. *Kural*, Chapter: 56, Verses: 555-556.
39. K.A.Nilakanta Sastri, *The Pandyan Kingdom from the Earliest Times to the Sixteenth Century*, London, 1929, p. 191.
40. C. Lakshmanan, *Nellai Mavatta Koilgal*, p. 212.
41. *A.R.E.*, 1915, Part II, Para 34.
42. Noboru Karasimha, *South Indian History and Society*: *Studies from Inscriptions A.D. 850-1800*, New Delhi, 1984, p. 105.
43. C. Lakshmanan, *op.cit.*, p. 212.

44. Noboru Karashima, *op.cit.*, p. 114.
45. *Ibid.*, p. 115.
46. E.I., Vol. XXII, p. 34.
47. *A.R.E.*, No. 127 of 1925.
48. *A.R.E.*, Nos. 318 & 324 of 1908.
49. *Idem.*
50. Rajan Gurukkal, *Social Formations of Early South India*, New Delhi, 2012, p. 15.
51. *A.R.E.*, No. 326 of 1908
52. *S.I.I.*, Vol. XX, No. 109, line12.
53. *S.I.I.*, Vol. III, No. 9.
54. *S.I.I.*, Vol. XXII, No. 360.
55. P.S.I., No. 375.
56. *A.R.E.*, No. 124 of 1935-1936; *A.R.E.*, 1935-1936, Part-II, Para 54.
57. P.S.I., No. 449.
58. P.S.I., No. 448.
59. P.S.I., No. 636.
60. *A.R.E.*, No. 91 of 1924; *A.R.E.*, 1923-1924, Part-II, Para 31.
61. P.S.I., No. 309.
62. P.S.I., No. 376.
63. P.S.I., No. 399.
64. *A.R.E.*, No. 81 of 1916; *A.R.E.*, 1916, Part II, Para 30.
65. P.S.I., No. 624.

Bibliography

Alagappan, N., *Economic Conditions in the Medieval Tamil Country*, Chidambaram, 1998.

Appadorai, A., *Economic Conditions in Southern India (1000-1500)*, Vol.I, University of Madras, Madras, 1936.

Chitra Madhavan, *History and Culture of Tamil Nadu*, Vol. I, New Delhi, 2005.

Mahalingam, T.V., *South Indian Polity*, University of Madras, Madras, 1967.

Nilakanta Sastri, K.A., *The Cōlas*, University of Madras, Madras, Second Edition, 1955.

-----------------, *The Pandyan Kingdom: From the Earliest Times to the Sixteenth Century*, Luzac & Co., London, 1929.

Noboru Karasimha, *South Indian History and Society: Studies from Inscriptions A.D. 850-1800*, Oxford University Press, Delhi, 1984.

Rajan Gurukkal, *Social Formations of Early South India*, New Delhi, 2012.

Thirumalai, R., *Land Grants and Agrarian Reactions in Cola and Pandya Times*, University of Madras, 1987.

10

Agrarian Patterns and Practices of Malaiyali Tribes of Pachaimalai Hills in Tamil Nadu

C. Premnaseer

In India, there are many tribal communities, have been living in the hilly regions as well as in plain areas since time immemorial. India has the second largest tribal population of the world next to African countries. Two hundred and fifty tribal groups are living in isolated regions of the country. These tribal groups are speaking about 105 languages and 225 subsidiary languages.[1] We find tribal settlements in the Eastern and Western Ghats of Tamil Nadu. The important hill ranges of Tamil Nadu are the Jawadhu hills and Yelagiri hills of the North Arcot district, the Kalvarayan hills of South Arcot district, the Pachaimalai and Kollimalai hills of Salem district, the Anamalai of Coimbatore, the Sitheri hills of Dharmapuri, the Palani hills of Dindigul and the Nilgiri hills of Nilgiris district. Most of the tribal communities in Tamil Nadu have been living in the hill regions and its surrounding places. The government of Tamil Nadu has recognised 17 tribes as primitive, out of 36 Scheduled Tribes. The Government of India identified six tribal communities as Primitive Tribal Groups based on a pre-agriculture level of technology, a stagnant or declining population, extremely low literacy, and a subsistence level of the economy. These six primitive tribal groups are Tōdās, Kōtas, Kurumbās, Irulās, Paniyans and Kāttunāyakans, who are mostly living in Nilgiris district and other parts of Tamil Nadu. Among them, Irulās and Kāttunāyakans are living throughout Tamil Nadu state including the Nilgiris district.[2]

Among the 36 Scheduled Tribes of Tamil Nadu the Malaiyalis tribes of Pachaimalai are identified as an important ethnic social group, have their unique lifestyle and culture. The Malaiyali tribal communities are not recognized as a primitive tribe but they are listed in the Scheduled Caste categories of Tamil Nadu. They have their own exclusive identity, cultural traditions and customs, mostly living in the following hilly areas of Tamil Nadu such as Kollimalai hills, Pachaimalai hills, Kalvarayan hills, Shervarayan hills, and Jawadhu hills. It is believed that they are migrated from the sacred place of Kanchipuram to these hills and settled for their livelihood. Later they shifted to Pachaimalai hills about ten generations' ago.[3]

The Pachaimalai hills, is an easternward extension of the Eastern Ghats, which literally translate to 'green hills' in English, are the unexplored lush green hill ranges, covered with dry evergreen and dry deciduous forests. These are located in the northwestern boarders of Trichirappalli district of Tamil Nadu. The total area is 14,122 sq.km. The hill range is about 2000 feet above the sea level and certain peaks are about 3400 feet high.[4] In hilly region the Malaiyalis (or hill men) were made a settlement during the time of Pallavas and Cholas periods.[5] There were four *nādus* in Pachaimalai Hills such as *Thenparanādu*, *Vannādu*, *Attinādu*, and *Kōmbainādu*. The *Thenparanādu*, *Vannādu*, and *Kōmbainādu* are situated in Thuraiyur taluk of Tiruchirappalli district and *Attinādu* is situated in Gangavalli taluk of Salem district.[6] Among the *nadus*, there were eighty-four settlements in Pachaimalai Hills.[7]

The Malaiyali tribes of Pachaimalai are mostly involved in agricultural activities, and hunting and gathering. As they are the traditional cultivators they have been cultivating crops like paddy, millets, pulses, tapioca, guava, jackfruit, mango, coconut, cashew nut, and vegetables, etc. The subsistence lifestyle, food habits, and organoleptic preferences of these tribes, as well as their dependence on monsoon rain for irrigation, have led them to cultivate and conserve local seeds for consumption and for sowing in the subsequent season.[8] This traditional practice is a blessing in disguise and has saved many forms of specific and intra-specific varieties of millets and paddy. The tribal members of the society traded with outsiders for the few necessities they lacked, such as salt and iron.[9]

Land Revenue Assessment

The cultivated land on the hills is divided into two categories: *ulavukādu*, land capable of being ploughed, and *punalkādu*, land which cannot be ploughed for cultivation, of which the cultivation is carried on by grain being dribbled in among trees and rocks wherever a few feet of soil is to be found.[10] The produce of the hill forests, excluding grain and the produce of the fruit-trees, was formerly rented out by government, but latterly a seigniorage has been collected by rangers appointed for the purpose of all fuel, charcoal, bamboos, brought down from the hills. The government had spent money for the promotion of forest economy for the period of five years from 1868 to 1873. The hill-tribes are allowed to cut whatever wood they may require for domestic purposes. A tax is also raised on the honey produced on the hills, from which about 60 Rupees a year is collected as tax from the honey collection.[11]

Property Rights and Inheritance

Pachaimalai Malaiyalis does not have personal property, which has a high value in terms of money-market because of their subsistence economy. After the death of a man, his properties have been handed over to his wife. After her death, the property is inherited by her children. Lands were equally shared (*sama-pangu*) among the sons in this region, but no share is given to women. However, few articles such as earthenware, aluminium vessels, basketry, tools, clothes, ornaments of cheap varieties were given to women.[12] In the case of cattle and other domesticated animals; they are shared among all the sons in equal proportions.[13]

Traditional Economy

The Malaiyalis of the Pachaimalai Hills is largely dependent upon their traditional economic pursuits. The traditional economy of the tribes is mostly based on the cultivation and collection of minor forest produce. Besides, other minor economic activities such as hunting and gathering of food are also practiced by them.[14] Since the tribes are coming in contact with the people of other cultures, some of them have been taking up modern economic pursuits also. Though, the traditional economic pattern have been in existence and the communities has been producing goods for consumption, distribution, and marketing.[15]

The economic conditions are classified under different categories such as subsistence, hunter-gatherers, foraging, slash and burn, and of course, settled agriculture. They have other subsidiary activities such as cattle herding, collection of minor forest products and occasional hunting. The Malaiyali system of agriculture is terraced and rain-dependent. Tapioca and paddy are the principal crops raised on a large scale, while vegetables and other cereals are cultivated in lesser areas and small scale.

Agricultural Practices

Tapioca Cultivation

Tapioca (*maravallikilangu* in the local language) is a dry land crop widely cultivated in the terraces of the hills. This crop has been introduced in the hills in recent times. It is a commercial crop cultivated on a large scale. The duration of the cultivation of Tapioca is from 10 to 12 months. Initially, the seed cuttings have been brought down from the Kolli Hills. The cultivation begins in the month of *Adi* and harvested in the same month next year (after about 12 months).[16]

There are no market centres in the region of Pachaimalai Hills, but market centres are available around Pachaimalai Hills. The nearest weekly market town is Thuraiyur. One can buy clothes, tools and implements, baskets, pots, betel leaves, areacanuts, tobacco, vegetable, and dry fish from this market.[17] Tapioca is marketed through businessmen who come from neighbouring towns like Āttur and Rāsipuram. The businessmen or *Kilangu* broker approach the tribal farmers and negotiate a price according to the quality of the product. Only a fixed rate to be paid to the farmers and this often depends on the distance between the road and the field gate. With increasing distance between the two points, there is a declining price offered as the distance involves transportation costs.[18] There was another method of price determination, that is, the crop is priced based on the bag of 100 kg each. Farmer gets the money after the transport and labour charges were deducted from the price negotiated, provides an account of the expenditures incurred in the cultivation of tapioca in a unit area of an acre.[19]

Agricultural Methods

Different agricultural methods were adopted in the process of wet and dry crop cultivation. The wooden ploughshare was used with iron teeth. The interesting and noteworthy point is that the ploughshare was made by one of the tribes of Top Sengāttupatti village on the top of the hill and not from the carpenters of the plains.[20]

From the European travellers' point of view the agricultural implements were too 'simple' and 'rude'. But they were sufficiently diversified and fitted for the conditions of native agriculture. There was a special implement for every operation and various kinds of soil. The hard black soil was cultivated with a heavy ploughshare, each drawn by two to three pairs of bullocks or buffaloes. For less hard un-irrigated land the medium-size plough was used. The ploughshare used on wetland was the smallest. A man could bear two such ploughshares, one on each shoulder. Besides these main types, there were several others, especially suitable for the different regions.[21]

The ploughshares were made of certain kinds of hardwood. For the light sandy soil, a wooden ploughshare was sometimes used.[22] Besides ploughshare, many varieties of harrows with wooden and iron teeth, seed-drills, hoes, sickles for crops and grass and so on, were used. Indian ploughshare had no mouldboard and therefore, properly speaking, it did not plough the soil but loosened it. But the turning of the layer in many parts of India, including the southern region, was unnecessary and sometimes even harmful because it might cause damage to the soil with acid and saline substances. The same should be said about the depth of ploughing. By British standards, the Indians ploughed little depth (3-5 inches). But deeper ploughing in Indian climatic conditions and under the then existing technology would lead to greater evaporation and over-drying of the soil.[23]

Paddy is the principal crop widely cultivated in the entire Pachaimalai Hills. The Malaiyali tribes have been cultivating *bhavāninellu (Bhavāni paddy)* in wetlands of the Top Sengāttupatti area of Pachaimalai region. In dry lands, people cultivated different paddy varieties such as *pulutikarunellu*, *mara nellu*, *thoonganellu*, *periyamalainellu*, and these belonged to a native variety. These native paddy varieties are found suitable for this hill climate. These crops do not require much water. No pesticides or manures are used for this cultivation. It is cultivated in the first season of the year (*Ādi*). The cultivable land was well ploughed 3 to 4 times before sowing the seeds. The compost is applied in the last plough (*sāl*) before the rain comes or after the rains, the seeds are sown in the soil. After the crop reaching 30 days, the field is ploughed again, as if to make the growth scanty. Hence the farmers use a special wooden plough, for destroying the thick growth of crops.[24] This process is simply known as the *payirkalappu* (thinning crop). Only after this process, the crop grows rapidly. It is also observed that many farmers apply manures in this cultivation with the advice of the agricultural department. Weeding takes place twice before reaping.

Paddy is cultivated in irrigated lands called *vayakādu* or wetland and *mēttunilam* called as dry land, where water is not possible to bear easily to dry land but water could be lifted by an oil engine. There are two main cultivating seasons each depending mainly on one of the two monsoons. The first, the southwest monsoon, sets in early in June but previous to this there are generally height showers towards the end of March and in April, followed by a good downpour in May. The early showers are utilised for ploughing the moisture-rich or damp soil, and in May, if enough rain is received or in June (*Ādi*), the dry crops are planted after a heavy shower.[25]

Apart from the paddy, there is the cultivation of minor millets and oilseeds such as *rāgi*, *chōlam*, *thinai*, *makkāchōlam*, *horse-gram*, and gingili. These crops were either cultivated in separate fields or if mixed, have been sown in the same field. After the introduction of tapioca in this region, the area under the other crops mentioned above has come down. Another crop locally called *mēttunel* (paddy of the elevated land or simply dry paddy), is a native variety growing in dry lands and has been brought from the Periyamalai Hills (Kolli Hills). It is normally sown in *Ādipattam* (July-August) and this crop does not require much water. It is thus grown with the occasional rainfall. As soon as wetlands are fully irrigated, they are usually ploughed and manured and ploughing is continued at regular intervals. The dry crops take three to six months to mature.[26]

Process of Cultivation

Slash and Burn Cultivation

Slash and burn cultivation is widely practiced in the entire Pachaimalai Hills. A patch of land is selected, which is either a *patta* land or *porambōke* on the slopes and they set fire in summer for the bushes due to small trunks are destroyed in the fire. After that, the tribes clean up the land for cultivation. The 'ash' is often used as the manure for nourishing the soil. After the rains start, in *Ādi* which is an auspicious Tamil month (May-June), *rāgi*, *chōlam* (jower), and *thinai* (millets) seeds are broadcast in the plot now ready after slash and burn. The soil is however upturned with the help of hoe or by ploughing (hoes are used in the hills while the plough is used in the plains).[27]

Ploughing and Sowing Seeds

The main activity in the process of cultivation is ploughing, which normally starts in the month of *Ādi*. The ceremony of first sowing is observed on either of the first days or the eighteenth day of the month *Ādi*, which is considered traditionally is a good day for broadcasting seeds.

Nursery

The seedbeds popularly known as the nurseries (*nātrrāngāl*) are first made ready. Ploughing is done after the rainfall, making the soils soft. The nursery beds are normally prepared close to the fields to be planted with paddy; near the main or wetland.[28] Only a fraction of a small plot of land is utilised for this purpose. For preparing '*nātrrāngāl*', the piece of land has to be intensively ploughed four to six times from different directions at right angles to the previous one.[29]

The field is frequently irrigated and the field is always in a puddle of mud, after ploughing. After a puddle is made of the soil, basal dressing is done using either the farm manure (green) or cattle manure. The manure is carried in baskets by men and women, in huge quantities if needed into the field. The manure is then spread out by hoe or pushed around by the feet. Then the field is ploughed again when the nursery is ready, the seeds soaked in water for almost a day/overnight for letting them sprout and then are broadcast. The seeds take almost a month to grow to be the seedlings that can be transplanted.[30] If the plant is ready for transplantation, the landowner fix an auspicious day for the transplanting the seedlings. In plucking the seedlings for transplanting, the workers start from one end of the field, using both hands. When the two hands are full, then they tie the seedlings together and thus make small bundles.

Transplantation

Transplantation work in the cultivation process is known as *nāthunaduthal*, that is, the planting of seedlings. For transplantation, the fields are ploughed a minimum of four times. Ploughing is always done by men, with the oxen tied to a ploughshare which is often done in the day, between early morning and 1 pm. Once the ploughing is over for the day, the labourer takes the oxen for a bath in the stream and to the shed for a massage and feed. They give the pair of bullocks some nutritious feed for the work performed by them.[31]

Hired ploughshares are procured for payment of Rs 500 at the end of the day of work. When the field is getting ready for the transplantation of paddy, a group of workers performs various tasks towards it. A puddle is generated, it is then levelled using the '*parambupalagai*', the levelling wooden plank, and planted with the seedlings. On the day of transplantation, it is women who pluck the seedlings in the nursery and transplant seedlings in the prepared field.[32] Between the nursery and field of transplantation, the seedlings are transported either as head loads or as cartloads (in *kathi* or small bundles), as the case may be. In any case, women perform these along with men.

Transplanting itself is a ritualistic process, in which, the smaller bundles are thrown from one end of the field. Women stand in a row and start transplanting from one end of the field. Women engaged in this work are professional in their execution and they do it fast. They are also adept at planting the seedlings some good distance from each clump Japanese method of transplanting, that is planting seedlings in regularly spaced rows to allow for aeration when in maturity is much practiced than the traditional practice of placing the clumps wherever the transplanter sees fit, but with gaps between successive clumps. Women normally work from 10 am to 5 pm or 7 am to 1 pm and 2 to 5 pm. The women workers are kith and kin. The wages paid to them Rs 100 per day. Twenty women are needed to transplant one acre of land.[33] Once transplanted, then the seedlings have to be cared for and nurtured into healthy plants for a good yield. In about one or two weeks the plants become firmly rooted in soil. Irrigation must be done throughout the cultivation, or at least until the harvest.[34]

Weeding

The paddy seedlings give rise to several new shoots (locally '*kilaipu*'). Weeding is done by plucking the weeds by hand and this is done mostly by women. Weeding of the paddy fields is done at least twice, and mostly by the landowners. Hill paddy is a long term crop and hence it flowers only after five months of growth.[35] However, a month afterward it will be ready for harvest. The farmers take care to see that the weeds do not suffocate the crop and that the required levels of water in the fields are maintained. Besides weeds, these plants also suffer from various other diseases. Villagers recognize the '*poonjai* ', means a condition in which the plant becomes white, with small white patches on the leaves. *Senchoorai* is another disease in which the leaves turn red or yellow '*poochivettu* ' (insect bite) affects the plant at the time of flowering the paddy stakes were cut by worms and the whole plant becomes white. The farmers use modern pesticides and insecticide for protecting the plant from diseases. The Demokran, BHC 10 percent (*milangaimarundhu* chilli medicine) are sprayed by both manually or by power sprayer. Hand sprayers are already supplied free by the Horticulture Department.[36]

Harvesting

First of all, the '*Karnel*' (also called *varanel*) of the *mēttunilam* (dry land) ripens and then the turn of the paddy on the wetland (*vayalkādu*) before the harvest. The farmers prepared the threshing floor, now-a-days, the lands are found nearer to the metalled roads, and hence the floor of the road could be used as the thrusting ground. Reaping is done by both men and women and the working hour is from 9 am to 1 pm and then 2 pm to 5 pm. Labourers are paid either in cash (Rs. 100 per day) or grains (4 *vallam* of paddy equivalent to 9.63 kg). They reaped the paddy and place them down on the stumps of paddy in sheave (bundle). Harvest is normally done in the day and the sheaves are left in the field overnight. On the following day, the sheave will be bundled which are carried to the threshing floor (the '*kalathumēdu*') in many a '*kattu*' (literally, a bundle of sheath tied together). The bundles are carried as head loads by men and women. Men then thresh the sheave, separating the paddy from the straw. This is manual work and hard work, performed in the sun. The separated paddy is heaped on the floor as a result of winnowing in the breeze.

Threshing

Paddy bundles are stacked on one side of the floor while threshing is done on the other. This process has to be set in motion with available, local groups of people. The men thresh while women pass the sheave to the threshing men. The straw resulting from it could be used as a feed for the cattle. Once threshed, the straw is spread thin for drying, if it requires drying in the sun otherwise, it is spread in a thin circular heap and the oxen tied one to another in a row of cattle are made to walk over the straw to further separate the leftover grains from the stalk. This is locally known as *pinaiadithal*. This process requires more attention to the facts of the length of threshing, *pinaiadithal*, and hay/straw supplies feed for the cattle in the 'off-season'. The hay/straw from the harvest will not be useful for thatching the roofs. For this purpose, paddy is harvested with long stalks and the threshing is done mostly by beating the sheaves (*thāl*) on the ground. Then the straw is gathered and used in thatching.[38]

Winnowing

When the threshing is over, and also when the grain separated by the *pinaiadithal* are gathered into a heap, then starts the process of winnowing. This is known as *nelthūthuthal*, which is done often with the 'Steve' (*muram*). In the process the grains are filled in the *muram* and then it is gradually winnowed, from a height, leaving the good grains to fall at the feet of the winnower while the lighter chaff (useless paddy husks) fall at a distance blown away by the wind.

Granary

The Malaiyalis tribes of Pachaimalai use their expertise and build their granaries (grain storage houses) and these are called the *Thombai*. There are two types of granaries one is the rectangular (almost like a house) and the other is the round type of cone-shaped. Making the granaries and the techniques of storing are indigenous. First of all, huge stones are erected on the soil. The stone slabs are laid on the stones in such a way there is a gap between the stones and slabs. Then, a huge round-shaped bamboo basket (barrel type), reinforced with red clayed mud, is fit with the slabs on the floor. The top of the grain storage is sealed with grass (ceval grass). The entrance is a hole that is sealed by a bunch of dried stems of the plants. Whenever the farmers need grains, they remove the grass lid and enter into the granary. Some of the granaries are divided by a hearth. It is helpful to put different grains in the same granary.[39] Generally, every farmer has at least one-grain storage in their house. The indigenous technology used for the construction of grain storage houses which protects the grains from rains and rodents. This technology is found to be eco-friendly.

House-Type Granary

The cost of construction of house-type granary is higher than that incurred in the round-type. It is found attached to the living quarters of the houses.[40] Usually, the bottom is made up of stones in round shape. The huge stone slabs are laid on the stones. It looks like a room; the walls are raised to 1.5 meters from the ground. The walls are then plastered with the red clay. In the entrance, there will be an opening made of a wooden door. Inside the granary room, it is divided into several portions. The upper part is by bamboo mats plastered with red clay. Above the clay carpet rectangular roof is covered by grass. After harvest, the grain is taken in baskets and simply dumped inside the barn. The rectangular type of granary is 5 meters long, two meters high and two meters wide. Agricultural produce is kept in the granary for two/three years. Whenever a marriage takes place in the village, or someone buys or sells land, a contribution is made to the granary in kind. The Pachaimalai tribes have learned many skills from their ancestors. This is one of them. The traditional grain storage houses are locally specific, effective and efficient too.[41]

Village Common Granary

A common granary is constructed by the villagers and this is looked after by the Ur Gounden and Moopan of the Malaiyali community. Every landowner among the tribes has contributed a certain quantity of products from the harvested millets and paddy which are kept in the common granary. When the elders impose fine on the tribal for any crime in the village panchayats that fine collection has to be given to the common granary.[42]

Another source of receipt of grains to the common granary is that of divorce. When any of the villagers are expected to meet expenses like that of a marriage, divorce and the grains can be drawn from the village granary and later repaid in the form of farm produce from the next harvest.[43] The grains for '*Ur Kangani* ', for his services, are given from the common granary. The grains needed for any common village festivals like the Pongal and the Mariamman Thiruvizha (Mariamman Festival) are drawn from the village granary.

Shifting cultivation

The rotation of cultivation of crops mainly on the mountain ridges in the forests. The tribes begin the work of shifting cultivation in the forest land by the end of January. The branches and leaves of the jungle trees in the lands are chopped off leaving a few of them sparingly for building garrets on the top of trees.[44] Up to one week the clearings in the fields are left to dry. Then they are burnt. The land at this stage is called *ponekkaadu* (burnt land). The sticks which are not affected by fire are picked up and collected. Those un-burnt sticks are termed *podulu* and the collections of such sticks are known as *podulu edukradhu*.[45] The sticks were collected and made use of fuel. On the other hand, the ash of the burnt wood and leaves is left in the field itself till the arrival of rains during monsoons. The monsoon showers moisten the fields with the absorption of the ash, and the field becomes ready for sowing. Before sowing, the land is levelled by means of *kalakkoththu* (hoe). The land at this stage is termed *paynga* (fresh land).[46]

The sowing was initiated by the headman after conducting a ritual in honour of *Pidāriyamman* (deity of the earth). A ceremonial feast also arranged during the rituals time. At the time of sowing a handful of seeds (maize or millet) are taken at the right hand by the shower, which was dropped into the holes made by the digging stick held in the left hand, and those holes were then covered with earth treading over it by a foot. The labourers were not orderly practiced sowing the seeds. But they sowed the seeds randomly; there is no systematic practice when sowing seeds like rows or lines.[47] Because of the above said types of sowing, the seeds are dibbled at random in all directions leaving gaps intermittently. However, each of the holes dibbled so is getting apart at a uniform distance of one foot each. The sowing of maize or millets is followed simultaneously by the sowing of the pulses in the same way. In doing so, men keep the maize seeds in a cloth bag hung over their shoulder while women carry the seeds in the folds of their *sari*.[48]

Starting from sprouting till ripe the grains, the tribal were involved to remove weeds at least twice with the help of hoe.[49] In addition to the weed, the small crops are to be guarded against the ravages of wild animals and birds. The entry of domestic animals into the field was avoided by the erected of the stone wall around it.[50]

No major rituals are connected with cultivation is observed after sown seeds till the *aravattom* (harvest) started when maize or millet had been harvested.[51] At the time of harvest both men and women were used to sing songs (folk songs). This was made them happy to work without tiredness. Before harvesting the crops, first they were offered to the God, and then they harvest grains and sold in the market.[52] Maize was harvested in the month of July-August, and millet harvested in October-November. Besides, castor cultivated along with the millets.[53]

Collection of Minor Forest Produces

Apart from the paddy and minor millet cultivations, the tribal people also involved in the collection of minor forest produces from their locality. The minor forest produce such as *konnapattai* (bark of cassia Officinalis), *sengapattai* (bark of cassia fistula), *màvalikelangu* (a kind of edible rhizome), *malankelangu* (tubers of hills), *kadukkāi-kottai* (gall nut) and *thēnu* (honey) are collected by the Malaiyalis of the Pachaimalai hills.[54] Bark of cassia Officinalis is used in tanning industries. It is available in plenty from January to May. The Bark of cassia fistula and that of *Terminaliachebula* are useful in the dying industries. They are collected during the summer months especially from February to April.[55] The edible tubers, viz., *malankelangu* are uprooted during the monsoon period (that is October-November). The tools employed in uprooting are *kadaparaikambi* (crowbar), and *kalakoththu* (hoe). For collecting tubers, the land should be in a moist condition. The collected tubers are boiled by immersing in water and taken as food.[56]

The minor forest products like the gall nut, soap nut (*sikakkai*), curry leaves, tamarind, and edible fruits like jack and gooseberries are collected and sold either to the co-operative society or in the nearby market towns. Now Gall nut is the only item purchased by the co-operative society. The Gall nut is collected primarily by women and children, from the interior forest. The dried Gall nuts were packed in gunny sacks that were sent to the market or exported to other countries.[57] The merchant used to purchase gall nuts from the tribes and sold it outside the market. The State Government has taken steps to purchase gall nuts directly from the tribes through co-operative society.[58]

Honey, as an important item of minor forest produce, fetches considerable remuneration for the tribes. Honey collection is termed pace *edukaradhu* and the honeycomb is termed *raattu*, in their dialect. There are two seasons for collecting honey viz., May-June and October-November. Honey was collected above the seasons from the combs which found to be sticking to cliffs, rocky crevices and the branches of giant trees.[59] Usually the tribes extract honey from such remote and inaccessible places using bamboo scaffolding or ladders. Honey obtained from such places is called *varathēnu*. The *poarthēnu* is extracted from the combs attached to the small types of trees. Honey is used for medicinal purpose; therefore, it has more demand in the markets.[60]

Medicinal Plants

The plants which are growing in the hills region are utilised by the natives for various medicinal purposes. The Pachaimalai Malaiyalis had a good knowledge of traditional medicine; it has been accumulated in the course of times. They have been collecting different varieties of plants for producing herbal medicinal through the conventional systems of *Āyurvēda*, *Unāni*, and *Siddha*, etc. In India, it is reported that there are traditional healers used 2500 plant species. There are 66 species of plants served as regular sources of medicine from Pachaimalai.[61] As a consequence of this long experience and practice; it has become an effective way of accumulation of rich knowledge on medicinal plants and its usage among the people. Use of herbal medicines in Tamil Nadu represents a long history of human interactions with the environment.[62]

The medicinal plants are used for traditional medicine; it contains a wide range of substances that can be used to treat unrelieved as well as infectious diseases. They had a vast knowledge about using the medicinal plants to secure different illness. It may be expected the tribal is accumulate the medicinal plants followed by preparing very important medicine.[63] A tribal man called Duraisamy is a *Siddha Vaithiyar* (physician) in Top Sengattuppatti of Pachaimalai hills, collected more herbal plant (medicinal plant), and made *Siddha* medicine for sales. Many people come from outside of Pachaimalai region for collection of *Siddha* medicine from him. However, *Siddha* medicine has given free to local people for headaches, stomach pain, fevers and snake bite, etc. Sometimes he used to go to the neighbouring villages for treatment for others when they need. Meantime he used to work in agricultural fields in his village otherwise he used to collect plants for preparing medicine. The collection of medicinal plants and identifying medicinal plants are traditional cultural habits.

Non-traditional Economy

Besides their traditional subsistence economy, the Pachaimalai Malaiyalis are also engaged in various other economic activities such as forest labour, Highways Department work, and animal husbandry.[64] The contractors of the Highways Department employ the tribes of the hill for their works. Since the tribes are hardworking people, the contractors employ them for constructing buildings, road laying, and other works.[65] The daily wage Rs 300 is given for men and Rs 150 for women. These sorts of jobs are available only during the summer months.

Rearing of pigs is found among the tribes without a single exception. As pork forms delicious food for them, the tribes of the hills spared more time of their daily routine in this rather than any other work. In front of each hut, we can see *panaasi* (water pot) made for dogs, an earthen pot for pigs over a tripod twig, the *pannimogudu*.[66] The earthen pot is filled with porridge, rice water and brine of millets. Besides, even if any waste food material such as banana skin is found it is also added into that pot. A ladle is always there on the pot. Whenever they want to nourish their pets they will call them by a peculiar sound. On hearing the call, the pigs are found to rush to the spot of food distribution.[67]

Milk and cow dung are the chief products obtained from the bovines. From milk, they prepare curd, buttermilk, etc. Dung is used to smearing the floor of their hut. The accumulated dung is put in pits and manure is prepared out of that, at the long run. They do not derive milk or mutton from their sheep or goat; rather than they used to sell in the market.[68]

Soil Conservation/Minor Irrigation Development

The Pachaimalai Hills received rains from the northeast monsoon. For the conservation of the wealth of the soils from erosion, the Soil Conservation Department has been undertaken numerous steps for protecting the hill people. The following benefits have identified under the scheme:

(i) Effective control of soil erosion and conservation of adequate soil moistures.

(ii) Increasing crop yields by about 20 percent on the average.

(iii) Recharging of groundwater and thereby improving the water table near the wells.

(iv) Removing the silt entering from the small tanks the ponds in the low lying areas.

There are water facilities from the time of rainy seasons when the tribal used to utilise for irrigation purposes. Sometimes stream water stored in small ponds or the low lying areas. During the dry season storage water can be used for irrigation in the methods of pumping from the ponds.[69]

Methods of Irrigation

There are three types of irrigation systems found in the Pachaimalai Hills. They are:

1. Manual water lift (*Yetram* or Mote).
2. Well irrigation (*Kinatrupasanam*, with oil pump sets, motor pump sets).
3. Stream Irrigation (*Odai Pasanam*).[70]

Manual Water Lift

Generally, on rainy days, the wells become full. The lift will not be more than 60 cm in height a tin of 20 liters capacity is used to lift the water manually. Only a single man is employed in this work. A small tract of paddy fields is irrigated by this method. In case of a large tract of paddy crop, there is a traditional method of lift which can be used. There is normally a pole erected near the well and a big bamboo is fixed to it in a way it could move up and down for lifting the water and at the well-end of the bamboo is tied a leather container locally known as '*kaveli*'. To balance when in operation, a stone is tied on the other extreme of the bamboo.[71]

The water lifter pulls the rope tied to the '*kaveli*' downwards and dips the container into the water by swinging it when full; he lifts the *kaveli* up and tilts the *kaveli* onto the channel taking water to the fields. This is being repeated as long as required. For smaller heights of stream smaller containers are used. For greater heights, the picota (*yetram*) or *kaveli* (manual) is used. In the case of the picota, men walk on the bamboo to make it easier for the man who lifts the water from the well, whereas in the case of the *kavalai*, oxen are used to lift water. The picota is nothing more than a long beam of bamboo with a bucket and rope tied at one extreme. It is lowered into and raised out of the well for lifting water by men. Generally, oxen are not used in the lifting of water in the Pachaimalai Hills.[72]

Well Irrigation

In Pachaimalai hills there are forty farmers owned wells. The size of them and their depths depend on the size of their landholdings. Wells are normally of 36 meters in size. The farmers are irrigated to the field from well during the time of the dry season. Otherwise, they have been depending on stream (*odai)* irrigation. Wells are filled by water in August and September (*Purattasi* in Tamil month) due to the raining season. During the rainy days, the well water spills onto the fields. Farmers construct channels facilitating the flow of water to the fields. There are 9 wells dug under the scheme of Jeevandhara Well Digging Scheme.[73]

The cost of digging the well is met by the government. This scheme was introduced in the area in the year 1991. Many farmers have got their own oil pump sets for lifting the water. It is also found to be only in summer months that they could use oil pump sets for lifting the water due to the high cost of diesel price. Many farmers spend more than a thousand rupees per crop season for lifting the water. There are twenty farmers have a free electrical connection. The protective walls around the wells are often destroyed by the rains. This is a common problem found in all hamlets of the Pachaimalai Hills. The reason for this is that of the soft ruminative black or red soil which is not strong enough to hold the stone walls intact.

Stream Irrigation

Many forest streams are flowing down the hill slopes. The farmers have made their wet terrace parcels of cultivable land near the forest streams and they make use of the streams for irrigation. The streams dry up only in summer months. The water flows in the streams for almost eight months in a year. The Forest and Soil Conservation Department have constructed several small and large *check dams* across the forest streams to help the farmers. These check dams arrest the runoff and control the soil erosion of the slopes. Paddy cultivation in Pachamailai hills is completely dependent on the stream water irrigation.[74]

Conclusion

The tribal economy is the traditional one. During the colonial rule, few Malaiyalis possessed lands. But in the early 20th century most of the tribes were lost their lands due to their indebtedness. Sometimes the moneylenders were occupied tribal's land when they are unable to repay their money to them. Otherwise, they transferred the land among themselves. As a result, they have no lands even for their cattle for grass. They are quite miserable due to alienation of lands and indebtedness. Since Independence, there was no alienation of lands, the government has passed Act and prohibited the transfer of land to non-tribal people. The Malaiyalis mostly are engaged in agricultural work in Pachaimalai areas. There is 70% of Malaiyali tribal working in the agricultural field as daily coolies. Cultivation of paddy is highly labour intensive from planting to harvest, it requires several labourers for undertaking all related activities.

The Malaiyalis are well-known cultivators in this region and having domestic animal (Ox) for the cultivation of lands. The principal crop cultivation is tapioca. Besides they have been cultivating paddy, *chōlam*, *varagu*, *thinai*, and *kēlvaragu* (*rāgi*). Commercial crops like chews nut also cultivating and exported to other parts of this country. They have been involving non-agricultural occupations too namely, animal husbandry, honey collection, and hunting, etc. In addition, they rear pigs, which is a potential source of income for the Malaiyali tribes.

References

1. M. Sundara Pandiyan, *Tribal Development in India*, Anmole Publication, India, 2001, p. 73.
2. Jakka Parthasarathy, "Problems of Indebtedness- Tribal Experience in the Nilgiris District", *Hill Area Development Programme*, Udhagamandalam, Tamil Nadu, August, 2007.
3. Edgar Thurston, *Caste and Tribes in South India*, Cosmo Publication, New Delhi, 1909, pp. 406-408; also see Paul Roche, "The

Marriage Ceremonies of the Malaiyalis of the Pachaimalai", *Asian Folklore Studies*, Vol. 39, No.2 (1980), p. 124.

4. Anusha Bhaskar and Lalit R. Samant, "Traditional Medication of Pachaimalai Hills in Tamil Nadu", India, *Global Journal of Pharmacology*, 6 (1), IDOSI Publications, 2012, p.47. See K.S.K. Velmani., *The Gazetteer of Tamil Nadu*, *Tiruchirappalli District*, Vol. II, Government of Tamil Nadu, Chennai, 1899, p. 1584.
5. Edgar Thurston, *op.cit*., p.406.
6. K.S.K. Velmani, *op.cit*., Vol. I, p. 321.
7. N.P. Periyasamy, *Thamash Non-Governmental Organization*, Pachaimalai, Thuriayur, 2008, p. 10.
8. Edgar Thurston, *op.cit*., p. 412.
9. Lewis Moore, *Madras District Gazetteer: Trichinopoly*, Vol. I, Cosmo Publication, New Delhi, 2000, p. 17; also see K.S.K. Velmani, *op.cit*., p. 17.
10. C. Maheswaran, *Ethnography of Pachaimalai Malaiyali Tribes*, Government Press, Madras, 2007, p. 27.
11. *Ibid*., p. 17.
12. *Annual Report of the Integrated Tribal Development Programme*, Salem District, 1992, p. 5.
13. C. Maheswaran, *op.cit*., p. 39.
14. H. Le Fanue, *Manual of the Salem District in the Presidency of Madras*, Vol. I, Government Press, Madras, 1883, p.137.
15. Personal interview with Kannan, Attinadu, Pachaimalai, Date: 18.08.2015.
16. Personal interview with tribal man Thuraisamy, Thenparanadu Panchayat, Pachaimalai, Date: 15.08.2015.
17. Personal Interview with Tribal leader Punavarai, Pachaimalai, Date: 22.3.2014.
18. Personal interview with Tribal man Arumugam, Thenparanadu Panchayat, Pachaimalai, Date: 16.08.2015.
19. *Ibid*.
20. C. Maheswaran, *op.cit*., p. 23.
21. Tapan Raychaudhuri and Irfan Habib (eds.), *The Cambridge Economic History of India*, Vol. I, c.1200- 1750, Cambridge University Press, Cambridge, 2008, p. 230.
22. J. Forbes, *Studies in Ancient Technology*, 8 Vols. Leiden, 2nd Edition, 1964, p. 394.
23. Tapan Raychaudhuri and Irfan Habib (eds.), *op.cit*., p. 231.
24. Personal interview with Tribal village headman Manickam, Thenparanadu Panchayat, Pachaimalai, Date: 15.08.2015.
25. Personal interview with Govintharaj, Thenparanadu Pachaimalai, Date: 18.08.2015.

26. Personal interview with Perumal, Thenparanadu Pachaimalai, Date: 18.08.2015.
27. Personal interview with Parathesi, Thenparanadu Pachaimalai, Date: 18.08.2015.
28. Personal interview with Periyasamy, Thenparanadu Pachaimalai, Date: 19.08.2015.
29. Personal interview with Karuppusamy, Thenparanadu Pachaimalai, Date: 19.08.2015.
30. Personal interview with Periyasamy, Thenparanadu Pachaimalai, Date: 19.08.2015.
31. Personal interview with Vembadiyan, Thenparanadu Pachaimalai, Date: 11.09.2015.
32. Personal interview with Manivel, Thenparanadu Pachaimalai, Date: 11.09.2015.
33. Personal interview with Kannan, Attinadu Pachaimalai, Date: 12.09.2015.
34. Personal interview with Rasu, Thenparanadu Pachaimalai, Date: 12.09.2015.
35. Personal interview with Muniyandi, Thunparanadu Pachaimalai, Date: 14.09.2015.
36. Personal interview with Karuppan, Attinadu Pachaimalai, Date: 20.09.2015.
37. Personal interview with Vembadi, Thenparanadu Pachaimalai, Date: 20.09.2015.
38. Personal interview with Marudai, Thenparanadu Pachaimalai, Date: 21.09.2015.
39. Personal interview with Andi, Thenparanadu Pachaimalai, Date: 21.09.2015.
40. Personal interview with Shanmugam, Thenparanadu Pachaimalai, Date: 21.09.2015.
41. Personal interview with Ponnusamy, Thenparanadu Pachaimalai, Date: 22.09.2015.
42. Personal interview with Manimaran, Thenparanadu Pachaimalai, Date: 22.09.2015.
43. Personal interview with Duraisamy, Thenparanadu Pachaimalai, Date: 23.09.2015.
44. Busnagi Rajanan, *Salem Cyclopedia- A Cultural and Historical Dictionary of Salem District Tamil Nadu*, Institute of Kongu Studies, 1992, p. 165.
45. V. Saravanan, *Tribal Revolts in India with reference to Salem District of Madras Presidency during the late 18th Century*, Artha Vijnana, Vol. IX, 1999, p. 63.
46. *Ibid*., p. 64.

47. *Ibid.*, p. 65.
48. Personal Interview with Tribal leader Punavarai, Pachaimalai, Date: 25.3.2014.
49. *Ibid.*
50. Interview with Sudha, Tribal Woman, Periyamangalam, Pachaimalai, Date: 12.4.2014.
51. *Ibid.*
52. C. Maheswaran, *op.cit.*, p. 22.
53. *Ibid.*, p. 22.
54. Interview with Krushnamoorthy, Tribal man, Vannadu Panchayat, Pachaimali, Date: 20.01.2014.
55. *Ibid.*
56. *Ibid.*
57. *Ibid.*
58. R.Sankar and Manimaran, "Socio-Economic condition of Pachaimalai Tribes", *Cognitive Discourses International Multidisciplinary Journal*, Vol. I, Issue 1, July 2013, pp. 112-118.
59. Personal Interview with village headman, Kombai Nadu, Date: 22.04.2014.
60. *Ibid.*
61. Anusha Baskar and Lalit R. Samant, *op.cit.*, p.47; also see S. Prabu and S. Vijayakumar, 'Ethnobotanical Study of Traditionally used Medicinal Plants in Malaiyali Ethnic People of Pachaimalai Hills, Tamil Nadu', *Journal of Pharmaceutical and Medicinal Research*, Vol. 2 (1), 2016, pp. 39-42.
62. Anusha Bhaskar and Lalit R. Samant, *op.cit.*, p. 47.
63. *Ibid.*, p. 48.
64. C. Maheswaran, *op.cit.*, p. 33, see R. Sankar and Manimaran, *op.cit.*, pp. 112-118.
65. *Ibid.*, p.34, see Lewis Moore, *op.cit.*, p. 17.
66. Personal Interview with Vembadi, Tribal man, Vannadu Panchayat, Pachaimalai, Date: 15.5.2014.
67. *Ibid.*
68. Busnagi Rajanan, *op. cit.*, p. 164.
69. Interview with Kaliappan, Top Sengottupatti, Pachaimalai, Date: 15.3.2014.
70. Personal interview with tribal men Duraiarasu, Attinadu Panchayat, Pachaimalai, Date: 16.08.2015.
71. Personal interview with tribal men Dharman, Thenparanadu Panchayat, Pachaimalai, Date: 17.08.2015.
72. *Ibid.*

73. P. Parimurugan, *Tribal economy and development among the Malaiyalis of Pachaimalai Hills in Tamil Nadu*, unpublished thesis, University of Madras, 1997, p. 153.
74. Personal interview with Mahalingam, Thenparanadu Pachaimalai, Date: 17.08.2015.

Bibliography

Annual Report of the Integrated Tribal Development Programme, Salem District, 1992.

Anusha Bhaskar and Lalit R. Samant, "Traditional Medication of Pachaimalai Hills in Tamil Nadu", India, *Global Journal of Pharmacology*, 6 (1), IDOSI Publications, 2012.

Busnagi Rajanan, *Salem Cyclopedia- A Cultural and Historical Dictionary of Salem District Tamil Nadu*, Institute of Kongu Studies, 1992.

Edgar Thurston, *Caste and Tribes in South India*, Cosmo Publication, New Delhi, 1909.

Forbes, J., *Studies in Ancient Technology*, 8 Vols. Leiden, 2nd Edition, 1964.

Jakka Parthasarathy, "Problems of Indebtedness- Tribal Experience in the Nilgiris District", *Hill Area Development Programme*, Udhagamandalam, Tamil Nadu, August. 2007.

Le Fanue, H., *Manual of the Salem District in the Presidency of Madras*, Vol.I, Government Press, Madras, 1883.

Lewis Moore, *Madras District Gazetteer: Trichinopoly*, Vol. I, Cosmo Publication, New Delhi, 2000.

Maheswaran, C., *Ethnography of Pachaimalai Malaiyali Tribes*, Government Press, Madras, 2007.

Parimurugan, P., *Tribal economy and development among the Malaiyalis of Pachaimalai Hills in Tamil Nadu*, unpublished thesis, University of Madras, 1997.

Paul, Roche, "The Marriage Ceremonies of the Malaiyalis of the Pachaimalai", *Asian Folklore Studies*, Vol. 39, No.2 (1980).

Periyasamy, N.P., *Thamash Non-Governmental Organization*, Pachaimalai, Thuraiyur, 2008.

Prabu, S. and S. Vijayakumar, 'Ethnobotanical Study of Traditionally used Medicinal Plants in Malaiyali Ethnic People of Pachaimalai Hills, Tamil Nadu', *Journal of Pharmaceutical and Medicinal Research*, Vol.2 (1), 2016.

Sankar, R. and Manimaran, "Socio-Economic condition of Pachaimalai Tribes", *Cognitive Discourses International Multidisciplinary Journal*, Vol. I, Issue 1, July 2013.

Saravanan V., *Tribal Revolts in India with reference to Salem District of Madras Presidency during the late 18th Century*, Artha Vijnana, Vol. IX, 1999.

Sundara Pandiyan, M., *Tribal Development in India*, Anmole Publication, India, 2001.

Tapan Raychaudhuri and Irfan Habib (eds.), *The Cambridge Economic History of India*, Vol. I, c.1200- 1750, Cambridge University Press, Cambridge, 2008.

Velmani, K.S.K., *The Gazetteer of Tamil Nadu, Tiruchirappalli District*, Vols. I and II, Government Tamil Nadu, Chennai, 1899.

Part III

Temple-Society Interface

11

The Medieval Tamil Society and Interpretation of its Caste with Class Formation – A Study

L. Thilagavathi and K. Thangapandian

The societal history of medieval Tamil country cannot be studied in isolation with a comprehensive study attempted on caste in its relations with religion, property ownership, and material production. The monarchy apart, right from the rule of the Pallavas down to the rise and decline of the Nayaks rule in Tamil Nadu, the caste factor with all its concomitant ramifications and manifestations seemed to have played a prominent role in bringing the above aspects to the fore.

The Pallava rule in Tamil country brought in a Pan-Indian focus for the first time, with caste and religion getting their sanctity and either of them remaining inseparably, like eye and its sight. By the 6th century C.E. the four-fold caste system *Chaturvarna* in its hierarchical model, as Brahmins sitting on the top of the social ladder followed by *Kshatriyas*, *Vaisyas*, and *Sūdras* became the social order of the day. The *Avarnas* were the *Panchamas* or *Chandālas* who were outcastes denied of all opportunities on par with the other four *Varnas*.

During the rule of the Pallavas itself, the growth in agriculture and a steady increase achieved in food grain production, trade and commercial activities, wars, and battles that had brought in wealth to the State, the emergence of towns and building of temples had resulted in generating a number of small and big occupations and ventures which in turn had produced umpteen number of sub-castes. The sub-castes like the principal castes had in the course of time had developed certain occupational ethics and features which in turn helped in enlarging the scope and rigidity of caste as a system and a societal concept. This trend continued during the Imperial Chola times on a bigger scale when "agriculturisation of economy" received special patronage at the hands of the ruling elite and the Vellalas and traders who mainly hailed from Vellala and artisan community, immigrant Brahmins, the emergence of more number of towns and cities, enlarged the constitution of the elite and the well-to-do class during the period. The later Pandya rule witnessed a more or less similar trend that existed during the Chola times. But slightly different was the trend that one could notice in the agrarian relations and production activities of the Nayak times when European traders monopolised the foreign trade and influenced the inland trade as also the entry of the immigrant Brahmins and non-Brahmin non-Tamils in the agrarian sector.

From the available sources of information, since the 6th century C.E., it was the avowed policy of the monarchy and the ruling elite, in particular, to grant lands and gifts to Brahmins, their inhabitations and temples. The donors considered the act as *dharma* which would ultimately help in sustaining their power in this world and usher in the good life in the other world after death. As a result, the number of donees increased from the Pallava times to the Chola and the later Pandya rule and it was more or less sustained during the rule of the Nayaks as well.

Up to the rule of the later Pandyas, not only the lands belonging to the Village, but also the Village as a whole were donated to the Brahmins. The fertile lands alone were granted to them.[1] Such of those lands, their production, and other activities pertaining to administration were in the hands of the donees the Brahmins only.[2] Along with Tamil speaking Brahmins, the immigrant Brahmins of non-Tamil origin were patronised from the days of the Chola rule and this continued during the rule of the Nayaks as well. As a consequence, among the Brahmin population, there emerged differences in the language spoken; and a kind of sub-culture and a number of sub-sects among them also emerged thus generating differences in their socio-cultural interaction.

In the due course of time, when more number of temples were built made of stone, such of those temples were also endowed with fertile lands and other gifts. Apart from individual and personal grants that the Brahmins enjoyed during medieval times, the administration of the Vedic Schools and *Dēvadāna* lands were brought under the control of the Brahmins. Besides, the *Chaturvēdimangalam* lands, which were obtained by the inhabitants of the Village wherein the Brahmins well-versed in four Vedas had the privilege of enjoying the large share from the land produce. During the rule of Nanndivarman Pallava III, the *Sabha* members of the *Videl Vidugu Chaturvēdimangalam*, the Siva Brahmins were entitled to 11/20 share of the produce earmarked for the temple. This is in addition to the *Mēlvāram* (an individual's share from the produce of the land.[3] In the agriculture sector, this had placed the Brahmin community at a higher economic plane, next to the king and on par with the Vellala landocracy.

From the imperial Chola times, the Vellalas and traders drew the attention of the monarchy which by and large, also believed to have belonged to their community. This apart it was considered monarchical *dharma* to part away with a share of the spoils of war to the learned Brahmins well-versed in Vedas. On the other hand, the Vellala landlords until the end of the later Pandya rule excelled in number and area of lands owned by them when compared with Brahmins. But the lands of Brahmins and *Dēvadāna* and *Chaturvēdimangalam* were fairly fertile and were well endowed with irrigation facilities.

In the villages, wherein the other non-Brahmins lived, apart from Vellala landlords, were the artisans, service communities like barbers, dhobis and other village servants too had owned small pieces of lands according to their merit and service.

In the *Brahmadēya* lands the Brahmins enjoyed exclusive property rights, despite their lands being cultivated by Vellalas, traders, artisans, untouchables, and other service communities. Besides, the *Brahmadēya* lands could be sold either to another Brahmin or temple or not to anybody else as also they could be bought and donated only to Brahmins and temples.[4]

The "agriculturisation of economy" effected on a large scale during the period of the Cholas under whose rule, more lands were either acquired or reclaimed or brought under cultivation. Here again, the Brahmin and Vellala landlords with no or minimum risk settled down with fertile lands whereas Vanmiahs of Tondaimandalam, Vettuva Goundas of Kongu Nadu and Maravas and Kallas of Pandianadu, the principal agricultural class attached to lands for their subsistence and had lands which were not fertile and could not be cultivated with much effort and labour. On the other hand, as expected, with minor hiccups notwithstanding, both Brahmin and Vellala landlords could operate as a single class representing landocracy along with its inherent class character, vis-a-vis., the small landholding and landless agricultural labour class who were always at the receiving end of the former. As far as Brahmin landocracy is concerned their power and economic influence spread and felt from the village to Nadu and from there to the empire. The immigrant Brahmins patronised by the Chola rulers, in the due course of time, too enjoyed the similar power and economic influence like their Tamil Brahmin counterparts. These kinds of Monarchy extending patronage to Brahmins from other states or regions continued during the period of the Nayaks as well. As a result, along with Tamil and Sanskrit, Telugu and Malayalam speaking Brahmins were also accommodated but this later addition could not enjoy the socio-economic status that was enjoyed by the immigrant Brahmins of the Chola times.

During the rule of the Cholas by 11th century C.E., with the surplus agricultural production, a new class of people, the traders either emerged or grew in numbers. They were traders doing trade both inland and foreign. Subsequently, a number of trade guilds also emerged. Traders who exported goods and commodities to foreign countries had guilds like *Nānādēsi-disai-āyirathainūtruvar* and *Nāngudisai-āyiram* which referred to guilds consisting of one thousand five hundred and one thousand members respectively. In fact, the traders flourished as a result of lucrative business enjoyed by them. Besides, there was also a great demand for artisans who thereafter gradually relieved themselves of the agricultural sector. The socio-economic status of the traders and merchants had improved due to their acquired wealth. They began to buy lands in the villages and donate them to temples.[5] In the cities and towns developed around temples and government buildings as also palaces, the contribution of traders and merchants were solicited.

In most of the *Brahmadēya* lands, the Vellalas seemed to have been the tenants. It is likely that the Vellalas might have demanded more economic rights for the lands they cultivated as tenants. Therefore, the Brahmin landholders could not show much interest in the development of land. As a result of this kind of development that took place in the *Brahmadēya* lands, the Brahmins in an attempt to relieve themselves of this stress might have paved the way for selling away lands to the temples and other bidders. The available inscriptional evidences testify to that. At *Thanjaivanavan Mādēvi Chaturvēdimangalam* in 1147 C.E. a few Brahmin landholders when they felt that they could not clear the land tax dues, sold their lands to temple. Also at *Anabaya Chaturvēdimangalam* in the *Cholamandalam* region, one weaver and one *Kodumbalur Kizhan* bought lands from *Battars* (the Brahmin priests and learned people belonging to that community) and donated to Vedaranyam temple.[6]

The Left-hand and Right-hand factions, a by-product of medieval socio-cultural upheaval, containing 98 castes and sub-castes each, did not contain any of Brahmin or Vellala high castes into their configurations. With a few exceptions, trading and other jobs doing artisan communities belong to Left-hand faction whereas the Right-hand faction included agriculture and its related jobs doing communities, both small peasants and the landless. In a riot that broke out as a result of enmity between the above two factions at *Gandhara Nadu* in *Rājamahēndra Chaturvēdimangalam*, the entire village was torched, the temple ransacked and the statues destroyed. Also, the rioters plundered the treasury of the temple.[7] This incident clearly shows the ire and opposition of the working masses against the Brahmin landocracy which bloated under the royal patronage and in the garb of religion. In fact, the available sources indicate that these two factions were engrossed with such conflicts of socio-cultural and economic significance till 18th century C.E. However, such conflicts did not bring in much change in the society with the power-wielding Brahmin-Vellala combine kept these factions, more or less under their control, and also kept them serving their interests forever.

On the other hand, there are incidents that go to prove that the monarchy always tried to protect the interests of the landocracy represented by Vellalas and Brahmins even if they were found guilty of gross misconduct or indulged in corrupt practices that brought discredit to the commoners as long as they remained loyal to the royalty.[8]

By and large, until the rule of Rajaraja I, the *Brahmadēya*, *Dēvadāna*, and temples in Vellala and non-Brahmin habitations, were largely under the control of the Brahmin officials and their representatives. Thereafter, due to urbanisation of society and the emergence of merchant class as a growing economic factor, they had to be accommodated in the administration of temples of any hue along with Brahmins and Vellalas. The trade guilds' role in the construction of new temples, renovation of old ones and land grants made to them could be significant during the rule of the Imperial Cholas and later.

The Vellalas to retain their power in the land and its ownership and to sustain it and to countenance the Brahminical hegemony in temples and its related activities established *mutts* across the Tamil country. Thiruvidaimarudur Maligai Mutt, Thiruvanaikaval Andar Embiran Thirumadam, Cholai Kudimadam, Thiruvarur Achara Mazhagiyal Thirumadam, Govindapputtur Thiruthonda Thogaiyan Mutt, Thiruchengottenkudi Thogaiyan Mutt, Thiruchengottenkudi Chiruthondan Mutt, Thiruthuraiyur Mutt, Thiruvaduthurai Mutt, Dharumapuram Mutt, etc. are some of them. They were the adjunct of temples. Besides they were the abodes of coaching religious and moral education and were to serve as dwelling places of saints and servants. The heads of these Mutts were *Achāryas* and *Gurukkals* who belonged to the Vellala community vis-a-vis. of Brahmins in their temples and Mutts.

From 11th century C.E. onwards, on the political and administrative plane, this development had left its impact. From *Ur* to *Nadu* and thereafter to *Perianādu*, like *Chithiramēzhi Perianādu*, the Vellala landocracy and the well-to-do held the reins of the government in their hands, in collaboration with the monarchy[9]. As a cause and effect, there was a steep increase in the number of land-owning Vellala castes; their participation in significant numbers in the army of the State, their acquiring additional responsibilities in urban temples had slowly and gradually tilted the political power balance in favour of the Vellalas in the State. On the other hand, on the cultural plane also, a kind of parity came to be maintained between the Vellalas and the Brahmins, replacing the unquestioned hegemony of the latter in this sphere.

The status quo enjoyed by both Brahmins and the Vellalas as belonging to high castes and as the dominant landowning class had witnessed a change under the rule of the Nayaks. It was under their rule, a unique kind of feudal system with Poligars as chiefs of *Pālayams* answerable to the Nayak rulers emerged and as a consequence, the linguistic association, hitherto enjoyed by the Brahmin and Vellala classes with their native Tamil kings was replaced and their local loyalties with the *Pōligār* chiefs was enforced. Nonetheless, there was a dent experienced by those hegemonic castes but not their influence and presence in the administration of the State under the Nayaks. This speaks of the class-formation of the above castes which determined the socio-economic and cultural life of the Tamils of medieval Tamil country, which as a result of it, had to suffer from the unbridgeable gap between the rich and the poor.

References

1. Udayendran Copper Plates, Aihole Inscription, Kasakudi Copper Plate and Karanthai Copper Plates.
2. *South Indian Inscriptions* (*S.I.I.*), Vol. XIV, No. 37.
3. *S.I.I.*, Vol. III, No. 3.
4. *S.I.I.*, Vol. XVII, Nos. 460 and 536.
5. *Annual Reports on Epigraphy* (*A.R.E.*), Nos. 14 of 1888; 120 of 1930.
6. *S.I.I.*, Vol. XVII, Nos. 460 and 536.
7. *A.R.E.*, No. 31 of 1937.
8. *A.R.E.*, 1913, Para 39; and *A.R.E.*, No. 184 of 1940-1941.
9. *A.R.E.*, No. 7 of 1900; No. 154 of 1903; No. 28 of 1911.

12

Ritual Functionaries: the Brahmins of Temple in the Kāvēri Delta Region (c. 850-1300 C.E.)

Sourav Sen

> "He (Brahmin) must never follow a worldly occupation for the sake of livelihood, but subsist by means of a pure, upright and honest livelihood proper to a Brahmin. One who seeks happiness should become supremely content and self controlled, for happiness is rooted in contentment and its opposite is the root of unhappiness."
>
> *Manusmriti 4.11 – 4.12*
>
> *Translated by Patrick Olivelle.*[1]

Prologue

The emergence of temples in early medieval South India was an important aspect not only in religious history but also in the social history of the people. Temple in south India during the early period played a vital role as a centre of socio-economic and cultural activities of people. It provides enormous employment opportunities to the dwellers around it. Those who are engaged with the temple's activities are known as in general terms as temple functionaries, who are the impetus of the temple. Among the temple functionaries' priest is one of the significant groups who are mostly belonging from the Brahmin community. Two categories of functionaries we find in the temple, namely, ritual functionaries and non-ritual functionaries. Any kind of works or practice related to the temple is always ritual; some performers involved in ritualistic performances directly and some performers are involved in non-ritual works in the temple garden, kitchen, and other activities. Mostly Brahmins were engaged in many temple activities and performed the ritual practices in the temple complex directly. The present endeavor aims to focus on ritual functionaries especially the Brahmin functionaries and their activities along with the temple compound under the Chōḻa period in Kāvēri delta region from the 9th to 13th century C.E.

The word '*Brāhmaṇ*' is derived from the root '*brh*' which means 'to expand' or 'to grow' and as such indicates that immensity which includes everything is conceivable; it is used in the Upanishad in both sense of masculine and neuter.[2] Its neuter form denotes prayers addressed to different gods[3], while its masculine form simply denotes the sage, the poet, the officiating priest or a special priest, designated as *Brāhmaṇ*.[4] Generally it means a person who learned and aware of *Brahma* (prayer), is known as Brahmin. From the Vedic age, the Brahmins occupied an important place in society. The *Puruṣasūkta*[5] of *Ṛgveda* speaks about the four-fold division of the *Vedic* society, where Brahmins are placed at the top of the pyramid of social hierarchy. It is stated that the Brahmins were originated from the mouth of *Ādipuruṣa*[6] henceforth they were in the high position in the *Vedic* and Later *Vedic* society and still this hierarchy is maintained in the present social structure too. The hierarchy of the four-fold division was created by the *Āryans* and it was introduced by them into the Tamil country as well. We find references to the four-fold caste division in the *Saṅgam* literature.[7]

Brahmin and Priest

Tolkāppiyam, the earliest grammar work of Tamil speaks about the four-fold caste division of early Tamil society, namely *Antanar* (Brahmin), *Arasar* (King), *Vaṇikar* (Traders) and *Vēlālar* (Agriculturalists).[8] In the early Tamil society, the Brahmins were referred to in different names. There are synonymous words to denote the Brahmin in Tamil such as *Antanar*[9], *Pārppanar*[10], *Vēdiyar*[11], *Vedāntar*[12], *Bhaṭṭar*[13], *Muppurinulor*[14], etc. In Tamil literatures, the *Antanar* (Brahmin) referred to as an educated class reciting the *Vedas* (*Marai*). Those who expert in Veda (*Marai*) were called as '*Maraiyōn*' and occasionally performed *vēlvi* or sacrifices.[15] Tolkāppiyar, the author of *Tolkāppiyam* mentioned that the *Antanar* were considered as the priestly class in the early Tamil society.[16] The priest is an important functionary of early medieval south Indian temple. They were the professional priest in Indian tradition and occupied virtual monopoly of almost all rituals within the temple institution.[17] The temple priest can communicate with the god through the ritualistic sacrifices.[18] Reciting and composing of Vedic hymns, performing sacrifices, and officiating as a priest were the foremost duties of the Brahmins who were became a mediator between the deity and the people.[19] In *Ṛgveda* it is noted that there are two different kinds of professions for the Brahmins; the composer of hymns[20] and officiating as priest.[21]

In south India, there are many references to the Brahmin priests of the Hindu temples.[22] D. Dayalan[23] argues that all the priests of the temples were not Brahmins. In some temples, the non-Brahmin priests also we find in Tamil Nadu. During the *Saṅgam* age, *Vēlaṉ* was the non-Brahmin priest in the Murugan temple.[24] They were mainly appointed to look after the religious affairs. During the prayer the non-Brahmin priests devotionally excited with madness they performed a dance which is called *veṟiyāḍal*.

A. L. Basham[25] emphasises two different types of Brahmins namely learned Brahmins and village Brahmins, which we find references from the early Indian literature. During the Pallava period learned Brahmins were known as *Bappabhaṭṭārakas* and *Nalkūrnarpārpār*.[26] They performed all the rites and practices of the Hindus and have enough knowledge of *Vedas*, *Vedāṅgas*, *Dharmaśāstras*, *Itihāsa*, *Purāṇa* and receive great respect in the temple as well as in the society, but the village Brahmins, who made much of their living by fortune. The learned Brahmins were not only specialised in the *Vedas* and *Vedāṅgas* but also specialised in the *Shaḍaṅga-Veda*. Prabhākara, one of the donees of the Jamalagama grant of Vikramāditya was a *Shaḍaṅgavid*[27], who is well-versed in the *Shaḍaṅga-Veda*. During the 9th century C.E. Trivikrama, one of the donees of the Sanjan plates of Amoghavarsha I, was a *Shaḍaṅgavid*.[28] The father of Narasimha Dīkshita, another donee of this grant was also a *Shaḍaṅgavid*.[29] Among the 536 *Brāhmaṇas* receiving land grants from Vīra Choḍa (11th century C.E.) *Shaḍaṅgavid* is also found.[30]

During the *Saṅgam* period, the service of the priesthood was mostly done by the both Brahmin and non-Brahmin. The Brahmins who seems to have immigrated from the north; spread out their brāhmanical ideas and cult almost in the *Saṅgam* period.[31] A. Sreedhara Menon discuss that the *Āryan* immigration to the south consisted mostly of Brahmin priests and instructors.[32] Though T. V. Kuppuswami[33] views that the migration of Brahmins into Tamil Nadu was slow, imperceptible infiltration, never stopping and never sweeping. From the 7th to 13th century C.E., in all Śaiva or Vaiṣhṇava temple inscriptions, there is mention of the terms like *Śaiva brāhmaṇas* (Śaiva priests), *Vaikhānasas* (Vaiṣhṇava priests)[34]; and their functions and responsibilities.

Brahmin Functionaries in Temple

The Brahmin functionaries played an important role in the temple sacrifices. The *Puṟanānūṟu*,[35] a classical Tamil poetic work describes numerous sacrifices performed by the Brahmins to the feet of god and recited the *Itihāsas* and *Purāṇas* in the temple. The equivalent reference has been brought in to light from the epigraphical sources too.[36] An inscription found at the famous Sōmanāth temple in Gujarat[37] mentioned that there were three thousand employees were maintained by the temple *dēvastānam*, out of them two thousand were priests. They were the only authorised and acceptable person to enter the holy premises of the *garbhagṛiha* of the temple. They are mentioned in the inscriptions as *Āchārya*, learned teacher of religious institutions, temple priests, temple attendant, royal preceptor, philanthropic preceptor, etc.[38] The learned Brahmins were appointed in south Indian temples for reciting *Tēvāram* or *Tiruppadigam*.[39] During the time of the Cholas an inscription of Parāntaka I found at Lālgudi and Allur regions of Thiruchirappalli district mentions about the Brahmins, those who were in service of singing *Tiruppadigam* in the temple.[40] The reciters were generally Brahmins but in the later periods, the non-Brahmins were also engaged in reciting the holy hymns, who were known as *ōduvār* to recite the *Tēvāram* or *Tiruppadigam*.[41] The Kurram plates,[42] a Pallava grant, narrate that a Brahmin scholar was appointed to recite the *Mahābhārata* in the local Śaiva temple. The Śaiva temple of Kāñchīpuram had five Brahmins to recite the hymns (*mantras*) who were known as *mantrāchāriyas* in the inscription.[43]

From an Uttaramallur inscription,[44] we come to know that a Brahmin *Brahmachārin* who was attached to the local temple, and he was well-versed in *Veda* and addressed from *Parāyaṇamārgam*. Two more inscriptions[45] both dated to 877 C.E. from the same place referred to a temple priest called *Vaikhānasa Dāmōdara Bhaṭṭaṉ* who was also well-versed in *Vaikhānasa āgama*. C. J. Fuller[46] has been discussed the duties of chief priests at Meenakshi temple in his work '*Servants of the Goddess: The Priests of a South Indian Temple*'. The chief priests of the temple are responsible for ensuring the duties and daily routine of the other priests. Further Fuller emphasised that the chief priests are supposed to represent the priests of the temple administration, which in turn the other priests should consult the chief priests on all matters relating to the temple rituals. An inscription of 983 C.E. from Gōvindaputtūr mentions that *Śhaivabrāhmaṇas* were offering in the temple bound themselves to be supervised by *Māhēśvara*.[47] The Brahmin functionaries can open and close the doors and windows of the sanctum sanctorum as well as the minor shrines too. In the temple, it is necessary for preparing *naivēdyam* or *prasādam* (holy or consecrated food) to god. In early days the *naivēdyam* or *prasādam* was mainly prepared by the priest himself but when temple became grow up in a large complex then the temple needs a functionary as a cook on a regular basis.[48]

Internal Hierarchy among the Brahmins

The Brahmins of southern India have maintained a hierarchy within their community by differing in languages, manners, and customs. In Kasakudi plates[49] of Nandivarman II dated 753 C.E. Brahmins were considered as *devas* on the earth, though according to their duties in the temple they possessed different statuses in the society. In *Saṅgam* age, there were no divisions among the Brahmins, but during the reign of Pallavas (c. 6th century C.E. and sometime before) the hierarchy among the Brahmins was grown up. Generally, the Brahmins were divided into *Vaiṣhṇavas*, *Śaivas* and *Vedic Brāhmaṇas*, etc. from the 7th century onwards.[50] Those who performed ritual practices in Viṣhṇu temples were known as *bhaṭṭas*[51], and in the later period, they were known as *bhaṭṭāchāryas*. Those who served in Śaiva temples were known as *Sivāchāryas*, *Sivabrāhmaṇas*, *Ananta śivāchārya*, *Gurukkaḷ*.[52]

The Tamil Brahmins are categorised into three broad divisions based on their professions. The first category was Vaiṣhṇavas and Samarthas, who were mainly known as Vedic Brāhmaṇas. The second category was formed by *Pañchakarma* who did domestic rituals for non-Brahmin communities. The third category consisted of *Gurukkaḷ* who engaged with the temple's activities.[53] Again the Vaiṣhṇavas and Samarthas are divided into various sub-sects. Among them *Vēdāmas*, *Brahachāranam*, etc. are important sub-sects of Samartha Brahmins and Vaiṣhṇava included *Thenkalai* (southerner) those who give priority to the Tamil texts and *Vadakalai* (northerner) for whom Sanskrit texts are primary for worshipping Viṣhṇu.[54]

In the temple, according to the ritualistic duties, the hierarchy was also possessed. C. J. Fuller[55] emphasised that the priests of the Meenakshi temple were *Ādiśaiva* sub-caste, generally considered to be Brahmins, but ranked below among all the ordinary, non-priestly Brahmin sub-castes. In *Pañcharatra* temples, any married Brahmin can perform as a priest, but in *Vikhānasa* temples, only qualified priests can perform as a priest and accomplish the rituals, who are known as *Vikhānasa archakkar*.[56] The Vaiṣhṇava priests do not intermarry with the ordinary Brahmins and they are given a low rank by the later periods.

The priests of the major Śaiva and Vaiṣhṇava temples in south India were divided into two groups; Brahmin priests and non-Brahmin priests. The non-Brahmin priests are the non-Sanskritic, mainly served as a priest in the temples of village deities. The Brahmin priests are generally known as *Śāstri*, are called as the classical *purohita* in Tamil Nadu.[57] The priests of the Meenakshi temple never perform as a domestic priest in Śaiva temples and similarly, it is ensured by the Vaiṣhṇava temple priest as well. The second category, however, the priests of non-Sanskritic temples served as village priests or *pūjāri*. They worshipped the village deities. These priests are almost always from the non-Brahmin community and their rank is below compared to the Brahmin priests in the caste hierarchy.[58]

The division and hierarchy of Brahmins are also maintained by the *gotras*. The *gotras* carry the origin and genetic transmission of physical and mental behaviours.[59] Sir Monier Monier Williams, Professor of Sanskrit at Oxford University in his work "*A Sanskrit-English Dictionary*" gives a different meaning to *gotra* and he imposes it to protection or shelter for cows, stable, race, lineage or kin. Hence the term *gotra* is considered to be equivalent to lineage. It broadly refers to people who are descendants in an unbroken male line from a common male ancestor. According to the Upanishad, the *gotra* means the hereditary of *Ṛiṣis* (sages).[60] The important sages were *Gautama*,[61] *Bharadwaj*[62], *Kāśyapa*[63], *Viśwāmitra*[64], *Āgastya*[65], *Ātreya*[66], etc. which were reflecting in medieval Tamil inscriptions.

All the ritual functionaries, those who perform the ritual in the sanctum sanctorum are from Brahmins background, the principal servants of the temple involved in the sacrifice and worship of the deities. The other functionaries were not directly associated with the temple sacrifice and worship in general, but they helped the priest to get the performance or activities have done. Apart from the Brahmin priest, there were other Brahmin non-priest performed some temple related activities. In temple, there were also some ritual performers namely, chanters, devotional singers, musicians, etc. performed some ritual duties during the worship and festivals. The hierarchy is reflected spatially by limits on access into the temple and is also represented in the hierarchical ranking of the *Āgamas*, *Vedas* and Tamil hymns.[67]

Privileges of the Temple Brahmins

The temple Brahmins are privileged for performing numerous ritualistic works. Firstly, all the *dakṣiṇā* (a gift for performing ritual activities) of the temple is going to the priest. These *dakṣiṇā* could be in cash or kind. According to their rank, they receive *dakṣiṇā*. At Tiruvallam 500 *kāḍi* of paddy was donated as a reward to the *Śivabrāhmaṇas* who performed *pūjās* to the deity.[68] The temple priests and the other temple functionaries got the appointment in the temple service, which was generally hereditary. The eligible successors of the temple functionaries had the right to hold the same post.[69]

The second most important privilege they enjoyed in the temple was the land grants. *Brahmadēya* and *Dēvadāna* are the two important land grants made to the Brahmin and temple respectively.[70] During the 9th-10th centuries C.E. in many inscriptions we find references to the Brahmin settlements such as *pārppanachēri*, *vāmanachēri* and *nāranachēri*.[71] The Brahmins became a pivotal community in the social and economic aspects with the supremacy of religious activities of the medieval Tamil country in the Kāvēri delta region. An adequate number of inscriptional records are available in the various temples of Rājarāja I about the Brahmin settlement.[72] Burton Stein in his book '*Peasant State and Society in Medieval South India*' pointed out that, the *Brahmadēya*s were the major settlements in the spatial network of Chōḻa ritual hegemony.[73] Rajan Gurukkal[74] speaks about the donations made to the Brahmins and he says that *Paṭṭakal* (*Bhaṭṭars* or Brahmin scholars), *Chattirar* (*Chaṭṭās* or armed Brahmins), and *Śānti* (temple priest) were among popular Brahmins, who received *virutti*, the land-lease as remuneration for their service in the temple. The Brahmin settlements were sometimes designated as *taṉiyūr*, literally a 'separate settlement' or 'free' or 'independent-settlement'.[75] The privileges enjoyed by the Brahmin families in those villages were; *archanā-virutti* (recitation of *Vedas*), *bhārata-vritti* (recitation of *Mahābhārata*), *purāṇam* (recitation of *Purāṇa*), *panchangam* (calendrical activities to provide the auspicious times for marriages), etc.[76]

The expansion of *Brahmadēya* villages or settlements is mainly based on the appearance of the temple. The temple became headquarter of the agrarian villages and the Brahmins were the officials. The Brahmins as temple's officials occupied the top rank in the social hierarchy and the other temple functionaries hierarchically structured based on their responsibilities in the temple service. According to their duties, the temple functionaries ranked in the social structure.

The *Brahmadēya* land was protected by the royal officers. Therefore, it can be assumed that the state power and the ritual power are negotiating somewhere to establish their sovereignty on the people.

The entire land in the village was divided into plots and these were distributed among the influential communities. The land rights held by each of the person was known as *paṅgu* (share). But in this case, all the Brahmins were not given equal share in the village land. Depending upon their importance and ritualistic services in the temple, the land was distributed. Sometimes more than one share was given to some Brahmins and most of the time the majority was allotted one share only.[77] For instance, P. Shanmugam[78] noticed that, in the case of *Nayadhīramaṅgalam*, one Brahmin alone consumed 15 shares and 99 persons were given one share only out of the total shares amounting to 132. In the *Udayachandramaṅgalam* 11 persons captured 3 shares while 48 persons were allotted 2 shares only. In such cases, the land right was given by single donee only. It is important to note that, while creating the *Brahmadēya* village sometimes the whole village was endowed to a single Brahmin, it is called '*ēkabhōga brahmadēya*'. Probably this led to the emergence of landlordism among the Brahmins, owning large, single villages or lands.

The Brahmins individually, as well as a community, had become influential landholders by the 10th century CE.[79] The private landownership appeared in the purely Brahmin villages. The alienation of landed property was very usual among the Brahmins. When the Brahmins became landlord with the power of religious rights, they captured important places in the administrative bodies of social and institutional sectors. Because of their religious dominance and intellectual pursuits, the Brahmins became the member of *sabhā*, were called *perumakkal*.[80] They were honoured as the judges[81] of the *sabhā* of the villages by the king.[82] But usually, they were elected or selected by the people of the village.[83] In the story of the Kūṭṟuva Nāyanār (during the Pallava period), it is mentioned that the temple priests of *Tillai* (Chidambaram) had the privilege of crowning the kings.[84] In a later period also we come across the adequate number of inscriptions found at the temple's wall of the Srirangam temple, which gives detail about the arrangements made by Jatavarman Sundara Pāṇḍya III to donate a village, temple, and land revenues to a group of learned Brahmins.[85] According to the duties, the Brahmins in the medieval south Indian temples hold the rank of administrators, treasurers (*Paṇḍārattār*), superintendents (*Dēvakaṉmigaḷ*), accountants (*Kōyil kaṇakku*)[86], etc. The Brahmins can interfere in local affairs also. In an epigraphic record, there is a mention of *Śivabrāhmaṇas* who wrote a document regarding the land transaction, at the request of *Ūrār* of Kilaikkattamachchi.[87] Gradually, the social status of Brahmins was high and they became an influential community in the medieval Tamil society.

Epilogue

It is necessary to note that the ritual functionaries were mostly from the Brahmin community, occupied an important position in the temples of the Kāvēri delta region. In medieval Tamil country, the temples were constructed mainly in fertile land, and the Kāvēri delta region was fertile, a suitable landscape for the construction of the temple. Burton Stein emphasised that the kings were not only patronised for the construction of the temple but also bestowed land to the Brahmins and other temple functionaries. Further, he says that there were two perspectives for donating the lands; firstly, to generate income from the land for bearing the cost of some ritualistic activities in the temple complex and secondly, to confirm as a productive place for patronage.[88] "Economically speaking, the *brahmadēya* was a product of Brahmanical ideology, sponsored and promoted by the royal authorities, developed into institutions of substantial political power and social dominance with economic privileges", says S. Chandni Bi in her work.[89] The Brahmins through the *Brahmadēya* settlement controlled the land and temple administration, in the course of which they legitimised the political power and social dominance.

Regarding the *Brahmadēya* land holding the Brahmins, were becomes the only consumer to enjoy the income or revenue of those lands. During the time of the *Bhakti* movement, the temple gained more popularity. The deity of the temple was coherent with the royal status. Thus, *uḍaiyār*, *perumāḷ* meant both the king and the deity and the *kōyil* meant both the temple and the palace. Gradually routine of services in the temple followed the services in the palace.[90] It is clear to see the representation of the principle of mutual benefit was established between them.

Through royal grants, private land endowments, gifts of gold and money, and other forms of donations by the devotees, the ritual functionaries of the temple who had possessed those endowments especially the Brahmins have become the majestic wealthy community in medieval south Indian society. With their absolute influence, they controlled the temple administration and temple related activities. Possibly the chief priest could perform as the administrator of the temples. When wealth turned the symbol of status the Brahmins became the top in the social hierarchy. The Brahmins and temples have an invisible tie-up with the political power and sacred domain or its agents.

Rajan Gurukkal[91] argues that the proliferation of *Jāti* was led by the emergence of temple functionaries especially the Brahmins with their ritual supremacy. Further, he states that "a temple-centered *brāhmaṇa* village was the corporation of *brāhmaṇa* landlords with the people associated with them as landed intermediaries, tenants, artisans, craftsmen, and tillers. The process of integration of a large number of such functionaries was evidently complex and the process of their absorption into a hierarchy of caste was all the more complex. However, we are able to draw certain influences and insights out of the temple records of the period".[92]

From the above discussion, we may summarise that the Brahmin functionaries according to their ritualistic services were engaged in temple activities as well as dominated in the social hierarchy. They were able to establish their authority over the temple, which helped them to establish their dominance throughout the state. In spatial arrangements of socio-religious and state politics and economy, the temple ritual functionaries played a vital role in the temple administration as multi-dimensional functionaries. The structure of a hierarchy was a common system of social differentiation, based on varying levels of ritual status positions in the sphere around Brahmins. Moreover, the adoption of devotional, temple-centered forms of ritual by Brahmins required extensive support which was provided by the people. The Brahmins established themselves in society as their savior only by reading religious texts and performing other sacred activities in the temple. For which they claimed to respect and endowments. Expansion of agrarian settlements through the creation of *Brahmadēya* villages and ritual activities often involved the superimposition of the superior rights of the Brahmins over the communal holdings and the clan families of the society. Yet, eventually in the later period gradually they became a separate group and enclosed themselves in a particular area but still, their ethical behaviour is continuously questioned by the scholars of the present day.

References

1. Patrick Olivelle, *Manu's Code of Law: A Critical Edition and Translation of the Mānava-Dharmasāstra*, New York, 2005, p. 124.

2. R.N. Sharma, *Brahmins through the Ages: Their Social, Religious, Cultural, Political and Economic Life*, Delhi, 1977, p. 1.
3. Muir: *Original Sanskrit Texts*, Vol. I, p. 242. (In Brahman neuter the accent is on the first syllable whereas in Brahman masculine on the last) cited by R. N. Sharma, *op.cit.*, p.1.
4. *Ibid.*
5. *Ṛg Veda*. X. 90, cited by R. N. Sharma, *op.cit.*
6. '*Brāhmaṇasyamukhamāsīt*' cited by Ranabir Chakravarti, '*Bharat-Itihaser Adiparva: Pratham Khanda, Prachintaṃa Kal Theke Anumanik 600 Khrishtabdo*' (in Bengali), Kolkata, 2009, p.114.
7. K. Mavali Rajan, "The Brahmins in the Early Tamil Society", *The Mirror*, Vol. 1, Assam, 2014, pp. 98-107.
8. *Tolkāppiyam*: 623, 625, 626, 632, 635.
9. *Tolkāppiyam*: 70, cited by K. Lakshmi, "The Priest under the Pallavas", in S. Ganeshram and C. Bhavani (eds.), *History of People and Their Environs, Essays in Honour of Prof. B. S. Chandrababu*, Madurai, 2011, p. 86.
10. *Puṟanāṉūṟu:* 34,7 Porul 75: 134, cited by K. Lakshmi, *op.cit.*
11. *Paripādal*, 11: 84, cited by K. Lakshmi, *op.cit.*
12. *Thirumalisai*, 9: 3-4, cited by K. Lakshmi, *op.cit.*
13. *Thirumāndiram*, 1-82: 4: 1, cited by K. Lakshmi, *op.cit.*
14. *Thondaradi Thirumalai*, 42, cited by K. Lakshmi, *op.cit.*
15. K. Mavali Rajan, *op.cit.*, pp. 100-101.
16. *Tolkāppiyam*: 626.
17. D. D. Kosambi, *An Introduction to the Study of Indian History*, New Delhi, 1975, p. 58.
18. Romila Thapar, *Cultural Pasts: Essays in Early Indian History*, New Delhi, 2013, p. 31.
19. D. Dayalan, *Early Temples of Tamilnadu: Their Role in Socio-Economic Life (c. A.D. 550-925)*, New Delhi, 1992, p.164.
20. *Ṛg Veda*. 1.64-45, cited by Chitrarekha Gupta, *The Brahmanas of India: A Study Based on Inscriptions*, New Delhi, 1983, pp. 22-47.
21. *Ibid.*, 1.15.5; II. 36.5; VI. 75.10; VII. 103.1,7,8, cited by Chitrarekha Gupta, *op.cit.*
22. K. Mavali Rajan, *Medieval Tamil Society and Agrarian Slavery*, Kolkata, 2014, p. 37; K. Karuppiah, *A Social, Cultural History of the Later Cholas: As Gleaned Through Epigraphy*, Delhi, 2010, p. 48.
23. D. Dayalan, *op.cit.*, pp.168-169.
24. K. K. Pillay, *A Social History of the Tamils*, Vol. 1, 2nd Edition, University of Madras, 1975, p. 485.
25. A. L. Basham, *The Wonder That Was India*, London, 1969, p. 140.

26. C. Minakshi, *Administration and Social Life under the Pallavas*, 2nd ed., Madras, 1977, p. 177.
27. *E.I.*, Vol. XXXVI, p. 316.
28. Chitrarekha Gupta, *op.cit.*, pp. 22-47.
29. *E.I.*, Vol. XVIII, pp. 249-250.
30. *Ibid.*,Vol. V, pp. 70 ff.
31. D. Dayalan, *op.cit.*, p. 164.
32. A. Sreedhara Menon, *A Survey of Kerala History*, Kerala, 1967, p. 96.
33. T. V. Kuppuswami, "The Brahmanas and Brahmanism in Saṅgam Literature", *BITCM*, July-December, 1978, p. 143.
34. R. Champakalakshmi, *Religion, Tradition, and Ideology Pre-colonial South India*, New Delhi, 2011, pp. 236-239.
35. *Puṟanāṉūṟu*: 166, cited by K. Lakshmi, *op.cit.*
36. *A.R.E.*, No. 467 of 1909.
37. *E.I.*, Vol. III, p. 227ff.
38. K. Mavali Rajan, 'Administrators, Artisans and Servants: Temple's Functionaries in Medieval South India', in K. Mavali Rajan (ed.), *Temple and Society in South India*, New Delhi, 2016, p. 78.
39. *S.I.I.*, Vol. III, No. 43.
40. *A.R.E.*, Nos.373 of 1903 and 99 of 1929.
41. K. A. Nilakanta Sastri, *Development of Religion in South India*, Madras, 1963, p. 113.
42. *S.I.I.*, Vol. I, p. 151.
43. *S.I.I.*, Vol. IV, No. 827.
44. *S.I.I.*, Vol. VI, No. 355.
45. *S.I.I.*, Vol. VI, Nos. 287, 288.
46. C. J. Fuller, *Servants of the Goddess: The Priests of a South Indian Temple*, New Delhi, 1991, pp. 75-78.
47. *S.I.I.*, Vol. XIX, No. 331.
48. C. N. Vasudevan, *Temples of Andhra Pradesh*, Delhi, 2000, p. 34; K. Mavali Rajan, "Administrators, Artisans and Servants: Temple's Functionaries in Medieval South India", p. 87.
49. *S.I.I.*, Vol. II, No. 73.
50. C. Minakshi, *op.cit.*, pp. 178-179.
51. *S.I.I.*, Vol. VI, Nos. 287, 288, 347.
52. *S.I.I.*, Vol. III, No. 45.
53. Andre Beteille, *Caste, Class and Power: Changing Pattern of Stratification in Tanjore Village*, England, 1965, p. 61.
54. Edgar Thurston, *Caste and Tribes of Southern India*, Vol. I, Madras, 1987, pp. 333-334.
55. C. J. Fuller, *op.cit.*, pp. 24-25.
56. *Ibid.*

57. K. Subramaniam, *Brahmin Priests of Tamil Nadu*, New York, 1974, p. 12.
58. C. J. Fuller, *op.cit.*, p. 25.
59. K. Lakshmi, *op.cit.*, p. 87.
60. *Ibid.*
61. *S.I.I.*, Vol. XII, No. 5.
62. *S.I.I.*, Vol. XVII, No. 199.
63. *S.I.I.*, Vol. II, Part III, IV and V, No. 531.
64. *S.I.I.*, Vol. III, Part III, IV and V, No. 422.
65. Edgar Thurston, *op.cit.*, p. 268.
66. *S.I.I.*, Vol. II, Part III, IV and V, No. 373.
67. C. J. Fuller, *op.cit.*, p. 47.
68. *S.I.I.*, Vol. III, No. 43.
69. *A.R.E.*, No. 40 of 1906.
70. B. K. Pandeya, "The *Brahmadēya* and *Dēvadāna* Land during the Cola Period", *Proceedings of the Indian History Congress*, Vol. 42, New Delhi, 1981, pp. 146-149.
71. *S.I.I.*, Vol. VI, No. 145.
72. *S.I.I.*, Vol. II, No. 74.
73. Burton Stein, *Peasant State and Society in Medieval South India*, Delhi, 1994, pp. 343-345.
74. Rajan Gurukkal, *Social Formations of Early South India*, New Delhi, 2010, p. 312.
75. Burton Stein, *op.cit.*, p. 152.
76. *Ibid.*
77. P. Shanmugam, '*Brahmadeyas* in the Pallava Country', in S. Rajagopal (ed.), *Kaveri: Studies in Epigraphy, Archaeology and History* (Professor Y. Subbarayalu Felicitation Volume), Chennai, 2001, p. 335.
78. *Ibid.*
79. Y. Subbarayalu, *South India under the Cholas*, New Delhi, 2012, p. 120.
80. K. Mavali Rajan, *op.cit.*, p. 102.
81. *A.R.E.*, No. 19 of 1917.
82. *A.R.E.*, No. 19 of 1917.
83. *A.R.E.*, No. 33 of 1919.
84. D. Dayalan, *op.cit.*, p. 167.
85. *S.I.I.*, Vol. XXIV, Nos. 223-228.
86. *S.I.I.*, Vol. VIII, Nos. 83, 96, 216, 289, 750.
87. *A.R.E.*, No. 341 of 1906.
88. Burton Stein, "The Economic Function of Medieval South Indian Temple", *The Journal of Asian Studies*, Vol. 19, No. 2, 1960, p. 164.

89. S. Chandni Bi, "Brahmadēyas verses Vellānvagai Villages: Socio Cultural Hierarchy in Medieval South India", in K. Mavali Rajan, et.al. (eds.), *Facets of Temple Culture: Perspectives on Religious and Social Traditions in Early Medieval India*, New Delhi, 2018, p. 46.
90. Kesavan Veluthat, *The Early Medieval in South India*, New Delhi, 2011 (Third Impression), p. 67.
91. Rajan Gurukkal, "The Making and Proliferation of *Jāti*: A Historical Inquiry", *Studies in History*, Vol. 31, No. 1, 2015, pp. 30-50.
92. Rajan Gurukkal, *Social Formations of Early South India*, p. 311.

Bibliography

Annual Reports on (South Indian) Epigraphy for the years, 1903, 1906, 1917, 1919, 1929, Archaeological Survey of India.

Basham, A. L., *The Wonder That Was India*, London, 1969.

Beteille, Andre, *Caste, Class and Power: Changing Pattern of Stratification in Tanjore Village*, England, 1965.

Chakravarti, Ranabir, '*Bharat-Itihaser Adiparva: Pratham Khanda, Prachintama Kal Theke Anumanik 600 Khrishtabdo*' (in Bengali), Kolkata, 2009.

Champaklakshmi, R., *Religion, Tradition, and Ideology Pre-colonial South India*, New Delhi, 2011.

Dayalan, D., *Early Temples of Tamilnadu: Their Role in Socio-Economic Life (c. A.D. 550-925)*, New Delhi, 1992.

Epigraphia Indica, Vols. III, V, XVIII, XXXVI, Archaeological Survey of India, New Delhi.

Fuller, C. J., *Servants of the Goddess: The Priests of a South Indian Temple*, New Delhi, 1991.

Ganeshram, S. and Bhavani, C. (eds.), *History of People and Their Environs, Essays in Honour of Prof. B. S. Chandrababu*, Madurai, 2011.

Gupta, Chitrarekha, *The Brahmanas of India: A Study Based on Inscriptions*, New Delhi, 1983.

Gurukkal, Rajan, "The Making and Proliferation of *Jāti*: A Historical Inquiry", *Studies in History*, Vol. 31, No. 1, 2015.

--------------, *Social Formations of Early South India*, New Delhi, 2010.

Karuppiah, K., *A Social, Cultural History of the Later Cholas: As Gleaned Through Epigraphy*, Delhi, 2010.

Kosambi, D. D., *An Introduction to the Study of Indian History*, New Delhi, 1975.

Kuppuswami, T. V., "The Brahmanas and Brahmanism in Saṅgam Literature", *BITCM*, July-December, 1978.

Mavali Rajan, K. (ed.), *Temple and Society in South India*, New Delhi, 2016.

Mavali Ranjan, K. (ed), "The Brahmins in the Early Tamil Society", *The Mirror*, Vol. 1, Assam, 2014.

----------------, *Medieval Tamil Society and Agrarian Slavery*, Kolkata, 2014.

Mavali Rajan, K. et.al. (eds.), *Facets of Temple Culture: Perspectives on Religious and Social Traditions in Early Medieval India*, New Delhi, 2018.

Menon, Sreedhara A., *A Survey of Kerala History*, Kerala, 1967.

Minakshi, C., *Administration and Social Life under the Pallavas*, 2nd ed., Madras, 1977.

Olivelle, Patrick, *Manu's Code of Law: A Critical Edition and Translation of the Mānava-Dharmasāstra*, New York, 2005.

Pandeya, B. K., "The Brahmadeya and Devadana Land During the Cola Period", *Proceedings of the Indian History Congress*, Vol. 42, New Delhi, 1981.

Pillay, K. K., *A Social History of the Tamils*, Vol. 1, 2nd Edition, University of Madras, 1975.

Rajagopal, S. (ed.), *Kaveri: Studies in Epigraphy, Archaeology and History* (Professor Y. Subbarayalu Felicitation Volume), Chennai, 2001.

Sastri, Nilakanta K. A., *Development of Religion in South India*, Madras, 1963.

Sharma, R. N., *Brahmins through the Ages: Their Social, Religious, Cultural, Political and Economic Life*, Delhi, 1977.

South Indian Inscriptions, Vols. I, II, III, IV, VI, VIII, XII, XVII, XIX, XXIV, Archaeological Survey of India.

Stein, Burton, "The Economic Function of Medieval South Indian Temple", *The Journal of Asian Studies*, Vol. 19, No. 2, 1960.

--------------, *Peasant State and Society in Medieval South India*, Delhi, 1994.

Subbarayalu, Y., *South India under the Cholas*, New Delhi, 2012.

Subramaniam, K., *Brahmin Priests of Tamil Nadu*, New York, 1974.

Thapar, Romila, *Cultural Pasts: Essays in Early Indian History*, New Delhi, 2013.

Tholkāppiyam: In English with Critical Studies, Madras, 1994 (Second Edition).

Thurston, Edgar, *Caste and Tribes of Southern India*, Vol. I, Madras, 1987.

Vasudevan, C. N., *Temples of Andhra Pradesh*, Delhi, 2000.

Veluthat, Kesavan, *The Early Medieval in South India*, New Delhi, 2011 (Third Impression).

Part - IV
Cultural Facets and Edifying Traditions

13

Economic Aspect of the Hero Stone Tradition in Early Medieval Karnataka

Priya Thakur

Introduction

The early medieval period in Karnataka represents the socio-political as well as religious developments with lasting implications. Recent archaeological and historical scholarship on the Middle Period points to both a high degree of regional diversity in political and economic organisation and a fluctuating degree of interregional commercial and political connectivity. Nevertheless, several consistent themes emerge: urbanisation and related transformations of settlement; monetisation and the increasing role of production for markets; the volatile relationship between long-distance exchange and local political and economic structure; the intensification of production; and the shifting roles of such specialised institutions as monasteries, temples, and guilds.[1]

Several global traditions of memorial art serve didactic functions; they aim to inspire heroic or pious behaviour among the living. For example, religious and political martyrs are memorialised to celebrate their selfless acts and to inspire the living.[2] The idea of heroism has always commanded appreciation and recognition from society. Such men, who altruistically pledged and gave their lives for the protection of their village people and property, were given the position of the hero, and later one can observe the trend of these heroes acquiring the status of a demigod in the village, especially in southern India.

In the remembrance and as a tribute of such lives, the relatives or community erected a stone slab in front of the village temple or in village boundaries which are termed as 'hero stones' by the historians. These stones represent the ancient traditional thought that fallen heroes are welcomed in heaven by the celestial beings and gods as it was believed that such supreme sacrifice was awarded in the form of immortality after death and material gains in life. In the Epic age, the emphasis came to be laid upon the heavenly rewards and this conviction is quite common in the military annals of India.[3] The whole idea of these hero memorial stones seems to create eternal memory of the deed of the hero and this idea was adopted by every social group. According to T.S. Sharma[4],

> *"There are various traditions and 'little' tradition located at different nodes, both in space and time, of a cultural web, and the 'subaltern' voice raised against a dominant strand of a culture is also engaged in dialogic transaction, and the give and take goes on unceasingly. The 'subaltern' encounters the 'imperial' often in a state of frisson, appropriates it to its cultural idiom, and even seeks legitimacy for it."*

Economic Aspects

Most of the hero stones are not inscribed and are of commemorative nature and the historians understand such story based on local folk legends and oral traditions and the artistic quality of its iconography. Such studies tend to focus on simple assumptions associated with hero stone traditions. The hero stones with inscriptions are most often very simple ones providing only details about the hero's name and the cause of his death. But the detailed inscribed hero stones are important as they throw light on the details related to the name of the hero, the reason of his death, name of the family member (s) who erected the memorial and may include, the grant or gift made by a higher authority or benefactor – a king, minister or feudal chief in recognition of his sacrifice. The majority of the inscriptions seen on the hero stones are simple to label inscriptions but often one can find more descriptive inscriptions that register grants to the families of the fallen heroes. This added an economical fervour to this memorial practice. This sentiment was elevated to the level of religious practice and hero stones gained importance.[5]

The valour and sacrifice of the heroes were recognised by the rulers and the public. According to Settar and Kalburgi,[6]

> "... *The age (early medieval times) expected chivalry from every able-bodied individual, just it expected charity from the wealthy citizen. The hero- whether a chieftain or a soldier- took upon himself the responsibility of defending and protecting the society, even at the cost of his life. Society, in turn, recognized his service and admired his courage as well his contribution; it also took upon itself the responsibility of providing for the family of the dead hero.... Assurance of spiritual, social, and economic gains, appears to have emboldened soldiers so much as to lead them to embrace death on the battlefield without anxiety.*"

Types of Grants

Several types of grants were made by the local corporate bodies, local chieftains or headmen as well as by rulers, and ranged from small plots of land for the dependents of a local hero to whole villages or even larger politico-geographical units depending on the hero's status and service.[7] The financial benefits provided to the close family members of a fallen hero were compensatory in nature. Kuppuswamy[8] analyzed the economic factors governing the memorial stones in Karnataka by examining the purpose, content, and procedure and proportion and value of grants made on such occasions. The hero's family was also offered some kind of gift or economical relief as evident from inscriptions. Such land grants were known as *bāḷagachu*, *kalnāḍu*, *śivane*, *koḍagi* or *nettara- koḍagi*.[9]

Land Grants

A number of records observed across southern India mention the land grant made to the family of the hero. One record states that Kuṛakālaramanāḷiyar, a servant of Siyegalla died fighting the enemies and some land was granted to the fallen hero as *bāḷgaḷachu* and another records a grant of land as *talgaḷachu*.[10] Lands, granted to military officers for distinguished bravery, were known as *bāḷgachu* or sword-washing grants that may have paid only a light tax, if at all they had to pay any, as the inhabitant's share.[11] One inscription from Chittoor district of Bāṇa period registers the grant of a plot of the wetland of five *kula* in sowing capacity by the king to a person named Gavunda on the occasion of a cattle-raid.[12] Another undated record from the same district states that Bāṇa king Bāṇarasa bestowed land of three *khaṁba* upon the family of a fallen hero Mādhavarasa who died after slaying several men and horses.[13] The Western Ganga inscription from Begur mentions that king Būtuga gave Maṇalera the Ātukūr twelve and village of Kadiyur as *bāḻgachu* grant as the award of his bravery.[14]

A circa ninth century inscription states that the Noḷamba-Pallava king honoured a dead warrior Tējamāni by granting to his family a *kalnāḍu* called 'Elemaṇḍala'.[15] This gift of *kalnāḍu* is also seen in a record of Śaka 899 (=977 C.E.) from Rayadurg taluk of Bellary district in Karnataka, which states that during the reign of the Noḷamba-Pallava king Maydammarasa, a chief made this gift to two men – one who fell fighting and the other who died as *kīḻgoṇṭe*.[16] Kīlgoṇṭe was an act of self-sacrifice by live burial or self-immolation. Many inscriptions mentioning the death of Western Gaṅga ruler Nītimārga inform about *kalnāḍ* grants.[17] This *kalnāḍ* term denotes stony land or uncultivable land. The Doḍḍahunḍi inscription of Western Gaṅga king Nītimārga and Satyavākya mentions about the *kalnāḍ* grant with the relinquishment of all taxes made by Satyavākya to his father's follower Agarayya, who killed himself after the death of the king.[18]

It was not always the rulers or the feudal chiefs who used to make such grants. An epigraph dated 1194 C.E. of Hoysala period from Bellary mentions that the *Mahājanas* made a gift of land to the son of the man Basaveya Nayaka, in recognition of the service rendered by the latter, who is said to have died in a fight against a band of thieves (*chōrayūtha*).[19] The *Mahājanas* represented the members of the village council.[20] The Nukkanahalli inscription from Kolar district of mid-ninth century registers a *kalnāḍ* grant of a village from the king to Nagagutta-arasa, who died fighting against the *Mahājanas* This grant was made to him with all exemptions (*sarva bādhā parihāra*).[21] An inscription of 1249 C.E. from Bandipura mentions a grant of 500 *poṇ* to the family of a hero and the family excavated a tank, raised a flower garden, a resting place and a hero stone in memory of the fallen hero. It further refers to an endowment (*stānam*).[22] A record of circa early eighth century mentions the death of the village watchman Jatta in a battle and was granted some land.[23] Another inscription of c. 1296 C.E. from Malluru village of Somwarpete taluk registers the death of Malleya, son of Boppagauḍi, in a battle that ensued between several *nāḍus* and Muḻḻūr fort. He was granted as *vīrasēse*, certain lands by the three hundred men of the village.[24]

Trade Guilds

During the early medieval period, well-organised merchant guilds were a major part of the regional economy with links to associations of producers such as potters, weavers, leather workers, market gardeners, and farmers. Different types of merchants operated on either a regional or an international scale, marketing such products as iron, textiles, livestock, and forest products including spices.[25] According to Hall,[26] local merchant guilds had monopolistic power within their marketing territory, the power that was negotiated with political leaders and could include landholding, management of temple finances and land, collection of taxes for the state, and even local political administration. Some guilds supported private armies and a record of 1100 C.E. from Chengalpattu District in Tamil Nadu records a convention involving both merchants and soldiers. This record mentions about an agreement that converts a town known as Ayyappuḷal of Kāṭṭūr into a *vīrapaṭṭinaṃ* or designated soldiers' settlement and gives some privileges to the soldiers of the place.[27] These merchant guilds were not committed to any political power and maintained neutrality due to their trans-border and trans-oceanic commercial transactions. The occurrence of names of several groups of warriors (*vīrar/ vīrakoḍiyār*) associated with these merchant guilds suggests that they had a tradition of protecting themselves.[28] Two records dated ninth century from Alattur in Gundlupet taluk of Mysore district mention cattle raids carried by a group of merchants led by Ammana Śeṭṭi, probably in Chola nāḍu to which they had gone for trade.[29] It is not clear that if these two heroes mentioned were defending their cattle or were aggressors.

Two other inscriptions dated 1013 C.E., referring to such cattle raids, come from Sorab taluk in Shivamogga district which mentions the death of two Seṭṭis of Midiypallaga.[30] Another record of circa tenth century, from Chamrajnagar taluk in Mysore district, registers grant made to the younger brothers of Pemmanna, the son of Beniyamma Śeṭṭi, who died fighting against Desinga.[31] This grant was made by the *samaya* which is a term used for an assemblage, company, or congregation.

Cattle Raids

The epigraphic reference to the cattle raids, termed as *tuṛugōl* in Kannada, and the importance given to the men who died while protecting the cattle (*tuṛuvan maguḷci*) indicate the prevalence of the pastoral economy in this region from the early historic period.

In the majority of the instances, the cattle raids used to be limited to local territories only. Hero stone from Kolar district of c. 780 C.E. records the death of a cowherd named as Uvlan together with an unnamed cowherdess in the defence of the cattle of Balla village. The family of the cowherd received five *koḷagas* of fields yielding one rice crop.[32] A record of c. 1195 C.E. mentions that the Brahmins presented a horse, a drum, and a *koḍagi* or rent-free estate to a man, whose son died while recovering the cows of the Brahmins from robbers.[33] Similar types of land grants are mentioned in various hero stone inscriptions from the region.[34] Hultzsch [35] mentions an epigraph from Kolar region where the *Gaṅgā* king Rachamalla assigned land for setting up the stone in memory of the hero who fell protecting the cattle. This inscription mentions a very interesting line in the end, '*let the Kaṇṇāḍagas (i.e. the Kanarese people) look after this stone*.' One record dated 1195 C.E. from Chikmanglur taluk mentions the award of a *vīra-koḍagi* together with an umbrella, horse and a drum to a man who died recovering the cows from robbers.[36]

There are references to merchants (śeṭṭis) and artisans engaged in cattle raid or in the rescue of the cattle, which show that cattle were maintained by all classes of people during this period. Cattle must have been sufficiently valuable economic assets for the men of different groups to have risked life and limb to increase their livestock by capturing the herds of the neighbouring village or to defend their own cattle and the cattle were valuable economic assets.[37] An inscription from Kadur taluk dated 1205 C.E. mentions the death of Bicha Sēṭṭi, who was the son of a bangle seller while recovering the cows from robbers.[38]

Military Context

The soldiers serving under the rulers or chiefs were given generous awards in the world and promised greater ones in the next. The hero stones or *vīragals* were erected in their memory by their family and friends and provisions were made for the maintenance of their families. The early Indian literature provides an interesting insight in to this concept of acceptance of death while serving ones' duty. In the śloka 324 of Chapter XIII titled *Rājadharma Prakaraṇa* in *Yājňavalkya Smṛti*, the sage states that, '*sa āhveṣu vadhyante bhūmyamartham parāṅgamukhāḥ' |akūṭairāyudhairyānti svargaṁ yogino tathā* ||324||, i.e., '*Those who in battles are killed for the sake of the land, without turning their face back fighting all the while with weapons which are not treacherous, they certainly go to heaven just as the Yogins do'*.[39] A very similar notion can be seen in an inscription from Tiptur taluk dated 1395 C.E. which states that *Chennēya Nāyaka fought with the Turukas, broke their army, and giving up his body in the service of his lord, ascended to Vayikuṅṭha... By two among men is the disk of the sun burst through, - he who is perfect in Yoga, and he who falls facing the foe in battle'*.[40]

The heroes who gave their life on their master's orders formed a kind of bravery with martial connotation – where the heroes were brave enough to accept or invite death but did not question the rationale behind it. The Kannada literature identified such heroes as *vēlevali*, *joḷavali*, *lenka*, etc. *Vēḷe* means time or occasion, *pāḷi* means duty or obligation; the principle and philosophy of the *vēlevalis* were to do their duty and fulfill their obligation whenever they were called upon. The jolavalis were a different group of men who declared their vow in return for subsistence. *Joḷa* means millet and *jolavalis* received subsistence from their masters.[41]

Veluthat [42] discusses the *vēlevali* and *garuḍa* traditions involving the individual soldiers attached to the chiefs taking the oath of unswerving loyalty to them even in death and states that this institution occurs in the Kannada records from the beginning of the ninth century in high number. The Mevundi inscription of 865 C.E. is one of the earliest records making a clear reference to the institution of *vēlevali*.[43] This record states that a *vēlavadica*, *Retteyana*, took the king for his real parents and that he took an oath to die if his master died. His master died while he was away and he could see only his master's body burning in the funeral pyre. He immediately cut his head off. Veluthat points out to the fact that there are rare examples of persons abrogating the oath of *vēlevali* who received punishment and highlights the notion of the instinct of self-preservation in conflict with obligations of a socio-political nature.

The term '*garuḍa*' was used in the Hoysaḷa records to denote the *vēlevalis*. The Hoysala records provide information about the *Garuḍa* tradition in which a soldier was sworn in to make him the *garuḍa* or the lifeguard of the king who bestowed on him the *toḍar* (anklet) which was worn on the left foot. It was made of gold with carved images on it.[44] By the 13th century, this *garuḍa* tradition had reached at its peak as reflected in inscriptions that mention one thousand of heroes (called as *lenkas*) died with Kuvaralakshma who committed garuda when his master Hoysaḷa Vīra Ballala died.[45] Hero stones erected in memory of these bodyguards are called Garuda pillars.

A Rastrakuta record of 932 C.E. from Harapanahalli taluk of Bellary district mentions the grant of some wet and dry fields to the family of a dead warrior.[46] An inscription dated c. 1148 C.E. from Davangere mentions the death of four men who died while doing their duty (as soldiers of a feudal chief) and hero stone were erected for each of them and land grants were made for them.[47] But there are examples where the men, who survived the battles, were awarded for their bravery through similar grants. An inscription of Hoysala period from Kadur district dated 1148 C.E. states that Heggade Getana with his two younger brothers, in his ruler's war, both in battle in the plain and in battle in the fort, slaying the enemies and putting them to flight, received a badge of honour and a headpiece for his elephant, together with praise and fame, and his ruler gave him a *koḍagi* or rent-free estate.[48] An inscription from Maddagiri taluk dated 1569 C.E. tells about the grant of a village as a *nettara-goḍigi* to Malapa-gauda whose son Aubhalaiya sacrificed his life.[49] Another record dated c. 920 CE mentions *kalnāḍ* i.e. the grant of land of specific limits to Bhimayya whose son Perggade Beṇāyya died fighting the Gaṅgā army.[50]

A.S. Altekar[51] mentions about a Bāṇa period inscription which chronicles *the death of an officer, who was successful in driving away the enemy, but who fell while pursuing him, as he was too much in advance of his column. His army put off their arms with which they had come, raised a lamentation, and made a gift to yield an annual income for him*. Another Bāṇa record mention about a provision to pay the pension to the dependents of the soldiers killed in war.[52]

Grants as Inheritance

The Belgali inscription from Hassan district of mid-tenth century C.E. registers the donation of the village of Belgali to Ankada Katayya, who was the *vēḻe* or loyal retainer of Mahādevi Revakānimmaḍi Gaṅga. This grant is for perpetuity and it is specifically stated that the royal and local tax officials were not to enter the village and the right of *abhyantra siddhi* or tax-free grant that vested in Ankada Katayya and his successors.[53] An epigraph from Chikmanglur taluk mentions that the Brahmins of Kuruvage, pleased with a man who died like a hero fighting with burglars, gave to his wife and children a large palanquin and a canopy to descend to his children's children.[54] An epigraph dated 1076 C.E. from the reign of Chālukya Jayasiṃha III records a permanent exemption from the house tax (*mane-deṟe*) to the heirs of a hero (whose name is not clear) on his death in a fight by a chief Bhīvarāya. The record also states that the inscribed stone was set up by the elder son of the hero and it was engraved by Sēnabōva Kallayya.[55] Similar record from Tiptur dated 1291 C.E. refers to the death of a hero, Sūlāyta Kannaya, in a cattle raid. The Hoysaḷa king Vir Ballala made a grant for the elder brother of the hero who erected the hero stone and his son made a well.[56]

An interesting record dated 1542 C.E. from Bhatkal taluk of North Canara district commemorates the heroic death of Yenkappa Nayaka while protecting the palace gate in a fight against enemies. The *Mahāmaṇḍalēśvara* Chennadevi Ammanavaru granted the land of sowing capacity of ten and a half *mudis* of paddy, belonging to the palace, after having de-tenanted it from the previous tenants to Naranadeva Nayaka, the brother of the fallen hero. The details of the boundaries of the gift land are specified in lines 7-13 of the inscription and then it is stated that the land should pass to the female descendants as gift (*pennige dāna*) or to the male descendants by right of succession. (*gaṇḍige mūla*).[57]

Socio-Religious Context

Kudarkot inscription dated circa the seventh century from Uttar Pradesh records the erection of a building for Brāhmins familiar with the three *Vedas*, by a person named Harivarman in memory of his son Takshadatta, who had died in a battle.[58] In Karnataka, similar instances are also observed. The *Bhakti* movement of the Śaivities overwhelmed southern India from 6th century C.E. and the religious faith of Śaivism postulated the highest heaven, Śivaloka, for the blessed ones. The heroes were naturally counted among the blessed, fit for nothing less than the Śivaloka, and thus achieved the highest glory and supreme bliss.[59] The hero stones became one of the socio-cultural indicators of the Śaivite growth in the region. The reliefs of hero stones depict the idea that potential for the spiritual liberation was no more confined to the merit of caste or birth but could be gained simply by worthy deeds by a person of any birth or gender thus reshaping a completely different kind of concept of assimilation of religion and individual identity.[60] The iconographical elements of the hero stones delineate the spread and integration of Śaivism in the pastoral and agrarian communities by providing a more conventional vision of religion. Depiction of the hero with folded hands intends to convey the ultimate destiny of the hero was attaining *Śivaloka* as a devotee thus clearly highlighting the underlying context of the *Bhakti* tradition.[61] This signified the salvation of the hero as the *svarga*, the abode of Indra, ceased to be the ultimate destiny of hero, instead, attaining *samipya* (closeness) of Śiva was projected as his final destiny.[62]

Some records specifically mention the setting up of a temple or worshipping of the stone by providing the grant for basic acts of reverence like lamp oil, incense or flowers. Two epigraphs from Chikkanayakanahalli taluk of Tumkur district refer to the direct religious connotation attached to hero stones – the first record mentions about the erection of a Śiva temple along with the hero stone as a memorial and the second inscription mentions that a grant of some wet land was given to two men named– Mādajī and Masaṇajīya, for conducting the worship of the *vīragal*.[63] A record of 1320 C.E. from Hindupur taluk registers the gift of wet and garden lands beneath a tank to those who were appointed to worship the hero-stone.[64] An epigraph of Hoysala period mentions a land grant to the family of the fallen hero with the last lines of warning that *whoever destroys the grant will incur the sin of killing Brahmins and cows at Varanasi; he will go to the world of pachamahāpātaka*.[65]

Conclusion

The hero stones are considered as one of the primary sources for providing information on the socio-economic, political as well as religious framework of the history of the region under study. Similar traditions of memorial stones dedicated to a fallen hero can be seen in neighbouring states of Maharashtra, Tamil Nadu, and Andhra Pradesh and Telangana. This shows the importance of these memorials as significant social documents. At the same time, these inscribed memorial stones throw light on the economical aid and social prestige offered to these heroes for their sacrifice. The nature and extent of these grants and awards are interesting details of the socio-economic status of the benefactor as well as the recipient. But it is very difficult to conclude on the adequacy of these grants since we do not have any information regarding the cost of living and the productivity of the land during the period under study, but they do seem to have been very limited in size in most of the examples. The criterion of these grants seems to be the scale of the conflict: purely local skirmishes received smaller grants and the death in a battle entitled larger grants.[66]

In conclusion, one can understand the important economical and social contexts reflected in these hero stone inscriptions which offer information about the recognition and financial reward for the ultimate acts of bravery for various causes by men and women. The grants along with the memorials provided a prestigious social status to the family members in their society and at the same time served as a formal monument dedicated to the memory of the hero.

References

1. K.D. Morrison, "Commerce and Culture in South Asia: Perspectives from Archaeology and History," *Annual Review of Anthropology*, Vol. 26, 1997, p. 88.
2. M. Belli, "Between Heaven and Hell: Salvation, Damnation, and Memorialisation in the Arts of Death," *Arts Orientalise: The Arts of Death in Asia*, Vol. 44, 2014, pp. 7-16.
3. U.P. Thapliyal, "Military Honours and Awards in Ancient India" *Annals of the Bhandarkar Oriental Research Institute*, Vo. 56 (1/4), 1975, pp. 236-240.
4. T.S. Sharma, *Dialogic of Cultures in Ancient Indian Literatures*, Indian Institute of Advanced Studies, Shimla, 2017, p. 12.
5. M.V. Krishnappa,. *Social and Economical Conditions of Karnataka, AD 400-1000*, University of Mysore, Prasaranga, 1994, p. 177.
6. S. Settar and M.M. Kalburgi, 'The Hero Cult: A Study of Kannada Literature from 9th to 13th century,' in G.H. Sontheimer and S. Settar (eds.), *Memorial Stones: A Study of their Origin, Significance and Variety*, Institute of Indian Art History, Karnatak University, Dharwad, 1982, p. 17.
7. M. Adiga, *The Making of Southern Karnataka: Society, Polity and Culture in the Early Medieval Period*, Orient Black Swan Publishers, Delhi, 2006, p. 177.
8. G.R. Kuppuswamy, 'Economic Factors Governing the Memorial Stones in Karnataka' in G.H. Sontheimer, and S. Settar S. (eds.), *op.cit.*, p. 307.
9. B.L. Rice, *Mysore and Coorg from the Inscriptions*, Archibald Constable and Co. Ltd. London, 1909, p. 171.
10. K.A.N. Sastri, *Epigraphia Carnatica* (*E.C.*), Vol. XVI: *Supplementary Inscriptions in the Tumkur District*, Government Press, Mysore, 1955, p. 82. Ins. Nos. Tm 94 and 99.
11. A.S. Altekar, *The Rāshṭrakūṭas and Their Times*, Poona Oriental Series No. 36, Oriental Book Agency, Poona, 1934, p. 224.
12. R. Shama Sastry (ed.), *South Indian Inscriptions (S.I.I.) (Texts), Kannada Inscriptions from the Madras Presidency*, Vol. IX, Part-I, Government Press, Madras, 1939, p. 4. Ins. No. 10.
13. *S.I.I.*, Vol. IX, Part-I, No. 11, pp. 4-5.
14. J.F. Fleet, 'Three Western Ganga records in the Mysore Government Museum,' in *Epigraphia Indica*, Vol. VI, E. Hultzsch, (ed.), Education Society's Press, Bombay, 1900-01, pp. 56-57.
15. *S.I.I.*, Vol. IX, Part-I, No. 20, pp. 9-10.
16. *S.I.I.*, Vol. IX, Part-I, No. 40, p. 23.
17. B.L. Rice, *Epigraphia Carnatica*, Vol. V: *Inscriptions in Hassan District*, Basel Mission Press, Mangalore, 1902, Ins. Nos. Ag 5, Ag 11 and Ag 27.

18. J.F. Fleet, *op.cit.*, pp. 44-45.
19. *S.I.I.*, Vol. IX, Part-I, pp. 336-37, Ins. No. 321.
20. A.S. Altekar, *op.cit.*, p. 199.
21. B.L. Rice, *op.cit.*, p. 10. Ins. No. Kl. 200
22. B.R. Gopal, (ed.), *Epigraphia Carnatica*, Vol. III. *Mysore District (Gundlupete, Nanjanagud and Heggadadevanakote taluks)*, Revised Edition, Institute of Kannada Studies, University of Mysore, 1974, p. 144. Ins. No. 187.
23. B.L. Rice, *Epigraphia Carnatica*, Vol. IX, Inscriptions in the Bangalore District, 1905, p. 34. Ins. No. Ng. 34.
24. B.R. Gopal, *Epigraphia Carnatica*, Vol. I, Revised Edition, Institute of Kannada Studies, University of Mysore, Mysore, 1972, pp. 51-52. Ins. No. 80 (45).
25. Meera Abraham, *Two Medieval Merchant Guilds of South India*, Manohar Publishers, Delhi, 1988.
26. Kenneth R. Hall, *Trade and Statecraft in the age of the Colas*, Abhinav Prakashan, Delhi, 1980.
27. Y. Subbarayalu and P. Shanmugam, 'Appendix 2: Texts of Select Inscriptions of the Trade Guilds.' in Noboru Karashima (ed.), *Ancient and Medieval Commercial Activities in the Indian Ocean: Testimony of Inscriptions and Ceramic-Shreds*, Taisho University, Tokyo, 2002, p. 239.
28. K. Rajan, *Churning the Ocean: Maritime Trade of Early Historic Peninsular India*, Manoo Pathippakam, Thanjavur, 2019, p. 185.
29. B.R. Gopal, 1974, *op. cit.*, p. 3. Ins. Nos. Gu. 36 and 37.
30. B.L. Rice, *Epigraphia Carnatica* , Vol. VIII. *Inscriptions in the Shimoga District*, Part II, Mysore Government Central Press, Bangalore, 1904, p. 8. Ins. Nos. Sb. 385 and 386.
31. B.R. Gopal, (ed.) *Epigraphia Carnatica, Mysore District (Chamarajanagar, Yalandur, Kollegal, Hunsur and Piriyapattana taluks)*, Vol. IV, Revised Edition, Institute of Kannada Studies, University of Mysore, Mysore, 1975, p. 4. Ins. No. Ch. 115.
32. B.L. Rice, 1905, p. 10. Ins. No. Mb 92.
33. B.L. Rice, 1901. *Epigraphia Carnatica. Vol. VI. Inscriptions in the Kadur District*, Mysore Government Central Press, Bangalore, p. 10. Ins. No. 47.
34. K.A.N. Sastri, *Epigraphia Carnatica*, Vol. XVI: *Supplementary Inscriptions in the Tumkur District*, Government Press, Mysore, 1955, pp. 80-82. Ins. Nos. Tm 87, 94, 95, 99.
35. E. Hultzsch, 'Three Memorial Stones,' in *Epigraphia Indica*, Vol. VII, Reprint, E. Hultzsch, (ed.) 1902-03, pp. 22-25. New Delhi, 1981, DGASI. p. 23.
36. B.L. Rice, 1902. *op.cit.* p. 56. Ins. Nos. 157-158.
37. M. Adiga, *op.cit.*, pp. 61-65.

38. B.L. Rice, 1901. *op.cit.*, pp. 24-25. Ins. No. 130.
39. S.C. Vidyarnava (tr.), *Yajnavalkya Smriti with the Commentary of Vijnanśvara called the Mitaksara, Book I: The Āchāra Adhyāya*, The Panini Office, Bhuvaneswari Asrama, Allahabad, 1918, pp. 405-06.
40. B.L. Rice, *Epigraphia Carnatica, Vol. XII. Inscriptions in the Tumkur District*. Mysore Government Central Press, Bangalore, 1904, p. 51, Ins. No. Tp. 44.
41. S. Settar and M.M. Kalburgi, *op.cit.*, p. 33.
42. K. Veluthat, 'The Nature and Significance of the Institution of Velevalli in Karnataka in Historical Perspective (A.D. 800-1300),' in *Proceedings of Indian History Congress*. Vol. 51, 1990, pp. 151-159.
43. C.R. Krishnamacharlu (ed.), *Bombay-Karnatak Inscriptions*, Vol. I, Part I, Government Press, Madras, 1940, Ins. No.11.
44. B.L. Rice, 1902. *op.cit.*, No. Bl. 112.
45. A.V. Narasimhamurthy, *Epigraphia Carnatica*, Vol. IX, *Bombay-Karnatak Inscriptions*, Vol. I, 1990, p. 9. Ins. No. Bl. 300.
46. *S.I.I.*, Vol. IX, Part I, No. 61, pp. 34-35.
47. B.L. Rice, *Epigraphia Carnatica, Vol. XI: Inscriptions in Chitaldoorg District*. Mysore Government Central Press, Bangalore, 1903, pp. 72-73. Ins. No. 115.
48. B.L. Rice, *Epigraphia Carnatica, Vol. VI. Inscriptions in the Kadur District*. Mysore Government Central Press, Bangalore, 1901, p. 7. Ins. No. 34.
49. *Ibid.*, p. 105, Ins. No. Md. 10.
50. *Ibid.*, p. 111, Ins. Nos. Md. 70 and 72.
51. A.S. Altekar, *op.cit.*, p. 252.
52. *Ibid.*
53. B.R. Gopal (ed.), *Epigraphia Carnatica, Vol. VIII. Hassan District*, Revised Edition, Institute of Kannada Studies, University of Mysore, Mysore, 1984, p. 8. Ins. No. Ag. 1.
54. B.L. Rice, 1901. *op.cit.*, p. 39. Ins. No. 44.
55. M.D. Nagaraju, 'Two Hero Stone Inscriptions from Guñjāvaṭṭi' in *Studies in Indian Epigraphy*, Vol. XLIV, 2019, pp. 107-08.
56. B.L. Rice. 1904. *op.cit.*, p. 49. Ins. No. Tp. 39.
57. R.S. Panchmukhi (ed.), *Karnatak Inscriptions, Vol. III. Part I. Āḷupas*. Dharwar: Kannada Research Institute, 1953, Ins. No. 13, pp. 37-39.
58. F. Kielhorn, 'A Stone Inscription from Kudarkot (Gavidhumat),' in *Epigraphia Indica*. Vol. I, Burgess, J.A.S. (ed.), Tracker & Co., Bombay, 1892, pp. 179-183.
59. N. Vanamamalai, "Hero Stone Worship in Ancient South India," in *Social Scientist*. Vol. 3 (10), 1975, pp. 40-46.

60. Priya Thakur, 'Sculptural Reliefs on Hero Stones reflecting Śaiva Iconography in Tumkur Region, Karnataka' in S.R. Bandyopadhyay and S.M. Adhikari (eds.), Śaiva Iconography: A Facet on Indian Art and Culture, Sagnik Books, Kolkata, 2018, pp. 66-72.
61. R.R. Hegde and P. Rao, 'Hero Stones in Medieval Karnataka and Changing Perception of After Life,' in *Kalā, The Journal of Indian Art History Congress*, Vol. XXIV, 2018, p. 95.
62. R. Sheshashastri, *Karnatakada Vīragallugalu*, Kannada Sahitya Parishat, Bangalore, 2004, p. 374.
63. K.A.N. Sastri, *Epigraphia Carnatica Vol. XVI: Supplementary Inscriptions in the Tumkur District*, Government Press, Mysore, 1955, Ins. Nos. Ck 67 and Ck 78.
64. *S.I.I.*, Vol. IX, Part I, p. 373. Ins. No. 354.
65. A.V. Narasimhamurthy, *Epigraphia Carnatica.* Vol IX. *Bombay-Karnatak Inscriptions*, Vol. I., 1990, Ins. No. Bl. 530.
66. M. Adiga, 2006, *op.cit.*, p. 182.

Bibliography

Abraham, M. 1988. *Two Medieval Merchant Guilds of South India.* Delhi: Manohar Publishers.

Adiga, M. 2006. *The Making of Southern Karnataka: Society, Polity and Culture in the Early Medieval Period.* Delhi: Orient Black Swan Publishers.

Altekar, A.S. 1934. *The Rāshṭrakūṭas and their Times.* Poona Oriental Series No. 36. Poona: Oriental Book Agency.

Belli, M. 2014. 'Between Heaven and Hell: Salvation, Damnation, and Memorialization in the Arts of Death,' in *Ars Orientalis: The Arts of Death in Asia.* Vol. 44. 7-16.

Fleet, J.F. 1900-01. 'Three Western Ganga records in the Mysore Government Museum,' in *Epigraphia Indica*, Vol. VI, Hultzsch, E.(Ed.). Education Society's Press: Bombay. pp. 40-57.

Gopal, B.R. (ed.).1972. *Epigraphia Carnatica. Vol. I.* Revised Edition. Mysore: Institute of Kannada Studies, University of Mysore.

Gopal, B.R. (ed.) 1974. *Epigraphia Carnatica, Vol. III. Mysore District (Gundlupete, Nanjanagud and Heggadadevanakote taluks).* Revised Edition. Institute of Kannada Studies: University of Mysore.

Gopal, B.R. (ed.) 1975. *Epigraphia Carnatica. Mysore District (Chamarajanagar, Yalandur, Kollegal, Hunsur and Piriyapattana taluks). Vol. IV.* Revised Edition. Mysore: Institute of Kannada Studies, University of Mysore.

Gopal, B.R. (ed.) 1984. *Epigraphia Carnatica. Vol. VIII. Hassan District.* Revised Edition. Mysore: Institute of Kannada Studies, University of Mysore.

Hall, K.R. 1980. *Trade and Statecraft in the age of the Colas*. Delhi: Abhinav Prakashan.

Hegde, R.R. and Rao, P. 2018. 'Hero Stones in Medieval Karnataka and Changing Perception of After Life,' in *Kalā, The Journal of Indian Art History Congress*. Vol. XXIV. 92-99.

Hultzsch, E. 1981 (Reprint). 'Three Memorial Stones,' in *Epigraphia Indica, Vol. VII*. Hultzsch, E. (Ed.) 1902-03. New Delhi: DGASI. pp. 22-25.

Kielhorn, F. 1892. 'A stone Inscription from Kudarkot (Gavidhumat),' in *Epigraphia Indica. Vol. I*. Burgess, J.A.S. (Ed.) Bombay: Tracker & Co., pp. 179-183.

Krishnamacharlu, C.R. (Ed.) 1940. *Bombay-Karnatak Inscriptions, Vol. I*. Part I. Madras: Government Press.

Krishnappa, M.V. 1994. *Social and Economical Conditions of Karnataka, AD 400-1000*. Prasaranga: University of Mysore.

Kuppuswamy, G.R. 1982. 'Economic Factors Governing the Memorial Stones in Karnataka' in Sontheimer, G.H. and Settar S. (eds.). *Memorial Stones: A Study of their Origin, Significance and Variety*. Dharwad: Institute of Indian Art History. Karnatak University. 307-312.

Morrison, K.D. 1997. 'Commerce and Culture in South Asia: Perspectives from Archaeology and History,' in *Annual Review of Anthropology*. Vol. 26. pp. 87-108.

Nagaraju, D.M. 2019. 'Two Hero Stone Inscriptions from Guñjāvaṭṭi' in *Studies in Indian Epigraphy*. Vol. XLIV. 107-08.

Narasimhamurthy, A.V. 1990. *Epigraphia Carnatica*. Vol IX. *Bombay-Karnatak Inscriptions, Vol. I*. Mysore: Prasaranga, University of Mysore.

Panchmukhi, R.S. (ed.). 1953. *Karnatak Inscriptions, Vol. III. Part I. Āḷupas*. Dharwar: Kannada Research Institute.

Rajan, K. 2019. *Churning the Ocean: Maritime Trade of Early Historic Peninsular India*. Thanjavur: Manoo Pathippakam.

Rice, B.L. 1901. *Epigraphia Carnatica. Vol. VI. Inscriptions in the Kadur District*. Bangalore: Mysore Government Central Press.

Rice, B.L. 1902. *Epigraphia Carnatica. Vol. V: Inscriptions in Hassan District*. Mangalore: Basel Mission Press.

Rice, B.L. 1903. *Epigraphia Carnatica. Vol. XI: Inscriptions in Chitaldoorg District*. Bangalore: Mysore Government Central Press.

Rice, B.L. 1904a. *Epigraphia Carnatica . Vol. VIII. Inscriptions in the Shimoga District. Part II*. Bangalore: Mysore Government Central Press.

Rice, B.L. 1904b. *Epigraphia Carnatica. Vol. XII. Inscriptions in the Tumkur District*. Bangalore: Mysore Government Central Press.

Rice, B.L. 1905. *Epigraphia Carnatica* Vol. IX. Inscriptions in the Bangalore District. Bangalore: Mysore Government Central Press.

Rice, B.L. 1909. *Mysore and Coorg from the Inscriptions*. London: Archibald Constable & Co.

Sastri, K.A.N. 1955. *Epigraphia Carnatica Vol. XVI: Supplementary Inscriptions in the Tumkur District*. Mysore: Government Press.

Settar, S. and Kalburgi, M.M. 1982. 'The Hero Cult: A Study of Kannada Literature from 9th to 13th century,' in Sontheimer, G.H. and Settar S. (Eds). *Memorial Stones: A Study of their Origin, Significance and Variety*. Dharwad: Institute of Indian Art History, Karnatak University. 17-36.

Shama Sastry, R. (Ed.) 1939. *South Indian Inscriptions (Texts), Kannada Inscriptions from the Madras Presidency*. Vol. IX-Part-I, Government Press: Madras.

Sharma, T.S. 2017. *Dialogics of Cultures in Ancient Indian Literatures*. Shimla: Indian Institute of Advanced Studies.

Sheshashastri, R. 2004. *Karnatakada Vīragallugalu*. Bangalore: Kannada Sahitya Parishat.

Subbarayalu, Y. and Shanmugam. P. 2002. 'Texts of Select Inscriptions of the Trade Guilds.' In *Ancient and Medieval Commercial Activities in the Indian Ocean: Testimony of Inscriptions and Ceramic-Shreds*, Karashima, N. (Ed.) Tokyo: Taisho University.

Thakur, P. 2018. 'Sculptural Reliefs on Hero Stones reflecting Śaiva Iconography in Tumkur Region, Karnataka' in *Śaiva Iconography: A Facet on Indian Art and Culture.* Bandyopadhyay, S.R. and Adhikari, S.M. (Eds.) Sagnik Books: Kolkata. pp. 66-72.

Thapliyal, U.P. 1975. 'Military Honours and Awards in Ancient India.' In *Annals of the Bhandarkar Oriental Research Institute*. Vo. 56 (1/4). pp. 236-240.

Vanamamalai, N. 1975. 'Herostone Worship in Ancient South India,' in *Social Scientist*. Vol. 3 (10). pp. 40-46.

Veluthat, K. 1990. 'The Nature and Significance of the Institution of Velevalli in Karnataka in Historical Perspective (A.D. 800-1300),' in *Proceedings of Indian History Congress*. Vol. 51. 151-159.

Vidyarnava, S.C. (tr.) 1918. *Yajnavalkya Smriti with the Commentary of Vijnanśvara called the Mitaksara. Book I: The Āchāra Adhyāya*. Allahabad: The Panini Office, Bhuvaneswari Asrama.

14

Bhakti Movement in Early Medieval South India – A Historiographical Study

S. Jeevanandam

Religion is one of the important cultural elements in the human world. It used to function as an ideological apparatus to fulfill the requirements of the existing social order. The ideological and structural changes in the religious institution witnessed the social transformation and it reflected in the transformation of the society from ancient to medieval and to modern. Therefore, historians are always shown their special interest in studying religion and its institution to understand the social process. In this context, studying the religious history of medieval South India is an important academic engagement in a better understanding of medieval Indian society. The various historical schools such as Orientalist, Nationalist, Communalist, Marxist, *Annales*, Subaltern, and Gender tried to approach the *bhakti* movement accordingly. This paper is trying to understand the different concepts of *bhakti* in early medieval south Indian society on the basis of the various historiographical traditions.

In general, the *bhakti* movement is considered as a reformative movement. The movement made a great impact in shaping the Indian society, culture, religion, and literature. The movement was a product of a transitional society when a number of changes were taking place in the economic, social and political spheres. It functions as an ideological tool for social construction. In medieval India, the *bhakti* movement played an important role in the social formation. The ideology of *bhakti* influenced society and it's reflected in philosophy, kingship, kinship, ritual, poetry, art, etc. However, the *bhakti* movement was popularly identified as a religious phenomenon. In this context, this particular paper is trying to comprehend the basic ideas of the medieval *bhakti* tradition of *Tamilakam*.

The *Bhakti* Movement

The *bhakti* movement of medieval south India was popular and widespread between the sixth to the tenth century C.E. It witnessed the socio-economic and cultural transition of society. The revival of the Brahmanism in the Indian subcontinent was deeply rooted in the concepts of *bhakti* ideology. *Bhakti* became an important cultural element that could integrate the different faiths and crystalise the caste structure. K.A. Nilakanta Sastri, the prominent historian of medieval India, stated *bhakti* as a synthesis movement that could synthesis the so-called Great and Little Tradition.[1] The prominent orientalist ideologue, Max Muller, mentioned that henotheism was mingled with *bhakti* to produce sectarianism of a produced character; this, in turn, was followed by efforts to blunt the edge of sectarian animosities and effect conciliation among the sects.[2]

Orientalist and their *Bhakti* Questions

European orientalism created a general interest for an intensive study of the ancient past and it was reflected in the historiography of India. Initially, scholars and audiences were all Europeans.[3] The orientalist reconstructed the glory of ancient Indian civilisation in the ancient past. The Royal Asiatic Society (1784) kindled the thirst for Indian antiquity and language. They had a special interest in Indian religion. H.H. Wilson and Henry Thomas Colebrooke were credited with the first discussions of *bhakti* in Western scholarship.[4] H.H. Wilson discussed the religious sect of medieval Indian history and his work was published in *Asiatic Researches Serials* between 1814 and 1815, and later it was published as a book, *Religious Sects of the Hindus* (1846).[5]

Europeans came to India with a notion of religious world history derived from the Bible.[6] Orientalist visualised the *bhakti* as a monotheistic movement. H.H. Wilson, M. Monier-Williams, and G.A. Grierson referred *bhakti* as a monotheistic reform movement; the first real instance of monotheism in India.[7] Max Muller linked the *Bhagavad*

Gita with one of the Aramaic religions, Christianity. Albrecht Weber, a scholar of Sanskrit, theorised the origin of *bhakti* from contact between Christians and 'Hindus' in the remote historical past.[8] Franz Lorinser compared the Brahmanical text, *Bhagavad Gita* with the New Testament, the final book of the Christian.[9] Max Muller believed *bhakti* as a reform movement, which criticised the caste structure. In the meantime, the orientalist referred *bhakti* saints as a reformer and compared the sixteenth-century *bhakti* saints, Chaitanya with the Martin Luther King of Medieval Europe.[10]

Vaishnavite Origin of *Bhakti*

The number of orientalist, nationalist and communalist historians positioned the Vedic origin of *bhakti*. In general, orientalist constructed the origin of *bhakti* with Vaishnava tradition. Max Muller was identified the Vedas as the foundation of India's 'true' religion.[11] He considered *bhakti* as a monotheistic tradition and centered on the Vaishnavite pantheon Vishnu, who was projected as a "God of love".[12] R.G. Bhandarkar, a professor of Sanskrit, traced the indigenous developments of Vaishnava religiosity. He discussed the antiquity of Krishna worship and Vaishnavism.[13] Norman Culter, a scholar of Tamil poetry and religion, mentioned the beginning of the word *bhakti* from Sanskrit root, *bhaj* and the conception was from the text, *Bhagavad Gita*.[14] R. Nagaswami, a historian, positioned Tamil devotionalism with the Vedic roots.[15]

The Madras School of Orientalism

There was a significant ideological difference consolidate gradually among the orientalist school. The early historians and Indologists were much concentrated on North India, above the region of Deccan. There was less importance paid by the historian to South India. The history of South India remained as periphery to the writing of Indian history in the twentieth century. V.A. Smith's *Oxford History of India* gave an outlook for the study of peninsular history and religious movement of the south.[16] In general, Colin Mackenzie's approach to the South Indian society became the starting point for the South Indian historical writings. After that, there was gradual attention given to the history of South India. The establishment of the Archeological Survey of Madras (1874) and the appointment of Hultzsch as epigraphist in 1886 marked a new epoch in the field of South Indian Archaeology.

In the meantime, Robert Sewell made a comprehensive list of the antiquities of provinces in 1882. Burgess and Natesa Sastri brought out the volumes of Tamil and Sanskrit inscriptions. Sir Walter Elliot produced his first account of South Indian coins. These strengthened the curiosity of the later South Indian historians. They tried to understand the indigenous nature of Tamil devotionalism, which was different from the Vedic origin. Interestingly, R.G. Bhandarkar established the theme of *bhakti* with the non-Brahman origin and delinked the Brahmanic influences.[17] According to him, the founder of the revival movement was a non-Brahmin called, Krishna, the prominent Vaishnava deity. The Brahmanic texts mentioned Krishna from a *kshatriya varna* (a non-Brahmin and belonged to the warrior caste).[18] R.C. Zaehner, a notable Indologist, also stressed the Dravidian origin of the *bhakti* movement.[19]

Marxist Approaches of *Bhakti*

The dominance of the Marxist perspective on the ancient Indian past became popular from the 1960s. The Marxist historians viewed religion, religious centers, and sectarian movement in the socio-economic context. They established *bhakti* as an ideology of submission as well as dissent.[20] D.D. Kosambi was the first scholar to establish the link between *bhakti* and feudalism. Later, his idea was elaborated and carried by R.S. Sharma. A similar approach was carried out by various scholars such as David Ludden, James Heitzman, Noboru Karashima, David N. Lorenzen, R. Champakalakshmi, N. Vanamamalai, K. Sivathamby, M.G.S. Narayanan, Rajan Gurukkal and Kesavan Veluthat.

The *bhakti* movement and the temple institution bridged social and cultural stress points in earlier centuries. The prevailing social inequalities on the land structure, especially the growing preponderance of *brahmadeyas*[21] and military tenures characterised the early medieval south Indian society as feudal[22] and the concept of *bhakti* and its movement provided an ideological base for the society. The devotional movement culminated in the process of the disintegration of tribal society and its organisation as a caste society. George W. Spencer stated that building a great temple has often served as the catalyst for the self-sustaining growth of a thriving religious and economic center.[23] The most significant religious development in medieval South India was the development of *bhakti* devotionalism and the infusion of popular Hinduism with the ideal of salvation through intense devotion to a personal deity.[24]

Noboru Karashima[25] and James Heitzman[26] studied the Chola Empire at a micro-level. They detailed the rise of the temples, distribution of the temples, socio-economic functions of the temples, the administration of Cholas, and the distribution of land and its classification. The Japanese scholar, Karashima became the first historian of South India to make an extensive use of computers and statistical methods in understanding the medieval south Indian society. He studied the inscriptions of Chola, Pandya and Vijayanagar periods to gauge the extent of the socio-economic changes in the South Indian region.[27] He detailed the Brahmanical influence over the medieval society and the power structure of Cholas and *brahmadeya* lands. He highlighted the establishment of *brahmadeya* land on the Kaveri valley under the royal order.

James Heitzman reopened the complex study of the Chola state after the publication of Burton Stein's book, *Peasant State and Society in Medieval South India*. He examined the urban culture, transactional networks, social relatives that grew up around medieval temples, which increasingly became the recipients of property and defrayed tax revenue from royal agents and local notables seeking afflictions with Chola court through a donatives rural culture. He argued that the temples provided the political and ritual culture which held together with the assemblages, the local and intermediate lords under Chola's legendary.

The earlier form of mystical *bhakti* was transformed into the temple centred religion under the imperial Cholas.[28] The royal patronage towards the *bhakti* poems propagated *bhakti* ideology in the state. The sacred and secular margin of state was narrow down. The later Chola Empire, Kulottunga II, patronage the Cekkilar in the composition of *Periyapuranam*. It inculcated the prominent Chola kings such as Kochchengannan and Vijayalaya as Nayanmars. The images of kings and queens were installed in the temple precincts. Kundavai, the sister of Rajaraja Chola I, installed the images of her parents as *tirumeni* (sacred body) in the temple. It indicated the views of sacred sovereignty that were comparable to Kushana notions of sacred kingship.[29]

R. Champakalakshmi dealt with the mingling of several factors of economic, political, and ideological in varying degrees of importance in early medieval urban process between the period of 600 C.E. and 1300 C.E. She surveyed the background of both history and literature of Vaishnavism in Tamil county from 300 B.C.E. onwards. She studied *Sangam* religious system and Vaishnava pantheon and its theistic developments. She compared the ancient Mayon with Vishnu. She pointed out that the merging point of the entire Vaishnavite cult in the second century B.C.E.[30] and the evolution of the concepts of ten avatars was between fourth and fifth century C.E. She vividly discussed the role of Alvars and their role in process of popularisation of Vaishnavite ideology in Tamil country and she quoted "Alvars as pearl divers in the ocean of divine qualities".[31]

M.G.S. Narayanan[32] and Kesavan Veluthat[33] discussed the sectarian aspects of the movement with the developments in the field of economy, society, and polity. They detailed how these religious changes to consolidate the new social and political order on the early medieval South Indian society. They stressed the importance of the *bhakti* religion and how it supported the consolidation of the new monarchy. Kesavan Veluthat demonstrated the direct linkages of the *bhakti* movement with the expansion of agricultural development and the formation of the state based on it.[34]

Burton Stein analyzed the peasant state, religion, and society in medieval South India.[35] He studied the South Indian agrarian system introduced a conceptual model of the medieval South Indian state, namely, a segmentary state.[36] He discussed the economic functions of temples and its legacy to agricultural development and its socio-economic impact on society. He visualised that the intensive agricultural development of the temple was seen to have had a central place in the dominantly agrarian economy of South India.[37] Stein further analyzed the social mobility of medieval South Indian sects. His works dealt with the incorporation of the so-called *sutra* function areas into the important Sri Vaishnava temples of Srirangam in *Tamilakam* and Tirupathi in the Telugu region beginning with the reforms of Ramanuja and subsequent exclusion of the same functionaries from there temples in the later period.

The Marxist historians discussed the social, political, religious and economic conditions of medieval South India. They did not give much attention to the distribution of religious centers of medieval Tamil country. Scholars such as Burton Stein, Noboru Karashima, James Heitzman and few others were attempted to discuss on the medieval temples and its economic impact. However, their study did not detail or rationalise the establishment of religious networks of the medieval world. George W. Spencer[38] studied the sacred geography of the medieval Tamil country. His work, *The Sacred Geography of the Tamil Shaivite Hymns* was exclusively studied the distribution of the Saivite centers on the basis of the *Tevaram* hymns.

Gender questions on *bhakti*

In general, religion was used to retain the patriarchal structure in society. The gender historians perceived the role of the women in the *bhakti* movement. They believed that the medieval *bhakti* movement was helped in the consolidation of the Brahmanical superiority and patriarchal values in society.[39] Vijaya Ramaswamy stated that Brahmin dominance and *Sudra* subordination as also the inbuilt gender inequality within a patriarchal structure of medieval South India.[40] Ironically, religion is considered as space for women to express her emotion relatively with other social institution and it created an alternate space for them.[41]

The *Bhakti* movement also opened the space for women.[42] Religious space was one of the spaces available to women in medieval times. Many women embraced *bhakti* and it provided them the space to define their own truths in voices that revision society, polity, relationships, and religions.[43] According to Rekha Pande, through the concept of *bhakti* women could challenge patriarchy and the mortal man to whom they were tied in a relationship of marriage by extending the definition of love to God and understanding his relationship with them in terms of a lover, a wife, a mistress, a friend, and a servant.

Vijaya Ramaswamy[44] also analyzed the different sectarian movements of South India and women in the South Indian religious system. She gave more attention to gender practices of the respective age and focused the range of writings of women poets and saints and through this array. Her work, *Walking Naked: Women, Society, Spirituality in South India*, analyzed women's spirituality, social, structural, and historical conditions under which it developed, and its nature and character as illustrated by the compositions. She studied these movements and women's lives in larger cultural, socio-economic, and political contexts, literary sources were remarkable. She was commendable in using the epics and of narratives and treatises. Vijaya Ramaswamy mentioned that *bhakti* movement as more feminine in nature rather than the masculine.[45] The central path of *bhakti* was love and union and separation are the central emotion in the literature.

Literary movement

The *bhakti* movement was initially identified as a literary movement. So many veterans worked with the hymns of Saivite and Vaishnavite sects. Kamil Zvelebil, A.K. Ramanujan, Indira Viswanathan Peterson, F. Kingley, and G.P. Philips were the most prominent among them.

`Kamil Zvelebil wrote *The Smile of Murugan* [46] in 1973. The book is a fragmentary collection of essays. It discussed the ancient and medieval Tamil society based on historical and sociological approaches. Kamil highlighted the unique features of Tamil and declared that the only Indian literature to spring up entirely independent from Sanskrit influences. In it, he discussed the greatness of saints of Saivite cult and the impact of Saivism on the medieval period. A.K. Ramanujan translated the medieval *bhakti* literature.[47] Indira Viswanathan Peterson's translated work titled 'Poems to Siva', [48] which is a collection of translated hymns of *Tevaram*. The work not only limited itself with translations but also made a clear survey of the religious history of Saivism and traced the lineage of *Tevaram* hymns on the basis of the account of Cekkilar's *Periyapuranam*. She compared the hymns of *Tevaram* with the earlier *puram* (outer world) poems and pointed out that the Tamil *Bhakti* cult was a model for the regional *bhakti* cult.[49] She explained things that were initiated by the hymns of Saivism and Vaishnavism. She considered the south Indian *bhakti* was the first literary expression of the emotional *bhakti* cult in India. The work studied the shrines where saints travelled and associated with, and it accounted for 274 shrines of Saivite sect which were mentioned in *Tevaram*. The work also highlighted that 269 shrines were situated in South India alone.

Conclusion

The popular *bhakti* movement of medieval south India received the academic attention. The nationalist historians considered *bhakti* as a synthesis movement, which synthesis the so-called Great and Little Tradition. The orientalist perceived *bhakti* as a monotheistic reform movement and largely placed the origin of the *bhakti* with Vaishnavism. There was a significant ideological difference consolidated gradually among the orientalist school. The south centric Madras School of Orientalism tried to understand the indigenous nature of Tamil devotionalism. The Marxist established *bhakti* as an ideology of submission as well as dissent in the feudal structures. The gender historians perceived the role of the women within the *bhakti* movement. They believed that the medieval *bhakti* movement helped in the consolidation of the Brahmanical patriarchy in society.

Notes and References

1. K.A. Nilakanta Sastri, *Development of Religion in South India*, Orient Longmans, Bombay, 1963, p. 9.
2. *Ibid*., (the quote was referred in *Development of Religion in South India* of K.A. Nilakanta Sastri).

3. S.P. Gupta, K.N. Dikshit and K.S. Ramachandran (eds.), *Some Aspects of India's History and Culture*, Crown Publishers, Madras, 1990.
4. Karen Pechilis Prentiss, *The Embodiment of Bhakti*, Oxford University Press, New York, 1999, p. 214.
5. N.N. Bhattacharya, *Indian Religious Historiography*, Munshiram Manoharlal Publishers, New Delhi, 1996, p. 241.
6. Leslie C. Orr, "Orientalists, Missionaries, and Jains: The South Indian Story", in Thomas R. Trautmann (ed.), *The Madras School of Orientalism: Producing Knowledge in Colonial South India*, Oxford University Press, New Delhi, 2009, p. 263.
7. Karen Pechilis Prentiss, *op.cit.*, p. 3.
8. Albrecht Weber, "An Investigation into the Origin of the Festival of Krishnajanmashtami." *The Indian Antiquary* 3 (1874), pp. 21-25; 47-52; 6 (1877), pp. 161-180, 281-301, 349-54.
9. M.F. Lorinser, "An Investigation into the Origin of the Festival of Krishnajanmashtami." *The Indian Antiquary* 2 (1873), pp. 283-296.
10. The quote was referred to in Karen Pechilis Prentiss, *op.cit.*, p. 3.
11. Max Muller, *A History of Ancient Sanskrit Literature: So Far as it Illustrates the Primitive Religion of the Brahmans*. Edinburgh: Williams and Norgate, 1860.
12. *Ibid*.
13. R.G. Bhandarkar, "Allusions to Krishna in Patanjali's Mahabhashya". *Indian Antiquary* 3 (1874), pp.14-16.
14. Norman Culter, *Songs of Experience: The Poetics of Tamil Devotional*, Indiana University Press, Bloomington, 1987, p. 1.
15. R. Nagaswami, *Art and Culture of Tamil Nadu*, Sundeep Prakashan, Delhi, 1980.
16. V.A. Smith, *The Oxford History of India*. Oxford University Press, Delhi, 1958.
17. R.G. Bhandarkar, "Basis of Theism, and its Relation to the So-called Revealed Religions", in Narayan Bapuji Utgikar (ed.), *Collected Works of Sir R.G. Bhandarkar*, Vol. II, Bhandarkar Oriental Research Institute, Poona, 1928, pp. 603-616.
18. R.G. Bhandarkar, "Allusions to Krishna in Patanjali's Mahabhashya", *Indian Antiquary* 3 (1874), pp. 14-16.
19. R.C. Zaehner, *Hinduism*, Oxford University Press, New York, 1966, pp. 125-146.
20. Rekha Pande, "The Bhakti Movement- A Historiographical Critique". *Journal of Historical Research*, Vol.10 (March, 2000), pp. 49-60.
21. *Brahmadeyas* were the lands, which donated to Brahmins in medieval South India.
22. R.N. Nandi, "Feudalism in South India", in *Social Science Probings*, People's Publishing House, New Delhi, 1984, pp. 33-59.

23. George W Spencer, "Religious Networks and Royal Influence in Eleventh Century South India", *Journal of the Economic and Social History of the Orient* 12, no. 1. (January, 1969), p. 43.
24. *Ibid*., p. 46.
25. Noboru Karashima, *South Indian History and Society: Studies form Inscriptions AD 850- 1800*, Oxford University Press, Delhi, 1984.
26. James Heitzman, *Gifts of Power: Lordship in an Early Modern State*, Oxford University Press, Delhi, 1997.
27. Noboru Karashima, *op.cit*., p. 17.
28. R. Champakalakshmi, *Trade, Ideology, and Urbanization: South India 300 B.C. to A.D. 1300*, Oxford University Press, Delhi, 1996.
29. Sita Anantha Raman, "Review on Trade, Ideology, and Urbanization: South India 300 B.C. to A.D. 1300 by R. Champakalakshmi". *The Journal of Asian Studies* 62, no. 1. (February, 2003), p. 308.
30. R. Champakalakshmi, *Vaishnava Iconography in the Country*, Orient Longman Limited, New Delhi, 1981, p. 12.
31. *Ibid*.
32. M.G.S. Narayanan, "The Role of Peasants in the Early History of Tamilakam in South India." *Social Scientist*, Vol. 16, no. 9. (September, 1988), pp. 17-34.
33. Kesavan Veluthat, "Religion, Symbols in Political Legitimating: The Case of Early Medieval South India." *Social Scientist*, Vol. 21, no. 1/2. (January-February, 1983), pp. 23-33.
34. Kesavan Veluthat, *The Early Medieval in South India*, Oxford University Press, New Delhi, 2009, p. 66.
35. Burton Stein, *Peasant State and Society in Medieval South India*, Oxford University Press, New Delhi, 1980.
36. *Ibid*., p. 260.
37. Burton Stein, "The Economic Function of a Medieval South Indian Temple", *The Journal of Asian Studies*, Vol. 19, no. 2. (February, 1960), p. 163.
38. George W. Spencer, "The Sacred Geography of the Tamil Saiva Hymns", *Numen* 17, fasc. 3. (December, 1970), pp. 232- 244.
39. Vijaya Ramaswamy, *Divinity and Deviance: Women in Virasaivism*, Oxford University Press, Delhi, 1996, pp. 1, 4.
40. *Ibid*.
41. Rekha Pande, *Divine Sounds from the Heart- Singing Unfettered in their Own Voices: The Bhakti Movement and its Women Saints (12th to 17th Century)*, Cambridge Scholars Publishing, Tyne, 2010, p. 8.
42. *Ibid*., p. 8.
43. *Ibid*., p. 2.

44. Vijaya Ramaswamy, *Walking Naked: Women, Society, Spirituality in South India*, Indian Institute of Advanced Study, Shimla, 1997.
45. Vijaya Ramaswamy, *Divinity and Deviance: Women in Virasaivism*, p. 28.
46. Kamil Zvelebil, *The Smile of Murugan: On Tamil Literature of South India*, E.J. Brill, Leiden, 1973.
47. A.K. Ramanujan (trans.), *Speaking of Siva*, Penguin Books Ltd, Middlesex, 1973 (reprint 1985).
48. Indira Viswanathan Peterson, *Poems to Siva: the Hymns of Tamil Saints*, Motilal Banarsidass Publication, Delhi, 1989.
49. *Ibid.*, p.10.

Bibliography

Albrecht Weber, "An Investigation into the Origin of the Festival of Krishnajanmashtami." *The Indian Antiquary* 3 (1874); 6 (1877).

Bhandarkar, R.G., "Allusions to Krishna in Patanjali's Mahabhashya". *Indian Antiquary* 3 (1874).

---------------, "Basis of Theism, and its Relation to the So-called Revealed Religions", in Narayan Bapuji Utgikar (ed.), *Collected Works of Sir R.G. Bhandarkar*, Vol. II, Bhandarkar Oriental Research Institute, Poona, 1928.

Bhattacharya, N.N., *Indian Religious Historiography*, Munshiram Manoharlal Publishers, New Delhi, 1996.

Burton Stein, "The Economic Function of a Medieval South Indian Temple", *The Journal of Asian Studies*, Vol. 19, no. 2. (February, 1960).

--------------, *Peasant State and Society in Medieval South India*, Oxford University Press, New Delhi, 1980.

Champakalakshmi, R., *Trade, Ideology, and Urbanization: South India 300 B.C. to A.D. 1300*, Oxford University Press, Delhi, 1996.

----------------, *Vaishnava Iconography in the Country*, Orient Longman Limited, New Delhi, 1981.

George W Spencer, "Religious Networks and Royal Influence in Eleventh Century South India", *Journal of the Economic and Social History of the Orient* 12, no. 1. (January, 1969).

----------------, "The Sacred Geography of the Tamil Saiva Hymns", *Numen* 17, fasc. 3. (December, 1970).

Gupta, S.P., K.N. Dikshit and K.S. Ramachandran (eds.), *Some Aspects of India's History and Culture*, Crown Publishers, Madras, 1990.

Indira Viswanathan Peterson, *Poems to Siva: the Hymns of Tamil Saints*, Motilal Banarsidass Publication, Delhi, 1989.

James Heitzman, *Gifts of Power: Lordship in an Early Modern State*, Oxford University Press, Delhi, 1997.

Kamil Zvelebil, *The Smile of Murugan: On Tamil Literature of South India*, E.J. Brill, Leiden, 1973.

Karen Pechilis Prentiss, *The Embodiment of Bhakti*, Oxford University Press, New York, 1999.

Kesavan Veluthat, "Religion, Symbols in Political Legitimating: The Case of Early Medieval South India." *Social Scientist*, Vol. 21, no. 1/2. (January-February, 1983).

----------------, *The Early Medieval in South India*, Oxford University Press, New Delhi, 2009.

Leslie C. Orr, "Orientalists, Missionaries, and Jains: The South Indian Story", in Thomas R. Trautmann (ed.), *The Madras School of Orientalism: Producing Knowledge in Colonial South* India, Oxford University Press, New Delhi, 2009.

Lorinser, M.F., "An Investigation into the Origin of the Festival of Krishnajanmashtami." *The Indian Antiquary* 2 (1873).

Max Muller, *A History of Ancient Sanskrit Literature: So Far as it Illustrates the Primitive Religion of the Brahmans.* Edinburgh: Williams and Norgate, 1860.

Nagaswami, R., *Art and Culture of Tamil Nadu*, Sundeep Prakashan, Delhi, 1980.

Nandi, R.N., "Feudalism in South India", in *Social Science Probings*, People's Publishing House, New Delhi, 1984.

Narayanan, M.G.S., "The Role of Peasants in the Early History of Tamilakam in South India." *Social Scientist*, Vol. 16, no. 9. (September, 1988).

Nilakanta Sastri, K.A., *Development of Religion in South India*, Orient Longmans, Bombay, 1963.

Noboru Karashima, *South Indian History and Society: Studies form Inscriptions AD 850- 1800*, Oxford University Press, Delhi, 1984.

Norman Culter, *Songs of Experience: The Poetics of Tamil Devotional*, Indiana University Press, Bloomington, 1987.

Ramanujan A.K. (trans.), *Speaking of Siva*, Penguin Books Ltd, Middlesex, 1973 (reprint 1985).

Rekha Pande, "The Bhakti Movement- A Historiographical Critique". *Journal of Historical Research*, Vol.10 (March, 2000).

---------------, *Divine Sounds from the Heart- Singing Unfettered in their Own Voices: The Bhakti Movement and its Women Saints (12th to 17th Century)*, Cambridge Scholars Publishing, Tyne, 2010.

Sita Anantha Raman, "Review on Trade, Ideology, and Urbanization: South India 300 B.C. to A.D. 1300 by R. Champakalakshmi". *The Journal of Asian Studies* 62, no. 1. (February, 2003).

Smith, V.A., *The Oxford History of India*. Oxford University Press, Delhi, 1958.

Vijaya Ramaswamy, *Divinity and Deviance: Women in Virasaivism*, Oxford University Press, Delhi, 1996.

------------------, *Walking Naked: Women, Society, Spirituality in South India*, Indian Institute of Advanced Study, Shimla, 1997.

Zaehner, R.C., *Hinduism*, Oxford University Press, New York, 1966.

15

Buddhist Monastic Orders and its Influence in Social and Cultural Life of People in Tamil Nadu

Palas Kumar Saha

"Sabbe satta sukhi hontu,
Sabbe hontu cha kheminos,
Sabbe Bhadrani Pussantu,
Ma kanchi Dukha magama"

"Let all being be happy, Let all beings live without fear, Let all being enjoy peace and happiness, and be free from all sorrows and troubles".

Social and cultural influence of Buddhism has a great value and significance in the recent context of national and International point of view. At the moment, the whole humankind is filled with deviations produced by political, economic, social, religious and racial reflection. There is no a single corner of the world today which is free from conflicts and disorder. Disharmony and unhappiness are ground of war and tension. The Buddhism has given a serious thought to the problem of social harmony and has made, in the past, a sincere effort to promote it through its numerous missionaries, monks, nuns and laymen. Buddhism covers about the entire humankind as well as pretty much all living creatures.

The present paper aims to discuss the Buddhist monastic orders and its influence in the social and cultural life of the people in Tamil Nadu. We saw the last glory of the Buddhism in India during early period and there was a total transformation in the social relations. Society is not only the caste system also the everyday life of the people. So keeping in mind the importance of the Buddhist structures from the cultural and social point of view an attempt has been made in this paper to study the impact of Buddhism in the social life of people. It is important to note that the social history of religious institution requires interdisciplinary approach to untiring the religious and social study of particular region and period. What was the role of kings, queens, householder, merchants, common people, and laymen in the monastery? And why the large number of Buddhist monastery became a great learning centre? What subjects were studied? What was the role of teachers and students in the monastic life has been discussed in the paper.

I

The 'Four Nobel Truth', 'The Eightfold Path' and the 'dependent origination' constitute the outstanding contribution of Buddhism. The *tri-ratnam* (*Buddha*, *Dharma* and *Sangha*) shows that the Buddha was greatest organiser, as he was the first to form the *Sangha* or the spiritual society. The Buddhism has a long history in Tamil Nadu. It has had indelible impact on the intellectual development and traditions. The Buddhism has contributed greatly to secular Tamil culture. If we compare to other regions of India there is comparatively less evidences on Buddhism in Tamil Nadu. Although it is proved that, in the northern regions many sacred ideologies such as Buddhism, Ajivikism, Brahmanism and Jainism associated with Indo-Aryan culture completed important part to the institutions of a society. The details about Buddhism in coastal Tamil Nadu could be obtained from the *Sangam* texts, mainly from the post-*Sangam* epics like *Silappadikaram* and the *Manimekalai*. Both the texts provide us with details indicating the coastal urban centres, had traits of Buddhism and the circumstances which prevailed in the post 1st century B.C.E. in Tamil Nadu.

The Buddhism not just attempted to realise a change in the human mind and soul through the proclaiming of its standards and its attention on harmony in human life, yet it likewise attempted to achieve social and political change in the society. The Buddhism whispered in an independent society where every man in the society has a say and equity in the status. It must be note that Buddhism essentially focussed on a basic existence with no materialistic needs. The followers of Buddha offered emphasis to the straightforward and honest life so as to accomplish enlightenment.[1] From the earliest starting point of the approach of Buddhism, it realised social, political and financial changes in the general public of that period. The social change was to be marked in all the spheres of the society, ranging from a small village to a kingdom. The political variations remember the progressions for the structures of the village organisations to the organisations of the kingdoms. In the monetary circle, it achieved changes in the horticultural examples. It focussed on agriculture which was considered as the backbone of the economy. The utilisation of iron was pervasive during this period which extraordinarily encouraged the agrarian movement.[2]

At various periods of its history and development, Buddhism achieved changes in the social, political, financial, linguistic and literary circles of the society. Both the *Hinayana* and *Mahayana* Buddhists attempted to acquire the change the general public in various manners in Tamil Nadu. According to L. Jayasuriya observation, Buddha's teachings influenced each segment of society whether it is social, political or economic.[3] The Buddhism had indicated remarkable endeavours so as to change social and geographical conditions of the people.

It is very important to discus about difference between the emergence of Jainism and Buddhism in the Tamil country. Their respective movement evidently seems to have followed similar paths into Tamil Nadu. From the sources coastal Kalinga, coastal Andhra, coastal Tamil Nadu and Sri Lanka evidently point to a coast allocation for Jainism which also give us information that these regions using the mercantile sea routes just as much as was in the case of Buddhism. In cooperation the groups had a base in southern Mysore or the ancient Vanavasa-Mahisamandala region. The sources points out that Jainism go through further south from Karnataka along the central hill range of south India and it seems that moved further south to the Madurai-Tirunelveli regions.[4] On the other hand, according to Hiuen-Tsang account and the studies on Buddhism in Kerala emphasis that Buddhism apparently had some base along the central hills of Tamil Nadu, especially in the areas through which trade linked Kerala and Tamil Nadu.[5]

The change in agrarian system, which generated the second phase of urbanisation (from 6th century BCE onwards) in India, a process which resulted in changes such as individual holding of land as against the communal holding of the later Vedic period. The emergence of *gahapati* as the head of a production unit viz. the household and recognition of the *gahapatis*, a rudimentary class, as a prosperous high-status group by the kings, Brahmins and others as reflected in the Buddhist and Jaina texts.[6] The Buddhism drew its nourishment not only from the patronage of kings (*ksatriyas*) and other high born (*ucca kula*) Brahmins but also from this new social category of *gahapatis* who serves as a link between the rural and emerging urban centre of the 6th century B.C.E. Artisans and craftsmen also supported the new religion but these social groups had a lower status, economic and not ritual, even in the Buddhist system of stratification.[7] From a *Srāmanic* religion of wandering ascetics or renounces seeking salvation, the needs of society and of the Buddhist *sangha*, transformed Buddhism itself into a religion of salvation for all (the *Mahayana*). Hence the role of the *gahapatis* was crucial to the growth of Buddhism and their continuing support essential for the *sangha's* pursuit of *nirvana* through *dāna* or gift to the *sangha*.

Accordingly support to the renouncers (*Srāmana*) became the innermost duty of the lay devotees (*Sravaka*). Work and growth of wealth for various socio-economic needs became equally vital. The assessment of enduring or settled organisation i.e. monastic establishments, located invariably in the border of towns/cities, was an important part of this process of change in the Buddhist organisation viz., the *sangha*, which was a associated institution, through which the orders and the laity were linked with each other as mutually supporting sections of a single community. Uma Chakravarti says that it was a change from *aranya-vasa* to *vassa-vasa* (*grama-vasa*) or retreats for rainy seasons and to the permanent *ashramas* outside important towns/cities, which were centres of social activity. The laity so became an important constituent of the Buddhist society and often exercised their influence upon the *sangha*.[8]

II

At the time of Asoka when he was became the emperor, he was responsible as a guardian of the people in the north as well as in the south up to Ceylon. Asoka in his edicts made the doctrines of the Buddha become popular. In addition to the edicts, Asoka sent missionaries to nine countries; Ceylon, Gandhara, Greece, Himavat, Aparantaka (the west coastal region), Mahisa (the central Narmada valley), Vanavasa (northern part of the Karnataka), Suvarna Bhūmi (lower Burma). Even Asoka sent his own son and daughter to spread Buddhism in the south India and Ceylon. Thus, the Buddhism came to south India through royal patronage.

From the 2nd century C.E. onward we find gradual spread of Buddhism in Tondaimandalam (Kanchipuram region) particularly, and during 250 C.E. till 550 C.E. marked as the Kalabhra period. During that period the Buddhism attained the peak period. Through the great stalwarts of both Theravada and Mahayana Buddhist monks like Buddhaghosa and Dinnaga crowding the *Viharas* of Kanchi particularly and visiting or living in the other parts of Tamil Nadu. The period between 250 C.E to 550 C.E. became the 'Golden age' of Tamil Buddhism.

Between the 6th to 11th centuries C.E. Vajrayana Buddhism became popular and during the 7th to 11th century C.E. was most glorious period for Buddhism, with the help of the Pallava and the Chola rulers. During this period, the merchant class and the Buddhist communities, who settled down from North India, Andhra, Ceylon, China and Srivijaya would have constructed many Buddhist shrines particularly for the Mahayana and Vajrayana deities. According to Suresh Pillai, these shrines might have been destroyed or modified or occupied by the Hindus when the Buddhists left Tamil Nadu or joined other faiths. According to excavations results at Kanchipuram and Kaveripattinam have proved the subsistence of the ancient *viharas* mentioned in the ancient literatures. Pallavanesvaram excavation at Kaveripattinam gives us evidences about the importance of Mahayana sect and the existence of a *vihara* of the sect. Further, K. Sundararajan's finding in the same site gives us a clear picture to accept the Vajrayana influence of Nagapattinam on this region.[9]

The inscriptions found in the Madurai caves at Arittapatti, Alakarmalai, etc., similar to those Sri Lanka inscriptions reveal the existence of the Theravada monks in the early periods.[10] According to K. Indrapala, the spread of Buddhism in Tamil Nadu and Ceylon as contemporaneous on the basis of Brahmi cave records of Alakarmalai in which *tavira* and *tavirai* (Buddhist Theravada monk and nun respectively) have been noticed.[11] Manjulika Swarup, the Ceylon monks were the first to introduce Buddhism to Tamil Nadu on the basic of the expression īlam (pertaining to Sri Lanka), the Brahmi inscription on the stone beds of the *Panchapāntava malai* approaching the Sri Lankan caves records.[12]

The *Mahavamsa* and *Dipavamsa* of Sri Lanka mention to the spread of Buddhism in Tamil Nadu during the 5th century C.E. Hiuen-Tsang speaks of the Buddhist ruins of Madurai and Kanchipuram. Due to the revival of Saivism and Vaishnavism, the Buddhism began to decline from the 7th century onwards and almost disappeared from the

14th century C.E. Between the 3rd and 7th centuries C.E. Buddhism was a popular and well established religion among the Tamils. The earlier literary works like *Silappadikaram* and *Kundalakesi* bear ample information about the place and position of Buddhism in Tamil Nadu besides explaining the teaching of the Buddha. The *Silappadikaram* contains some rare references to Buddhism. The well-known dancer Madhavi met with difficulties of life and understood the miseries of the world. In her concern to remember her only daughter *Manimekalai* from all kinds of suffering, she allowed her to be converted to a Buddhist nun and embrace Buddhism. *Manimekalai's* conversion was done ceremoniously against the wish of the members of her family. Madhavi entered into a Buddha *vihara* to receive religious instructions. She became a nun not withstanding her birth as a professional dancer.[13]

The*Manimekalai* is composed as a Buddhist epic written to impress upon the people the value, wealth and worth of the religious doctrines. This epic contains full of religious teaching. The ideas, philosophy, ethics and the principles of Buddhism are explained in an easy way for the quick understanding of the people. As a work of literature, it is very affluent in Buddhist ideas and thoughts through episodes, explanatory preaching, answering questions and argumentation the epic, tries to state clearly the principles and doctrines on Buddhism. G. John Samuel[14] views that the epic *Manimekalai* as a harmonious combine of the philosophical elements of almost all the sects of the Sathavira School as well as the Mahayana School. The *Manimekalai* the epic of Tamil Buddhism assimilates many aspects of the different schools of Buddhism including the later *Mantrayana* and Tantric schools.

According to G. John Samuel "the first foremost Tamil Buddhist epic *Manimekalai* can be deemed as the finest flower that blossomed as a result of the cultural synthesis between Buddhism and Tamil culture."[15] It can be described as the first Indian epic born out of the Tamil soil owing to its success in blending artistically the Buddhist ethical codes which have taken their origin in North India with the indigenous Tamil culture. It reflects a social milieu in which the various sects of Buddhism lived in harmony in Tamil Nadu without giving much importance to their sectarian differences.

We learn numerous things about the social role of Buddhism in Tamil Nadu from Buddhist literary work *Manimekalai*. The *Manimekalai*, mainly aims at propounding Buddhist doctrine. The name *Manimekalai Turavu* (the renunciation of *Manimekalai*) confirms the idea that it was only written narrate the events leading to the renunciation of *Manimekalai*, the daughter of Kovalan and Madhavi, a renowned and endowed courtesan of the city of Pukar.[16]

At the point when Buddhism came to Tamil Nadu it needed to confront a society which had an alternate point of view. The people of Tamil Nadu were inclined to everyday life and were very little inspired by post-existence or so far as that are concerned renunciations. There are stray references in *Sangam* poems to mean the temporariness of the world essentially after a war and not many references to eternal life.[17] The thought after death could have come to Tamil Nadu with the relocation of Aryans into the South India. As gathered from the *Sangam* writing of the Tamils before the time of *Silappatikaram* and *Manimekalai* the fundamental concern was with the life right now very little significance was given to life after the death.[18]

Manimekalai, the daughter of Kovalan is the main character the author Sattanar created in the epic *Manimekalai*. It is to be noticed that the name Manimekalai is given to her by her father Kovalan after the sea goddess Manimekalai, whose story is found in the *Jataka* stories.[19] Sylvan Levi who has considered this story is of the conclusion that this story should have begun in the south and at a later stage it almost certainly been joined among the other *Jataka* stories.[20] As indicated by *Silappatikaram* the name has given to Manimekalai in light of the fact that the goddess Manimekalai had helped one of the ancestors of Kovalan, during a journey in the sea.[21] It is additionally realised that Kovalan and his progenitors were devotees of Buddhism.[22] In this manner, most presumably the narrative of Manimekalai was well known in Tamil Nadu, maybe more among the Buddhist society. In choosing Manimekalai as the main character the author has made significant innovation. Manimekalai belongs to the group of courtesans who are considered only as entertainers of the wealthy men in the city with their arts and sex. In comparison with married and chaste women, the courtesans were looked down upon and they were not respected by rest of the society. Even if a woman wanted to renounce she was expected to have a basic status in the society.[23]

III

The growth and spread of Buddhism in Nagapattinam, Kanchipuram and Kaveripattinam are known from this epic. The female goddesses were added to the tradition of Buddhism and supernatural capacities of the monks were believed and respected. We know that the *Jataka* stories were very well known in Tamil Nadu, which might have led to further impact on the literature. The *Manimekalai* gives us the best information of Buddhist thought and ideas. The epic was highly philosophical and argumentative. The birth of Lord Buddha, his teachings and the developed stages of Buddhism are well brought out in their nature, the non-soul theory, the three steps towards the attainment of Nirvana and such theories are found explicitly stated.[24]

From Hiuen-Tsang records we know about the condition of Buddhism in Pandya country.[25] According to him, in Malakuta very few monasteries were in preservation and there were only a small number of monks. There were 100 of Deva temples and perceived adherents of various sects, particularly the *Digambaras*, who were many. He also mentions about the Avalokitesvara cult are dealt with in detail by Shu Hikosaka.[26] Thus, Buddhism was in a dominant position in Tamil Nadu, at the height of prosperity in the so called "dark age" of the Kalabhra kings.

In the Tamil literary works like *Tirukkural*, *Silappadikaram*, *Virasoliyam* and *Kundalakesi* Buddhism has influenced, to an outstanding extent. As well as, we can find response to Buddhism in the Tamil work *Nilakesi*, a Jaina work. Hiuen-Tsang when he visited to Tamil Nadu in the 7th century C.E., observed the Buddhists in Kanchi and Pandya country living in harmony in spite of sectarian differences among them, particularly for the lay Buddhists of Tamil Nadu.[27] The Buddhism was a "Happy blend of the healthy elements of the various Buddhist sects as well as the vital parts of Tamil culture." According to G. John Samuel, this religious tolerance and harmony was characteristic of Tamil Buddhism.[28]

In south India the Kanchipuram and Amaravati was great centre of Buddhist learning and culture. When Hiuen-Tsang visited Kanchi in 640 C.E., in Dravida, there were some 100 monasteries with 10,000 monks. Prominent monks such as Buddhamitra, Acharya Buddhaghosa, Buddhadatta, Bodhidharma, Dharmapala and Dinnaga were Tamils, which is also mentioned by Mylai Seeni Venkataswamy in his book, "*Bavuthamum Tamizhum*" in Tamil none of them was native of Sri Lanka. There were close intellectual, religious and cultural contacts in early times between the Theravada centres of Sri Lanka and the Theravada centre of coastal Tamil Nadu such as Kanchipuram, Nagapattinam and Kaveripattinam, till the Buddhist monks went out from these learned centres as missionaries of Buddhism. Dinnaga, a celebrated Buddhist logician was a student of Nalanda and later lived in Kanchi. According to T.R. Sesha Iyengar, it is a reasonable to support that Asoka's world missionaries to Ceylon passed through the

Tamil country in spite of the statement in the *Mahavamsa* that they flew in the air and arrived in Ceylon.[29]

Thus, the socio-cultural relationship between Tamil Nadu and Sri Lankan Buddhism was very interesting. Girnar inscription of Asoka refers to South Indian mission of Asoka at Cholanadu, Pandyanadu and Ceylon. This mission would have spread only Theravada in both the region.[30] In the 1st century B.C.E. two Tamil Buddhists, Sena and Guttika ruled Ceylon. Buddhism should have spread in Tamil Nadu in the 1st century B.C.E. In this period, as invited by Dutthagamani Abhaya for the foundation stone laying ceremony, the Pallava *bhoga* monks led by the monk Mahadeva visited Sri Lanka. In the 4th century C.E. Vaitulya Vada monks were displaced from Ceylon by the king Gothabhaya came to Tamil Nadu and resided at Kaveripattinam.[31] Monk Sanghamitra residing at Kaveripattinam spread Mahayana Buddhism; he tried to undermine the *Mahavihara* monks in Ceylon. The tooth relic was brought to Ceylon after the demise of Mahasena the loyal disciple of Sanghamitra. The Mahendra festival was originated by his son Sri Megavarna in 362 C.E. In 1476 C.E., the monks of Burma who had been to Ceylon, visited the Bhadarikarama of Nagapattinam when their ship wrecked, and worshipped an image of Buddha in a cave constructed as commanded by the emperor of China on the seashore where the Tooth relic was deposited by Hemamala and her husband in the course of its transit to Sri Lanka in the 4th century C.E.[32]

Now we shall proceed to look at some specific example of Influence of Buddhism on the religious and social life of the people of Tamil Nadu. There are ample evidence to show that after the disappearance of Buddhism from Tamil Nadu the Hindu adopted many Buddhist ceremonies and form of worship. If one makes a critical study of the *'Utsavas'* (religious rituals) in the Hindu temples of Tamil Nadu, one will be able to notice many important in them. It is now a usually accepted fact that Buddhism has left its influence on the forms and methods of religious worship in all places where it had once flourished. But in many places the influences of Buddhism on Hindu forms of worship seems to be more distinct and permanent. One of the reasons for this is that Buddhism as such did not disappear from Tamil Nadu, but it only dissolved itself into the sea of Tamil Nadu Hinduism. Tamil Nadu Hinduism is elastic enough to accommodate in its folds religious systems of any form or variety. When Buddhism was absorbed into Hinduism in Tamil Nadu some of its impressive ceremonies and forms of worship which had become very popular, were continued in Hindu temple.

If we see in Kanchipuram, especially in some localities like Kama-Kotamatha near the Kamakshi Amman temple, Vaikuntha Perumal temple, Ekambareswarar temple, Pallavamedu, Jnana Prakasa Svanugalmath, etc., yielded Buddhist remains. The excavation conducted at the site of Kamakshi Amman temple brought to light vestiges of *stupa*, *chaityas* and *vihara* besides few copper coins belonging to Rudra Satakarni, coin moulds and *Buddhapada* slabs, datable from 1st century B.C.E. to 4th century C.E.[33] Here several Buddha images of a later date (9th century C.E.) were also unearthed. Among them the seated images of Buddha in *Virasana* posture in *dhyāna mudra*, another seated on lotus in *yōgamudra* and an image in *bhumisparsa mudra* are important.[34] While one is headless, the other is both without its head and hands. Several images including the *Mahāparinirvana* scene belonging to the later medieval period were found in the niches on the compound wall of the Ekambareswara temple.[35] The image measures about 2 feet. The face is lightly scratched. The *prabha* over the head of the Buddha is rather Hindu workmanship.[36] A seated image (3 feet 9 inc.) of Buddha (in *dhyāna mudra*) was found datable to later Vijayanagara or Nayaka period; suggest the survival of Buddhism even up to the Vijayanagara period. On the southern *prakara* towards the right of the side entrance in the same direction are found sculptured on granite slabs, now built into wall, seven Buddha all are in seated position. Of these, there are on the similar type of slab while the rest are on different ones.[37] It is important to note that all the images of the Buddha found in Ekambaresvara temple have initially come from a ruined shrine of the Lord which must have existed in the surrounding area of this great Siva temple. Though Buddhism was eventually compressed out of the country it had left its impress upon Hinduism. Most of the accessories of modern Hinduism such as temples, devotion of images, *'utsavams'* and religious processions were all borrowed from Buddhists. These explanations are no doubt very far-reaching in their nature. They should only be taken to mean that Hinduism borrowed many of the ceremonies and habits of Buddhist worship.

The Buddhist monks were pioneers in the field of education. The role played by Buddhist monks in the spread of learning in Tamil Nadu deserves special mention. They had various charity establishments associated with their *viharas* and these served as centres for the spread of learning. Monasteries turned into cultural centre both for the monks and the laity. It was the monastery that communicated education both to the members of the order and the lay followers; it was the monastery that arranged for the general population; it was the monastery that infatuated the biggest library and helped the cause of the development of books by getting them copied.[38] The *Manimekalai* refers to Kanchi as a well-known centre of Buddhist culture in the early centuries of the present era. It is true that no architectural monuments have been discovered still now, but historically, Kanchipuram was a centre of education and was known as the *ghatikasthanam*, or "place of learning". The Kanchipuram has given great Buddhist scholars and also was a great centre for learning for both Hinayana and Mahayana form of Buddhism. The city was also a religious centre of advanced education for Jainism and Buddhism between the 1st and 5th centuries C.E. Kanchipuram gave room to every school of Buddhism and it was the meeting place of the Buddhist leaders not only from the central India, Andhra Pradesh, Southern Tamil Nadu, but also from the foreign countries like Sri Lanka, China, Burma, Java and other Southeast Asian countries. It is quite clear that Kanchipuram was the pre-eminent seat of Buddhist culture, in the early period.

The contribution of merchant class, to a religion is found in Tamil Buddhism too. For the sake of Malaya merchant class, the Nagapattinam Sailendra *vihara* was built. This *vihara* just built for the sake of the merchant caused the revival of Buddhism in Tamil Nadu and it was a centre for the propagation of Vajrayana form of Buddhism. Such religious communities are capable of influencing the society quickly. Merchant community played an important role in the Buddhist monastic society. There is a close relationship between Buddhism and trade which is largely due to the dependence of the Buddhist monastic community on donations from lay supporters.[39] Ideally, Buddhist monks and nuns were required to reject all worldly possessions and thus to depend on the lay community for supply of all their necessities, including food, clothing, shelter, and medicine. In practice, donations to Buddhist monasteries included a wide range of materials necessary to maintain the monks and nuns. There were the needs of considerable economic surpluses to sustain large-scale Buddhist institutions. In return for material donations to Buddhist monasteries, monks and nuns were available to give religious instruction and donors received religious merit (*punya*), which was often shared with relatives, teachers, political supporters, and 'all beings' (*sarvasattva*).

The increase of economic production system leads to the breakup of old social classes[40] and appearance of the new ones such as the free peasants and farmers, [41] merchants and craftsmen.[42] One of the most significant factors in this case was the emergence of the merchants.

These merchants were relatively wealthy but their rank in the social structure under the Brahmanism was quite low, the third position which was repulsive to them.[43] Due to the strengthening of trade and commerce these traders become more and more affluent and started playing a crucial role in the contemporary politics and economics. D.D. Kosambi points out that "traders had become so wealthy that the most important person in an eastern town was generally called the *shresthi*. The term not known earlier, is derived from the word for 'superior', or 'pre-eminent'. Even absolute, despotic king treated them with respect, though they had no direct voice in politics.[44]

IV

The seven *Viharas* at Kaveripattinam is quite interesting. It will be noted that the seven numbers seems to be a very auspicious number to Buddhist religion. On the other hand Buddha is said to have made seven steps immediately after birth. The Manimekalai, collected with the intension of exaltation of Buddhism, is crucial for the study of the various Buddhist establishments at Kaveripattinam. It is very important that Manimekalai, the heroine of the poet-philosopher Sattanar, started as a Buddhist novitiate in Puhar, and is made to visit all the key centres of Buddhism in Tamilakam, *Ilam* (Ceylon) and South-east Asia, she adopted the robes of *Pikkuni* under the tutelage of Aravana Adikal, the head of the Vihara of Puhar.[45]

The subsistence of seven *Indira viharas* at Puhar is mentioned in the epics. The mention to the *Indira vihara* of Puhar and Mapoti occurs in the *Silappadikaram*, when Kovalan narrates a dream to the Brahmana named Matalan.[46] After leaving Puhar for Madurai, Kovalan and Kannaki are said to have crossed the outer gate of this city and then passed by the seven *viharas* known as *Indira vihara*.[47] From the account of *Silappadikaram*, it is clear that this Buddhist establishment was located in the outskirts of the urban area. The epic also states that *Māsāttuvān* after hearing of his son Kovalan's unreasonable implementation by the Pandya king dismayed of worldly life and joined the Buddhist Sangam establishments in the *Indira vihara* of Puhar.[48] This *vihara* is also mentioned in the *Manimekalai*.[49] The *Indira vihara* seems to be very popular at that time and was considered to be impressive to contrast it with other *viharas*. At the same time as describing the Chera capital Vanci, Manimekalai mentioned a *vihara*, which is said to be as beautiful as the *Indira vihara* of Kaveripattinam.[50] It is very interesting to note that, Sattanar speaks of a small pavilion made of precious stone in a park called *Upavana*. A model of the Buddha's footprint was worshipped there.[51] Moreover the same writer declares that Killivalavan, a Chola king transformed the prison into a Buddhist monastery at the request of the nun Manimekalai.[52]

The Buddhist site at Kaveripattinam, found a Buddhapada away from the *vihara* to its south. The Buddhapada has a small vessel cut between the long toes of the feet and proposed for the relic offerings of bone remains and gold flowers, which were customarily deposited in it, related to the *acharyas* or the Buddha as the case may be, which it venerated. The Buddhapada is also apparently of the Theravada school. The Buddhapada match up shows the auspicious symbols such as the *purnaghata*, *svastika* and *srivatsa*, etc. The four significant incidents of the Buddha's life ending with *chaitya* worship demonstrating *mahaparinirvana* are also depicted on the slab; during the 3rd -4th C.E. From the available evidence suggests that the monastery belonged to the 4th-5th century C.E.

Many Buddhists from T'ang dynasty of China visited Nagapattinam possibly to see the Buddhist centres.[53] The *Guruparamparai* of 12th century C.E. records that Tirumangai Alvar, one of the Vaishna Alvar of 8th-9th century robbed the gold image of Buddha from Nagappattinam and used the gold out of it for the development of Ranganatha temple at Srirangam. The description of an area referred to as *Tuta* which means an 'earthen tower' inside the flat land of Patan (Nagapattinam) in the *Daoyi Zhiluels* refers to the existence of a brick tower which had a Chinese inscription. The inscription quoted in the *Daoyi Zhilue* refers to the existence of the brick tower as the eighth moon of the third year of Xianchun (1267 C.E). It's miles stated within the *Daoyi Zhilue*, an significant 14th century Chinese work on the nations within the southern sea stretching from Southeast Asia to West Asia that the Chinese people came to *Tuta* and engraved the inscription.[54]

Marco Polo of Venice visited Nagapattinam in the 13th century on his way to China and describes an eastern *stupa* in the flat land of Pa-tan (Nagapattinam) as follows, "It's miles surrounded with stones. There is a *stupa* of earth and brick many feet high. It bears the following Chinese inscription: The work turned into completed in the 8th moon of the third year Hien chw'en (1267 C.E). It is related that those characters have been impressed by some Chinese in imitation of inscriptions on stone of those countries; as much as the present time they've no longer been destroyed".[55] The existence of Buddhist edifice constructed by the king of China at Nagapattinam is also attested to by the Kalyani inscription. The Kalyani inscriptions are located at Zaingganaingm the western suburb of the Pegu. They contain ten stone slabs with inscriptions on each aspect. The language of the first three stones is Pali and that of the relaxation is Talaing, being a translation of the Pali textual content. Dhammaceti or Ramadhipati, the king of Pegu put up these inscriptions in 1476 C.E.[56] According to the inscription, a group of *Theras* visiting Ceylon, being shipwrecked, travelled strolling to Nagapattinam and there they visited the site of the Patarikarama monastery. They worshipped an image of the Buddha in a cave built at the behest of the Maharaja of Cinadesa.[57] It is well known that a broken brick tower had been standing in Nagapattinam till 1867 whilst it becomes pulled down by the Jesuits.[58] It became variously referred to as the Putuvelikopuram, vintage Pagoda, Black Pagoda and Jaina Pagoda.[59] Sir Charles Valentyn (1725) referred to as Pagood China (i.e. Chinese Pagoda).[60]

During the Pallava period Buddhism had a smooth sailing in coastal Tamil Nadu. In fact Buddha was considered by the Hindus as their god and included as an incarnation of Vishnu. According to the Pallava inscription, in the Adivaraha cave at Mamallapuram Buddha while enumerating the ten incarnations of Vishnu.[61] The sculpture of standing Buddavatara Vishnu was carved in one of the niches on the walls of the Vaikuntaperumal temple at Kanchipuram constructed during the period of Nandivarman II Pallavamalla (731-796 C.E.). Huge number of Buddha images discovered from the 7th century to 14th century in and around Kanchipuram, pointed out that it remained as a significant centre of Buddhism. A remarkable image among them is the large standing Buddha of about 7th century hailed from the location of the Kamatchi temple.[62]

From the records it is seen that Kanchipuram became an incredible centre of Buddhism whilst Anuradhapuram turned into in Sri Lanka. Well-known Buddhist teachers such as Aravana Adigal, Manimekalai, Dinnaga, Bodhidharma, the commentator Achariya Dhammapala, Aniruddha and Buddhaditiya lived in this city. The prevailing Tirumalai Vaishnavaite shrine turned into previously a Buddhist centre. Here too we found a large number of rock caves. Ashoka characters (of the *Brahmi* scripts) are observed in them. V.R. Ramachandra is of the opinion that, these were occupied by Buddhist monks. Similarly Buddhist towns and villages existed in the Pandya country. This region was the birth place of Achariya Dhammapala, Vajrabodhi and other Buddhist scholars.[63]

V

Many Buddhist teachers in south India made their valuable contributions to Tamil, Pali and Sanskrit literatures. They composed numerous works on a diffusion of topics along with religion, philosophy, history, grammar, astronomy and medicine. Reference to their works is found in Tamil literatures and other historical records. It is most unfortunate that of the large number of books written from the 3rd to the 14th century C.E. only very few are available today.[64] The Jains and Buddhists propagated their faith in the local languages. The Buddhist monks who came to South India studied the local language, preached and wrote books for the teaching and learning of the native residents. Although their literary works were destroyed by enemies they have left enduring marks of their influence. During the 4th century the famous commentator Achariya Buddhadatta lived in Buddhist cities such as Uragapura (Uraiyur), Kaveripattinam, and Bhutamangalam and wrote a number of commentaries in Pali. Rhys Davids mentions that, he took material for his commentaries from the Buddhist literature available to him in Tamil. In the paraphrase of the *Nilakesi* and *Virasoliyam* there are extracts from which books the extracts were taken. There is no question that many Buddhist works in Tamil existed during the heyday of Buddhism.[65]

The Buddhism flourished in coastal Tamil Nadu is abundantly proved by Buddhist ruins, the present day customs, manners and ideas of Buddhist origin and the books written by Buddhist authors of South India. Further, there may be proof of many Tamil Buddhist teachers, in cooperation of lay and monastic, who graced the land of their birth.[66] In the beginning, Buddha resisted the consumption of women in the *sangha*, he later admitted women from all walks of existence. Within the preliminary level the monks had little relation with lay society.

It is difficult to provide any particular date on which Buddhism becomes introduce to the south of India. However there are references to show that Buddhism was known in South India during the time of the Tamil works, *Maduraikanchi*, *Silappadikaram* and *Manimekalai*. Around 600 C.E. the Pallava ruler Mahendravarman wrote a farcical play which adequately testifies to the Buddhist existence in Kanchipuram. The play gives us information to a Buddhist monk reminiscing over a wonderful meal of fish and meat that he has just eaten at the house of a rich Buddhist merchant. On his way back to the royal Buddhist monastery, he wonders why the Buddha, who allowed his monks so many luxuries, should not have given them those two added pleasures which would have made life perfect- wine and women.[67]

At some stage in the Chola era also, Buddhism was widespread in the Tamil country. The broad-minded attitude adopted by the Tamil kings is clearly reflected by the information contained in the bi-lingual Larger Leiden plates.[68] According to this inscription, Rajaraja I, in his twenty first regnal years (1005 C.E.) gave the village named Anaimangalam to the *Cudamanivihara* at Nagapattinam built by Maravijayottungavarman of the Sailendra dynasty, and the lord of Sri Visaya (Srivijaya) and Ketah (Kadaram) in the name of his father Cudamanivarman. This *vihara* has been praised in glowing terms in this inscription as being 'surpassingly beautiful' (*atiramaniyam*) and 'equalling the mountain Meru in loftiness' (*kanakagiri-sammaunati-vibhavam*). After the death of Rajaraja I, his son Rajendra I issued an enduring edict to be made for this village which had previously been granted by his father. This inscription poetically states that this king ordered that "as long as Sesa, the Lord of all serpents holds the entire earth, so long may this *vihara* last in this world as endowment."[69] To continue the story of the Tamils contribution to Buddhism, we witness that in the reign of Voharaka Tissa (269-291 C.E.), some Vaitulyans came to Sri Lanka and the new doctrine of Mahayanism became popular with the monks of the Abhaygiri *vihara*. At the same time, there lived a learned monk by the name of Sanghamitra in the Chola country who visited the island to spread the new sect.

VI

The history of Buddhism in *Tamilakam* have often ended up in general surveys of the religious history of the region within which Buddhism played only a marginal role, despite its contribution to the history of ideas, philosophy and social norms through the literary and intellectual pursuits of the Buddhists in the vernacular language and literature. The importance of the archaeological evidence for Buddhism that continued occurrence of Buddhist sites at coastal region, which shows that the Buddhist religion survived, where trade flourished and to a lesser extent in the interior where temples controlled by Brahmins.

Despite the fact that practically all the religions of the world have confidence in the standards of harmony, in Buddhism, it is the above all else embodiment of life. Peace is especially integral to the fundamental quality of Buddhism. Peace in Buddhism can be followed to Buddha's lessons and his own particular manner of life. The Buddha's goals are to make peace among the people depend on his teaching in his everyday life. Buddha's teaching and lifestyle are not only very simple but also in practical. In Buddha's way of thinking, harmony is the method for accomplishing salvation. In Buddhism, one needs to observe certain guidelines of profound quality so as to accomplish salvation. Buddha has focussed on certain ethical standards which are particularly basic for driving a significant and restrained life which will control one towards *nirvana*. All through Buddha's time, the followers of Buddha were leading a very moral, truthful and peaceful life which was based on freedom, justice, and love. Buddha also determined on the obligation of fellow felines among people and the communal service in human life. Buddha also concentrated on equality among people and justice in the society.

References

1. Carl Olson, *Different Paths of Buddhism: A Narrative-Historical Introduction*, London, 2005, pp. 68-70.
2. Alok Kumar Verma, "A Critical Study of Mahayana Buddhism in South India". *International Refereed Journal of Reviews and Research* (online), Council of Scientific and Industrial Research, Vol. 5, Issue 6, 2017.
3. L. Jayasuriya, "Buddhism, Politics and State Craft", *International Journal of Buddhist Thought and Culture*, University of Virginia, 2008, pp. 41-47.
4. P.B. Desai, *Jainism in South India and some Jaina Epigraphs*, Solapur, 1957, p. 25; also see A. Ghosh (*ed*.), *Jaina Art and Architecture*, Vol. I, Delhi, 1974, pp. 92-103.
5. S. Beal, *Si-Yu-Ki: Buddhist Records of the Western World*, London, 1906, pp. 230-234; P.C. Alexander, *Buddhism in Kerala*, Annamalainagar, 1949, pp. 5-7.
6. Uma Chakravarti, *The Social Dimension of Early Buddhism*, Oxford University Press, Delhi, 1987, p. 61.
7. G. John Samuel (*ed*.), *Buddhism in Tamil Nadu: Collected Papers*, Chennai, 1998, p. 73.
8. Uma Chakravarti, *op.cit*., pp. 61-62.
9. John Samuel (*ed*.), *op.cit*., p. 24.
10. *Ibid*., p. 25.
11. K. Indrapala, "Buddhism among the Tamils: A.D. 1000-1500", *Proceedings of the 5th International Conference, Seminar of Tamil Studies*, Vol. 2, edited by M. Arunachalam, International Association of Tamil Studies, Madras, 1981, pp. 12-27.
12. Manjulika Swarup, "How did Buddhism come to Southern India", *The Maha Bodhi Journal*, Mahabodhi Society of India, Vol. 94, Calcutta, 1986, pp. 102-105.

13. K. Krishna Murthy, *Studies in Buddhism*, Delhi, 1996, pp. 29-31.
14. G. John Samuel (*ed.*), *op.cit.*, p. xvi.
15. *Ibid.*
16. U.Ve. Swaminatha Iyer (*ed.*), *Manimekalai*, 1st Edition. Madras, 1998, lines 97-98.
17. U.Ve. Swaminatha Iyer (*ed.*), *Purananuru*, 6th Edition. Madras, 1963, pp. 71, 134, 141, 236.
18. G. John Samuel (*ed.*), *op.cit.*, p. 200.
19. W.H.O. Rouse (*trans.*), *Sangha Jataka Stories of the Buddha's former Births*, Vol. IV, Cambridge, 1901, Story No. 442.
20. *The Indian Historical Quarterly*, Vol. VI, No. 4, New Delhi, 1930, p. 614.
21. *Silappadikaram*, Canto. 15 lines 25-40.
22. *Manimekalai*, Canto. 28 Lines 25-31.
23. John Samuel (*ed.*), *op.cit.*, p. 201.
24. K. Krishna Murthy, *op.cit.*, pp. 29-31.
25. S. Beal, *op.cit.*, pp. 228-229.
26. Shu Hikosaka, *Buddhism in Tamil Nadu: A New Perspective*, Madras, 1989.
27. S. Beal, *op.cit.*
28. G. John Samuel (*ed.*), *op.cit.*, p. xv.
29. T.R. Sesha Iyengar, *Dravidian India*, Vol. I, Madras, 1925, p. 162.
30. *Ibid.*
31. *Ibid.*
32. T.N. Ramachandran, *The Nagapattinam and other Buddhist Bronzes in the Chennai Museum*, Madras, 1992, pp. 18-19.
33. B. Subrahmanyam, *Buddhist Relic Casket in South India*, New Delhi, 1998, p. 19.
34. T.A. Gopinath Rao, "Buddhist Vestiges in Kanchipuram", *Indian Antiquary*, Vol. XLIV, 1915, p. 128.
35. D. Mitra, *Buddhist Monuments*, Calcutta, 1971, p. 197.
36. C. Minakshi, "Buddhism in South India", *South Indian Studies*, *Society of Archaeological*, *Historical & Epigraphical Research*, Vol. II, Madras, 1979, p. 87.
37. *Ibid.*
38. P.C. Alexander, *Buddhism in Kerala*, Annamalainagar, 1949, p. 168.
39. T.W. Rhys Davids, *Questions of King Milinda*, Oxford, 1890, p. 4.
40. Hirakawa Akira, *A History of Indian Buddhism from Sakyamuni to early Mahayana*, tr. and ed. by Paul Groner, Honolulu, 1993, p. 15.
41. D.D. Kosambi, *The Culture and Civilization of Ancient India in Historical Outline*, Vikas Publishing House, New Delhi, 1970, p. 109.

42. Hirakawa Akira, *op.cit.*
43. Romila Thapar, *History of Early India from the origins to A.D. 1300*, London, 2003, p. 144.
44. Kajal Barua, "Tracing the Socio-economic Roots of the Buddhist Concept of Universal Monarch (Cakkravatti)", *South Asia Culture, History & Heritage*, International Association for Asian Heritage (IAAH) and Centre for Asian Studies, University of Kelaniya, Sri Lanka, 2015, pp. 4-12.
45. *Manimekalai*, canto. 15 lines 55-59.
46. *Silappadikaram*, canto. 10 lines 11-14.
47. *Silappadikaram*, canto. 27 line 92.
48. *Silappadikaram*, canto. 27 lines 90-95.
49. *Manimekalai*, canto. 26 line 55; canto. 28 line 70.
50. *Manimekalai*, canto. 28 lines 69-71.
51. *Manimekalai*, canto.3 lines 59-66; canto.5 lines 95-105; canto. 6 lines 11-12.
52. *Manimekalai*, canto 19. lines 157-162.
53. Huimin Bhikkhu, *et.al.*, "*Buddhist Eminent Monks Tracks and the Sea Silk Road in Tang Dynasty*," Vietnam in the East Asian Buddhist Traditions and Electronic Cultural Atlas Initiative, Vietnam Buddhist University, Ho Chi Minh City, 2007, p.
54. *Ibid.*
55. T.N. Ramachandran, *op.cit.*, p.14.
56. *Indian Antiquary*, Vol. XXII, 1984, pp. 29-51.
57. *Ibid.*, p.45.
58. *Ibid.*, pp. 224-227.
59. *Ibid.*, p. 224.
60. *Ibid.*
61. K.R. Srinivasan, *Cave-temples of the Pallavas*, ASI, New Delhi, 1964, p. 173.
62. T.A. Gopinath Rao, *op.cit.*, pp. 127-129.
63. P.H. Dharmmaratana Mahathera, *Buddhism in South India*, Kandy, 1968, p. 11.
64. *Ibid.*, p. 15.
65. *Ibid.*
66. *Ibid.*, p. 19.
67. P. Pal, *A Port-Pourri of Indian Art*, Mumbai, 1988, pp. 55-57.
68. Chithra Madhavan, *History and Culture of Tamil Nadu*, New Delhi, 2005, pp. 268-269.
69. *Ibid.*

Bibliography

Alexander, P.C, *Buddhism in Kerala*, Annamalai University, Annamalainagar, 1949.

Alok Kumar Verma, "A Critical Study of Mahayana Buddhism in South India". *International Refereed Journal of Reviews and Research* (online), Council of Scientific and Industrial Research, Vol. 5, Issue 6, 2017.

Beal, S, *Si-Yu-Ki: Buddhist Records of the Western World*, Kegan Paul, Trubner & Co., London, 1906.

Carl Olson, *Different Paths of Buddhism: A Narrative-Historical Introduction*, Rutgers University Press, London, 2005.

Chithra Madhavan, *History and Culture of Tamil Nadu*, Vol. I, (Up to C.A.D.310), D.K. Print World Ltd., New Delhi, 2005.

Desai, P.B, *Jainism in South India and some Jaina Epigraphs*, Jaina Samskrti Samrakshaka Sangha, Solapur, 1957.

Dharmmaratana Mahathera, P.H, *Buddhism in South India*, Kandy, 1968.

Gopinath Rao, T.A, "Buddhist Vestiges in Kanchipuram", *Indian Antiquary*, Vol. XLIV, 1915.

Ghosh, A (*ed.*), *Jaina Art and Architecture*, Vol. I, Bharatiya Jnanpith, Delhi, 1974.

Hirakawa Akira, *A History of Indian Buddhism from Sakyamuni to early Mahayana*, tr. and ed. by Paul Groner, Honolulu, 1993.

Huimin Bhikkhu, *et.al.*, *"Buddhist Eminent Monks Tracks and the Sea Silk Road in Tang Dynasty,"* Vietnam in the East Asian Buddhist Traditions and Electronic Cultural Atlas Initiative, Vietnam Buddhist University, Ho Chi Minh City, 2007

Indian Antiquary, Vol. XXII, 1984.

Jayasuriya, L, "Buddhism, Politics and State Craft", *International Journal of Buddhist Thought and Culture*, The University of Virginia, 2008.

John Samuel, G (*ed.*), *Buddhism in Tamil Nadu: Collected Papers*, Institute of Asian Studies, Chennai, 1998.

Kajal Barua, "Tracing the Socio-economic Roots of the Buddhist Concept of Universal Monarch (Cakkavatti)", *South Asia Culture, History & Heritage*, International Association for Asian Heritage (IAAH) and Centre for Asian Studies, University of Kelaniya, Sri Lanka, 2015.

Kosambi, D. D, *The Culture and Civilization of Ancient India in Historical Outline*, Vikas Publishing House, New Delhi, 1970.

Krishna Murthy, K, *Studies in Buddhism*, Delhi, 1996.

Manimekalai, *Manimekalai*, canto. 15 lines 55-59.

Minakshi, C, "Buddhism in South India", *South Indian Studies, Society of Archaeological, Historical & Epigraphical Research*, Vol. II, Madras, 1979.

Mitra, D, *Buddhist Monuments*, Sahitya Samsat, Calcutta, 1971.

Pal, P, *A Port-Pourri of Indian Art*, Mumbai, 1988.

Ramachandran, T. N, *The Nagapattinam and other Buddhist Bronzes in the Chennai Museum*, Madras, 1992.

Rhys Davids, T.W, *Questions of King Milinda*, The Clarendon Press, Oxford, 1890.

Romila Thapar, *History of Early India from the origins to A.D. 1300*, Penguin Book Ltd., London, 2003.

Rouse, W.H.O (*trans*.), *Sangha Jataka Stories of the Buddha's former Births*, Vol. IV, Cambridge, 1901.

Sesha Iyengar, T.R, *Dravidian India*, Vol. I, Madras, 1925.

Shu Hikosaka, *Buddhism in Tamil Nadu: A New Perspective*, Madras, 1989.

Silappatikaram, canto. 27 lines 90-95.

Srinivasan, K.R, *Cave-temples of the Pallavas*, ASI, New Delhi, 1964.

Subrahmanyam, B, *Buddhist Relic Casket in South India*, New Delhi, 1998.

Subrahmanyam, B, *Buddhist Relic Casket in Andhra Pradesh*, Hyderabad, Ananda Buddhist Vihara Trust, 1999.

Uma Chakravarti, *The Social Dimension of Early Buddhism*, Oxford University Press, Delhi, 1987.

16

Mahendravarman I: an Artist who built a Kingdom

Sreebarna Ghosh

The Pallava dynasty has an enormous contribution to developing south Indian temple architecture. Their experimentation on forms, modes, and techniques not only set a new trend of architecture but also influenced the contemporary temple style of neighbouring dynasties. The Pallavas started their temple building activity with cave temples, a common traditional architecture, in a challenging medium. Excavating cave temple on hard stones like granite and gneiss was their first declaration of uniqueness to the contemporary society.[1] Mahendravarman I (c. 590-630 C.E.), the second king of the Pallava dynasty, was believed to be the initiator of new temple architecture in South India, which was supported and developed by his successor as well as the successor of the Pallava dynasty. The Pallava temple tradition which later represents the beginning of south Indian temple architecture has its first foundation step in Cave temple at Mandagapattu. The inscription at the Mandagapattu cave mentioned the cave as brick less, timber less, metal less and morter less mansion,[2] which sounds like a satisfactory announcement by Vichitrachitta for making something which is either unique or never attempted before. However, rock-cut cave temple by that time was the most popular and common architecture accepted and adapted by all major religions in India.

Mahendravarman I the successor of the Pallava king Simhavishnu, ruled *Tondaimandalam* from c.590 to 630 C.E. Although he didn't have political achievements like his son Narasimhavarman but he initiated two trends in the political and cultural history of the Pallava dynasty - the Pallava-Chalukya feud and making of the temple. These later became the honorary responsibility of the Pallavas and were followed sincerely by his successors. Mahendravarman was a person of many talents and he likes to be introduced by them. He has taken several *virudas* like *Mattavilāsa*, *Gunabhara*, *Satrumalla*, *Chettakari*, etc. complementing his diverse talent and seldom used the name Mahendravarman. His other great contribution was writing two famous plays *Matavilāsaprahasana* and *Bhagavadajjuka* which continued in south India long after the decline of the Pallava dynasty. Although he was defeated by Pulakesin II and lost his northern province yet his Tiruchirappalli cave inscription shows his territory was extended till river Kaveri. It is believed that he was converted from Jainism to Saivism by Appar, a famous Bhakti saint.[3]

Mahendravarman I is generally accepted as an artist and creator, who introduced the rock-cut cave temple in his territory and the rock-cut architecture cross the threshold and began its journey in south India. K.R. Srinivasan mentioned him as an originator of rock-cut architecture depending on Mandagapattu inscription.[4] The *viruda* 'Vichitrachita' of the same inscription has been explained by T.N. Ramachandran as an outcome of the 'murmured protest' of the masons against Mahendravarman's new invention of rock-cut architecture.[5] While this inscription let scholars think that Mahendravarman was first to introduce rock-cut architecture in south India the caves at Undevalli in Andhra Pradesh and Malayadi-k-kurichi in Tirunelveli raised doubt in this regard. M.S. Mate argued that the Pallava cave temple of Mahendravarma wasn't an exclusive phenomenon but rather has its roots in the rock-cut architecture of the lower Deccan especially of the Andhra region.[6] They are architecturally and stylistically similar to the Brahmanical caves of Lower Krishna Region, especially with the Undavelli caves at Guntur. G. Subbiah shows the Malayadi-k-kurichi cave temple at Tirunelveli excavated by the Pandya King Maran Chedan on the 17th year (4th decade of 7th century) of his reign was stylistically finer than the cave temples of Mahendravarman.[7] So he concluded that fundamentals of South Indian rock-cut architecture, which was credited to Mahendravarman, was a parallel development and was flourishing in the different parts of south India. Marilyn Harsh put another argument saying not only Mahendravarman was an originator of rock-cut architecture in south India but also he was the artist and patron of Mahabalipuram, generally assigned to his son Narasimhavarman.[8]

Rock-cut cave first appears in the Indian scenario under the patronage of Asoka and his successor in the Barabar hills of Gaya. The Udaygiri and Khanda Giri in Orissa, made during the time of Kharavela were for the Jain monks. It is after or contemporary to the later, making of the rock-cut cave become a trend in Deccan, especially in western Deccan and continued for more than millennia. Before the 6th century CE the caves in western Deccan were mostly donated for the Buddhist institution but there were also cave temples dedicated to deities of Hinduism and Jainism. However, the political rivalry between three dynasties- Chalukya of Badami, Pallava and Pandya also encouraged a cultural competition which spread this rock-carving architecture further south. The Early Chalukya and the Pallavas, both dynasties were temple builder but the Pallava kings of Simhavishnu lines initiated their journey and instigate the Dravidian form of temple architecture.

Since the 6th century CE onwards temple building becomes an integral part of South Indian polity. The temple not only housed the idol but also represented the political valour and cultural glory of the King. However, the religious architecture includes an active social rationale that motivates both the purpose as well as the arrangement of the building. In ancient India, temples were built of perishable materials and were used for worship only. Rock-cut cave architecture served three main purposes- durability, seclusion, and devotion. The monastic religions like Buddhism, Jainism, and Ajivikas adapted to this mode of architecture because of their religious rituals. Every layout of rock-cut architecture displays the function and the purpose of the dweller. Although in general, it seems that every rock-cut cave has a common layout yet uniqueness of every cave reveals their different functions. The Ajivikas used the caves for isolation, Jain monk used the caves for teachings and sometimes for Sallekhana, and finally Buddhist monks first used them as temporary Vassavasa and later transformed them into permanent institutions.

The cave architecture associated with Buddhism differs from other rock-cut architecture due to additional *Vihara* or cells for living. The two separate ground plans for two different functions in Buddhism alone played an important role in the development as well as in the evolution of rock-cut architecture in India. Later the Brahmanical cave temples in western Deccan, influenced by the earlier style, turned the cells into individual shrines. The purpose of the rock-cut cave involves two groups- the occupant or receiver and the donor or builder. The reason of occupants mostly involves religious rituals, but the purpose of the donor or builder includes a larger horizon from gaining religious merit to the humble display of political virtues. The purpose of the donor can also alter the appearance of rock-cut architecture. While Pallava king Mahendravarman I introduced the first rock-cut cave in his territory what was his purpose? Was it solely religious, expression of political virtues, or an experiment to present something new?

Mahendravarman I build Mandagapattu cave temple and claimed it to be brick less, timber less, metal less and morter less mansion dedicated to Vishnu, Shiva, and Brahma. The inscriptions found at Mandagapattu raises two opposing arguments regarding Mahendravarman's contribution to introducing rock-cut architecture in south India. One group believes that he was a great artist and introduced rock-cut architecture in the south. While the other group argues that the cave temple of Mahendravarman owes its origin to the cave temple of lower Krishna Valley, hence it wasn't a new introduction. These two groups argued whether to call Mahendravarman an inventor or not. However, among all discussion what was the intention of Mahendravarman in making those temples left unanswered. The Mandagapattu inscription, which raises these arguments and the cave temples build by Mahendravarman throws some light on his purpose. The inscription mentions- the brick less, timber less, metal less, and morter less temple, which is a mansion for (the Gods) Brahma, Isvara, and Vishnu was caused to be created by the King Vichitra-chitta.[9]

The inscription mentions three things clearly- the king, the deity, and the medium of the temple. The first line which understood as a proclamation of introducing a new technique is a complicated synonym of the rock-cut temple. Mahendravarman I had a keen sense of humour with a poetic mind. Instead of writing stone temple he put it in a poetic manner and introduced himself as Vichitra Chitta. He didn't mention anywhere it is a new technique or a unique style but the presentation of the word played with the mind of the reader and let them think this endeavour was one of a kind. While in reality, all it revealed was the material used for contemporary structural temples and the fact these caves didn't have wooden doors or windows. This inscription also shows a complicated exposition of simple matter which was another expertise of Mahendravarman. So to understand the main purpose of making cave temples, it is necessary to understand the site formation as well as the architecture of the cave.

K.R. Srinivasan divided the rock-cut temples of Mahendravarman I into four groups:[10]

- First group comprises of cave temples at Mandagappattu, Pallavaram, Mamandur II and Kurananilmuttam.
- The second group includes Vallam I, Vasantesvara cave temple.
- The third group comprises of Mahendravadi and Mamandur I.
- Fourth group has Dalavanur, Tirchirappalli and Siyamangalam.

Stylistically there are more cave-temples belong to Mahendra period. However, to understand the King's impetus to contribute to rock-cut temple making and their contribution to south Indian cave temple, only a few sites will be discussed here. The following cave temples which were directly made by the king or can be corroborated with his inscription are the primary concern of this paper.

Lakshita Cave temple: This cave (Fig.1) is situated in the Hill of Mandagapattu in Viluppuram of South Arcot district. This cave was the first conscious attempt of Mahendravaraman to build a rock-cut temple in his territory. This cave, also known as Mandagapattu cave, was dedicated to trinity and named after Mahendravarman's

Fig. 1: Mandagapattu Cave temple.

one of the Viruda Lakshita.[11] The temple faces north overlooking an irrigation tank. The cave is divided into two part- Mukhamandapa and Ardhamandapa both have two pillars and two pilasters. The pillars are massive square pillars with octagonal shape in the middle. The facade is plain and two dwārapālas are carved on either side. Three shrine chambers for trinity are carved on the back wall.

Pallavaram cave temple: The cave temple at Pallavaram has been converted into a Durgah. But the existing drawing shows it had an almost the same simple plan as Mandagapattu. The *Mukhamandapa* and *Ardhamandapa* had four pillars and two pilasters creating five openings for five shrines at the back wall. These pillars are the same as Mandagapattu, except the second pillar on the right side has the octagonal portion at the bottom. This cave had no *dwārapālas*. The most important contribution of this cave is the inscription carved on the architrave of both rows of pillars which mentioned a list of *Virudas* of Mahendravarman I. The King liked to be known by multiple *Virudas*, so a list of *Virudas* leading with the name 'Sri Mahendra Vikarama' was a conscious attempt of divine legitimisation.

Rudravaliswaram cave temple (Mamandur II): The hill on the Mamandur and Narasapalaiyam village has four cave excavations. This hill also acts as a natural dam for a large irrigation tank Chitramegha-tataka attributed to Mahendravarman I. On the southern side there are two caves (Fig. 2) contemporary to Mahendravarman. There is no inscription of Mahendravarman in this cave but the neighbouring cave Mamandur I is certainly made by Mahendravarman. This cave has an identical ground plan with Mandagapattu. The facade is plain and has three shrines at the back wall. Probably this temple also was dedicated to trinity.

Fig. 2: Mamandur Cave temple 1 and 2.

The above-mentioned caves from first group have direct or indirect inscriptional reference to suggest they were made by Mahendravarman himself. The Kurananilmuttam temple is discussed by K.R. Srinivasan because of its architectural similarities with Mahendra period cave temples. These three caves were either devoted to trinity or multiple God. Their plan and stylistic executions are almost identical except for some sculptural additions. These were the earliest attempt of the king. The only cave mentioned in the second group is Vallam I. The architectural similarities and mention of Mahendravarman's *viruda* in early Tamil date this cave contemporary to the king.[12] However, the Tamil inscription suggests this temple was made by Kandasena, the feudatory of Mahedravarman.[13] The cave temple at Vallam is a fine example of the imitation of royal endeavour by the feudatory rulers.

Mahendravadi Cave temple: Mahendravadi cave (Fig. 3), situated in the North Arcot district is one of the few temples dedicated to Vishnu. The cave temple is also known as Mahendra Vishnugriha is located near an irrigation tank. The temple faces east and has a single shrine chamber, at the back wall guarded by two doorkeepers. The facade, on the other hand, is very simple and devoid of doorkeepers. The front pillars are the same as the earlier one except the square portion has lotus ornamentation. The *Mukhamandapa* and *Ardhamandapa* each have two pillars and pilasters. The inscription found at the cave mentioned the Mahendravishnugriha, which is created by Gunabhara on the bank of Mahendra-tataka situated in Mahendrapura.[14] It is interesting to note that everything was named after Mahendravarman, but while king is introducing himself he choose the *Viruda* Gunabhara, not Mahendra Vikrama or varman.

Fig. 3: Mahendravadi Cave temple- 1.

Mamandur I: Adjacent to Mamandur cave I (Fig. 2) this cave temple is made by Mahendravarman. Architecturally and ornamentally Mamandur I is almost identical with Mahendravadi cave except the former have only an oblong *Ardhamandapa* and the doorkeepers are absent completely.

Satrumalla cave temple, Dalavanur: The cave temple at Dalavanur in South Arcot district is situated on the Panchapandavamalai hill. This cave (Fig. 4) temple is dedicated to Lord Shiva. The facade of the temple faces south but the shrine on the west wall of the temple faces east. The facade, guarded by two doorkeepers, has two ornamented pillars and pilasters. The architrave of the facade is consists of curved Kapota ornamented with five kudu arches with Gandharva faces inside. The two middle pillars are ornamented with lotus medallion design and the corbel is curved with beautifully ornamented makara torana above the middle entrance. The shrine chamber on the western wall has a pillared porch. The pillar inside has a square base and slightly tapered octagonal shaft with cross corbel on the top. The shrine has two doorkeepers on either side. The Linga and Pitha of the shrine chamber are curved separately. Inscription describes that this temple was built by King Narendra Satrumalla and named as Satrumallesvaralaya.[15] There are two more Tamil inscriptions in this cave temple among them one is dated 9th century is a verse written by Brahmamangalavan Sellan Sivadasan.[16] The subject is however same with the earlier inscription.

Fig. 4: Dalavanur Cave temple 1.

Lalitankura cave temple, Tiruchirappalli: The cave temple is situated on the top of Uchchi-p-pillaiyar-malai also known as Tayumanasvami hill. The location, sculptural execution, and the engraved inscriptions indicate this cave had some strategic importance. The cave is situated near an important Jain resort. The facade of the cave has four pillars and two pilasters forming five openings. The square pillars have an octagonal shaft in the middle. The square part in the bottom and top of the pillar has lotus medallion. Behind the facade, there is an oblong *mandapa* with a row of pillars in front of the back wall. The pillars are symmetrical with the facade pillars. The shrine chamber is on the eastern wall of the *mandapa* flanked by two identical doorkeepers. On the opposite wall of the shrine, the western wall of the *mandapa*, there is a large bass relief of Shiva as a Gangadhara (Fig. 5). This panel becomes more meaningful with two inscriptions engraved on either side of the panel. However, another inscription refer to the cave as Lalitankura-Pallavesvara-griham made by the king Lalitankura.[17]

Fig. 5: Gangadhar Panel at Tiruchirappalli Cave temple.

Avanibhajana cave Temple, Siyamangalam: Siyamangalam cave temple is situated in North Arcot district near a large irrigation tank. These rock-cut cave temples from the central shrine of structural Stambhesvara temple made in the later period by the Pallavas, Cholas, and Vijayanagara rulers. The facade has two pillars and two pilasters. The oblong *mandapa* is divided by another row of pillars and pilaster. The shrine chamber at the back wall has a projecting front with doorkeepers on either side. The shrine is added separately. The inscription mentions that the cave was made by Lalitankura and named as Avanibhajana Pallavesvaram for good deeds.[18] An inscription from a stone nearby suggests that there was a famous Jain seat very near to this cave.[19]

The cave temples of Mahendravarman stylistically were very simple in their execution. Nevertheless, the location of these caves reveals four common features: adjacent to irrigation tank, Jain retreats nearby, dedicated to multiple Gods, and finally naming the cave temple after his *viruda*. Although these features weren't common in every cave but they draw a pattern together. Often rock-cut temple of Mahendravarman I has been compared with existing Buddhist or Jain cave temples, especially due to the lotus medallion ornamentation on the pillar. The lotus medallion basically was very common ornamentation seen in different parts of India with the different religious associations in Mathura, Maharashtra, and Andhra Pradesh, etc. Second, the caves of Mahendravarman have a similar ground plan with Undavalli and Udaygiri caves, but they do not have any similarities with the rock-cut architecture of western Deccan. The making of rock-cut architecture for Buddhist institutions was a cumulative effort and they generally functioned as *Vihara* for both Monks and Gods. The Brahmanical cave temples of western Deccan in the early seventh century were making progress but they seldom had any donatives inscriptions. Which lead to the most important question- what was Mahendravarman's purpose in making them, and do they have any other function apart from religious worship?

The rock-cut cave temples of Mahendravarman I is in most cases situated near an irrigation tank.[20] The water supply from river wasn't sufficient in *Tondaimandalam*, hence several irrigation tanks were built by Pallava rulers.[21] Mahendravarman I not only made these tanks but also carved rock-cut cave temples very close to them. Two well-known irrigation tanks attributed to the King are Mahendra Tātaka and Chitramegha Tātaka adjacent to which Mahendravarman made Mahendravadi and Mamandur caves respectively. The inscription in Mahendravadi mentioned the building of this cave near Mahendravadi Tātaka. It shows that the irrigation tank was either built before the cave or they were contemporary. The association of the water body with the Brahmanical temple is a very common feature in India. The binding of the major agricultural tools with religious perception was probably a conscious attempt of the ruler.

Jain caves were mostly situated in a secluded place and carved on the rocky hill. Dalavanur, Tiruchirappalli and Siyamangalam are three cave temple sites which have Jain beds situated on the top of the hill. The presence of Jain beds and sculptures of Jain Tirthankara on the hilltop was a common feature in Tamil Nadu. The Jain retreats[22] were might have worked as a guide to choose the location of the cave. However, Mahendravarman is believed to be Jain in his early life, so he was probably aware of their existence and used it as a guide for finding a suitable hill to excavate a cave temple.

The name of the temples conveys an important message for the devotees as well as for the donors. Mahendravarman was initially Jain but later converted to Saivism but he dedicated his cave temples to different Gods like Trinity, Vishnu, and Shiva. He also built Pallavaram cave with five shrine chambers at the back wall which must have had five different Gods. Mahendravarman constructed many cave temples for different deities and named them after his *Viruda*. He has always used multiple *Virudas* to mention the builder and the temple name separately. The Mandagapattu cave temple, made by Vichitrachitta, was a tribute to Trinity and called Lakshitayatana.[23] Mahendravadi was dedicated to Murari (Vishnu) and named Mahendra-Vishnugriha but the inscription informs that it was carved by Gunabhara.[24] The cave at Dalavanur dedicated to Shiva made by Narendra Satrumalla was named after him as Satrumallesvaralaya.[25] The cave temples at Tiruchirappalli was named as Lalitankura-Pallavesvaragriham and constructed by Pallava King Lalitankura.[26] Siyamangalam was made by Lalitankura and named as Avanibhajana Pallavesvaram.[27]

All these features reveal Mahendravarman I choose his cave temple sites and excavated them strategically. Mahendravarman was ruling from the Kanchipuram and his Tiruchirappalli cave inscription shows that he extended his territory as far as the bank of the Kaveri on the south. *Tondaimandalam* was included the modern districts of Nellore, Chittoor, North and South Arcot, and Chingleput. All the cave temples claimed to be made by the King are situated within this region. These rock-cut temples were developed as a parallel growth to the political and personal achievements of Mahendravarman. To comprehend these developments carefully a chronological understanding of these caves is necessary. These caves do not give any direct date, but the location of the temple, the architectural development, the deity, and finally the *Viruda* of the king helps to get a probable chronology. The four groups mentioned by K.R. Srinivasan, according to architectural developments, already suggested a chronological order. Mandagapattu inscription shows that it was Mahendravarman's first attempt of a rock-cut cave in his territory. He called himself 'Vichitrachitta' either because of his inventive attempt or as T.K. Ramachandran suggested[28] he liked the nickname given by the mason and architect for his whimsical choice of medium. Whatever may be the reason, it is definite that this was Mahendravarman's first conscious attempt of making rock-cut cave during his time, within his territory.

The Mandagapattu is situated in the South Arcot district. Mahendravarman in the early period of his reign lost the northern part of Kanchipuram to Pulakesin II in the battle of Pullaluru. It was probably after this battle, he made his first inventive temple in the southern area of *Tondaimandalam*. The Mandagapattu being the earliest one, the location, inscription, and architectural execution

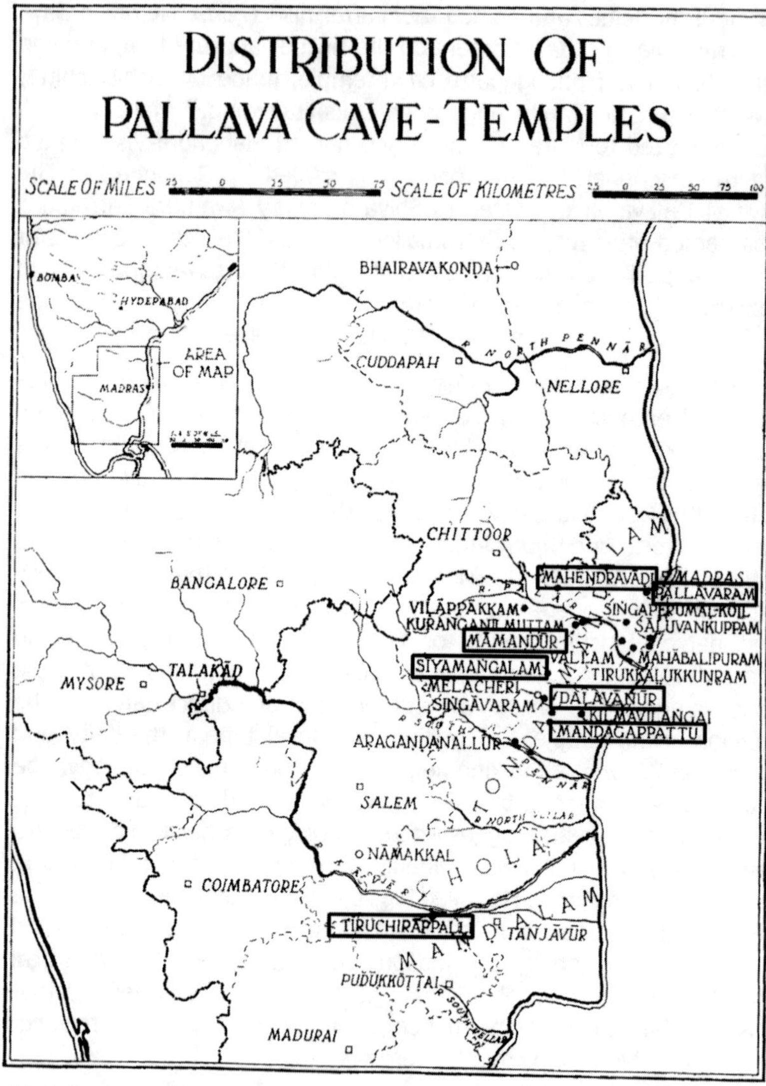

Distribution of Rock-cut cave temple made by Mahendravarman I.
(K.R. Srinivasan, Cave Temples of the Pallavas, Archaeological Survey of India, New Delhi, 1964.)

suggest, if not last Tiruchirappalli cave temple was made at the last period of his reign. The Dalavanur and Siyamangalam can be earlier or contemporary to Tiruchirappalli cave but they are certainly later than the rest of the caves.

The Mandagapattu was dedicated to the trinity. The Pallavaram and Mamandur caves must have been built soon after. The Pallava King built an irrigation tank for agricultural purposes, and Mahendravarman was attributed to two big tanks- Mahendra tātaka and Chitramegha tātaka which are situated very near to three caves built by him. These works for agricultural development must have been done in the early period of his reign. It is no coincidence that most of these early caves are situated near the irrigation tank. The Pallavaram cave has a long list of *Virudas* attributed to Mahendravarman. These *Virudas* were in Sanskrit, Tamil and Telegu language and represent the diverse nature of the king. This list was probably done to testify his other works in different parts of the territory. T.K. Ramachandran[29] has beautifully described different *Virudas* and the King's perspective for accepting them so there is no point in discussing every *Viruda* here. However, few among them are important to understand his motive. His middle stage includes Mahendravadi and Mamandur I. The Mahendravadi cave, Mahendra tataka, and Mahendrapur testify that by the time of its making Mahendravarman had already managed to set up a town with a proper irrigation system which can serve up to 7-8 mile distance.[30] Here he mentioned himself as Gunabhara who split the rock to make this temple. The Mahendravadi cave is carved out from a huge boulder. The inscription reflects immense pride in making this temple completely by him, which wasn't possible. There are remains of fort wall very near to the Mahendra tātaka. It is possible that Mahendravarman built a fort here and developed agriculture and township and this was an important centre of his territory as well as his reign. It is the only temple where everything was named after his royal name Mahendravarman which was very rare for the king. Mahendravadi cave marks the middle phase of his rock-cut temple making. After Mahendra-Vishnugriha the final part of his rock-cut temple initiated with the blessing from Lord Shiva.

After Mahendravadi cave almost every cave was donated to Shiva. It is known that he was converted from Jainism to Shaivism by Appar. This conversion influenced him which can be seen from his three best Shiva cave-temple at Dalavanur, Tiruchirappalli and Siyamangalam. Whether it is a coincidence or intentional selection, is a matter of argument but all these three caves were situated adjacent to existing Jain retreats. Considering his conversion these three cave temples show excellent diplomatic balance. These three sites must have strategic importance, as even long after Mahendravarman's reign his successive kings made addition or contribution to the cave.

The Dalavanur was made by Narendra Satrumalla and named as Satrumallesvaralaya, the abode of Satrumalla's lord.[31] The *Viruda* Satrumalla must have been come after defeating some kings or conquering certain territories. This theory further supported by late prose engraved in the same cave by Sivadasa. He mentioned that the cave was built by Narenda Pottaraiyan who brought great joy in the south of Venbettu (Dalavanur) with his cruel bow bristled with arrow.[32] Mahendravarman probably solved certain political issues and made this temple to commemorate the victory. It was probably a very popular issue in that period, so neither the king nor Sivadasa took time to elaborate on the incident. In this phase, Mahendravarman denoted the Shiva of each rock-cut temple after his own *Viruda*.

The Tiruchirappalli Cave situated at the furthest south of Pallava territory, was the epitome of both political as well as religious prowess of the king. The temple known as Lalitankura-pallavesvaragriham was constructed by the King Lalitankura.[33] However, this temple is more important because of its Gangadhar panel and two inscriptions[34] (Fig. 5) describing why this cave was built. Mahendravarman made this temple for Shiva as Shiva wanted to see the great power of the Chola or River Kaveri from a temple on earth. So he builds a temple on that hill, which was Diadem of Chola power and the temple was a chief jewel of splendour. As Shiva has a history of falling in love with rivers, Parvati also stayed with him to remind that Kaveri is beloved of the Pallava king. This inscription is the ultimate display of pride and confidence to the most worthy opponent as well as to the devotee of the Shiva. Mahendravarman claimed himself as a very close friend as well as an opponent of Shiva. He praised Chola kingdom and doing so he uplifted the status of his temple which symbolise declaration of his political achievements. The conversation with Lord Shiva made him equal to the Gods. The Tiruchirappalli cave was the ultimate roar of Lalitankura-Pallavesvara from the summit of his reign.

The cave at Siyamangalam, made by Lalitankura was named as Avanibhajana Pallavesvara temple.[35] The only one made for the merit and good deeds of the builder. The title Pallavesvara and also the cause of building suggest this was probably the last cave temple build by Mahendravarman. After the Tiruchirappalli, Avanibhajana Pallavesvaralaya was a final tribute of the king. This cave later expanded by the Pallava, Chola, and Vijayanagara kings.

Mahendravarman was a talented person and contributed to a different sphere of artistic creation. His creativity probably was advanced for the contemporary society for which he has been criticised and also praised. Mahendravarman took his criticism as well as achievements and wore them through his *Virudas*. He was an artist and contributed to art, architecture, and literature of the Pallava period. However, he was neither originator nor the inventor of rock-cut architecture in south India. The similarity of Undavalli cave architecture with cave temples of Mahendravarman wasn't a coincidence.[36] He was well aware of rock-cut architecture associated with monastic religions. His *Viruda* 'Chettakari' and his early Jain association support that view. But his involvements accelerate the rock-cut architecture in South India and begin its journey in *Tondaimandalam*. Mahendravarman's contribution towards rock-cut architecture was personalisation of a cooperative endeavour. The Vichitrachitta made Mandagapattu cave and didn't use wood, metal or morter. The Gunabhara spilt the rock and made Mahendravadi cave temple. The Buddhist or Jain caves are basically group effort and in most cases, they were made according to the functions and requirements of the *sangha*. The patron can modify the paintings or ornamentation but the basic ground plan has to be according to their religious need. The *Vinaya* text mentioned in order to make *Vihara* the monk and donor both has to consult and take the approval of the *sangha*.[37] But he presented it as an individual effort which encouraged his contemporaries as well his successor. Narasimhavarman or Mamalla's experimentation of a contribution of Pallava architecture was the fruit of his father's enthusiasm. Mahendravarman I was definitely influenced by earlier architecture but he established a trend stylized according to his requirements. This style was new in *Tondaimandalam* and royal patronisation makes it popular. So this cave-temple architecture influenced local kings like Skandasena,[38] a vassal of the king who donated Vallam I cave temple during his reign, shares the same architectural features. This solves the problem of distribution of rock-cut cave temple, stylistically similar to Mahendra period architecture, all over south India.

The making of rock-cut temples by Mahendravarman I was more of a political endeavour than the religious one. He took a common tradition and presented it in an innovative way. He certainly wasn't the first king who introduced rock-cut architecture in South India, yet he was definitely the first one in making rock-cut temples very popular and accessible by everyone. These temples secured the kingdom with political advancement and religious authority. The distribution of these caves will show the *Tondaimandalam* is surrounded and guarded by his cave temples (see map). These rock-cut temples are reflection of Mahendravarman's reign, a political endeavour presented in a religious platform.

References

1. K.R. Srinivasan, *Cave Temples of the Pallavas*, Archaeological Survey of India, New Delhi, 1964, p. 26.
2. *Epigraphia Indica* (E.I.), Archaeological Survey of India, 1923-24, Vol. XVII, p. 17.
3. Noboru Karashima, (ed.), *A Concise History of South India Issues and Interpretations*, Oxford University Press, 2014, p. 85.
4. K.R. Srinivasan, *op.cit.*, p. 5.
5. T.N. Ramchandran, "The Royal Artist Mahendravarman", *Oriental Research*, Madras, 1933, Vol.VII, p. 221.
6. M.S. Mate, "Origin of Pallava Art: The Undavalli Caves", *East and West*, Vol. 20, No. 1/2 (March-June 1970), pp.108-116.
7. G. Subbiah, "Malayadi-K-Kurichi Rock-Cut Temple-its Date and Significance", *Proceedings of the Indian History Congress*, 1978, Vol.39, Volume I, pp. 104-109.
8. Mailyn Harsh, "Mahendravarman I Pallava: Artist and Patron of Mamallapuram", *Artibus Asiae*, Vol. 48, No. 1/2 (1987), pp.109-123.
9. *E.I.*, Vol. XVII, p.17.
10. K.R. Srinivasan, *op.cit.*, pp. 37-38.
11. *Ibid.*, p. 47.
12. *Ibid.*, pp. 61-63.
13. T.N. Ramchandran, *op.cit.*, p. 230.
14. E. Hultzsch (ed.), *Epigraphia Indica and Record of the Archaeological Survey of India*,1896-97, Vol. IV, pp. 152-53.
15. Konow, Sten (ed.), *Epigraphia Indica and Record of the Archaeological Survey of India*, 1913-14, Vol.XII, pp.225-226.
16. V. Venkatasubba Ayyar, *South Indian Inscription*, The Pallavas, Vol. 12, No.11, p. 7.
17. K.R. Srinivasan, *op.cit.*, p. 79.
18. E. Haltzsch (ed.), *Epigraphia Indica*, Archaeological Survey of India, New Delhi, 1981, Vol.VI, p. 320.
19. K.R. Srinivasan, *op.cit.*, p. 91.
20. *Ibid.*, p. 49.
21. Noboru Karashima, (ed.), *op.cit.*, pp. 93-94.
22. K.R. Srnivasan, *op.cit.*, p. 79.
23. K.R. Srnivasan, *op.cit.*, p. 47.
24. *E.I.*, Vol. IV, p. 153.
25. *E.I.*, Vol. XVII, p. 225.

26. *S.I.I.*, Vol. XXII, No. 9.
27. *E.I.*, Vol. VI, p. 320.
28. T.N. Ramchandran, *op.cit.*, pp. 220-221.
29. *Ibid.*, pp. 226-229.
30. *E.I.*, Vol. IV, p. 152.
31. *E.I.*, Vol.XII, p. 225.
32. *E.I.*, Vol. XII, p. 226.
33. *S.I.I.*, Vol. XII, No.9, p. 6.
34. *S.I.I.*, Vol. I, Nos. 33 and 34.
35. *E.I.*, Vol. VI, p. 320.
36. M.S. Mate, *op.cit.*, pp. 113-116.
37. F. Max Mullar (ed.), *The Scared Book of the East*, Vol. XIII, 1881, pp. 8-9.
38. T.N. Ramchandran, *op.cit.*, p. 230.

Bibliography

Epigraphia Indica (E.I.), Archaeological Survey of India, Relevant Volumes.

Haltzsch, E. (ed.), *Epigraphia Indica*, Archaeological Survey of India, New Delhi, 1981, Vol. VI.

Hultzsch, E. (ed.), *Epigraphia Indica and Record of the Archaeological Survey of India*, 1896-97, Vol. IV.

Konow, Sten (ed.), *Epigraphia Indica and Record of the Archaeological Survey of India*, 1913-14, Vol. XII.

Mailyn Harsh, "Mahendravarman I Pallava: Artist and Patron of Mamallapuram", *Artibus Asiae*, Vol.48, No. 1/2 (1987).

Mate, M.S., "Origin of Pallava Art: The Undavalli Caves", *East and West*, Vol. 20, No. 1/2 (March-June 1970).

Max Mullar, F. (ed.), *The Scared Book of the East*, Vol. XIII, 1881.

Noboru Karashima (ed.), *A Concise History of South India Issues and Interpretations*, Oxford University Press, 2014.

Ramchandran, T.N., "The Royal Artist Mahendravarman", *Oriental Research*, Madras, 1933, Vol.VII.

Srinivasan, K.R., *Cave Temples of the Pallavas*, Archaeological Survey of India, New Delhi, 1964.

Subbiah, G., "Malayadi-K-Kurichi Rock-Cut Temple-its Date and Significance", *Proceedings of the Indian History Congress*, 1978, Vol. 39, Volume I.

Venkatasubba Ayyar, V., *South Indian Inscription*, The Pallavas, Vol. XII, No. 11.

17

Territorial Administrative Divisions of Medieval Tamil country: An Epigraphical Study on Pandya Country

R. Govindaraj

The Pāṇḍya rulers divided the empire in to major as well as minor administrative units in medieval order. The study and classification of the administrative divisions referred to in the inscriptional records of particular area reveal approximate extent of the territory. Thus, the historical geography of a political set up can be visualised and demarcated by realising the extent of the administrative divisions. The present endeavour is an attempt to investigate territorial administrative division of Pāṇḍya country up to 13th century CE. The administrative divisions referred to in the inscriptions of the region have been examined and identified with their modern parallels as accurately as possible. In the following pages the salient features of territorial appellations like *Maṇḍalam*, *Vaḷanāḍu*, *Nāḍu*, *Kūṟṟam*, *Muṭṭam* and *Irukkai* are discussed in a brief manner.

The Tamils from very early times knew the geographical varieties which characterised the land. Perhaps, after generations of observation they found that there were such as hilly tracts, forest lands on the plateaus, fertile cultivable lands in the delta- areas and in river valleys and coast land in this country. It was natural that they should have thought of the sea coast, for, in Tamiḻnāḍu even the most interior place was no more than a hundred and fifty miles from the nearest sea – shore. The interest in the sea was very pronounced.[1]

Historical Geography

The Tamil country in the *Sangam age* was ruled by the three crowned monarchs and many minor chieftains too. The country comprised of the entire area to the South of a line that may be drawn to connect Bangalore with Madras. It was called *Tamiḻakam* or Tamiḻnaḍu. The major political divisions of the country were the Chōḻa Nāḍu,[2] the Pāṇḍya Nāḍu and the Chēra Nāḍu. The Chēra Nāḍu in particular was called Kuḍanāḍu.[3] (meaning western country) though Kuḍagu or Kuḍagu-nāḍu in restricted sense came to mean modern Coorg only. The Chēra himself was called Kuṭṭuvan, as they ruled over Kuṭṭanāḍu. Ptolemy's 'Cottonara' from which pepper was exported to Rome was evidently Kuṭṭanāḍu. The Chēra land being hilly was the Kuriñji of Tamil literary known.[4]

The Chōḻas held way over the fertile Kāvēri-delta region. Agriculture was the chief occupation of the people of the Chōḻa country. Agricultural land is called as '*marudam*' of Tamil literary convention. Surprisingly enough, the entire land was naturally apportioned among the three crowned monarchs; one ruling over 'Kuriñji', another over 'Mullai' and yet another over the 'Marudam' Neydal and Pālai, being coastal tracts and desert land respectively formed only a small part of the country.[5]

The Pāṇḍyas ruled over the predominantly pastoral districts of the Tamil country i.e., Dindugal, Theni, Madurai, Tirunelveli, Thoothukudi, Sivagangai and Virudhunagar districts. The Pāṇḍya Nāḍu, situated in southern most region of Tamiḻnāḍu, was ruled by the Sangam Pāṇḍyas, Kaḷabrahs, Early Pāṇḍyas, Chōḻas, medieval Pāṇḍyas and Second Pāṇḍyas. After second Pāṇḍyan Empire the Pāṇḍyas Nāḍu came under the control of Muslim invaders. The Muslim invaders ruled this country for about six decades. In 1371 C.E. Kumara Kambana a prince of Vijayanagara Empire, put an end to the Muslim ruler and the power was transferred to Vijayanagara Empire. Vishwanatha Nayakkar introduced *Nayaka* rule in the year of 1529 C.E. which lasted up to 1736. It was then ruled by the Arcot Nawabs and finally came under the control of British East India Company. It is surrounded by the Bay of Bengal in the east and on the southern side by the Indian Ocean. On its western part is the densely forested Western Ghats. The Western Ghats divides the *Pāṇḍya Nāḍu* from *Chēra Nāḍu* and in its north-west is *Kon˙gu Nāḍu* (Coimbatore region). The North West boundary extends up to the Veḷḷāru River near Pudukkottai. This river divided the two countries viz., Pāṇḍya Nāḍu and Chōḷa Nāḍu.

During the Pandya rule the territorial administration was divided into different units. The classification of the administrative divisions referred to in the inscriptional records of particular area reveal approximate extent of the territory. Thus, the historical geography of a political landscape can be visualised and demarcated by realising the extent of the administrative divisions.[6] The salient features of territorial appellations like *Maṇḍalam*, *Vaḷanāḍu*, *Nāḍu*, *Kūṟṟam*, *Muṭṭam* and *Irukkai* are discussed in the succeeding pages. The present attempt is mostly based on inscriptional sources. Earlier there are number of studies had done in the field of territorial administrative aspect, like the Political Geography of the Chola country by Y. Subbarayalu (1973), Pandya Country by V. Vedachalam (1996) and R. Tirumalai (2003), Pudukkottai region by Rajavelu (2003) and Kanchipuram region by C. Santhalingam (2003). These studies mainly focus the various aspects of the administrative structures of the respective region.

Accordingly the ancient Tamil country was divided into *Nāḍus*, like Chōḻa Nāḍu, Chēra Nāḍu, Pāṇḍya Nāḍu, Toṇḍai Nāḍu, and Koṅgu Nāḍu. The Pāṇḍya Nāḍu was divided into *Vaḷanāḍus* and the *Vaḷanāḍus* were further divided into *Nāḍus*, *Kūṟṟam*, *Muṭṭam* and *Irukkai*. Later the *Nāḍu* was further sub-divided into Ūr.[7] In the beginning it was called as Pāṇḍya Nāḍu. During the period of Rājarāja I, it was changed into *Rājarāja - Vaḷanāḍu* and remained in the same name till 991 C.E. Later it was renamed as *Rājarāja Maṇḍalam* and this name continued up to 1012 C.E. It was again renamed as *Rājarāja Pāṇḍya Nāḍu* during the Chola period. Some parts of the southernmost area were controlled by the chieftains *Āye Vēḷir*. These chieftains were ruling as the subordinates of the Pāṇḍya kings. At the same time, another chieftain family called *Muttaraiyar* was ruling in the Pudukkottai region under the Pāṇḍyas.[8]

Maṇḍalam

The 'Chōḻa-Maṇḍalam', whose territorial extent has been fairly determined, did not come into existence until 1009 C.E.[9] Earlier the Chōḻa country was known by the name *Chōḻa Nāḍu* (or *Chōnāḍu*) and was smaller in extent. The *Nāḍu* units mentioned as belonging to the *Chōḻa Nāḍu* until 1009 C.E. The Chōḻa-Maṇḍalam is referred to for the first time in an inscription of 1009 C.E.[10] Along with this, it seems, some of the conquered territories were given new names; Toṇḍai-Nāḍu alias Jayaṅkoṇḍa Chōḻamaṇḍalam, Pāṇḍi Nāḍu alias

Rājarāja - Maṇḍalam, Nuḷamba-Pāḍi alias Nigarilachōḻa-Pāḍi and Īḻam alias Mummuḍichōḻa-Maṇḍalam. During the reign of Rājendra I, Gaṅga-Pāḍi was given the name of Muḍikoṇḍachōḻa-Maṇḍalam. We hear about an officer called *Maṇḍala-Mudali* in connection with the *Maṇḍalams* other than Chōḻamaṇḍalam. An inscription of Kulōttuṅga I informs that the king issued an order in his 12th year (1082 CE) from Kanchipuram to *Toṇḍaimānār* who was acting as the *Maṇḍala-Mudali* at Talaikkādu alias Rājarājapuram in Muḍikoṇḍachōḻa-Maṇḍalam asking the later to constitute a new *Brahmadēya* and make necessary entries in the *puravuvari* and that the same king issued another order in his 34th year (1104 CE) to the then *Maṇḍala-Mudali*, Rājēndra Chōḻa-*Brahmādirājar* asking him to make entries, regarding some additional grant of land to the same *Brahmadēya*, in the *puravuvari* of Muḍikoṇḍachōḻapuram. Similarly a *Maṇḍala-Mudali*[11] (of Pāṇḍimaṇḍalam) is mentioned in another inscription of the same king.

Vaḷanāḍu

The term *'vaḷam'* means fertile and *'nāḍu'* means country, hence the term *'valanādu'* denotes fertile country. The *Vaḷanāḍu* is an administrative division practiced since first Pāṇḍya Empire. More than ten *Vaḷanāḍu* divisions seem to have existed in the Pāṇḍya country such as Vaikuṇṭa Vaḷanāḍu[12] (represented Nanguneri taluk, 867 CE). Parāntaka Vaḷanāḍu[13] (Srivaikuntam taluk 875 CE), Amithaguṇa Vaḷanāḍu[14] (Tiruchendur and Srivaikuntam taluk 879 CE), Vaḻuthi Vaḷanāḍu[15] (Srivaikuntam taluk 879 CE). Māṉavīra Vaḷanāḍu,[16] and Srivallabha Vaḷanāḍu[17] (both are represented Tiruchendur taluk). The above mentioned *Vaḷanāḍu* divisions were represented before the regime of Rājarāja I and they all *Vaḷanāḍu* situated in Tirunelveli district only. During the days of Rājarāja Chōḻa I, Pāṇḍya Nāḍu was called as Rājarāja Vaḷanāḍu.[18] The Pāṇḍya Nāḍu's biggest administrative unit Nāḍu now came to be changed as *Maṇḍalam*. This unit was introduced by *Rājarāja Chōḻa*. The *Maṇḍalam* unit is equalent to Nāḍu. From the year 1012 C.E. onwards Pāṇḍya Nāḍu was called as Rājarāja Maṇḍalam[19] (Kovilpatti, Ambasamudram and Nanguneri taluks). Entire Pāṇḍya country was divided by four administrative units namely; Rājēndrachōḻa Vaḷanāḍu[20] (in between the part of Vellaru and Vaigai River at Present Paramakudi, Sivagangai, Arantangi, Tirumeyyam and Tiruppattur Taluks); the tract to the south and east of Madurai was named as Madurāntaka Vaḷanāḍu[21] (in between the part of Vaigai and Vaipparu rivers at present Rajapalayam, Srivilliputtur, Sattur, Aruppukottai, Sivagangai and Mudukulattur taluks); Muḍikoṇḍachōḻa

Vaḷanāḍu[22] (in between the part of Vaipparu and Tāmiraparaṇi rivers at present Tenkasi, Ambasamudram, Sankarankovil, Kovilpatti, Tirunelveli and Thoothukudi districts) and Uthamachōḻa Vaḷanāḍu [23] (in between the part of Tāmiraparaṇi and Kanyakumari present at Tiruchendur, Srivaikuntam and Nanguneri taluks).

Some of the other Vaḷanāḍus are Kēraḷasiṅgavaḷanāḍu,[24] (Tirupattur, Pudukkottai, Sivaganga regions), Mudurai udaiya Vaḷanāḍu [25] (Sivagangai taluk), Arumoḻidēva Vaḷanāḍu,[26] Pāṇḍikulasani Vaḷanāḍu,[27] Varaguṇa Vaḷanāḍu[28] (Tiruvadanai taluk), Chōḻapāṇḍya Vaḷanāḍu[29] (Tirupattur taluk), etc. Present Madurai district have had only one Vaḷanāḍu i.e., Madurāntaka Vaḷanāḍu which survived in the name of Madurōdaya Vaḷanāḍu upto fourteenth century, etc.[30]

Nāḍu

The term 'Nāḍu' indicates an ancient territorial division. This term has been existence from the *Sangam* period upto Nāyaka period in Tamil country. During the Pallava period the term Nāḍu connotes two different meanings. The first one is used for indicating a bigger territorial division, called *Periya - nāḍu*. It was derived from dynastic name like Chōḻa Nāḍu, Chēra Nāḍu, Pāṇḍya Nāḍu, Toṇḍai Nāḍu and Koṅgu Nāḍu. The second one is a smaller territorial division, i.e., Āṉmar Nāḍu, Teṉkallaga Nāḍu etc. These are revenue and administrative units. These bigger and smaller territorial divisions continued during the Pāṇḍya and Chōḻa period also.[31] There were three terms often in use to denote the cluster or group of villages. They are Nadu, Kurram and Muttam.[32]

The *Nāḍu* (with synonym '*Kūṟṟam*') is the very key to the political geography of the Pāṇḍya country. It was a very important limb of administrative system of the period under study and it was basic unit of the then agrarian society. For a clear understanding of the subject it is necessary to distinguish and recognize at this stage itself the two different but inter linked aspects regarding this unit, viz. *Nāḍu*, the territorial unit and *Nāḍu*, the assembly. In inscriptions the distinction is well maintained by the use mostly of them *Nāṭṭār* to indicate the latter.[33]

The term *Nāḍu* has another significance referring to the collective body of the *Nāḍu* consisting of its occupants the *Nāṭṭār*. In the sense, it may refer to the *Veḷḷāḷar* or *Veḷḷāṉvagai* occupants in some instances specifically cited by Y. Subbarayalu, as the Mannarkudi inscription of Rājarāja III clearly conveys.[34]

The Earliest Reference for Nāḍu

The Tamil Brahmi inscription found at Sittannavasal refers to Erumi-Nāḍu, a territorial unit.[35] Palaeographically, this inscription is dated to the 3rd or 2nd century B.C.E. The *Sangam* poem *Aganānūṟu* mentions about Erumai - Nāḍu.[36] These are the earliest reference to *Nāḍu*, in Tamil Nadu and Karnataka regions. The *Erumai-Nāḍu* (present Mysore) located in southern Karnataka region.[37] The discovery of three important inscriptions at Pulankurichi dated to the 5th century CE gives the earliest and authentic evidence of the territorial divisions, which existed in Tamil country. These inscriptions mention three territorial units namely Kūdalūr Nāḍu (Kudalur), Ollaiyūrkūṟṟam and Muttūṟṟukūṟṟam. The inscriptions of succeeding periods provide amble evidence for the continuous existence of the above territorial units.[38] The Vēḷvikuḍi copper plate dated to the 770 CE gives the authentic evidence of territorial division, which existed in Pāgaṉūr Kūṟṟam (present Vadipatti taluk of Madurai district).[39]

Nāḍu- Agricultural Region

The *'Nāḍu'* has the generic sense of 'land' or 'country'. But we have some specific evidences from literature that 'Nāḍu' signified something more than this generic aspect. In a *Puṟanānūṟu* verse,[40] a Chēra king is extolled as scion of a family of benevolent rulers who had the good fortune of being obliged by the hills, the forests and the *Nāḍu* under this rule.[41] Here *Nāḍu* is clearly distinguished from hills and forests. It is implicated the civilised and inhabited space of the country. And this is supported by the *Paṭṭiṉapālai* wherein it is stated that the Chōḻa king Karikala created *Nāḍu* (*Nāḍu-ākki*) by clearing forests (*kāḍu koṉṟu*)[42] taking clue from this can it not be suggested that *Nāḍu* was basically an agricultural region? If the suggestion is valid, the *Nāḍus* could not have artificial administrative divisions. They could be only groupings of agricultural settlements, whose formations would have been influenced by natural factors conducive to agriculture, like slope, soils, water supply, etc. This suggestion is well warranted as will be shown in sequel after dealing with problem of *Nāḍu*, the assembly.[43] The Pāṇḍya country had more than hundred *Nāḍus*. They were divided basically for agriculture settlements. The Pāṇḍya Nāḍu had innumerable water resources for agriculture and fertile soil for cultivation. Agriculture was an important field for revenue of the Pāṇḍya government. The kingdom had natural resources such as channels, rivers, tanks, wells etc.[44] Even though *Nāḍu* was divided for administrative purpose, it was basically created on the basis of geographical reasons.

Nāḍus in the Pāṇḍya Country

The *Nāḍu* was a sub-division of *Valanāḍu* which would be equated to the modern *taluks* such as Kāṉa Nāḍu in Virudharājabhayaṅkara Vaḷanāḍu (Pudukkottai region), Poygaiyūr Nāḍu in Vaḍakarai, Rājarāja Vaḷanāḍu, Kō-Nāḍu in Kaḍalaḍaiyā-tilaṅgai-koṇḍa-Chōḻa-Vaḷanāḍu, Kīḻvembu Nāḍu[45] (Tirunelveli District), Tirumalai Nāḍu[46] (Sivagangai district), Anda Nāḍu[47] (Palani), Āri Nāḍu[48] (Sankarankovil taluk), Sāla Nāḍu (northern portion of Tiruchuli and eastern part of Kariapatti), Kañai-irukkai Nāḍu[49] (eastern part Tiruchuli), Paruthikuḍi Nāḍu[50] (western region of Tiruchuli), Pūṅgā Nāḍu[51] (Aruppukottai), Poḻiyūrnāḍu,[52] Vayalūr Nāḍu[53] (eastern part of Paraipatti), Venbu Nāḍu[54] (eastern part of Aruppukkottai), Aḷaṟṟu Nāḍu[55] (southern part Aruppukkottai), Irunjōḻa Nāḍu[56] (Sattur), Karunīlakkudi Nāḍu[57] (northern part of Sivakasi), Venbaikudi Nāḍu[58] (southern part of Sivakasi), Malli Nāḍu[59] (southern part of Srivilliputtur), Kaṇḍa Nāḍu (northern part of Srivilliputtur), Ānmar Nāḍu[60] (Rajapalayam), Vaigāvūr Nāḍu[61] (Palani), Karaikōṭṭu Nāḍu[62] (Dindugal). The present Madurai district had been divided into several Nāḍus viz., Seṅgudi Nāḍu[63] (Southern Part of Tirumangalam taluk), Teṉmuṭṭanāḍu[64] (Tirumangalam taluk), Teṉparappu Nāḍu[65] (Melur and Madurai North), Vaḍaparappu Nāḍu[66] (Melur) and Teṉkallaga Nāḍu[67] (Usilampatti taluk).

Kūṟṟam

The *Vaḷanāḍu* was sub-divided into the *Kūṟṟam*s. The *Kūṟṟam* is a territorial division means just a divided part. The word *Kūṟṟam* which existed from *Sangam* period was a division of territory during the ancient period particularly in the Pāṇḍya country.

Milaḻaik Kūṟṟathudaṉē
....Muthūṟṟuk Kūṟṟathaik Koṇḍa[68]

The above verses of *Puṟanāṉūṟu* mentioned the two Kūṟṟam namely, *Milaḻai* and *Muthūṟṟu Kūṟṟams*. The former was located in Arantangi, Tirumeyyam taluks and the later in Tiruvadanai taluk. This usage confirms that *Nāḍu* and *Kūṟṟam* are more or less synonymous. Y. Subbarayalu's interpretation on the same lines is attested by the evidence. Several *Ūr's* contain in one constituency that one constituency called as *Kūṟṟam*. The first epigraphical evidence on this territorial division is found in the Pulankurichi inscription of the 4th and 5th century C.E. The inscription also refers to *Muthūṟṟu Kūṟṟam* and *Ollaiyūr Kūṟṟam*.[69] The *Kūṟṟam* is said to be either *Nāḍus* or units bigger than *Nāḍus* but there were *Kūṟṟams* smaller than the *Nāḍus* too.[70] For the administrative convenience, the early and later Pāṇḍyas divided the territory into *Kūṟṟam*.

Kūṟṟam in the Pāṇḍya Country

There were several Kūṟṟams in the Pāṇḍya kingdom e.g. Thuvvūr Kūṟṟam, (Paramakudi region),[71] Milaḻai Kūṟṟam[72] (Arantangi region), Tirukkāṉappēr Kūṟṟam[73] (Sivagangai region) and Muthūṟṟu Kūṟṟam (Tiruvadanai region).[74] Pāgaṉūr Kūṟṟam was also mentioned in the Vēḷvikuḍi copper plate which seeks about the earliest Pāṇḍya grant. Arumbūrkūṟṟam, Koḻūvūrkūṟṟam[75] also noticed in the Pandya inscriptions.

Muṭṭam

There were three terms often used to denote the cluster or group of villages. They are Nāḍu (Teṉkallaga Nāḍu present Usilampatti taluk), *Kūṟṟam* (Pāgaṉūr Kūṟṟam present Vadipatti region) and *Muṭṭam* (Kīḻraniya- *Muṭṭam* and Mēḻraniya- *Muṭṭam* present Melur region). Kīḻ and Mēlraniya- *Muṭṭam* on the eastern and south-western side of Alagarkovil hills appear to follow the geographical delineation. The *Muṭṭam* seems to refer, among others, a village or township or it may mean side or slope of the hills or mountains which formed a natural boundary or delimitations.[76]

In the inscriptions of the Pandya country we find references to the various Muttam. They are Kēralạsiṅgavalạnāṭṭu Mēlai Tiruttiyūrmuṭṭam[77] (Paganeri Sivagangai taluk), Kīḻai Tiruttiyūrmuṭṭam[78] (Siruvayal Sivagangai taluk), Veṇbaikudi nāṭṭu Thuḍaiyaṉūr muṭṭam,[79] Teṉ- *Muṭṭa* Nāḍu[80] (Tirumanickam), and Vaḍa-Muṭṭa-Nāḍu[81] etc.

Irukkai

Irukkai means in Tamil is a habitation settlements and which is equal to Nāḍu or taluk level administrative unit. The Irukkai settlements are the lowest unit in the Pāṇḍya country. The Venbunāṭṭu-Seṅgāṭṭirukkai, Kañai-Irukkai, Achaṅkāṭṭirukkai, Vaḍavallaitirukkai,[82] (Ilayangudi taluk), Teṉvallaitirukkai[83] (Paramakudi taluk), Sevvirukkai Nadu, Kaḷatirukkai[84] (Sattur taluk) are some of the habitation settlement Irukkai we find in Pandya inscriptions.

Other Divisions

The *Kurram*, *Nāḍu*, *Muṭṭam* and *Irukkai* were sub-divided into micro level administrative divisions such as *Ūr*, *Kuḍi*, *chaturvēdimaṅgalam* or *Brahmadēyams*, *Nallūr*, *Nagaram*, *Pattinam*, *Puram* and *Perunteru*.

Ūr and Kuḍi

The *Ūr* is a common suffix for various types of settlements. Mostly, these settlements were very old agrarian settlements. According to the Tamil grammatical traditions, *ūr* is a suffix for settlements located in the Marudam land.[85] There are some of the *ūr* settlements in the Pāṇḍya country namely, Tēṉūr,[86] Pāgaṉūr,[87] Tiruvēḍagam and Tirumāttūr.[88]

Kuḍi

Another frequently used suffix for naming the place is *kuḍi*. This is synonym to the suffix *'Ur'* as *kuḍi* also denotes agricultural village. The *Kuḍi* is also widely used for a settlement of people belonging to the same blood or a settlement of people with close relationships with each other.[89] Some of the *kuḍi* settlements are, Veṭṭikuḍi,[90] Malaikuḍi,[91] and Kalkuḍi.[92]

Maṅgalam / Nallūr

It is generally believed that *maṅgalam* and *nallūr* were the settlements of *Brahmins* and the villages connected with temples. Usually royal names were added to the prefix of *maṅgalam* and *nallūr*. The meaning of them, signify the auspices settlement.[93] They are Chōḻāntaka-chaturvēdimaṅgalam,[94] the city Chōḻākulāntaka-chaturvēdimaṅgalam,[95] Parāntaka-chaturvēdimaṅgalam,[96] Jananātha-Chaturvēdimaṅgalam[97] and Vīranārāyana-chaturvēdimaṅgalam.[98] Kulasēkaramaṅgalam,[99] Adhijaya-maṅgalam,[100] Viḷakkamaṅgalam[101] Srikarana Mangalam,[102] Virudharāja Bayaṅgaranallūr,[103] Mūvāyiranallūr[104] and Vīraiyaviḍaṅganallūr.[105]

Piḍagai settlements (Villages or Suburbs)

The village is the smallest administrative unit of a country. Several villages together formed a unit or a division of administration. Village or *grama* is different from the *ur* which is a bigger unit. Inscriptions state that certain areas outside the official village boundaries were considered to be under the village's administrative jurisdiction. Such areas were usually designated Pidagai (Padagai or "hamlets"), Pāl, and Puram. The village does not simply mean the area of land which comprises of the habitation area of that village. It also contains, for all administrative purposes, the surrounding lands the owners of which are normally, the residents of the village. Some big villages, which were religious or commercial centers or Brahmadēyas, had some suburbs which were indicated by the terms *Pidagai* (*Padagai*), *Pal* and *Puram*.[106]

References to the Pidagai or Padagai settlements are abundance in the inscriptions of the Pandya country. An inscription from Sengundrapuram in Virudhunagar district mentioned Sengudinattu Sengudi Nagaramana - Mēlpidagai (mēl or mēṟ means in Tamil west).[107] The same district Mettuppatti village record says that Veṇbunāṭṭu Nagur Merpidagai (Pidagai of Vembunāṭṭu Nagur),[108] Tirunelveli district, Ambasamudram taluk Tiruvalisvaram temple inscription speaks about Rājarājapāṇḍināttu Mudikoṇḍa Chōḻavalaṇāṭṭu Mulliṉāṭṭu Brahmadēyam Sri Rājarājacharuppēdimaṅgalattu Mēlpidagai Mērūr (Pidagai of MulliṉNāḍu Brahmadēyam Sri Rājarājacharuppēdimaṅ galam).[109] The same district same taluk Erichchavudaiyar temple inscription mentions Rājarājapāṇḍi Nāṭṭu Muḍikoṇḍa Chōḻavalaṇāṭṭu Mulliṉāṭṭu Sri Rājarājacharuppēdimaṅgalattu Teṉpidagai (Pidagai of Sri Rājarājacharuppēdimaṅgalam,[110] same district and same taluk Mannarkovil temple inscriptions says about Rājarājapāṇḍināttu Mudikoṇḍa Chōḻavalaṇāṭṭu Mulliṉāṭṭu Sri Rājarājacharuppēdimaṅgalattu Pidagai Pāmbunāri, Pidagai Kadayattu, Pidagai Pulikuḷam[111], Madurai district Alagarkovil inscriptions says that Veṇbunāṭṭu Vāṉavaṉmahadēvi chaturvēdimaṅgalattu Pidagai (Pidagai of Vāṉavaṉmahadēvi-chaturvēdimaṅgalattu)[112], Kēraḷasiṅgavaḷanāṭṭu Tirukkottiyur Pidagai (Pidagai of Kēraḷasiṅgavaḷanāṭṭu Tirukkottiyur);[113] Madurai district Melur taluk Sokkalingapuram inscription mentions Rājēndrachōḻa Chaturvēdimaṅgalattu Mēlpidagai (Pidagai of Rājēndrachōḻa Chaturvēdimaṅgalattu);[114] same taluk Panangadi village inscriptions mentions about Rājēndrachōḻa Chaturvēdimaṅgalattu Dāmōdaramaṅgalam (Pidagai Damodaramangalam of Rājēndrachōḻa Chaturvēdimaṅgalam).[115] An Alagarkovil temple inscription mentions Tirumāliruñchōlai Nallūrpidagai;[116] same temple inscription mentions the Pāgaṉūr Kūṟṟattu Māṅgāikkuḍi Pidagai,[117] Chōḻāntakachaturvēdi-maṅgalattu Mēlpidagai Paṭṭakuṟichi;[118] Vikramangalam temple inscription mentions Teṉpidagai[119] and Madurai Sundaresvara temple inscription mentions about Brahmadēyam Aḍukkalạipuramāṉa Koḍimaṅgalamāṉa Muḍittalaikoṇḍa Pāṇḍyachaturvēdimaṅgalattu Māttūr Pidagai.[120] Some inscriptions from Pandya country speak of Pāl, which is equivalent term to suburbs. Usilampatti taluk Anaiyur temple inscription mentions about Vadapāl Thachaguḍi;[121] Alagarkovil inscriptions mention about Sri *Chōḻakulāntaka Chaturvēdimaṅgalattu Kīḻpāl* and *Chōḻasigāmaṇinallūr* Vaḍapāl.[122]

Nagaram, Puram and Perunteru

The term '*nagaram*', '*perunteru*' and '*teru*' denote the settlement of mercantile groups. The *Nagaram* generally means a city or town, was a commercial centre and the settlement place of merchant group of the medieval Tamil country. The *nagaram*, settlement was also referred to as *perunteru* or simply *teru*. Most of the commercial centre were named after the king's names or titles.[123] For instance, the merchant town belongs to Pāganūr Kūrram *Rājarājapperuntervu*[124] is named after the Chola king Rājarāja I.

The *Puram* is a name given to the merchant settlement. We find frequent usage of the term *puram* in Pandya inscriptions. The villages with *puram* suffix are named after kings and poets. Parākramapāṇḍyapuram,[125] Kulasēkarapuram,[126] Srivallavapuram,[127] *Porunthalāna Dēvēndiravallavapuram*[128] were some of the *puram* belongs to Pāganūr-*kūrram* region. *Vikramachōḻapuram*[129] is belongs to Tenkallaganāḍu, which is located on the western part of Pāganūr-*kūrram* and Kēraḷānthakāpuram[130] belongs to the region of Nerkuppainādu.

Conclusion

On the basis of detailed study of the Pandya inscriptions, it is important to note that the territorial administrative divisions were existed in the Pandya country, such as *Maṇḍalam, Vaḷanāḍu, Nāḍu, Kūrram, Muṭṭam and Irukkai*. These kinds of administrative units were practiced into throughout ancient and medieval Tamil region. After the arrival of Vijayanagara and Nayaka rulers the traditional territorial administrative units were abolished by the Nayaks. They introduced new administrative units called *Palayam* and *Sirmai* instead of Tamil administrative units *Mandalam* and *Valanadu*.

Place names containing personal names or epithets of the kings and the officials are found largely in the *Brahmadēyam* and mercantile villages. The varieties of townships and larger territorial divisions, the *Nāḍus* and *Vaḷanāḍus* were already formed and found adopted. They should have been the crystallisation of centuries of continuing in the 8th and 9th centuries CE. The creation of the *Kūrram* and the *Nāḍu* territorialising had already been established. Pāṇḍya's several copper plates elaborately describe how these settlements came to being established. The *ūr, kuḍi, maṅgalam, nallūr, piḍagai, nagaram, perunteru* and *puram* settlements were very important local administrative units looked after the local self government.

References

1. S. Sundararajan, *Ancient Tamil Country: Its Social and Economic Structure*, Navrang, New Delhi, 1991, p. 22.
2. *Purananuru*, 166, 181.
3. *Ibid*, 17, 177
4. S. Sundararajan, *op.cit.*, p. 30.
5. *Idem.*
6. E. Sreedhar, *Historical Cultural Geography and Ethnography of Andhra under The Vijayanagara From XIV to XVII Century A.D.*, Unpublished Ph.D. thesis submitted to Sree Krishnadevaraya University, Anantapur, 2011, p. 23.
7. K.V. Raman, *History of Pandyas*, Government of Tamil Nadu, Chennai, 1977, p.146.
8. *Idem.*
9. Y. Subbarayalu, *Political Geography of the Chola Country*, Madras, 1973, p. 14.
10. *Idem, A.R.E.*, No. 22 of 1922.
11. Y. Subbarayalu, *op.cit.*, p.14.; *I.P.S.*, No. 126.
12. *S.I.I.*, Vol. XIV, No. 19.
13. *E.I.*, Vol. XXI, No.17.
14. *S.I.I.*, Vol. XIV, No. 16 (A).
15. *Idem.*
16. *Idem.*
17. *Idem.*
18. *A.R.E.*, No. 415 of 1906.
19. *Idem.*
20. *S.I.I.*, Vol. XIV, No. 145.
21. *Ibid.*, No. 145.
22. *Ibid.*, No. 136.
23. *Ibid.*, No. 131.
24. *Ibid.*, No, 233.
25. *S.I.I.*, Vol. V, No, 303.
26. *S.I.I.*, Vol, XIV, No. 145.
27. *Ibid*, No. 157.
28. *Ibid*, No. 225.
29. *Ibid, No.* 145; *A.R.E.*, No. *284 of 1916.*
30. K. V. Raman, *op. cit.*, pp.147-148.
31. K. Pannerselvam, "Idaiyarrur – Nadu: A Study of its Name and History", *Studies in Indian Place Names*, Vol. XXXII, The Place Name Society of India, Mysore, 2012, p. 110.

32. R.Tirumalai, *The Pandyan Townships, Historical Geography of the Pandyan Kingdom, Part-I*, Chennai, 2003, p. 8.
33. Y. Subbarayalu, *op.cit.*, p.19.
34. R. Tirumalai, *op.cit.*, p. 17.
35. *Tamil Brahmi Inscriptions*, 2006, p. 55.
36. *Ahana_nūṟu*, 253.
37. *Tamilnadu Tholpalankalam*, 1979, p. 33.
38. S. Rajavelu, *Historical and Cultural Geography and Ethnography of Pudukkottai Region Up to AD 1800*, unpublished Ph.D Thesis, Tamil University, Thanjavur, 2003, pp. 23-24.
39. *Pandiyar Cheppedugal Pattu*, p. 22.
40. *Puṟanānūṟu*, 17.
41. Y. Subbarayalu, *op. cit.*, p. 32.
42. *Paṭṭiṉappālai*, 1. 283.
43. Y. Subbarayalu, *op. cit.*, pp. 32-33.
44. A.J. Dinakaran, *The Second Pandyan Empire (A.D. 1190 - 1312)*, Madurai, 1987, p. 168.
45. *S.I.I.*, Vol. XIV, No. 195.
46. R. Tirumalai, o*p.cit.*, p. 121.
47. *A.R.E.*, Nos. 155 of 1908 and 409 of 1907.
48. *AR.E.*, Nos. 243 and 246 of 1940-41.
49. T.S. Sridhar, *Virudhunagar District Inscriptions (V.D.I.)*, Vol. I, 2008, p.103.
50. *Ibid.*, p. 65.
51. *Ibid.*, p. 95.
52. *Ibid.*, p. 86.
53. *Ibid.*, p. 180.
54. *Ibid.*, p. 13.
55. *S.I.I.*, Vol. XIV, No. 16 A.
56. T.S. Sridhar, *Virudhunagar District Inscriptions*, 2008, Vol. I, p.223.
57. *S.I.I.*, Vol. XIV, No. 258.
58. *Ibid.*, No. 106.
59. *Ibid.*, No. 91.
60. *Ibid.*, No. 205.
61. *S.I.I.*, *Vol. V*, No. 287.
62. *Ibid.*, No. 290.
63. *S.I.I.*, Vol. XIV, No. 125.
64. T.S. Sridhar, *Madurai District Inscriptions*, Vol. II, 2008, p. 2.
65. *Ibid.*, Vol. I, 2006, p. 11.
66. T.S. Sridhar, *Alagarkovil Inscriptions*, 2010, p. 41.

67. *S.I.I.*, Vol. V, No. 303.
68. *Puranānūru:* 24.
69. Y. Subbarayalu, The *Pulankurichi Inscriptions, Kaveri: Studies in Epigraphy, Archaeology and History*, Chennai, 2001. p. 2.
70. K.V.Raman, *op.cit.*, p. 146.
71. Y.Subbarayalu (et.al.), *Naadu and Uur in Medieval Tamilnadu (800 A.D.)*, Thanjavur, 2014, p. 10.
72. *Idem.*
73. *Idem.*
74. *Idem.*
75. *S.I.I.*, Vol. XIV, No. 5.
76. R. Tirumalai, *op.cit.*, p. 8.
77. *A.R.E.*, No. 55 of 1924.
78. *A.R.E.*, No. 58 of 1924 and 330 of 1949-50.
79. T.S. Sridhar, *Virudhunagar District Inscriptions*, Vol. I, 2008, p.152.
80. T.S. Sridhar *Madurai, District Inscriptions*, Vol. II, 2008, pp. 2 and 11.
81. *Ibid.*, p. 62.
82. R. Tirumalai, *op.cit.*, p. 174.
83. *A.R.E.*, No.33 of 1931-32.
84. *S.I.I.*, Vol. XIV, No. 16.
85. S. Rajavelu, *op.cit.*, p. 64.
86. *Ainguṟunūṟu 54, Verse 1-3; A.R.E.*, No.132 of 1910.
87. *Tamil Brahmi Inscriptions*, p. 30.
88. *S.I.I.*, Vol. XIV, Nos. 84 and 85.
89. S. Rajavelu, "Place Names of Pudukkottai region in Tamilnadu", *Studies in Indian Place Names* (Bharatiya Sthalanama Patrika), Vol. XXIX, The Place Names Society of India, Mysore, 2010, pp. 85 and 86.
90. *S.I.I.*, Vol. XIV, Nos. 84 and 85.
91. *S.I.I.*, Vol. XIV, Nos. 223 and 223 B.
92. *Ibid.*, No. 229.
93. S. Rajavelu, "Place Names of Pudukkottai region in Tamilnadu", p. 88.
94. *S.I.I.*, Vol. XIV, No. 224.
95. *S.I.I.*, Vol. V, No. 301.
96. M. Chandramurthy and V. Vedachalam, *Parakramapandyapuram*, Madurai, 2002, pp. 14 and 15.
97. *A.R.E.*, Nos.132 and 134 of 1910.
98. *A.R.E.*, No. 332 of 1918.
99. *S.I.I.* Vol. XIV, No.223.

100. *S.I.I.*, Vol. V. No. 294.
101. *S.I.I.*, Vol. XIV. No. 224.
102. *A.R.E.*, No. 683 of 1905.
103. *A.R.E.*, No. 606 of 1926.
104. *S.I.I.*, Vol. XIV, No. 229 A&B.
105. *A.R.E.*, No.130 of 1910.
106. Y. Subbarayalu, *Political Geography of the Chola Country*, p. 91.
107. T.S. Sridhar, *Virudhunagar District Inscriptions*, pp. 267 - 268.
108. *Ibid.*, p. 61.
109. *S.I.I.*, Vol. XIV, No. 141.
110. *Ibid.*, No. 162.
111. *Ibid.*, Nos. 144 and 145.
112. T.S. Sridhar, *Alagarkovil Inscriptions*, p. 14.
113. *Ibid.*, p. 170.
114. T.S. Sridhar, *Madurai District Inscriptions*, p. 167.
115. *Ibid.*, pp. 188-190.
116. T.S. Sridhar, *Alagarkovil Inscriptions*, p. 133.
117. *Ibid.*, p. 130.
118. *S.I.I.*, Vol. V, No. 294.
119. *Ibid.*, No. 303.
120. *A.R.E.*, No. 274 of 1941-42.
121. Sitharam Gurumurthi, *Madurai District Inscriptions*, p. 177.
122. T.S. Sridhar, *Alagarkovil Inscriptions*, pp. 172-173.
123. S. Rajavelu, "Place Names of Pudukkottai region in Tamilnadu", pp. 86 and 87.
124. T. V. Mahalingam, *A Topographical list of Inscriptions in the Tamilnadu and Kerala States*, Vol.V, New Delhi, 1989, p. 112.
125. *S.I.I.*, Vol. V, No. 295.
126. M. Chandramurthy and V.Vedachalam, *op. cit.*, p. 32.
127. *S.I.I.*, Vol. V, No. 298.
128. *Dindugal District Archaeological Guide*, 2007, pp. 204-205.
129. *Madurai District Archaeological Guide*, 2005, p. 153.
130. *SII*, Vol. XIV, No. 215.

Bibliography

Annual Report on South Indian Epigraphy (various years): 1905, 1905, 1910, 1916, 1918, 1924-25, 1926-27, 1931-32, 1940-41, 1941-42, 1949-50.

Chandramurthy, M and V. Vedachalam, *Parakramapandyapuram*, Madurai, 2002.

Dinakaran, A.J. *The Second Pandyan Empire (A.D. 1190 - 1312)*, Madurai, 1987.

Epigraphica Indica, Vol. XXI.

Mahalingam, T.V, *A Topographical list of Inscriptions in the Tamilnadu and Kerala States*, Vol.V, New Delhi, 1989.

Pannerselvam, K, "Idaiyarrur – Nadu: A Study of its Name and History", *Studies in Indian Place Names*, Vol. XXXII, The Place Name Society of India, Mysore, 2012.

Puṟanāṉūṟu: 24

Rajavelu, S, "Place Names of Pudukkottai region inTamilnadu", *Studies in Indian Place Names* (Bharatiya Sthalanama Patrika), Vol. XXIX, The Place Names Society of India, Mysore, 2010.

Raman, K.V, *History of Pandyas,* Government of Tamilnadu, Chennai, 1977.

Sitharam Gurumurthi, *Madurai District Inscriptions.*

South Indian Inscriptions (in various Volumes): Vol. V and Vol. XIV.

Sreedhar, E, *Historical Cultural Geography and Ethnography of Andhra under The Vijayanagara From XIV to XVII Century A.D.*, Unpublished Ph.D. thesis submitted to Sree Krishnadevaraya University, Anantapur, 2011.

Sridhar, T.S, *Virudhunagar District Inscriptions*, Vol. I, 2008, Vol. I.

__________, *Alagarkovil Inscriptions.*

Subbarayalu, Y, *Political Geography of the Chola Country*, University of Madras, Madras, 1973.

____________, The *Pulankuṟichi Inscriptions*, *Kaveri: Studies in Epigraphy, Archaeology and History*, Chennai, 2001.

Subbarayalu, Y, *et.al.*, *Naadu and Uur in Medieval Tamilnadu (800 A.D.)*, Thanjavur, 2014.

Sundararajan, S, *Ancient Tamil Country: Its Social and Economic Structure*, Navrang, New Delhi, 1991.

Tamil Brahmi Inscriptions.

Tirumalai, R, *The Pandyan Townships, Historical Geography of the Pandyan Kingdom, Part-I,* Chennai, 2003.

Index

B

L

M

N

O

P

T